MANAGING WITH INTEGRITY

MANAGING WITH INTEGRITY

An Ethical Investigation into the Relationship between Personal and Corporate Integrity

Augustine Chennattu

FORTRESS PRESS
MINNEAPOLIS

MANAGING WITH INTEGRITY
An Ethical Investigation into the Relationship between Personal and Corporate Integrity

Cover image: iStock © 2019; Abstract triangle shaped background: Modern architecture in Milan stock photo by ilbusca

Cover design: Emily Wyland

Paperback ISBN: 978-1-5064-5042-1

eBook ISBN: 978-1-5064-5043-8

This book is dedicated to my parents

and other family members,

for their kindness, love and

endless support throughout my life.

ACKNOWLEDGMENTS

Completion of this book was indeed a powerful experience of interpersonal relationships and relational human existence. First of all, I thank God for guiding and strengthening me all throughout my academic pursuit. I owe much to all the authorities of Fortress Press for taking the responsibility of publishing this book. I recall with sincere gratitude His Grace Mar George Njaralakattu, Archbishop of Tellicherry, Mar Joseph Pamplany, and His Grace Emeritus Mar George Valiyamattam, for their support and encouragement to pursue my research. I remember with much affection and gratitude my parents, sisters, brother, and all other family members for their love and spiritual and emotional support always, especially during my research. As one can imagine, the most influential person behind this project as a source of inspiration was Prof. Johan Verstraeten. His in-depth knowledge on the subject, insightful suggestions, timely corrections, encouraging support, and above all, friendly attitude have helped me immensely to complete this project. A BIG "Thank You" to you, dear Prof. Verstraeten. I extend my sincere gratitude to all my professors, the staff of the Secretariat and library and the Research Unit of Theological and Comparative Ethics at K. U. Leuven. I owe much to my students and colleagues at St. Joseph's Pontifical Seminary, Mangalapuzha, Aluva, who always challenged me with their wisdom.

Dr. Augustine Chennattu
St. Joseph's Pontifical Seminary
Mangalapuzha, Aluva, Kerala, India.
biju.chen@gmail.com

CONTENTS

Preface.......... 1

Introduction.......... 3

Part 1: An Analysis of Corporate Integrity

1. Corporate Integrity Theories.......... 9
2. Corporate Moral Agency Debate and Corporate Integrity.......... 51
3. Theories of Corporate Social Responsibility (CSR) and Corporate Integrity.......... 75
4. Corporate Reputation and Corporate Integrity.......... 97

Part 2: The Role of Personal Integrity in Corporate Ethics

5. Working Definition of Personal Integrity.......... 105
6. Role of Personal Integrity in Organizational Contexts.......... 125
7. Theory of the Fundamental Option and Personal Integrity.......... 139

Part 3: Personalist Approach to Corporate Integrity Theories

8. Ethical Reasons and Foundations for Personalist Approach to Corporate Integrity.......... 159
9. A Personalist Approach to Corporate Integrity Theories.......... 207

Conclusion.......... 231

Bibliography.......... 239

PREFACE

In business as well as in public administration, integrity is a necessary condition for the creation of organizations without unethical conduct. Integrity enables individuals to act in the perspective of life as a whole. It allows them to overcome the disconnection between work and life, and to configure life in view of the realization of fundamental values and norms. As such, integrity characterizes a person whose life is coherent, consistent, and who is capable of "walking the talk."

The problem, however, is that many integrity studies focus quite exclusively or unilaterally on either the individual or the organization. They often neglect the *interaction* between the individual and the institutional level of action. In this regard, Father Augustine Chennattu's book fills a gap. Conscious of the complex and holistic nature of integrity, it proposes a lucid, nuanced, and insightful approach, based on an extensive overview of the different interpretations with regard to both individual and corporate integrity. More precisely, Augustine Chennattu maps the different distinctions and theories in such a way that the reader gets a clear insight into the complexity of integrity in the indispensable strategies that are required to improve the situation.

The seven descriptive ethical chapters serve as building blocks for the construction of an alternative approach, which is not only an argument for a more dynamic interaction between individual and institutional integrity but also an argument, within this interaction, for the logical priority of personal integrity. This reflects Augustine Chennattu's inspiration from the personalist philosophical tradition, and particularly of Luc Bouckaert's contribution to it.[1]

Father Augustine Chennattu's book is the result of solid research in the context of his doctoral project that he has successfully completed and defended under my supervision at the Catholic University of Leuven. In comparison to the existing literature on the topic, Augustine Chennattu's

[1] Luc Bouckaert is co-founder and former president of the European SPES Forum (*Spirituality in Economics and Society*).

book is not only an enrichment of classical business ethics, and as such a contribution to a scholarly conversation, but also an indispensable guide for leaders and managers who want to develop a meaningful context in which ethical behavior is made possible.

Prof. Dr. Johan Verstraeten
Leuven, June 25, 2018

INTRODUCTION

The book is situated within the broader context of the emerging interests of people to eradicate unethical organizational conduct. The massive outcry against corruption and public opinion puts leaders, top managers, and employees under strong social and political pressures. At present, the establishment of corporate ethics is attempted through the introduction of corporate integrity theories. Although the main elements of corporate integrity theories such as codes of conduct, corporate structures, and culture play an important role in the corporate ethics, they are insufficient because they do not immediately present a solution to solve all corporate ethical dilemmas.

Fragmentation of the self in the workplace is one of the challenges that comes from the absolutization of the compliance-based approach in corporate ethics. Naturally, managers and employees with better educational backgrounds can easily be driven by selfish interests that ignore the interests of the other, perhaps less empowered or intellectually able stakeholders in corporate structures. Moreover, modern corporate ethics fails to confront the challenges of compartmentalization. Corporate integrity theory encourages the fragmentation of self in corporate life because of the negligence of personal integrity of managers and employees.

Another potentially alarming modern sign of unethical business is the calculation of business success in terms of efficiency, maximization of profit, and production. This tendency is boosted by the campaign of India's Modi government elected in 2014 to "Make in India," which encourages multinational and domestic companies to manufacture their products in India by way of new investments. The concept of ethics is used in business structures with an instrumental purpose. As a result, both the political and corporate worlds neglect the value of non-instrumental dimensions of business operation. This creates a situation in which managers and employees experience meaninglessness and fragmentation of their lives. Furthermore, they come to see business as nothing more than pursuit of "success" that is translated to them as profit maximization, thus justifying corruption as a means of achieving this preconceived notion of "success."

Moreover, business ethics can be instrumentalized by managers, employees, and shareholders of corporations to attain economic results, and such instrumentalization leads to unethical corporate conduct. In the context of conflicts of interest, efficiency, maximization of profit, production, instrumentalization of ethics, and moral dilemmas, decisions depend on the moral integrity of managers and employees. In this context, moral creativity and personal involvement are necessary to make corporate ethics possible, and this depends directly on the personal integrity of managers and employees. This book argues for the combination of personal integrity on the one hand and on the other hand corporate codes, ethical structure, and culture in such a way that it contributes to overcome instrumentalization in corporate ethics, and as a result reduce the possibility of unethical corporate conduct. Therefore, this book aims at demonstrating the need for incorporating the formation of personal integrity together with other elements of corporate integrity theories for better corporate ethics.

Personalistic economics rationality is used as a basis for incorporating personal integrity of managers and employees in corporate integrity theories. It holds the importance of the relational dimension of all stakeholders in economic decisions. It implies that the primary motivation of an economic decision must be non-instrumental, whereas profit (instrumental) is a secondary motivation. To implement this personalist approach to corporate integrity theories, the book argues that an ethics of doing is by itself insufficient because of the complexity and uniqueness of each corporate context that naturally leads to different behaviors. What is required is an ethics of being along with an ethics of doing. Therefore, I suggest in this book a personalist approach to corporate integrity, which consists of both an ethics of being and an ethics of doing, which are more relevant to personalistic economics thinking.

The book consists of three parts. First, it comes across corporate integrity theories as a current method for implementing ethics in the corporate world, which is a compliance-based approach. The book critically evaluates corporate integrity theories and highlights aspects that they have missed, making these theories more complete and effective. The book focuses on the existence of corporate integrity theories in relation to the background of corporate moral agency and social responsibility debates. This allows my argument to shed light on the underlying inner spirit of corporate integrity theories, that is, methodological collectivism, its shortcomings, and the negligence of personal integrity of the people who have decision-making power in a corporation.

Second, by analyzing various definitions of personal integrity the book contributes to clarification of the meaning of personal integrity. I depict the personal integrity of managers and employees to be crucial in situations of corporate conflicts of interest and dilemmas. The book shows the correlation of the personal integrity concept with the Christian ethical concept of fundamental option, and therefore the discussion enhances Christian ethics.

Lastly, the possibility of a personalist approach to corporate integrity, which is the combination of the ethics of doing and the ethics of being, is the main discussion point of this book. I hope that this book serves as an ethical guide for managers, employees, politicians, clergy, candidates for priesthood, and business students for forming a vision regarding organizational ethics.

PART I

AN ANALYSIS OF CORPORATE INTEGRITY

CHAPTER ONE

CORPORATE INTEGRITY THEORIES

Introduction

The corporate integrity theory[1] is proposed as a solution to unethical corporate conduct. Integrity is a complex and dynamic reality, which should be understood as an essential element in both personal as well as organizational life. In this chapter, I introduce and critically analyze corporate integrity theories. At the end of the detailed analytical and critical study of the corporate integrity theories, I point out its limitations and argue for a more comprehensive approach.

1 Meaning of Corporate Integrity

In the business world there are diverse uses of the term "integrity." Indeed, "integrity is quite possibly the most commonly cited morally desirable trait in the world of business."[2] Many corporate integrity initiatives have a compliance-based policy, employing instruments such as "a code of conduct,[3] training in relevant areas of the law, mechanisms for reporting and investigating potential misconduct, audit, and control[4] to ensure that

[1] I concentrated on the corporate integrity theories of Muel Kaptein (Professor of Business Ethics and Integrity Management at RSM Erasmus University, Netherlands), Johan Wempe (Professor at Saxion University of Applied Sciences), and Marvin T. Brown (Professor of Business and Organizational Ethics at the University of San Francisco, California).

[2] Robert Audi and Patrick E. Murphy, "The Many Faces of Integrity," *Business Ethics Quarterly* 16, no. 1 (2006): 3.

[3] Corporate codes of conduct are an explicit statement of behavioral ideals, prohibitions, and suggestions in a corporation. There are three types of codes of conduct in corporations such as corporate code of conduct for behavioral conduct, corporate codes of conduct aimed at values, and corporate codes of conduct for social responsibility. Clarity, comprehensiveness, and enforcement are characteristics of a good corporate code of conduct. Cf. Dinah Payne and Frédéric Dimanche, "Towards a Code of Conduct for the Tourism Industry: An Ethics Model," *Journal of Business Ethics* 15, no. 9 (1996): 1004.

[4] Corporate ethical audit means the "regular, complete and documented measurement of compliance with the company's published policies and procedures." Cf. John Rosthorn,

laws and company standards are being met."[5] Furthermore, integrity has a strict normative connotation, which implies that "acting with integrity is the same as acting ethically or morally."[6] However, in general, the notion of corporate integrity as compliance with ethical norms and rules is not widely accepted. Overemphasis on integrity as a notion of compliance with rules denotes that "something is seriously wrong within a company."[7]

Corporate integrity is defined as the corporate conditions that stimulate the careful resolution of corporate moral problems. These conditions and corporate efforts are localized in corporate culture and structure.[8] In a broader sense, corporate integrity refers to the "realization of the legitimate moral expectations of a corporation in a coherent manner."[9] In this regard, corporate integrity is the coherence between corporate intentions, related conduct, and their consequences. Moreover, corporate integrity refers to the justifiable social role that corporations fulfill.[10] From the standpoint of corporate social responsibility, corporate integrity is also relational, which in turn demands engaging and responding to all stakeholders in a responsible manner. Therefore, so as to achieve corporate integrity, corporations "must be conscious of all relationships in which they participate, engage with all their constituencies in responsible ways, meet their reasonable expectations, and be considered a partner ensuring a sustainable future."[11] This stakeholder relationship is not merely motivated by an instrumental mentality[12] but it is a responsible engagement with other stakeholders, irrespective of any benefit. Moreover, relational wholeness refers to the "whole range of relationships; internally, externally, and with societies at large."[13] Integrity, in this sense, refers to the extent to

---

"Business Ethics Auditing: More Than a Stakeholder's Toy," *Journal of Business Ethics* 27, no. 1/2 (2000): 11.

5 Lynn Sharp Paine, "Managing for Organizational Integrity," *Harvard Business Review* 72, no. 3/4 (1994): 111.

6 Richard T. DeGeorge, *Competing with Integrity in International Business* (Oxford: Oxford University Press, 1993): 5.

7 Daryl Koehn, "Integrity as a Business Asset," *Journal of Business Ethics* 58, no. 1/3 (2005): 126.

8 Muel Kaptein and Johan Wempe, *The Balanced Company: A Theory of Corporate Integrity* (Oxford: Oxford University Press, 2002): 152–153.

9 Kaptein and Wempe, *The Balanced Company*, 153.

10 Kaptein and Wempe, *The Balanced Company*, 154.

11 Thomas Maak, "Undivided Corporate Responsibility: Towards a Theory of Corporate Integrity," *Journal of Business Ethics* 82 (2009): 363.

12 Instrumental theory of stakeholder management means "the contract" i.e., a metaphor for the relationships between the firm and its various stakeholder groups. The firm will gain competitive advantage if it is able to develop relationships with its stakeholders based on mutual trust and cooperation. Cf. Thomas M. Jones, "Instrumental Stakeholder Theory: A Synthesis of Ethics and Economics," *The Academy of Management Review* 20, no. 2 (1995): 423.

13 Maak, "Undivided Corporate Responsibility," 363.

which an organization maintains relational wholeness. Marvin T. Brown defines a corporation as "an organization constituted by on-going verbal and non-verbal communication patterns."[14] According to him, corporate integrity is the character of the above-mentioned communication patterns of a corporation.[15]

Although there are various definitions of corporate integrity, ultimately, it stands for the integration of the various demands of stakeholders. Thus, a corporation should always make morally justifiable corporate decisions and also conduct itself in such a manner. There are different methods or theories used to achieve corporate integrity within a corporation. In the following section, I analyze and evaluate the various corporate integrity theories.

2 Theories of Corporate Integrity

Various theories of corporate integrity have been proposed as solutions to corporate misconduct, including corporate corruption, structural, and contextual moral issues, which create corporate dilemmas that emerge from the debate over conflicts of interest and corporate social responsibility. Generally, unethical corporate business practices reflect "the values, attitudes, beliefs, language and behavioral patterns that define an organization's operating cultures."[16] As a solution to this corporate problem, many companies implement a compliance-based ethical approach. The essence of such programs is to "prevent, detect, and punish illegal violations."[17] However, organizational ethics are more than rules and punishments. The theory of corporate integrity is an alternative approach, which might vary in content but tries to define a way that puts into action the efforts of companies to shape their businesses according to moral values and virtues along with the compliance approach.

My literary research enabled me to divide the theories of corporate integrity into two: social contract-based theory and corporate civic citizenship-based theory. Social contract-based corporate integrity theory attempts to develop an organizational culture and structure to promote efficient fulfillment of stakeholders' interests.[18] Civic citizenship-based corporate integrity theory presents corporations as a member of the civil society. Consequently, it "allows us in business ethics to also include the

---

[14] Marvin T. Brown, "Corporate Integrity and Public Interest: A Relational Approach to Business Ethics and Leadership," *Journal of Business Ethics* 66, no. 1 (2006): 14.

[15] Cf. Brown, "Corporate Integrity and Public Interest," 14.

[16] Lynn Sharp Paine, "Managing for Organizational Integrity," *Harvard Business Review* 72, no. 3/4 (1994): 106.

[17] Paine, "Managing for Organizational Integrity," 106.

[18] Kaptein and Wempe, *The Balanced Company*, 250.

civic realm in our horizon."[19] Since corporations take part in civic morality,[20] "business ethics can safeguard the integrity of corporations as well as, the integrity of civil society and of democratic institutions."[21]

2.1 The Social Contract-Based Theory of Corporate Integrity

As explained before, there are three types of relationships in organizational life: (1) the relationship between stakeholders and corporations, (2) the relationship between employees and corporation, and (3) the relationship among employees. Often the moral quality of these relationships is compromised by conflicts of values and interests. The central concern is balancing corporate interests with stakeholders' interests. It is easy to define such relationships in a contractual way as "social contract theory is based on the idea that the authority of moral principles can come from the agreement of those affected."[22]

Muel Kaptein and Johan Wempe apply this contract model[23] to business ethics, however, with emphases on different parts.[24] The contract model is grounded in two philosophical traditions: the legal tradition, which

---

19 Brown, "Corporate Integrity and Public Interest," 13.

20 Civic morality is the fulfillment of the duties and responsibilities of a citizen in a society. Civic morality includes "paying taxes, high regard for environment and animals, and concern about discrimination against civic minorities, the elderly and the handicapped." Cf. Geoffrey Hunt, "Moral Crisis, Professionals and Ethical Education," *Nursing Ethics* 4, no. 1 (1997): 33.

21 Brown, "Corporate Integrity and Public Interest," 13.

22 Allan J. Kimmel, N. Craig Smith, and Jill Gabrielle Klein, "Ethical Decision Making and Research Deception in the Behavioral Sciences: An Application of Social Contract Theory," *Ethics and Behavior* 21, no. 3 (2011): 237.

23 In the history of business ethics there are two comprehensive solutions for the corporate dilemmas: the market model and the contract model. According to the market model, if everyone pursues one's own self-interest, then the optimal solution for the whole will naturally follow. Every citizen must be free to maximize their own self-interest and government interference must be minimal that paves the way for fair competition.The contract model tries to solve the tension that is created by corporate dilemmas by creating a situation where stakeholders are entering into a fictional contract in which agreements are settled. These agreements create mutual benefits. Cf. Kaptein and Wempe, *The Balanced Company*, 200–201.

24 There are differences in the use of the contract model in business ethics. Robert Hessen's contract model states that "The contract model holds that a corporation is simply and literally a voluntary association of individuals, united by a network of contracts, who are entitled to exactly the same rights and legal protections as all other individuals and organizations. It holds that corporations are not the recipients of special privileges, that they do not require governmental permission to exist, and that their "charters" do not contain any promise (express or implied) to place public service ahead of private profit." Cf. Robert Hessen, "A New Concept of Corporations: A Contractual and Private Property Model," *Hastings Law Journal* 30, no. 5 (1979): 1330. Through a series of writings, Donaldson described that contract in business is a contract between corporations and individual members of society. Cf. Thomas Donaldson, *Corporations and Morality* (New York: Prentice-Hall, 1982): 42. Manuel G. Velasquez sees contract as the relationship between customers and

can be traced back to Roman law and the socio-political tradition, which was developed by political philosophers.[25] Legal contract theory involves safeguarding the possibility of cohesive forms of social cooperation and complex transactions. This theory is used as the foundation for the relationship of rights and obligations of citizens and the state. The core aim is the same in both traditions; to keep the balance between the rights and interests of individuals and collective rights. In this respect, the contract model is relevant to the corporate context; a corporation is formed by a hypothetical or implicit contract, which is similar to the way society engages in a political contract, with employees and stakeholders being the involved parties. Therefore, a corporation is perceived as a common project of all parties concerned.[26] Moreover, the contract serves as the foundation for the moral obligation of corporations to promote the well-being of stakeholders because corporations exist due to an implicit contract between corporations and their stakeholders.[27] I provide a more detailed analysis of stakeholder theory toward the end of this chapter in the discussion on corporate social responsibility and corporate integrity theories.

Kaptein and Wempe propose a corporate social contract theory, which is the "integration of transaction costs, and agency theory[28] into the

---

a business firm. Cf. Manuel G. Velasquez, *Business Ethics: Concepts and Cases* (New York: Prentice Hall, 1992): 270–273. We will have a detailed explanation of it later.

25 Political theory uses social contract theory as a device to grasp the role of government within a society. Enlightenment writers like John Locke (1632–1704), Thomas Hobbes (1588–1679), and Jean-Jacques Rousseau (1712–1778) used social contract widely in their formation of political theories. Cf. Thomas W. Dunfee, "Social Contract Theory," in *Encyclopedic Dictionary of Business Ethics*, eds. Patricia H. Werhane and R. Edward Freeman (Oxford: Blackwell Publishers, 1998): 585. See also Donaldson, *Corporations and Morality*, 35–39. See also Kaptein and Wempe, *The Balanced Company*, 200–201.

26 Kaptein and Wempe, *The Balanced Company*, 200–201.

27 Thomas Donaldson, *The Ethics of International Business* (New York: Oxford University Press, 1989): 57–59. See also Donaldson, *The Ethics of International Business*; Mathew Illathuparambil, *Business Ethics* (Tiruvalla: Macfast Publications, 2005): 136.

28 Transactional cost theory is pioneered by R.H. Coase. Cf. R. H. Coase, "The Nature of the Firm," *Economica* 4, no. 16 (1937): 386–405. See also Eric T. G. Wang, "Transaction Attributes and Software Outsourcing Success: An Empirical Investigation of Transaction Cost Theory," *Info Systems Journal* 12 (2002): 155. Transactional cost theory holds that corporations were created to generate greater prosperity through efficient production. This theory contains three elements; form-specific advantages that include a corporation's capacity to know unique assets and transactional advantages; country-specific advantages that state that some advantages are always located with some countries for business; and international advantages that state that there are relative benefits when a corporation serves a foreign market. Cf. Alan M. Rugman and Alain Verbeke, "A Note on the Transnational Solution and the Transaction Cost Theory of Multinational Strategic Management," *Journal of International Business Studies* 23, no. 4 (1992): 761–771. Agency theory of corporation explains the relationship between shareholders, principles (shareholders of the corporation), and the agents (executives of the corporation). Cf. Luh Luh Lan and Loizos Heracleous, "Rethinking Agency Theory: The View from Law " *Academy of Management Review* 35, no. 2 (2010): 294–314.

stakeholder theory.[29] The acknowledgement of a normative element in these theories leads to the contract model of a corporation."[30] The theory emphasizes that a corporation is a place where a strong relationship exists between corporations and stakeholders. According to Henk Van Luijk, integrity in the corporate domain is formed from the background of stakeholder relations whereby corporations are established by contract.[31] Contracts create trust between stakeholders and corporations: it follows that corporations have to fulfill their obligations toward stakeholders, and stakeholders are obliged to legitimize corporations. The existence of various obligations can, however, result into conflicting obligations within a corporation.[32]

In order to ensure that contracts are binding, corporations and stakeholders have to overcome obstacles of bounded rationality[33] and opportunism.[34] In a corporate context, the managerial decision-making process is described as a bounded rational decision model. This model explains how managers actually make decisions based on the limitations of the human mind. In this model, a corporate system demands that managers employ the right criteria to weigh different stakeholder interests to overcome the obstacle of bounded rationality in a difficult situation.[35] Opportunism plays an important role in the destruction of corporate success because the future existence of the corporation depends upon the stakeholders. If stakeholders feel that the corporation is not just, then they may withdraw their support from further cooperation.[36]

---

[29] Stakeholder theory is an attempt to give a normative and instrumental basis for including stakeholders in managerial decision making. Cf. Andrew Crane and Trish Ruebottom, "Stakeholder Theory and Social Identity: Rethinking Stakeholder Identification," *Journal of Business Ethics* 102, no. 1 (2011): 77.

[30] Kaptein and Wempe, *The Balanced Company*, 215.

[31] Henk Van Luijk, "Integrity in the Private, the Public, and the Corporate Domain," in *Corporate Integrity and Accountability*, ed. George G. Brenkert (London: Sage Publications, 2004): 48–49.

[32] Kaptein and Wempe, *The Balanced Company*, 215.

[33] Bounded rationality is a condition that influences the decision making process. Generally, bounded rationality implies that "there are limits to the ability of stewards to align their interests with those of the organization, as well as limits to the ability of owners to properly evaluate the pro-organizational intentions, abilities, and actions of stewards." Cf. James J. Chrisman, Esra Memili, and Kaustav Misra, "Nonfamily Managers, Family Firms, and the Winner's Curse: The Influence of Noneconomic Goals and Bounded Rationality," *Entrepreneurship Theory and Practice* 38, no. 5 (2013): 1103–1104.

[34] Opportunism is a strong self-interest seeking tendency. In the background of contracts "opportunism refers to calculated efforts to mislead, distort, disguise, obfuscate, or otherwise confuse, as well as for the tendency to renege on previous commitments in the light of new opportunities." Cf. Kaptein and Wempe, *The Balanced Company*, 234.

[35] John E. Fleming, "A Suggested Approach to Linking Decision Styles with Business Ethics," *Journal of Business Ethics* 4, no. 2 (1985): 138.

[36] Kaptein and Wempe, *The Balanced Company*, 234–235.

2.1.1 Corporate Integrity for Protecting Corporate Stakeholder Contracts

Corporations have a personality that is generally interpreted as corporate culture, a concept widely described as "shared values, principles, traditions, and the way of doing things that influence the way organizational members act."[37] Corporate behavioral principles and qualities are articulated by the corporate founders. If corporate principles and qualities are deeply held and widely shared within corporate culture, then it has a greater influence on employees' behavior generally as well as during any business conduct as the overarching goal is to uphold cultural values. Openness, clarity, discussibility, supportability, and consistency are key important corporate qualities and principles.[38] Corporate principles and qualities vary from one corporation to another and the articulation of corporate behavioral principles and qualities are different for each author as there is no set of absolute guiding principles that could provide for their form or substance.

In order to safeguard stakeholder interests, which are part of the social contract, authors such as Kaptein, Wempe, and Van Luijk propose that corporate behavioral principles such as openness, empathy, fairness, solidarity, and reliability, ought to be used as criteria for resolving corporate conflicts and dilemmas. In order to work out these principles clearly, a corporate culture, structure, and corporate intentionality are necessary.[39] There are seven corporate qualities that are proposed by Kaptein and Wempe. These are: clarity, sanctionability, discussibility, visibility, supportability, achievability, and consistency. These are embedded in the corporate culture as well as its structure, and additionally help employees engage responsibly when confronted with different conflicts and dilemmas within the context of the social contract. The result of both behavioral principles and corporate qualities in the corporate arena is the advantage of mutual sustainability.[40] As a result, there will not be many possibilities for safeguarding selfish interests and corporate corruption while conducting business. The theory of the corporate integrity model for Kaptein and Wempe is the sum total of corporate behavioral qualities and corporate behavioral principles in corporate culture, structure, and the resulting mutual sustainable advantage.[41]

---

37 Stephen P. Robbins and Mary Coulter, *Management* (New Jersey: Pearson Prentice, 2009): 62.

38 Robbins and Coulter, *Management*, 62. See also Mats Alvesson, *Understanding Organizational Culture* (London: Sage Publications, 2002): 59.

39 Luijk, "Integrity in the Private, the Public, and the Corporate Domain," 47. See also Kaptein and Wempe, *The Balanced Company*, 237.

40 Kaptein and Wempe, *The Balanced Company*, 250.

41 Kaptein and Wempe, *The Balanced Company*, 257–259.

2.1.2 Corporate Behavior Principles

In order to form a corporate integrity theory, Kaptein and Wempe propose five behavioral principles based on inductive research[42] combined with a deductive approach.[43] Corporate behavioral principles are essential components of binding contracts and the main aim of these principles is to safeguard the relationships between a corporate actor and its stakeholders. These behavioral principles lead to certain qualities of corporate conduct[44] and there is a reduction in possibilities for corporate corruption.

2.1.2.1 Principle of Openness

Openness is the main corporate attitude that can be used to overcome both bounded rationality and opportunism. Openness can exist in different forms such as transparency, honesty, receptivity, and vulnerability.[45] Transparency is defined "as an individual's subjective perception of being informed about the relevant actions and properties of the other party in the interaction."[46] Through the mutual exchange of information, the relationship between corporations and stakeholders can become very strong because transparency works as a source of external stakeholder satisfaction. Furthermore, transparency leads a corporation to consider stakeholders as an autonomous agent. Otherwise, companies could use contracting partners as a mere means to an end,[47] which could result in corporate corruption.

Stakeholder dialogue is also a proposed method to achieve more corporate transparency. The logic behind stakeholder dialogue is that while it is impossible to satisfy all stakeholder interests, through stakeholder dialogue, "stakeholders will be confident that companies are dealing with their interests with the necessary care. [...]. This can be done in two ways:

---

42 Generally, inductive research approaches "reasons through moving from a specific case or a collection of observations to general law, i.e. from facts to theory." I have taken this quotation from the following source. Cf. Gyongyi Kovacs and Karen M. Spens, "Abductive Reasoning in Logistics Research," *International Journal of Physical Distribution & Logistics Management* 35, no. 2 (2005): 132.

43 Deductive research is the conscious movement from "a general law to a specific case." Cf. Kovacs and Spens, "Abductive Reasoning in Logistics Research," 132.

44 Kaptein and Wempe, *The Balanced Company*, 236–237.

45 Kaptein and Wempe, *The Balanced Company*, 238–239.

46 Andreas Eggert and Sabrina Helm, "Exploring the Impact of Relationship Transparency on Business Relationships: A Cross-Sectional Study among Purchasing Managers in Germany," *Industrial Marketing Management* 32, no. 8 (2003): 101.

47 Eggert and Helm, "Exploring the Impact of Relationship Transparency on Business Relationships," 104. See also Charles Garofalo and Dean Geuras, "Administrative Leadership and Transparency," in *Ethics and Integrity in Public Administration Concepts and Cases*, ed. Raymond W. Cox (London: M. E. Sharpe, 2009): 74–75.

by informing stakeholders, for example, by means of an annual report, and also by communicating with each other."[48]

In business contracts, honesty of information is desired. Contractors must have the right information to be able to trust the information, that is, view it as honest. As Thomas Donaldson writes, "productive organization must avoid deception and fraud."[49]

In stakeholder relationships, there should not only be an exchange of trustworthy information but also a mutual receptivity of this information. The principle of receptivity "refers to the ability of contractors to listen to and acknowledge the problems, questions, and suggestions of fellow contractors."[50] Every contract will, however, have its positive and negative consequences depending on the process to which it agrees or requires compliance. Vulnerability refers to the willingness of the contracting parties to be corrected by third parties and institutions.

2.1.2.2 Principle of Empathy

The principle of empathy refers to the idea that contractors (corporations and stakeholders) should have the ability to see the potential benefits and damages of their actions and intentions. Moral blindness diminishes an actor's capacity for foresight with respect to the advantages and disadvantages of a potential contract. Contractors must be very careful to find out the consequences of the implementation of their plans.[51] Generally, empathy can be defined as a "unique ability to understand the world of others and to reconfigure our own understanding to apprehend the world of other people."[52] Moreover, it can be described as the imagination of corporate contractors, "in particular the ability to see and acknowledge the full mixture of potential benefits and harm that may ensue from the action or inaction of potential contractors."[53] If corporations and stakeholders lack this ability, then they will lose what could have otherwise grown to be a lasting contractual relationship.

This ability helps managers and executives of corporations to "feel as others are feeling" in their relationship with external and internal

---

48 Muel Kaptein and Rob Van Tulder, "Toward Effective Stakeholder Dialogue," *Business and Society Review* 108, no. 2 (2003): 208.

49 Donaldson, *Corporations and Morality*, 53.

50 Shelby D. Hunt and Scott Vitell, "A General Theory of Marketing Ethics," *Journal of Macromarketing* 6, no. 1 (1986): 5.

51 Kaptein and Wempe, *The Balanced Company*, 242.

52 Samuel Michael Natale and Sebastian A. Sora, "Ethics in Strategic Thinking: Business Processes and the Global Market Collapse," *Journal of Business Ethics* 94, no. 3 (2010): 310.

53 Kaptein and Wempe, *The Balanced Company*, 242. See also LaRue-Tone Hosmer, "Lessons from the Wreck of the Exxon Valdez," *Business Ethics Quarterly* 8, no. 1 (1998): 109–122.

stakeholders.[54] Empathy can be worked out in different ways for individual managers. It can be "(a) an affective state [or] (b) [...] the observation or imagination of another person's affective state."[55]

2.1.2.3 Principle of Fairness

Kaptein and Wempe explain that corporate fairness is a primary principle for solving corporate conflicts and dilemmas. Moreover, it is an essential principle of a contract.[56] Generally, "The principle of fairness in corporate governance is not the form of fairness that ethics of justice is embedded in, namely the equitable allocation of resources and implementation of rules, but the equitable care distributed toward all stakeholders."[57]

A contractor must be free from potentially exploitative situations that compel the contracting partner to act irrationally in response to a threatening behavior by the other party to the contract. If managers were to use intimidation, aggression or blackmail toward an employee, then that manager is abusing their position of power. When there is a difference in wealth and power among the contracting partners, fairness is indispensable. Moreover, many studies document that fairness in corporate life creates positive attitudes and behavior from internal and external stakeholders, because it creates trust and acceptance among stakeholders.[58]As a result, in a corporate context, all stakeholders should have the same opportunity to enter into a relationship with the corporation. This means that both the corporation and the internal stakeholders of the corporation must be bias-free, independent, and objective. Furthermore, fairness in the business behavioral principle demands the rejection of unjustifiable discriminatory treatment and exploitation of the other contracting parties.[59]

2.1.2.4 Principle of Solidarity

The principle of solidarity is the connective link between different stakeholders. According to Jerry M. Calton and Lawrence J. Lad, a contract can be formed with free consent only on the condition that there is an opt-out

---

54 Natale and Sora, "Ethics in Strategic Thinking," 310.

55 Natale and Sora, "Ethics in Strategic Thinking," 310.

56 Kaptein and Wempe, *The Balanced Company*, 243–244.

57 Luu Trong Tuan, "Corporate Social Responsibility, Ethics, and Corporate Governance," *Social Responsibility Journal* 8, no. 4 (2012): 552.

58 Bernhard Streicher, Verena Graupmann, and Silke Weisweiler, "A Spoonful of Fairness: Training in Fairness Principles Helps Communicate Bad News," *International Journal of Training Research* 12, no. 1 (2014): 73. See also Tom R. Tyler, "Social Justice: Outcome and Procedure," *International Journal of Psychology* 35, no. 2 (2000):117–125. See also Roy J. Lewicki, Carolyn Wiethoff, and Edward C.Tomlinson, "What is the Role of Trust in Organizational Justice?," in *Handbook of Organizational Justice*, eds. Jerald Greenberg and Jason A. Colquitt (Mahwah: Lawrence Erlbaum, 2005): 247–270.

59 Kaptein and Wempe, *The Balanced Company*, 243–244.

clause within the contract.[60] Contractors must have the right to terminate the contract if there are unforeseen major fundamental changes in the conditions of the relationships, which should be defined with precision by the working of the clauses included in the contractual agreement. However, "although contractual relations do entail the right to re-evaluate the contract in the light of new circumstances, the parties concerned should at the same time respect the value the contract represent to other contract partners and resist opting out too readily"[61] and that results in corporate solidarity. Thus, the principle of solidarity is a matter of trust between the corporate actors and their stakeholders.

2.1.2.5 Principle of Reliability

Since corporations exist by a contract, all explicit and implicit promises are to be kept by corporations and stakeholders. Corporate reliability requires "sufficient coherence and uniformity in the behavior of the different constituencies comprising the corporation as a contracting party."[62] Moreover, reliability refers to the independent stand of corporations in the face of conflicting interests and dilemmas. Reliability also requires that corporations give careful attention to contractual obligations and that they are not governed by powerful influences.[63]

These principles are considered the foundation of all contracts in a corporate context. Corporations, which fail to retain the basic behavioral principles, are considered morally incompetent and stakeholders have what is deemed a moral right to withdraw from an existing contract. The practicability of these principles depends upon the way in which both parties expend the effort to fulfill it. Authors such as Van Luijk consider that if these behavioral principles are alive in public conduct, then there is integrity in the public domain.[64]

2.1.3 Corporate Ethical Qualities

Based on these contractual principles, Kaptein and Wempe systematically arranged seven corporate virtues in corporate structure and culture. These virtues are the result of the above-mentioned corporate behavioral principles, but on the other hand, the behavioral principles are also a result

---

60 Jerry M. Calton and Lawrence J. Lad, "Social Contracting as a Trust-Building Process of Network Governance," *Business Ethics Quarterly* 5, no. 2 (1995): 284.

61 Kaptein and Wempe, *The Balanced Company*, 244.

62 Kaptein and Wempe, *The Balanced Company*, 245.

63 Todd R. La Porte, "High Reliability Organizations: Unlikely, Demanding and at Risk," *Journal of Contingencies & Crisis Management* 4, no. 2 (1996): 60–71.

64 Luijk, "Integrity in the Private, the Public, and the Corporate Domain," 46–47.

of corporate virtues. Here "[...] contexts stimulate conduct and conduct builds the context, principles and qualities are interrelated."[65]

Corporate virtues are necessary for corporate ethical conduct and guide the organization's ability to stimulate the ethical conduct of its employees by overcoming dilemmas.[66] The organization's integrity was evaluated upon the degree to which these dilemmas existed and how executives of those organizations responded to it.[67]

2.1.3.1 Clarity

Kaptein defines corporate clarity as "the extent to which the organization makes ethical expectations, such as values, norms, and principles concrete and understandable to employees."[68] It is thus related to the employee's functions in the corporation. Moreover, corporate clarity specifies how employees should treat the assets of the corporations, describing what the job-related responsibilities of the employees are and defines what stakeholders expect of employees.[69] If a corporation does not attempt to define what is acceptable and unacceptable, the situation would give too much freedom to employees. Subsequently, excess freedom can result in vagueness of corporate actions and responsibilities, thereby leading to many unethical practices among employees, including corporate corruption.[70] Furthermore, vagueness and too much freedom produce "further risk of vague or unclear normative expectations such that employees may hide behind their ignorance or deliberately keep themselves uninformed, which leads to excuses and rationalizations."[71]

Corporate clarity determines the reaction of employees to observed wrongdoings and unethical practices in the corporate world. If corporate clarity is greater, the "greater the responsibility employees will feel to uphold it, and the greater the likelihood that employees who observe wrongdoing will confront the wrongdoer(s), report to management, and

---

65 Kaptein and Wempe, *The Balanced Company*, 258.

66 Muel Kaptein, "Developing and Testing a Measure for the Ethical Culture of Organizations: The Corporate Ethical Virtues Model," *Journal of Organizational Behavior* 29, no. 7 (2008): 923–947.

67 Muel Kaptein and Piet van Reenen, "Integrity Management of Police Organizations," *International Journal of Police Strategies & Management* 24, no. 3 (2001): 281–300.

68 Muel Kaptein, "From Inaction to External Whistleblowing: The Influence of the Ethical Culture of Organizations on Employee Responses to Observed Wrongdoing," *Journal of Business Ethics* 98 (2011): 516.

69 Muel Kaptein and Jan Van Dalen, "The Empirical Assessment of Corporate Ethics: A Case Study," *Journal of Business Ethics* 24 (2000): 102.

70 Muel Kaptein, *Ethics Management: Auditing and Developing the Ethical Content of Organizations* (Boston: Kluwer Academic Publishers, 1998): 77–78.

71 Kaptein, "Developing and Testing a Measure for the Ethical Culture of Organizations," 925.

call the hotline."[72] However, according to Kaptein, the relation between external whistle blowing[73] and clarity is less clear because external whistle blowing is only possible when corporate norms are compatible with stakeholders or societal norms.[74] However, it is quite logical to conclude the importance of corporate clarity since "when an organization has no explicit standards to distinguish right from wrong, external reporting is less likely because it is more difficult to hold the organization accountable for conduct that has not been defined as wrong than when the organization violates its own standards."[75]

2.1.3.2 Consistency

According to Kaptein and Wempe, corporate "consistency concerns the degree to which the organizational expectations toward the moral conduct of employees are coherent, univocal, unambiguous, and compatible."[76] The management of a corporation is considered as the referent group for the employees in corporations. The influence of management's conduct on employees' conduct depends on the intensity and frequency of contact between management and employees.[77] High levels of contact with management can influence the actions of employees in several ways, such as: (1) management action can be seen as an example for corporate conduct because it is idolized, (2) what management rewards and punishes influences the employees, (3) and a consistent ethical climate within the company is promoted by higher ranking management.[78] Even the emotions that higher ranking managers display toward corporate projects have the potential to influence an employee's behavior and thus, performance

---

[72] Kaptein, "From Inaction to External Whistleblowing," 516. See also David B. Greenberger, Marcia P. Miceli and, and Debra J. Cohen, "Oppositionists and Group Norms: The Reciprocal Influence of Whistle-Blowers and Co-Workers," *Journal of Business Ethics* 6, no. 7 (1987): 527–542.

[73] Whistle blowing can be divided into external and internal whistle-blowing. If employees were to report the corporate unethical behavior of an employee to an internal corporate authority, then it is internal whistle-blowing. External whistle blowing, however, refers to the "reporting the offense to an outside agency, such as a professional organization or the press." Cf. Abraham Mansbach and Yaacov G Bachner, "Internal or External Whistleblowing: Nurses' Willingness to Report Wrongdoing," *Nursing Ethics* 17, no. 4 (2010): 483.

[74] Marcia P. Miceli, Janet P. Near, and Charles R. Schwenk, "Who Blows the Whistle and Why?" *Industrial and Labor Relations Review* 45, no. 1 (1991): 118. See also Kaptein, "From Inaction to External Whistleblowing," 516.

[75] Kaptein, "From Inaction to External Whistleblowing," 516.

[76] Kaptein and Wempe, *The Balanced Company*, 252. See also Kaptein and Dalen, "The Empirical Assessment of Corporate Ethics," 102.

[77] Dove Izraeli, "Ethical Beliefs and Behavior among Managers: A Cross-Cultural Perspective," *Journal of Business Ethics* 7, no. 4 (1988): 263–271. See also Kaptein and Wempe, *The Balanced Company*, 252.

[78] Robert C. Ford and Woodrow D. Richardson, "Ethical Decision Making: A Review of the Empirical Literature," *Journal of Business Ethics* 13, no. 3 (1994): 212.

due to the simple need to please the boss, an approach very dominant in most cultures across the world.[79]

Moreover, there is a positive relation between congruency of senior managers and reporting corporate wrongdoing to managers.[80] When managers are not perceived as role models, then employees are not inclined to whistle blow. The "less the employees will be able to rely on the intervention of management to stop the wrongdoing [...] the more they will be required to take action themselves."[81] Employees will likely be reluctant to report wrong-doing due to fear of institutional bullying.

2.1.3.3 Sanctionability

The corporate moral quality of sanctionability refers to the reward and punishment structure for both managers and employees as a result of positive and negative actions. If the corporation does not punish the unethical behavior of internal stakeholders, then the corporation shows ambivalence regarding the handling of dilemmas.[82]

Reward leads to repletion and punishment leads to avoidance of particular acts based on the theory of deterrence.[83] Based on concrete examples, Kaptein concludes that unpunished unethical behavior can create similar forms of unethical behavior because unpunished unethical behavior communicates an impression to perpetrators that their behavior would not be punished.[84] Similarly, "the lack of recognition of ethical behaviour diminishes the willingness of employees to act ethically and increases the likelihood of resorting to unethical behaviours."[85]

Sanctions are applied to employees if they mishandle corporate assets, or if functional responsibilities are deliberately neglected so that stakeholder's expectations are deliberately ignored. Furthermore, unpunished unethical behavior of employees and managers would work as an incentive for continuing unethical behavior in the future.[86]

---

79 Ethel Brundin, Holger Patzelt, and Dean A. Shepherd, "Managers' Emotional Displays and Employees' Willingness to Act Entrepreneurially," *Journal of Business Venturing* 23 (2008): 222.

80 Kaptein, "From Inaction to External Whistleblowing," 517.

81 Kaptein, "From Inaction to External Whistleblowing," 517.

82 Kaptein and Dalen, "The Empirical Assessment of Corporate Ethics," 102. See also Kaptein and Wempe, *The Balanced Company*, 254–256.

83 Loren Falkenberg and Irene Herremans, "Ethical Behaviours in Organizations: Directed by the Formal or Informal Systems?," *Journal of Business Ethics* 14, no. 2 (1995): 133–143. See also Muel Kaptein, "Understanding Unethical Behavior by Unraveling Ethical Culture," *Human Relations* 63, no. 6 (2011): 851.

84 Kaptein, "Understanding Unethical Behavior by Unraveling Ethical Culture," 851.

85 Kaptein, "Understanding Unethical Behavior by Unraveling Ethical Culture," 851.

86 Kaptein, *Ethics Management*, 67–106.

2.1.3.4 Achievability

Achievability in corporate culture requires that "ethical expectations should be practicable."[87] The quality of achievability refers to the manner in which a corporation helps employees to meet ethical expectations when they are faced with one or more of the three dilemmas. These dilemmas correspond to different expectations, which cannot be satisfied simultaneously: however, they can be properly balanced. Therefore, corporations should provide employees with the means to achieve corporate expectations and stakeholder expectations or at least the means to keep a balance when dealing with dilemmas such as necessary resources, sufficient authority, sufficient timing, knowledge, skills, and information.[88] Moreover, achievability implies that management should not ask immoral requests of employees that are contrary to common or personal moral values because "if there is sharp division between personal values and values at work, then unethical conduct will occur sooner rather than later."[89]

Achievability is important in corporate ethical conduct "because the more pressure the employees are under to perform and meet targets and the fewer resources they have available, the higher is the risk of [...] wrongdoing."[90] Lack of achievability creates high-pressure corporate culture and in "such a high-pressure culture, managers and employees may also start to think that other matters, such as meeting financial targets, are more important than complying with ethical standards. These factors create conditions for rationalizing unethical behaviour thus increasing the likelihood that unethical behaviour will occur."[91]

2.1.3.5 Supportability

Supportability in the organizational-corporate context refers to how much support is stimulated among employees for the careful use of corporate assets, adequate coordination between employees, and fulfilling stakeholder interests. Negative employee experiences have the potential to turn them against the corporation's success, but if employees receive sufficient support from the corporate management, then they will be more likely to overcome dilemmas and conflicts. A lack of supportability and unfair treatment in a corporate context creates distrust and hostility among employees and consequently leads to ethical problems.[92] Employment

---

87 Kaptein and Wempe, *The Balanced Company*, 252.

88 Linda Klebe Trevino, "Ethical Decision Making in Organizations: A Person-Situation Interactionist Model," *The Academy of Management Review* 11, no. 3 (1986): 613–614.

89 Kaptein, *Ethics Management*, 84–85.

90 Kaptein, "From Inaction to External Whistleblowing," 518.

91 Kaptein, "Understanding Unethical Behavior by Unraveling Ethical Culture," 849.

92 Linda Klebe Trevino et al., "Managing Ethics and Legal Compliance: What Works and What Hurts," *California Management Review* 41, no. 2 (1999): 142. See also Kaptein and

dissatisfaction is the main cause of unethical behavior in the corporate context. Supportability helps employees "to integrate the interests of the corporation, their co-workers, and external stakeholders."[93]

According to Kaptein, another dimension of supportability in corporate culture is the "extent to which the organization stimulates identification with the ethics of the organization amongst employees."[94] When employees identify with corporate ethical standards, they will not only be more motivated to stand for those corporate ethical standards at the time of conflicts of interests and dilemmas but they also take action to correct corporate actions, which are against corporate ethical standards through either confrontation, reporting, or calling a hotline.[95]

2.1.3.6 Visibility

Visibility and clarity are different within the corporate context. Clarity refers to the employee's responsibilities whereas visibility denotes the "degree to which the effects of one's conduct are visible to the actor, to those who are affected by it, and to the co-workers, and supervisor who are directly involved."[96] David L. Carter, in his investigation of police corruption, states that failure to detect corruption reinforces the safety of the practice. Fear of being caught decreases unethical acts within a corporation. Therefore, visibility is a precondition for correcting corporate misconduct.[97]

Corporate visibility can be perceived horizontally and vertically. Vertical visibility means that there is an awareness of unethical behavior of employees in both spheres; top-down (manager to employees) and bottom-up (employees to managers). Horizontal visibility refers to the degree to which co-workers are aware of the unethical conduct of fellow workers.[98] If there was to be visibility in the corporate context, then the consequences of the treatment of corporate assets, consequences of employee's work, and the consequence of how the stakeholder expectations are fulfilled, would

---

Dalen, "The Empirical Assessment of Corporate Ethics," 102. See also Kaptein and Wempe, *The Balanced Company*, 253.

93 Kaptein and Wempe, *The Balanced Company*, 253.

94 Kaptein, "From Inaction to External Whistleblowing," 518.

95 Tom R. Tyler and Steven L. Blader, "Can Businesses Effectively Regulate Employee Conduct? The Antecedents of Rule Following in Work Settings," *The Academy of Management Journal* 48, no. 6 (2005): 1154. See also Kaptein, "From Inaction to External Whistleblowing," 518.

96 Kaptein, *Ethics Management*, 88.

97 David L. Carter, "Drug-Related Corruption of Police Officers: A Contemporary Typology," *Journal of Criminal Justice* 18, no. 2 (1990): 88–89.

98 Kaptein and Wempe, *The Balanced Company*, 253–254.

be visible. When corporate visibility is absent, the possibility for ethical misconduct rises.[99]

2.1.3.7 *Discussability*

The quality of discussability refers to the extent to which employees can critically examine ethical issues and moral dilemmas within the corporation. The possibility of criticism has both horizontal and vertical dimensions, as in the case of visibility. An organization that is closed to discussion neither encourages nor accepts criticisms and thus prevents potentially enriching discussion.[100] According to Kaptein, "ethics becomes a problem in most companies not because of ethical differences or ignorance but rather because it is just not part of their conversation."[101]

The corporate quality of discussability is possible when corporations encourage a democratic atmosphere. However, in authoritarian organizational structures, employees are expected to follow orders or do what is assigned to them from above within the hierarchal structure. If the quality of discussability exists in the corporate structure, then it welcomes internal and external criticisms of stakeholders and the possibility of ethical conduct is high.[102]

These qualities are interrelated. If all these qualities are embedded in a corporate context, then that context is an ideal corporate climate. By calculating the degree to which these qualities have become part of the corporate climate, we can trace corporate intentionality. If all these qualities are present in the corporate culture, then this culture will also have a positive feedback on corporate assets, employee responsibility, and stakeholder expectations.[103]

2.1.4 The Purpose of Social Contract-Based Corporate Integrity

The dilemmas, conflicts of interests, and corporate political illegal relations are all real ethical challenges within the corporate world, which in turn lead to corporate unethically related conducts. Corporate integrity helps employees and managers of a corporation to create a "balance between conflicting values, norms and ideals, pursuing equilibrium in the corporate ambitions and demands."[104] Moreover, contractual relationships

---

[99] Carter, "Drug-Related Corruption of Police Officers: A Contemporary Typology," 85–98. See also Kaptein and Dalen, "The Empirical Assessment of Corporate Ethics," 103.

[100] Kaptein and Dalen, "The Empirical Assessment of Corporate Ethics," 103.

[101] This quotation is originally from Solomon and Hanson but I have quoted it from the following source. Cf. Kaptein, *Ethics Management*, 90.

[102] Kaptein, *Ethics Management*, 105–115.

[103] Muel Kaptein, "Integrity Management," *European Management Journal* 17, no. 6 (1999): 632.

[104] Kaptein and Wempe, *The Balanced Company*, 227.

within a corporation between various stakeholders fulfill the aim of obtaining a sustainable mutual advantage, which is only possible by creating a balance where there are tensions surrounding contractual obligations.[105]

Social contract-based corporate integrity is advocated as having a sustainable advantage for both contracting parties, which directly depends upon the prior-stated corporate ethical qualities and corporate ethical behavior principles. Corporate structures, culture, and intentionality contain corporate ethical qualities that are part of the corporate context. Behavioral principles are the criteria for ethical corporate behavior and relationships. However, both conduct and context are interrelated because "context stimulates conduct and conduct builds context."[106] The consequences of the prior-stated corporate context and conduct result in a "mutual sustainable advantage through balancing conflicting values, norms and ideals."[107] The blameworthiness of a company depends on the degree to which the prior-stated criteria are disregarded. This integrity model contains three perspectives. The basic thinking behind the theory is that good intentions are converted into good deeds that thus create the desired effects, thereby leading to a sustainable advantage. In short, "input, conduct and output are the three lines of approach relevant in determining the coherence of a corporation's ethics."[108] My critical remarks in this regard will be presented later.

2.1.5 The Implementation of the Social Contract-Based Corporate Integrity

There are four stages in the implementation of corporate integrity; these are management commitment, development of a code of ethics, implementation of a code, and auditing of its effectiveness in practice.[109]

2.1.5.1 Management Commitment

The first step to form corporate integrity is to enhance and ensure the interest and commitment of the senior management of the company concerned. Generally, commitment of managers is expected for financial, strategic, ethical, and operational success. However, the commitment of managers to establish corporate ethics is not for one-sided instrumental

105 Kaptein, *Ethics Management*, 27.

106 Kaptein and Wempe, *The Balanced Company*, 258; 148–149; 257–258.

107 Kaptein and Wempe, *The Balanced Company*, 257–258.

108 Kaptein and Wempe, *The Balanced Company*, 260.

109 Muel Kaptein and Scott Avelino, "Measuring Corporate Integrity: A Survey-Based Approach," *Corporate Governance* 5, no. 1 (2005): 46. See also Kaptein and Wempe, *The Balanced Company*, 264–265.

benefits.[110] Moreover, "manager's commitment to ethics [...] will capture the attention of employees, holding employees accountable to ethical expectations. They will define ethical roles not only through ethics policy documents, memos, and other communications, but also through more deeply embedded organizational activities whose implications are difficult to avoid."[111]

According to Kaptein and Wempe, senior management should take initiatives to implement corporate integrity. In this process, senior managers should consult and discuss dilemmas with stakeholders as well as consider stakeholder expectations and code inclusions.[112]

2.1.5.2 Development of Codes of Ethics

Kaptein illustrates that the formation and implementation of codes of conduct is the most important and thus significant step to establishing corporate integrity. From a general point of view, a corporate code of conduct is the totality of a corporation's business values, principles and standards.[113] By taking into consideration various levels of corporate codes of conduct,[114] Kaptein and Mark S. Schwartz define a business code as "a distinct and formal document containing a set of prescriptions developed by and for a company to guide present and future behavior on multiple issues of at least its managers and employees toward one another, the company, external stakeholders, and/or society in general."[115] To be more

---

110 Gary R. Weaver, Linda Klebe Treviño, and Philip L. Cochran, "Integrated and Decoupled Corporate Social Performance: Management Commitments, External Pressures, and Corporate Ethics Practices," *The Academy of Management Journal* 42, no. 5 (1999): 543.

111 Weaver, Treviño, and Cochran, "Integrated and Decoupled Corporate Social Performance," 543.

112 Kaptein and Wempe, *The Balanced Company*, 263–265.

113 Sandra A. Waddock, Charles Bodwell, and Samuel B. Graves, "Responsibility: The New Business Imperative," *The Academy of Management Executive* 16, no. 2 (2002): 132–148.

114 Corporate codes of conduct are explained through different names such as business principles, corporate credo, corporate philosophy, corporate ethics, corporate ethics statements, corporate practice etc. Cf. Amartya Sen, "Economics, Business Principles and Moral Sentiments," *Business Ethics Quarterly* 7, no. 3 (1997): 5–15. See also George C. S. Benson, "Codes of Ethics," *Journal of Business Ethics* 8, no. 5 (1989): 305–319. See also Gerald E. Ledford, Jon R. Wendenhof, and James T. Strahley, "Realizing a Corporate Philosophy," *Organizational Dynamics* 23, no. 3 (1995): 5–19. See also Patrick E. Murphy, "Corporate Ethics Statements: Current Status and Future Prospects," *Journal of Business Ethics* 14, no. 9 (1995): 727–740. Corporate codes of conduct can have different objects and levels such as internal and external. An internal level code states how employees treat each other and corporate assets whereas an external level code deals with the treatment of external stakeholders. There are formal corporate codes of conduct, which are approved by and informal corporate codes of conduct that are unwritten corporate customs and laws. Cf. Muel Kaptein and Mark S. Schwartz, "The Effectiveness of Business Codes: A Critical Examination of Existing Studies and the Development of an Integrated Research Model," *Journal of Business Ethics* 77 (2008): 113.

115 Kaptein and Schwartz, "The Effectiveness of Business Codes," 113.

precise, corporate codes of conduct include "board and management oversight, employee communication and training, auditing and monitoring plans, hotlines, disciplinary and enforcement mechanisms, response protocols, and the like."[116]

2.1.5.3 Implementation of a Code

Implementation of codes of conduct defines corporate responsibilities, principles, and virtues. The code is kept in a written form and it "indicates the way in which the rights of stakeholders will be respected and the way in which company representatives will express the company's responsibilities."[117] Furthermore, corporate culture and structures are formed in accordance with the code's spirit.[118] The formation and implementation of corporate codes of conduct in corporate structures and culture are also conducted by consulting both internal and external stakeholders.[119] The moral integrity of managers and employees are crucial in the implementation of a code of conduct because it can be done with an instrumental mentality.

2.1.5.4 Auditing the Effectiveness of the Code

A corporate audit has two directions. First, a corporate audit is related to corporate codes of conduct by which the organization is expected to function. Second, a corporate audit aims to review the positive and negative aspects of corporate ethics and to give directions for any future improvements that can be made.[120]Auditing of corporate ethics also includes social auditing,[121] which is defined as "a review to ensure that an organisation gives due consideration to its wider and social responsibilities to those both directly and indirectly affected by its decisions, and that a balance is achieved in its corporate planning between these aspects and the more traditional business related objectives."[122] Review and improvement of corporate social responsibility is the prime aim of corporate social auditing.[123]

116 Kaptein and Avelino, "Measuring Corporate Integrity: A Survey-Based Approach," 47. See also Paine, "Managing for Organizational Integrity," 111.

117 Muel Kaptein and Johan Wempe, "The Ethics Report: A Means of Sharing Responsibility," *A European Review* 7, no. 3 (1998): 136.

118 Kaptein and Avelino, "Measuring Corporate Integrity: A Survey-Based Approach," 47–48.

119 Kaptein and Wempe, *The Balanced Company*, 265.

120 Peter Kok et al., "A Corporate Social Responsibility Audit within a Quality Management Framework," *Journal of Business Ethics* 31 (2001): 291.

121 Kok et al., "A Corporate Social Responsibility Audit within a Quality Management Framework," 291.

122 G. Vinten, "Modern Internal Auditing," in *Current Issues in Auditing*, eds. Michael Sherer and Stuart Turley (London: Paul Chapman Publishing, 1991): 233.

123 Kok et al., "A Corporate Social Responsibility Audit within a Quality Management Framework," 291.

Auditing as part of the implementation of corporate integrity shares the same aims as the above-mentioned auditing of corporate ethics. Further, Kaptein and Wempe state that "the auditing process includes checking whether the code is honored in practice, the auditing results are communicated and adjustments are needed."[124] However, the uniqueness of Kaptein and Wempe's view lies in the fact that they reduce corporate integrity to corporate codes of conduct, as is clear from the different steps of the implementation of corporate integrity. My critical remarks on this view will be presented at the end of this chapter.

2.2 Civic Citizenship-Based Corporate Integrity

Civic citizenship-based corporate integrity theory is largely related to corporate social responsibility. Corporate citizenship theory builds on the stakeholder theory as well as the corporate agency theory, by emphasizing an inclusion of business organization in the civic context.[125] From moral agency theory, a corporation is seen as an active member of the civic society, thereby sharing equal rights and duties with other members of the civic society.[126]Among corporate social responsibility theories, "the citizenship theories of corporations see corporate responsibility emerging from their location in civil society. This theory provides a strong platform for developing a civic perspective of corporate integrity."[127] However, corporate citizenship theory does not clarify what corporate obligations are, and whether corporate obligations are the same in regard to the charitable acts conducted by corporations. Furthermore, corporate social responsibility theory gives considerable regard to the community, which concurs with a stakeholder view. In this situation "corporate citizenship theory plus the corporate agent and stakeholder theories give us a strong foundation

---

124 Kaptein and Wempe, *The Balanced Company*, 264. See also Kaptein and Wempe, "The Ethics Report: A Means of Sharing Responsibility," 138.

125 There are different corporate social responsibility theories i.e. corporate citizenship theories, stakeholder theory etc. Corporate citizenship theory considers corporations as members of civil society. Therefore, corporations have duties and responsibilities just as citizens. Cf. Jeanne M. Logsdon and Donna J. Wood, "Business Citizenship: From Domestic to Global Level of Analysis,"*Business Ethics Quarterly* 12, no. 2 (2002): 157–158. According to stakeholder theory, corporations have to keep overall stakeholder relationships. This is necessary for the survival and existence of corporations. Cf. R. Edward Freeman and William M. Evan, "A Stakeholder Theory of the Modern Corporation: Kantian Capitalism," in *Ethical Issues in Business: A Philosophical Approach*, eds. Thomas Donaldson and Patricia H. Werhane (New Jersey: Prentice-Hall, 1996): 312–313.

126 Charles J. Fombrun, "Three Pillars of Corporate Citizenship: Ethics, Social Benefit, Profitability," in *Corporate Global Citizenship: Doing Business in the Public Eye*, eds. Noel M. Tichy, Andrew R. McGill, and Lunda St. Clair (San Francisco: New Lexington Press, 1997): 28.

127 Marvin T. Brown, *Corporate Integrity: Rethinking Organizational Ethics and Leadership* (Cambridge: Cambridge University Press, 2005): 21.

for continuing our movement toward a civic perspective of corporate integrity."[128]

The relationship between economy and civil society[129] is disputable, and dominant views hold that the two entities are part of very different realms, and additionally they have their own rules and values. I would call civil society as direct and indirect stakeholders; however, corporations are naturally very different from the civil society[130] because business is always related to profit, whereas civil society is more readily concerned with human dignity, and equality of rights, and considers individual as an end rather than a means to an end.[131] However, controversial views exist as to whether corporations and government belong within the category of civil society.[132]

---

128 Brown, *Corporate Integrity*, 21.

129 Until the mid-eighteenth century, civil society was seen as the "political association, or state, or the government." Cf. Gnana Patrick, "Civil Society and Church as Critical Interrogators," in *Church's Engagement in Civil Society*, eds. Antony Kalliath and Francis Gonsalves (Bangalore: Indian Theological Association, 2009): 1. It is very clear from the statement of John Keane that "to be a member of a civil society was to be a citizen, a member of a state and, thus, obliged to act in accordance with its laws and without engaging in acts harmful to other citizens." Cf. John Keane, "Despotism and Democracy," in *Civil Society and the State: New European Perspectives* ed. John Keane (New York: Verso, 1998): 38. After the middle of the eighteenth century, civil society is, however, distinguished from the state and the political associations. During this period, civil society is considered as the area "wherein the individual could freely undertake his socio-cultural and economic endeavours independent of the imperial state." Cf. Patrick, "Civil Society and Church as Critical Interrogators," 2. This view is based on liberalism. Therefore, civil society is considered independent of state and economic sphere. For the last three decades, the concept of civil society has been considered a third sphere, free from state and free from market and economy. The third sphere refers to the open society formed on the basis of the freedom of the individual to associate. This concept acknowledges the danger of inequality. The basic critical question is whether all people are equally able to form associations. Cf. Patrick, "Civil Society and Church as Critical Interrogators," 2–6. From a general point of view, civil society is defined as "a zone of freedom for individuals to associate with others and for groups to shape their norms, articulate their purposes, and determine for themselves the internal structure of group identity and authority." Furthermore, "civil society refers essentially to the so-called 'intermediary institutions' such as professional associations, religious groups, and labour unions, citizen advocacy organizations that give voice to various sectors of society and enrich public participation in democracies." Cf. Robert C. Post and Nancy L. Rosenblum, "Introduction," in *Civil Society and Government*, eds. Robert C. Post and Nancy L. Rosenblum (Oxford: Oxford University Press, 2002): 3.

130 Petr Kopecký and Cas Mudde, "Rethinking Civil Society," *Democratization* 10, no. 3 (2003): 5.

131 Yoshikazu Sakamoto, "An Alternative to Global Marketization: East Asian Regional Cooperation and the Civic State," *Alternatives: Global, Local, Political* 24, no. 2 (1999): 147.

132 Few authors held that "in principle, similar considerations pertain to the relationship between civil and economic society, even if historically, under capitalism, economic society has been more successfully insulated from the influence of civil society." Cf. Jean L. Cohen and Andrew Arato, *Civil Society and Political Theory* (Cambridge: MIT Press, 1992): 10.

On the other hand, Brown argues that both businesses and corporations are set in the context of civil society.[133] Therefore, "the relationship between corporations and the systems in which they exist form a civic perspective of corporations."[134] Furthermore, dependency of a market economy on social capital and the rules of society show the relationship between society and economy. Both the civic perspective and the civic context allow corporations to overcome the temptation to privatize ethics.[135] There is a close link between the corporate civic perspective and Aristotle's idea of virtue here. Moreover, Robert Solomon is of opinion that "Aristotle, for whom life was supposed to fit together in a coherent 'whole', it is the same holistic idea—that business people and corporations are first of all part of a larger community—that drives business ethics today."[136] Brown also argues that corporations are not only a part of the community in which they operate but also an active citizen of the community.[137]

Assuming that corporations are citizens in civil society, corporate integrity includes the relational aspects of integrity. There are five dimensions of corporate relations: "the cultural, interpersonal, organizational, civic, and natural. Each of these dimensions can either block or enable corporate integrity."[138] According to Brown, "the complete picture of corporate integrity would consist of verbal and non-verbal communication patterns that are open to disagreements and differences conscious of human relationships, guided by a worthwhile purpose, engaged in civic cooperation, and promotes prosperity for all natural communities."[139]

2.2.1 Corporate Cultural Dimension of Integrity

The clear image of corporate culture is expressed by communication patterns, which are sometimes quite different. Various forms of communication take place in an organizational culture, including stories, rituals, and rites.[140] Generally, there are two types of communicative models: the

---

133 Brown, "Corporate Integrity and Public Interest," 12.

134 Brown, "Corporate Integrity and Public Interest," 12.

135 Privatization of ethics refers to ethics that does not consider society. Cf. Brown, "Corporate Integrity and Public Interest," 12.

136 Robert C. Solomon, "Aristotle, Ethics and Business Organizations," *Organization Studies* 25, no. 6 (2004): 1022.

137 Brown, *Corporate Integrity*, 20–21.

138 Brown, *Corporate Integrity*, 9.

139 Brown, "Corporate Integrity and Public Interest," 15.

140 Corporate stories describe the experience of the organization members. Corporate stories include a company's heritage, excellent decisions of past managers etc., that provide examples that people can learn from in the future. They transmit the value culture of organizations. Weekly meetings and semi-annual reviews can be seen as part of organizational rites and rituals. Cf. Linda Suny Myrsiades, "Corporate Stories as Cultural Communications in the Organizational Setting," *Management Communication Quarterly* 1, no. 1 (1987): 85–120.

post office model and the contextual model.[141] The communication context includes not only family and civic relationships but also relationships at work. The contextual model of communication focuses on work within corporate life.[142]

According to Pearce W. Barnett, there are four different types of communication patterns: monocultural communication, ethnocentric communication, modernistic communication, and cosmopolitan communication.[143] These patterns differ in "how they establish coherence, coordination, and how they treat others and their resources, and how they interpret the logic of their actions."[144] Monocultural communication is based on traditional culture whereby people treat others as members. However, the basic beliefs of the community are considered as sacred and static, and that they should communicate as they have done in the past. Ethnocentric communication is the same as monocultural communication, except that people consider other fellow colleagues as "non-native" to the organization. From this perspective, other people, traditions, and groups are different, but at the same time they are considered inferior nevertheless. Modernistic communication rejects traditional beliefs and thus, people place their beliefs in progress. Modernistic communication is an integral part of corporate cultural communications. Contrary to the above-mentioned communication patterns, cosmopolitan communication gives more importance to coordination rather than to coherence. This communication pattern integrates different cultures and stories as well as reflections on this integration.[145]

Cosmopolitan pattern of communication values the importance of the various parts of the whole mass. Thomas Maak, in his theory of corporate integrity, observes that "just like individuals, for corporations to have true integrity, they must be conscious of all relationships in which they

See also Suellen J. Hogan and Leonard V. Coote, "Organizational Culture, Innovation, and Performance: A Test of Schein's Model," *Journal of Business Research* 67, no. 8 (2014): 1610.

141 The post office model sees communication as an isolated act. Here, communication is the exchange of ideas by individual isolated members. The contextual model says that one's communication is based on the idea that one is an integral part of the society. Cf. Brown, *Corporate Integrity*, 33.

142 Brown, *Corporate Integrity*, 34–35.

143 Pearce W. Barnett, *Communication and the Human Condition* (Carbondale: Southern Illinois University Press, 1989): 91–196.

144 Brown, *Corporate Integrity*, 41. Coherence in communication means the interpretation of one's own environment and experience. Coordination is the integration with one's own fellow human beings and nature. Mystery is the meaning of life that is brought about by both coherence and coordination. Treatment of resources refers to how people relate to stories, myths, and rituals which provide coherence. Treatment of others in cultural communication refers to how cultural communication responds to people outside of their group. Cf. Barnett, *Communication and the Human Condition*, 31–32.

145 Brown, *Corporate Integrity*, 41–45. Brown originally took these ideas from Barnett Pearce. Cf. Barnett, *Communication and the Human Condition*, 30–180.

participate."[146] Cosmopolitan communicators accept disagreement as a chance to learn and it is not a relativist position. Moreover, "they are willing to stand for the inclusiveness of communication practices, which rests on the principle of respect for others. [...] Cosmopolitan communicators are open to engaging with others to find the best solution when they disagree about the right one."[147] Therefore, since integrity is understood as the moral wholeness of the person, the cosmopolitan pattern of communication expresses integrity.

The dialogical relationship is considered as a precondition for corporate communication integrity. For such a perspective, one can refer to Martin Buber who has articulated the relational aspect of human existence, expressed as an "I-Thou" relationship. This is a person-to-person relationship, whereby the other is considered as a person in the truest sense of the word.[148] In a corporate context, stakeholders are to be considered as the other; both corporation and stakeholders are true persons. Since communication takes place between one person and another, integrity demands it be open "because the stakeholder involvement strategy takes the notion of the stakeholder relationship to an extreme. Companies should not only influence but also seek to be influenced by stakeholders, and therefore change when necessary."[149] Joseph A. Petrick and John F. Quinn observe in their management integrity theory that the "communication theory of integrity prefers to stimulate change fervidly in a highly assertive and progressive manner."[150]

However, many modern corporate systems consider efficiency as their highest value,[151] as part of the culture of modern technology. A modernistic culture believes that only maximization of productivity and profitability are the main thrusts of modernity. A weakness of this idea is the lack of integrity, because if a business seeks higher efficiency, then this reduces the awareness of stakeholders. Brown suggests that in order to have integrity, businesses have to move from modernism to cosmopolitan communication.[152]

In order to have integrity at the cultural level, corporations have to form cosmopolitan conversations, which are open to different cultures

---

146 Maak, "Undivided Corporate Responsibility," 360.

147 Brown, *Corporate Integrity*, 53–54.

148 Martin Buber, *I and Thou*, trans. R. Gregor Smith (New York: Charles Scribner's Sons, 1958): 4.

149 Mette Morsing and Majken Schultz, "Corporate Social Responsibility Communication: Stakeholder Information, Response and Involvement Strategies," *Business Ethics: A European Review* 15, no. 4 (2006): 328.

150 Joseph A. Petrick and John F. Quinn, *Management Ethics: Integrity at Work* (London: Sage Publications, 1997): 84–85.

151 Kaptein and Wempe, *The Balanced Company*, 164.

152 Brown, *Corporate Integrity*, 67–68.

and disagreements. The world of technology may not encourage this but it should never hinder it either. The barriers of such openness are "the lack of curiosity, the fear of scarcity, and the absence of boundaries."[153] The capacity to overcome these barriers is included in the dialogical process with external stakeholders and co-workers.[154] Corporate integrity is the gradual process of creation. In this context, Brown states that there is a possibility for cosmopolitan communication in corporate cultures with stakeholders producing and inspiring a vision of corporate cultural integrity.[155]

2.2.2 Corporate Interpersonal Dimension of Integrity

The main concern of the interpersonal dimension of corporate integrity is relational wholeness in the corporate context. An interpersonal dimension of integrity should facilitate the relationship of cooperation among co-workers, stakeholders, and managers that is necessary to effectively solve complex employee/employer issues. The corporate interpersonal dimension of integrity concentrates on conversations among stakeholders and managers in terms of relational awareness.[156]

There are different images for relationships in societal orders and business practices. Let us analyze these in order to pinpoint the meaning of the corporate interpersonal dimension of integrity. The master and servant image represents the work relationship very accurately.[157] This image includes three criteria: "(1) the master must have the right to control the physical conduct of the servant; (2) the master must consent to receive the service; and (3) the master must expect to receive some benefit from the service."[158] This model is not suited to corporate interpersonal relationships. However, a more adequate model can be found in the "law of reciprocity." The law of reciprocity states that "everyone who does anything for someone else expects to be paid back eventually in one form or another."[159] It does not mean that a work relationship within corporations is only for the gain of money. However, Lawrence C. Becker considers reciprocity

153 Brown, *Corporate Integrity*, 54–57. Conversation is blocked by the monocultural conversation context because they have no interest in others. Promotion of curiosity is the only way to move beyond monocultural patterns. Ethnocentric context presumes that the resources of knowledge and skills are rare. So they try to remain in their ethnic group. If they understand that resources are plenty, they will move to openness. There should be boundaries for any openness. It is not the blind acceptance of other cultures. Cf. Brown, *Corporate Integrity*, 54–57.

154 Brown, *Corporate Integrity*, 68.

155 Brown, "Corporate Integrity and Public Interest," 14–15.

156 Brown, *Corporate Integrity*, 101.

157 Brown, *Corporate Integrity*,76–77.

158 Jeffrey D. Kahn, "Organizations' Liability for Torts of Volunteers," *University of Pennsylvania Law Review* 133, no. 6 (1985): 1440.

159 Allen Cohen and David Bradford, *Influence without Authority* (New York: John Wiley, 1991): 29–29.

as a deontic virtue, which for him is "a disposition to obey a moral obligation."[160] Furthermore, reciprocity is the balancing of mutual benefits.[161]

The teamwork image asserts that corporate relationships consist of the cooperation between employees and managers who share a common vision to develop new strategies for the solving of problems. However, the entrepreneurial image states that in a workplace, individual creativity makes the conversation livelier and contributes to creating stronger working relationships. According to the family relationship images, such as the mother and child image, and family dinner image, the core criteria for the relationship is the fundamental need for security. Although this image is not directly related to the corporate context, one cannot ignore the security aspect of such a relationship. Brown states that a caring and thereby a securing corporate environment would benefit from individuals' creativity and knowledge. The ideal image of civic relationship's core message is that members of corporations have the right to participate.[162] That means, "people should have opportunities to deliberate with others about the arrangements of their work life."[163] Furthermore, in this scenario, workers are considered citizens in the workplace and have a civil right to participate in corporate working life, namely through the means of employee feedback programs and collective bargaining. The fundamental question is: What should be the real image of corporate interpersonal dimensions of integrity? In sum, "when we add reciprocity to the notions of secure and civic dimensions of relationship, meeting the challenge of interpersonal integrity would require conversations that promote secure civic reciprocal relationship."[164]

Corporate interpersonal relational awareness acknowledges that work relationships are not only relationships at work, but rather they also include the other relationships of workers as members of a family and civil society. The key foundation of these relationships is reciprocity, which upholds that no one is to be exploited to another person's advantage. That means corporate exchanges should benefit the relational wholeness of the stakeholders.[165] Maak, in his theory of corporate integrity, explains relational wholeness by stating that: "just like individuals, for corporations to have true integrity, they must be conscious of all relationships in which they participate, engage with all their constituencies in responsible ways,

---

160 Lawrence C. Becker, *Reciprocity* (Chicago: University of Chicago Press, 1986): 112. I have taken this author and his view from the following source. Cf. Brown, *Corporate Integrity*, 79.

161 Becker, *Reciprocity*, 112.

162 Brown, *Corporate Integrity*, 74–100.

163 Brown, *Corporate Integrity*, 98.

164 Brown, *Corporate Integrity*, 100.

165 Brown, "Corporate Integrity and Public Interest," 15.

meet their reasonable expectations and be considered partners in ensuring a sustainable future."[166]

The image of secure civic reciprocity of corporate relationships gives strong guidance to many daily issues arising in the workplace. Under the condition of non-tyranny, this would mean that equality and publicity are present. When this happens, there is the possibility of secure conversations, which would increase civic participation in corporate life. Safety and participation in corporate life go hand in hand.[167] Given the situation of business oriented dilemmas, the possibility of safety and participation provides for an environment whereby "various stakeholders could become involved in the process of public deliberation about their common challenges and possible joint solutions."[168]

2.2.3 Corporate Integrity as Worthwhile Corporate Purpose

There are two types of organizations, for-profit and non-profit. In economics, profit is generally defined as "the return to owners of business firms or investors in other financial ventures after the cost of operations, including taxes."[169] The sources of profit are attributed differently and the equitable distribution of profits is the main overarching theme within business ethics. The existence and operations of for-profit corporations are aimed at the maximization of profit; on the contrary, non-profit organizations exist for the public good.[170] Anne E. Preston states that in non-profit organizations, people are ready to spend their labor to achieve a public good.[171] Moreover, "non-profit organizations are able to offer employees a workplace where they can assist in the production of a good or service in which they find an intrinsic value."[172]

While there are certain similarities between for-profit and non-profit organizations, they are ultimately different in their end goal.[173]

166 Maak, "Undivided Corporate Responsibility," 363.

167 Brown, *Corporate Integrity*, 102.

168 Brown, *Corporate Integrity*, 102–103.

169 Bill Shaw, "Profit and the Profit Motive," in *Blackwell Encyclopedic Dictionary of Business Ethics*, eds. Patricia H. Werhane and R. Edward Freeman (Malden: Blackwell Publishers, 1997): 517.

170 F. Neil Brady, "Profit," in *Blackwell Encyclopedic Dictionary of Business Ethics*, eds. Patricia H. Werhane and Edward Freeman (Oxford: Blackwell Publishers, 1997): 518. See also Eric Kong, "The Development of Strategic Management in the Non-Profit Context: Intellectual Capital in Social Service Non-Profit Organizations," *International Journal of Management Reviews* 10, no. 3 (2008): 282.

171 Anne E. Preston, "The Nonprofit Worker in a For-Profit World," *Journal of Labor Economics* 7, no. 4 (1989): 440.

172 Matthias Benz, "Not for the Profit, but for the Satisfaction? Evidence on Worker Well-Being in Non-Profit Firms," *KYKLOS* 58, no. 2 (2005): 158.

173 Clyde Eiríkur Hulla and Brian H. Lio, "Innovation in Non-Profit and for-Profit Organizations: Visionary, Strategic, and Financial Considerations," *Journal of Change*

Nevertheless, both have a legal personality and they have a private nature as opposed to governmental organizations. Non-profit organizations do not distribute profit to the owners as it is to be reinvested, whereas the distribution of profit is a standard practice in for-profit organizations. Both are self-governed. For-profit and non-profit organizations tend to have a positive relation with stakeholders. Profit is ultimately the result of serving the stakeholders, hence Brown is of the opinion that both for-profit and non-profit managers aim to satisfy their stakeholders.[174] Managers and boards of directors "felt a responsibility to treat employees well, wanted a good relationship with their suppliers, and felt obliged to return something to their communities."[175] Furthermore, Amartya Sen states that every successful organization might have concerns serving the public benefit.[176] Moreover, Maak, in the theory of corporate integrity, identifies worthwhile corporate purposes as the commitments of corporations, which they undertake voluntarily.[177]

Individual persons can make decisions in accordance with their own intentions and deliberations. However, a "corporation's purpose resides in the good that it is designed to pursue."[178] Corporations have non-agent centered purposes, while natural persons have agent centered purposes. Both can use their worthwhile purposes as criteria for the evaluation of their actions. People can determine how they can achieve their purposes, whereas corporations working through a group of individuals have to accept internal decision-making structures to achieve corporate purposes.[179]

Solomon interprets corporations as a community. He states that "if we consider corporations first of all as communities—not legal fictions, not monolithic entities, not faceless bureaucracies, not matrices of price/earnings ratios, net assets, and liabilities—then the activities and the ethics of business become much more comprehensible and much more human."[180] The specificity of a corporation as a community is that it is a shared community with shared wealth, purpose and responsibilities. The stakeholder enters into its traditional community by internalizing the traditions, customs, and expectations, of corporations.[181] Brown makes

Management 6, no. 1 (2006): 55.

174 Brown, *Corporate Integrity*, 120–123.

175 Brown, *Corporate Integrity*, 115.

176 Amartya Sen, "Does Business Ethics Make Economic Sense," *Business Ethics Quarterly* 30, no. 1 (1993): 45–55.

177 Maak, "Undivided Corporate Responsibility," 362.

178 Brown, *Corporate Integrity*, 128.

179 Brown, *Corporate Integrity*, 128. See also Peter A. French, "The Corporation as a Moral Person," *American Philosophical Quarterly* 16, no. 3 (1979): 207–215.

180 Robert Solomon, *Ethics and Excellence: Cooperation and Integrity in Business* (Oxford: Oxford University Press, 1992): 150.

181 Robert C. Solomon, "The Corporation as Community: A Reply to Ed Hartman," *Business Ethics Quarterly* 4, no. 3 (1994): 273.

a distinction between internal corporate purpose (as a community), and external corporate purpose (as an agent). He states that internal corporate purpose is related to the corporate character that is a good community.[182] A corporate character is defined as, "the seat of the virtues necessary for a corporation to engage in practices with excellence, focusing on those internal goods thereby obtainable, while warding off threats from its own inordinate pursuit of external goods, and from the corrupting power of other institutions with which it engages."[183] The production of goods and services is the external purpose of corporations. When a corporation attains cultural openness and relational wholeness, then the internal purpose of a corporation is attained. Furthermore, a good corporate character or a good corporate community requires the relationship of a secure civic reciprocity.[184]

Furthermore, the civic perspective of corporations perceives corporations as parts of civil society, and corporate members as citizens. At the organizational level, corporate integrity refers not to the profit of a corporation but the corporation's functions within society. Therefore, a worthwhile purpose of both for-profit and non-profit corporations is to meet human needs and to enhance human life. These purposes have to be developed by engaging in dialogue with other agents of society, by taking into account the social and environmental needs as well as the taste of consumers. At the same time, the civic perspective of corporations allows both economic and managerial functions such as wealth creation and high performance.[185]

2.2.4 Civic Cooperation as Corporate Social Integrity

Civic cooperation includes the relationship of corporations with civil society and local government or city government. As we have already seen, a "civil society is most commonly defined as a set of organizations that operate between the state, the family (individual; household), and [...] the economic production (market; firms). Supposedly, civil society is independent from the state in financial terms."[186] However, the relationship between civil society, government, and corporations are "in terms of different sectors such as market sector, government sector, and third sector that includes associations not controlled by the market or government."[187]

182 Brown, *Corporate Integrity*, 129.

183 Geoff Moore, "Corporate Character: Modern Virtue Ethics and the Virtuous Corporation," *Business Ethics Quarterly* 15, no. 4 (2005): 661.

184 Brown, *Corporate Integrity*, 130.

185 Brown, *Corporate Integrity*, 130–132.

186 Kopecký and Mudde, "Rethinking Civil Society," 5.

187 Brown, *Corporate Integrity*, 144. See also Kopecký and Mudde, "Rethinking Civil Society," 5.

Furthermore, the economy is not a free system but a part of civil society. Although business, government, and civil society are interrelated, they are managed by different strategies.[188]

There are three types of strategies; threat, exchange, and integration, for managing government, business, and civil society respectively. In the threat strategy, people are compelled to do something to avoid punishment. The exchange strategy is based on mutual reciprocity. A collaborative work is the key character of the integrative strategy of a civil society. However, a detailed examination shows that the three strategies are included in each group but not in the same proportion. The integrative strategy of civil society works in the context of exchange relations. The threat strategy of government protects both civil society and business in order to facilitate their smooth functioning.[189] "Civil society needs to be seen as both containing market exchanges and restraining the rule of law, so government does not become tyrannical, but does protect civil society and the market."[190] The possibility of the domination of civil society by corporations is high as they tend to control the media, press, as well as other information sources within societal structures considered to be essential to everyday lives and practices. Here, governments should actively protect democratically essential practices.[191]

Civic cooperation as corporate social integrity requires a positive relationship between corporations, civil society, and governments. Cooperation between civil society, governments, and corporations create mutual benefit for all parties. In the occasion of conflicts of interest, cooperation "would recognize the need to go beyond positions or arguments based on rights or power, and toward the joint identification of solutions based on mutual interests."[192] Furthermore, since civil society is the context of the very existence of corporate actors, cooperation between corporations and civil society is a prerequisite.[193]

As Maak observes, "corporate integrity requires sound relating as well as being consciously embedded in one's whole range of relationships; internally, externally, and with societies at large."[194] Every government shares the mission to create a good environment to facilitate human flourishing. So, how do corporations relate to the mission of the government or local

188 Krishan Kumar, "Civil Society: An Inquiry into the Usefulness of an Historical Term," *The British Journal of Sociology* 44, no. 3 (1993): 379.

189 Brown, *Corporate Integrity*, 147–149.

190 Brown, *Corporate Integrity*, 148.

191 Brown, *Corporate Integrity*, 149.

192 Ralph Hamann and Nicola Acutt, "How Should Civil Society (and the Government) Respond to 'Corporate Social Responsibility'? A Critique of Business Motivations and the Potential for Partnerships," *Development Southern Africa* 20, no. 2 (2003): 268.

193 Brown, *Corporate Integrity*, 158–159.

194 Maak, "Undivided Corporate Responsibility," 363.

governments? First, corporations have to acquire integrity on the cultural, interpersonal, and organizational levels by forming communication patterns that are open to agreements and disagreements, promote secure civil reciprocal relationship, and are pursuing worthwhile purposes. If corporations overcome the challenges of cultural, organizational, and interpersonal level of integrity, they would find a place in civil society. On this level, "business corporations have an obligation not to prevent and sometimes to promote the mission of a city,"[195] and thereby contribute to human flourishing.[196]

2.2.5 Natural Environmental Integrity

As explained earlier, the social integrity of corporations entails the promotion of human flourishing. A healthy natural environment is an essential element in human flourishing. In this respect, it is considered an inalienable right.[197] Corporations share civil obligations because "corporations are part of communal life and they contribute to communities in which they operate and they are expected to act as good global citizens."[198] Corporate cosmopolitan conversations open the door to move toward creating a corporate natural environmental integrity. There are four basic themes in these cosmopolitan conversations: "asking right questions, practising the principle of subsidiarity, selecting the appropriate boundaries, and promoting natural prosperity."[199]

Brown proposes various steps to attain natural integrity at the corporate level. Asking the right questions inevitably helps find the right solutions to existing environmental problems. These solutions can also include the policies of environmental programs, implementation of the process of environmental policies and strategies, and environmental audits. Correct questions lead to a reflection and dialogue with stakeholders about correct action plans.[200] Such studies necessitate the principle of subsidiarity, which supports the process of looking at issues at the lowest level of corporations. Here they have to consider all stakeholders in order to solve natural environmental issues. This endeavor reveals corporations' limitations or boundaries in their relationship with nature. An awareness of this

195 Brown, *Corporate Integrity*, 160–161.

196 Brown, *Corporate Integrity*, 166.

197 Richard H. Guerrette, "Environmental Integrity and Corporate Responsibility," *Journal of Business Ethics* 5, no. 5 (1986): 409. See also Eugene Sadler-Smith, "Toward Organizational Environmental Virtuousness," *The Journal of Applied Behavioral Science* 49, no. 1 (2013): 132.

198 Maak, "Undivided Corporate Responsibility," 363.

199 Brown, *Corporate Integrity*, 198.

200 Lynn Brewer, Robert Chandler, and O.C. Ferrell, *Managing Risks for Corporate Integrity: How to Survive an Ethical Misconduct Disaster* (Ohio: Thomson Higher Education, 2006): 252–253.

limitation guides corporations to formulate better attitudes and actions that lead to natural prosperity.[201]

Corporate natural environmental integrity helps corporations to stop environmentally hazardous businesses and enter into environmentally friendly businesses. Corporate natural environmental integrity "calls for the inclusion of corporations in the natural environment so that all of nature, both human and non-human communities, prospers together."[202] In summary, corporations need to embrace sustainability; "in addition to seeking financial gains, companies must actively seek harmony with the natural environment—to leave the fewest possible 'footprints on the planet'. One of a corporation's primary stakeholders must be nature, both in the regions where it operates and globally."[203]

2.2.6 Connection between Five Dimensions of Corporate Integrity

The corporate cultural dimension of integrity stands for cosmopolitan communication with stakeholders; that is, openness to agreements and disagreements, and learning from them. Cultural integrity leads corporations to maintain positive relationships between employees, stakeholders, and managers (integrity as relational wholeness) and this relational wholeness is known as the interpersonal dimension of corporate integrity. Since corporations exist through corporate cultural communication and interpersonal relational wholeness, corporations should also have the worthwhile purpose of enhancing human flourishing in addition to their economic purposes.[204]

Furthermore, the previously mentioned three levels of corporate integrity provide a strong foundation to promote cooperation between corporations and local governments, allowing them to work together for human enhancement. Such a relationship is known as corporate social integrity. Finally, corporate relations to stakeholders reach their highest fulfillment through environmental integrity. Having achieved environmental integrity, corporations exemplify sustainable business practices.[205]In summary, these five dimensions of corporate integrity are connected because corporations move from one dimension to another. I believe that one dimension cannot stand without the other, and that corporate integrity is the sum total of the integration of corporations with the various realms of stakeholders or systems in which they operate.

---

201 Brown, *Corporate Integrity*, 198–203.

202 Brown, "Corporate Integrity and Public Interest," 15.

203 Paul Shrivastava and Stuart Hart, "Creating Sustainable Corporations," *Business Strategy and the Environment* 4 (1995): 160.

204 Brown, *Corporate Integrity*, 209; 129; 106–107.

205 Brown, *Corporate Integrity*, 208–220.

2.2.7 Designing Civic Perspective Corporate Integrity

In terms of implementing the civic perspective of corporate integrity, Brown concentrates on the formation of appropriate corporate contexts.[206] In this attempt, he relies on J. Richard Hackman's explanation of the characteristics of effective teams. According to Hackman, real teams have the following characteristics: interdependent work of all members to the team, a common purpose, structure and context of the team for an enhanced performance, and expert coaching to achieve desired results.[207] Brown sees Hackman's characteristics of effective teams as equivocal to the implementation of civic perspectives of corporate integrity. According to Hackman, an effective team can be formulated by "creating the conditions that increase the chances that moments of greatness will occur—and moreover, can provide a little boost or nudge now and then to help members take the fullest possible advantage of these favorable conditions."[208] Moreover, he also states that once the conditions are established, groups will move toward their set objectives.[209]

Similarly, Brown views the civic perspectives of corporate integrity as the sum total of five dimensions of corporate integrity: proper corporate mission, polices, structure, culture, and contexts.[210] Discussing cultural and interpersonal dimensions of corporate integrity requires "looking at corporate policies and procedures, corporations could then look at how they might engage in cooperative conversations with civic and government agencies."[211]

3 Critical Assessments of Theories of Corporate Integrity

Both "social contract-based" and "civic citizenship-based" corporate integrity theories attempt to safeguard stakeholder interests. Both theories hold that corporations cannot exist isolated from society, hesitating to define wealth creation as the only aim of corporations. Corporate integrity is perceived by both theories as a direct link between either different ethical conduct principles or various dimensions of a corporation's relationship with stakeholders. Corporations are explained by both theories as on-going communication patterns. Furthermore, corporate integrity theories pay attention to corporate ethical challenges such as corporate moral agency, social responsibility, and corporate reputation.

206 Brown, *Corporate Integrity*, 222.

207 J. Richard Hackman, *Leading Teams: Setting the Stage for Great Performances* (Boston: Harvard Business School Press, 2002): 212.

208 Hackman, *Leading Teams: Setting the Stage for Great Performances*, 253.

209 Hackman, *Leading Teams: Setting the Stage for Great Performances*, 254.

210 Brown, *Corporate Integrity*, 223.

211 Brown, *Corporate Integrity*, 165.

Generally, social contract-based theories of corporate integrity suggest that corporate integrity is the balancing of different claims and obligations. According to Kaptein and Wempe, the reason for the balancing of corporate act is often reduced to the efficiency of production and services. Brown states that corporate efficiency is not a criterion for corporate integrity. A company can make dangerous agricultural pesticides in an efficient way but this does not mean the company has a high degree of corporate integrity. Corporate integrity demands more than mere efficiency. It must stand for an ethical purpose without denying the economic motive.[212] Kaptein and Wempe also state that the consequence of corporate integrity is sustainable mutual advantage. They define sustainable mutual advantage as a corporation's positive influence on the environmental as well as social and economic realms of society. If the purpose of corporate existence is efficiency of production and services, how can we hope to have a positive influence on stakeholders using corporate integrity? I am of the opinion that the social contract-based corporate integrity theory neglects the moral purpose of a corporation.

Furthermore, the social contract-based corporate integrity theory attempts to create an ethical corporate culture, as well as behavioral principles and structures with the hope that they will lead to ethical corporate behaviors. The corporate ethical structure, culture, and corporate conduct are related to or embedded in corporate codes of conduct. In the collective context, however, a code of conduct is not sufficient to form ethical behavior, even if one may assume that it helps to a certain extent. It is indeed positive to note that Kaptein later highlights the importance of personal integrity in politics and within government structures. He states that rules, spirit of rules, unwritten rules, and character of a person are important to develop integrity in politics and government. He writes that "personal integrity creates integrity in environment."[213]

The civic-based corporate integrity theorists define corporations as members of civil society while giving importance to the civic context and structure of corporations. They propose five dimensions of civic-based corporate integrity, namely: the cultural, interpersonal, organizational, civic, and the natural. Corporate integrity is seen as the sum of these five corporate integrity dimensions. I appreciate the attempt to combine both shareholder interest and public/stakeholder interest by considering that a corporation is a member of the civil society. However, there is no clear indication in this theory of cultural difference in the civic context. From the

212 Brown, *Corporate Integrity*, 8–9.

213 Muel Kaptein, "The Servant of the People: On the Power of Integrity in Politics and Government," 233, accessed February 4, 2017, http://www.rsm.nl/about-rsm/news/detail/3304-new-book-on-integrity-in-politics-and-government-written-by-rsm-professor/, http://ssrn.com/abstract=2498730.

civic perspective of corporate integrity, the different ethical contexts presented within various states or cultures will be a challenge imposed upon multinational corporate actors. Moreover, although Brown accepts the role of organizational leadership to promote corporate integrity, he fails to recognize the importance of the personal integrity of managers.

In short, in civic-based corporate integrity, cultural, interpersonal, organizational, civic, and natural dimensions are worked out by the individuals involved. These dimensions help corporations to become actors within civil society. Furthermore, social contract-based corporate integrity requires ethical corporate behavioral principles and corporate qualities for managers and employees. Both the social contract and civic perspectives acknowledge that corporate integrity theories attempt to create corporate integrity by taking into consideration corporate policies, missions, culture, structure, and codes of conduct. I think that in both cases, corporate integrity depends directly upon the integrity of managers and employees together with ethical corporate structure and culture, because managers and employees act on behalf of corporations and corporations cannot act by themselves.

Similarly, Donald C. Menzel explains various tools for integrity building in organizations, such as ethics training[214] (character formation), the implementation and enforcement of codes of ethics, the taking of professional oaths, ethics audits, healthy human resource management, and the establishment of hotlines.[215] Although he does not develop this theory much, he acknowledges the importance of the character of managers and employees in organizational integrity development. On the other hand, Mollie Painter-Morland sees business ethics as "part of everyday business practice and not mere compliance with legislation and regulations."[216] According to her, corporate ethics must give priority to people's sense of self and their values. She writes, "It is in, and through, the interactions between our sense of self, the power relationship in which we function, and the truth that we tacitly possess, that the fabric of morality is woven."[217] Taking these positions into consideration, I argue that corporate integrity is a matter of individual integrity together with ethical corporate context, culture, structure, and codes of conduct. In the following section, I shall

214 He believes that there are two models of ethics training in the US. The first one is compliance training that is concentrated on laws and regulations. The second one is the integrity model that gives more importance to character formation. Cf. Donald C. Menzel, *Ethics Management for Public Administrators: Leading and Building Organizations of Integrity* (New York: M.E. Sharpe, 2012): 77–78.

215 Menzel, *Ethics Management for Public Administrators*, 77–116.

216 Mollie Painter-Morland, *Business Ethics as Practice: Ethics as the Everyday Business of Business* (Cambridge: Cambridge University Press, 2008): 290.

217 Mollie Painter-Morland, *Business Ethics as Practice*, 291.

draw a detailed critical analysis of the above-mentioned elements, which are indispensable to corporate integrity theories.

3.1 Corporate Integrity and Codes of Conduct

It is clear that corporate codes of conduct play a vital role in the formation of corporate integrity. Corporate integrity theories aim to promote the well-being and interests of both internal and external stakeholders. Codes of conduct are a set of prescriptions that are developed by a company for the present and future behaviors known as ethos.[218] Such basic rules are necessary as ethical behavior and ethical conduct are the basis for corporate integrity. Moreover, if a company has codes of conduct, which are too limited in scope or coverage, criticisms may follow from external stakeholders and consequently, the company will be forced to renew the codes. Furthermore, if a company fails to implement codes of conduct, that company will have to face the criticisms and pressure of external stakeholders to implement them properly.[219] Therefore, codes of conduct give way to external pressures for the formation of ethical conduct and these "pressures have increased with the recent fall of Enron and the renewed calls for greater corporate integrity."[220] Codes of conduct give special attention and guidelines to the environmental or social aspects of corporate behavior along with the quality and efficiency of production, which help the formation of different dimensions of corporate integrity.[221]

Codes of conduct alone are insufficient for corporate integrity because they are the general statements of business principles. If corporations have corporate integrity, they would then be able to balance conflicting values, ideals, and moral theories. I doubt whether a code of conduct alone is sufficient to ameliorate all corporate dilemmas, but I would be careful not to degrade the value of a corporate code of conduct with regard to limiting unethical corporate behavior. An independent external monitoring system is necessary to ensure that codes of conduct are applied to the daily functioning of corporations. Since codes of conduct give general statements and prohibitions, they do not do anything for the improvement of the social conditions. For example, "it can be argued that an outright ban on the use of child labour can bring about deterioration in the livelihoods of the most vulnerable families, who depend on the additional income that children bring in."[222]

---

218 Kaptein and Schwartz, "The Effectiveness of Business Codes," 113.

219 Waddock, Bodwell, and Graves, "Responsibility," 132.

220 Waddock, Bodwell, and Graves, "Responsibility," 132.

221 Rhys Jenkins, *Corporate Codes of Conduct: Self-Regulation in a Global Economy*, 28–29, accessed 7 October, 2014, http://www.adapttech.it/old/files/document/18111JENKINS.pdf.

222 Jenkins, *Corporate Codes of Conduct:Self-Regulation in a Global Economy*, 29.

3.2 Corporate Integrity and Ethical Corporate Culture

An ethical corporate culture is a necessary precondition for the implementation of corporate integrity. As already seen in chapter one, at a concrete level, organizational culture consists of "behavioural patterns, language, rites, rituals, heroes, and stories etc., which are very difficult to interpret in isolation but rather easy to observe."[223] An important characteristic of corporate culture is the fact that "corporate culture has its roots in history, national culture etc."[224] Thus, traditions that exist in corporations are taken from important elements in their culture and are thus indispensable for their analysis. Rituals, stories, and myths of organizations explain how corporations solved their crises/dilemmas in the past. It is also important to note that organizational culture is not static.[225] However, in corporate culture, evolution happens gradually and continuously by adding new elements to the daily functioning while corporate functioning elements are moved or strengthened. This is obviated by the fact that corporate culture is linked to corporate structure.[226]

Organizational culture works as a source for organizational integration; the integration of different groups and people into one coherent group. Because of integration, consistency, and consensus should be reached among the members of a corporation.[227] "The integration perspective suggests that an organization has a single culture that is clearly identifiable and potentially measurable, and that employees are committed to supporting it."[228] Integration makes members of the organization aware about corporate interests.[229] Corporate culture is also a source of differentiation because corporations have "complex, many-faceted sets of sub cultures, within one overarching culture, interacting to manage their diverse and often competing interests and objectives."[230] Subcultures originated due to organization by departments and groups within corporate structures as well as the dissimilar experiences of various departments.[231]

---

223 Volkert Johannes Batelaan, *Organizational Culture and Strategy: A Study of Cultural Influences on the Formulation of Strategies, Goals and Objectives in Two Companies* (Amsterdam: Thesis Publishers, 1993): 56. See also Harrison M. Trice and Janice M. Beyer, "Studying Organizational Cultures through Rites and Ceremonials," *The Academy of Management Review* 9, no. 4 (1984): 653–669.

224 Batelaan, *Organizational Culture and Strategy*, 57.

225 Batelaan, *Organizational Culture and Strategy*, 57.

226 Batelaan, *Organizational Culture and Strategy*, 57–58.

227 Debram Eyerson and Joanne Martin, "Cultural Change: An Integration of Three Different Views," *Journal of Management Studies* 24, no. 6 (1987): 625.

228 Naomi Stanford, *Corporate Culture Getting It Right* (New Jersey: John Wiley & Sons, 2011): 4.

229 Batelaan, *Organizational Culture and Strategy*, 136–137.

230 Stanford, *Corporate Culture Getting It Right*, 4.

231 Batelaan, *Organizational Culture and Strategy*, 137–138.

It is my conviction that a strong organizational ethical culture helps members of corporations to overcome conflicts between personal interests and organizational interests. Ethical corporate culture is a stimulus for the correct corporate decision making in contested dilemmas and it is linked with employee performance.[232] From this perspective, corporate culture boosts corporate integrity.

However, it is clear that corporate culture alone is insufficient for the development of corporate integrity. Since organizational culture forces excessive integration, "the members easily become prey to self-complacency that in the end may result in corporate blindness."[233] Employees and managers of the corporation "may lose their urge for introspection and self-criticism by primarily focusing on past success instead of analyzing current and future development."[234] The main ethical concern is the conflict of interests and dilemmas between internal and external stakeholders. Corporate integrity is a proposed way to protect stakeholders' interests in a justifiable manner. Since corporate culture is not an answer to all corporate conflicts of interest and dilemmas, corporate integrity is more than corporate ethical culture; individual creativity and individual moral integrity are also important in corporate ethical life along with corporate culture because it is an individual who interprets and applies corporate culture in daily corporate practices. Moreover, individual creativity is essential to give personal meaning to the work.

As mentioned previously, corporate culture is a source of differentiation. Although cultural pluralism is good for the functioning of various departments, it may also lead to ambiguity due to defective communication between departments "in such a way that mutual expectations regarding responsibilities and tasks become frustrated because of different 'values and meanings', misinterpretations and divergent interests that have been institutionalized."[235] The possible differentiation in organizational culture leads to uncoordinated perspectives on corporate aims and perspectives. In this situation, "people no longer concern themselves with the duties of others and lose the sense of corporation as a corporate body. As a result, no one sees or takes responsibility for the bigger picture."[236] It allows Many Hands Dilemmas in corporate life;[237] this diminishes or blocks corporate integrity.

---

232 Stanford, *Corporate Culture Getting It Right*, 77–85.

233 Batelaan, *Organizational Culture and Strategy*, 145.

234 Batelaan, *Organizational Culture and Strategy*, 145. Originally this idea is from Kenneth R. Andrew's book, *The Concept of Corporate Strategy*. I took this idea from the above mentioned book.

235 Batelaan, *Organizational Culture and Strategy*, 147.

236 Kaptein and Wempe, *The Balanced Company*, 169.

237 Kaptein and Wempe, *The Balanced Company*, 166–169.

3.3 Corporate Integrity and Corporate Structure

As discussed earlier, organizational structures refer to the job and the content of the job that persons or groups fulfill within the organization. The distribution of tasks and responsibilities is facilitated via organizational charts and decision-making processes. They include "tasks and rules that set down who makes what decisions, what responsibilities belong to which functions, and which procedures should be followed."[238]

Corporate structures must fit with the corporation's strategy. Moreover, they must be "in tune with the human resources, culture, and management process required to move the firm toward its stated objectives."[239] There are four different structure types, which are used by companies. First, there is a centralized functional structure that is made up of different centralized units with a single manager at the top. In such a structure, power is centralized. Second, a division structure is made up of decentralized organization based on different independent groups with one top manager. Third, the holding company system is made up of separate business units held together by financial control systems. Finally, a matrix structure is organized under two managers, that is, a general manager who performs the roles of power balancing, decision co-ordinating, and standard setting, and a matrix manager who is in charge of the company production.[240]

Organizational structures have a positive impact on corporate integrity. Wempe states that corporate integrity is localized in the corporate structure.[241] The tasks, responsibilities, strategies, rules, regulations, and procedures are made clear to all managers and employees through the corporate structure. The actions and decisions of the employees and managers are guided by the corporate structure.[242] A transparent corporate structure has a potential to reduce conflicts of interests and dilemmas within corporate life. If there is no clear corporate structure, this leads to Many Hands Dilemma.[243] Corporate structures lay out the corporate mission, policies, and codes of conduct of a company as well as open up space for people to use reason and make ethical judgments.[244] Moreover, some authors believe that if the formal organizational structure includes organizational rewards systems, performance evaluation systems, and so on, this would increase

---

238 Kaptein and Wempe, *The Balanced Company*, 148.

239 Paul J. Stonich, *Implementing Strategy: Making Strategy Happen* (Cambridge: Ballinger Publishing Company, 1982): 47.

240 Stonich, *Implementing Strategy*, 49–61.

241 Johan Wempe, *Market and Morality: Business Ethics and the Dirty and Many Hands Dilemma* (Amsterdam: Eburon, 1998): 186.

242 Wempe, *Market and Morality*, 186.

243 Kaptein and Wempe, *The Balanced Company*, 168–169.

244 Wempe, *Market and Morality*, 144–154.

the ethical behavior of managers and employees.[245] As such, structure stimulates ethical corporate behavior. If this structure promotes ethical corporate behavior, it also leads to corporate integrity.

However, corporate structure alone is insufficient to the achievement of corporate integrity. Although corporate structure is an essential element, it is missing the link with the personal integrity of managers and employees. Wempe states that corporate integrity is expressed in various forms such as "the careful use of one's authority and the means one has available to carry out the function, judging fairly and objectively, [and] respecting one's co-workers."[246] It is uncontested that along with the ethical corporate structure, personal integrity of managers and employees play an important role. Neither corporate structure nor codes of conduct can form clear solutions to conflicts of interest and dilemmas. From this perspective, moral imagination, personal creativity, and prudence are all dependent upon the personal integrity of managers and employees, making them indispensable in decision-making processes.

Conclusion

We analyzed various dimensions and theories of corporate integrity. The concrete background of corporate integrity theories are the ethical challenges of corporate culture such as dilemmas, conflicts of interest, unethical conduct, social responsibility debate, and so on. Authors propose two different types of corporate integrity theories that are social contract and civic perspective-based corporate integrity theories. Social contract-based corporate integrity theories try to create an ethical corporate culture, behavioral principles and structure, and in the hope that this would lead to ethical corporate behaviors. However, civic-based corporate integrity theories suggest that a corporation is a member of the civil society. It is important to integrate the civic context and structure of corporations. Civil society is a whole and corporations are part of the whole. Corporate integrity helps corporations mesh with the whole. Codes of conduct, corporate culture, and structure are important for corporate integrity but they alone are insufficient because individuals are the real constitutive elements and decision makers of corporations. It is uncontested that along with the ethical corporate structure, personal integrity of managers and employees play an important role. Summing up my critical reflections, I can conclude that corporate integrity is a matter of individual integrity in an ethical corporate context.

---

245 Harvey S. James, "Reinforcing Ethical Decision Making through Organizational Structure," *Journal of Business Ethics* 28, no. 1 (2000): 43–58.

246 Wempe, *Market and Morality*, 185.

CHAPTER TWO

CORPORATE MORAL AGENCY DEBATE AND CORPORATE INTEGRITY

INTRODUCTION

Corporate moral agency is a basis for business ethics. The debate as to whether corporations possess moral agency or not leads one to neoclassical[1] economic theory rooted in eighteenth century economic thinking. There are three different views of corporate moral agency: amoral, functional, and autonomous. In this chapter, I explain the historical background of the corporate moral agency debate. Second, I describe different views of corporate moral agency as well as critically demonstrate the relation and contribution of corporate integrity theories to them.

1 HISTORICAL BACKGROUND OF CORPORATE MORAL AGENCY

Contemporary business ethics is theoretically rooted in the philosophy of neoclassical economist Adam Smith.[2] His writings mark a revolutionary step in the field of economics and ethics. Furthermore, he played an important role in the formation of the idea of a liberalized-market economy. Smith lived in a world where there was a close relation between religious values and business concepts. His major concern was to free economics and business from the domination of religion, especially from Christianity

---

1 Neoclassical economics is a theory that gives subjective preference to producers and consumers. It maximizes the value of agents and individual freedom. Cf. Anton D. Lowenberg, "Neoclassical Economics as a Theory of Politics and Institutions," *Cato Journal* 19, no. 3 (1990): 620.

2 Adam Smith (1723–1790) was a Scottish social philosopher and political economist. His ideas gave a great boost to the Scottish Enlightenment. He was the author of several books and is known as the Father of modern economics and capitalism. Adam Smith was deeply influenced by Stoic philosophy. His main aim was to free economics from the hands of theology. Cf. See also Adam Smith, *The Wealth of Nations*, vol. 2 (London: J. M. Dent and Sons Ltd., 1964): 5–10.

and the state for the creation of wealth.[3] He legitimized self-interest as the driving force behind wealth creation. He believed that government would understand this driving force and move toward free market measures to maximize wealth.[4]

In his work, *Wealth of Nations,* Smith suggests that self-interest is the dominant motivating factor within economics. Smith shows how market operates in connection with self-interest and how self-interest benefits society. Smith writes that "it is not from the benevolence of the butcher, the brewer, or the baker, that we expect our dinner, but from their regard to their own interest. We address ourselves, not to their humanity but to their own interest."[5] Furthermore, Smith presents the pursuit of self-interest as the basic element of a free market. If each person acts to maximize their self-interest in a competitive market, then this increases production and consumption of desired goods. As such, self-interest, according to Smith's account, is the most efficient means of attaining the optimal social outcome.[6]

Several misunderstandings of Smith's views exist. These are caused by the superficial interpretation of the *Wealth of Nations* and *The Theory of Moral Sentiments.*[7] Although he writes about self-interest in *Wealth of Nations,* in his former work, *The Theory of Moral Sentiments,* he states that benevolence is not only a primary virtue but also the scarcest virtue.[8] Moreover, social passions and the virtue of self-command are necessary.[9] According to Patricia H. Werhane, for Smith, "social passions are a motivating force equal to self-interest [...] and without [them] no economy

[3] The concept of free market was articulated by Adam Smith with the main idea that if individuals and firms work in accordance with their self-interest in a competitive market, then it allocates resources in an efficient manner. That means "a system of organizing economic activity in which the owners of resources, land, labor, and capital make the decisions determine how those resources are utilized." Cf. Mark Eaker, "Free Enterprise," in *Encyclopedic Dictionary of Business Ethics*, eds. Patricia H. Werhane and R. Edward Freeman (Oxford: Blackwell Publishers, 1998): 283.

[4] W. H. Shaw and Vincent Barry, *Moral Issues in Business* (Belmont: Wadsworth Publishing Company, 1998): 22.

[5] Adam Smith, *An Inquiry into the Nature and Causes of the Wealth of Nations*, vol. 1 (London: J. M. Dent and Sons Ltd, 1964):13.

[6] Edwin R. A. Seligman, "Introduction," in *An Inquiry into the Nature and Causes of the Wealth of Nations* (London: J. M. Dent and Sons Ltd, 1910): 7.

[7] Smith's writings were not only considered inconsistent but also contradictory with regard to "human motivation, human conduct, and virtue." His first work, *The Theory of Moral Sentiments*, presents morality, motivation for moral behavior, and moral judgments, whereas in his later work *Wealth of Nations*, he concentrates on economic activities and economic behavior. Cf. Patricia H. Werhane, *Adam Smith and His Legacy for Modern Capitalism* (Oxford: Oxford University Press, 1991): 9.

[8] Adam Smith, *The Theory of Moral Sentiments* (New York: Arlington House, 1969): 354.

[9] Smith, *The Theory of Moral Sentiments*, 52–54.

could operate."[10] Therefore, it is not correct to criticize Smith for defending the "narrow" concept of self-interest. Selfishness and self-interest are, moreover, different in Smith's idea. This is concluded from the observation of Edwin R.A. Seligman:

> Smith's concern within the *Wealth of Nations* was an analysis of the economic situation and a consideration of the motives and conditions that make for wealth, rather than for wider conception of welfare in general. [....] he took economic life as he found it and he explained more clearly and conceptually than any of his predecessors the influence of the factor of self-interest in the business world.[11]

Smith's idea of justice is founded upon refraining from injuring others. As Jacob Viner observes, "justice is a negative virtue; it consists of refraining from injury to another person and from taking or withholding from another what belongs to him. [...] Smith considered justice, so understood, to be the necessary foundation of a viable society."[12] In summary, Smith presents a market system where harmony depended upon benevolence, that is, the disposition to do good, and whose survival depends upon justice.[13]

Moreover, Smith presents both self-interest and justice as fairly related concepts as he writes that "every man, as long as he does not violate the laws of justice, is left perfectly free to pursue his own interest in his own way, and to bring both his industry and capital into competition with those of any man, or order of men."[14]

In summary, Smith's emphasis is on the individual responsibility rather than on the rejection of corporate responsibility.[15] Smith does not state anything about corporate moral agency. However, he holds that the individual and the collective will, even when unintended by the actors, contribute to the public good. Starting from individual responsibility and freedom, he suggests that the invisible hand[16] controls market transactions, regulates

---

10 Werhane, *Adam Smith and His Legacy for Modern Capitalism*, 11.

11 Seligman, "Introduction," 7–8.

12 Jacob Viner, "Adam Smith," in *Essays on the Intellectual History of Economics*, ed. Irwin (Princeton: Princeton University Press, 1968): 252.

13 Harvey S. James and Farhad Rassekh, "Smith, Friedman, and Self-Interest in Ethical Society," *Business Ethics Quarterly* 10, no. 3 (2000): 665.

14 Smith, *The Wealth of Nations*, 180.

15 Patricia H. Werhane, "Business Ethics and the Origins of Contemporary Capitalism: Economics and Ethics in the Work of Adam Smith and Herbert Spencer," *Journal of Business Ethics* 24, no. 3 (2000): 185–186.

16 Adam Smith used the "invisible hand" as a metaphor. He used it in different contexts in his writings with the following five different interpretations: In his work, *Wealth of Nations,* he used "invisible hand" to present a condition wherein human beings intend to benefit only for themselves in a particular manner, but in the act of creating that benefit, they also produce a benefit for society. (2) It is a price mechanism, the force that brings all markets together. (3) Invisible hand is a completion, and as such it is good because

self-interest, and produces economic growth and well-being.[17] Later ethicists were deeply influenced by his free market capitalist thinking but were led to different views on the topic of corporate moral agency.

2 The Amoral Corporation

According to the amoral view, corporations are legal beings and the laws can bind them but they are, however, not moral entities; only natural persons are moral agents and only natural persons have moral responsibility.[18] The amoral model rejects the existence of the corporate moral responsibility and holds that we cannot ascribe corporate moral responsibility to stakeholders,[19] who create corporations in accordance with their interests. John Ladd states that corporations are incapable of having moral agency and corporations are simply a complex tool of personal moral agents who are involved in it.[20] When individuals work in a company they act for that company and their actions are understood as part of the act of the business by which they are employed. Therefore, such action cannot be morally evaluated from an individual perspective. If the employer acts against the company, their actions are to be morally evaluated because they are acting at their own risk.[21] Moral responsibility in this view is purely attributed to human beings.[22]

2.1 Free Society and Moral Agency of Corporation

Friedrich Von Hayek is a distinguished intellectual who embraced the free market concept of Smith. He was a proponent of the neoclassical

completion is good. (4) Invisible hand is a process by which human beings acquire perfect knowledge and skills, and gradually it creates benefit to the individuals as well as nations. (5) Invisible hand is viewed as a prime mover.

I would prefer the interpretation of Jerry Evensky that if the individual wanted to enjoy the fruit of the liberal society, then "invisible hand" must not only co-ordinate individual choices but it must also shape individuals into constructive social beings. Cf. William D. Grampp, "What Did Smith Mean by the Invisible Hand?" *Journal of Political Economy* 108, no. 3 (2000): 441–465. See also Jerry Evensky, "Retrospectives: Ethics and the Invisible Hand," *The Journal of Economic Perspectives* 7, no. 2 (1993): 197–198.

17 Werhane, "Business Ethics and the Origins of Contemporary Capitalism," 186.

18 David Ciepley, "Beyond Public and Private: Toward a Political Theory of the Corporation," *American Political Science Review* 17, no. 1 (2013): 154.

19 Stakeholder can be explained in wider and narrower senses. In the wider sense it includes "any group or individuals who can affect or is affected by the corporation," and in the narrower sense it includes only "those groups who are vital to the survival and success of the corporations." Cf. Samantha Miles, "Stakeholder: Essentially Contested or Just Confused?," *Journal of Business Ethics* 108 (2012): 290. See also John Hasnas, "The Normative Theories of Business Ethics: A Guide for the Perplexed," *Business Ethics Quarterly* 8, no. 1 (1998): 25.

20 John Ladd, "Morality and the Ideal of Rationality in Formal Organizations," *The Monist* 54 (1970): 499–500.

21 Richard T. De George, *Business Ethics* (New Jersey: Pearson Prentice Hall, 2006): 184.

22 Kevin Gibson, "Toward an Intermediate Position on Corporate Moral Personhood," *Journal of Business Ethics* 101 (2011): 72.

conception of corporations, the notion that one cannot ascribe responsibility to corporation or to the stakeholders who constituted the corporation. He is primarily concerned with safeguarding a free society.[23] Hayek perceives freedom as a necessary component of morality and maintains that people can be responsible for their actions only if they are free. He states that "economic freedom is thus an indispensable condition for all other freedoms, and free enterprise is both a necessary condition and a consequence of personal freedom."[24] He firmly asserts that freedom creates individual responsibility by denying all kinds of hard determinism and affirming freedom of choice. One's individuality, which one expresses in acts rather than circumstances, is developed by society and in that sense there is an "indirect guidance" for individual actions. Hayek accepts such forms of indirect determinism, but this does not mean that he absolves an agent from individual responsibility.[25]

According to Hayek, people have the right to receive compensation in accordance with their work and services in a free society. A free market permits people to use their abilities to maximize personal utility. Furthermore, he was of the opinion that in order for a societal order to remain free, its corporations must be amoral agents as this is the only means by which to efficiently organize the market. Hayek rejects the view that primary corporate objectives are determined by the interests of managers and employees. He claims that the shareholder's interests are, in fact, the highest corporate objectives.[26] However, through Hayek's perspective, the roles of corporate integrity theories are nil. Corporate integrity theories stand for not just the shareholders but also for both internal and external stakeholders.

2.2 Corporation as an Artificial Person for Profit

Milton Friedman argues in line with Smith's thought. Accordingly, he believes that corporations are artificial persons and cannot have moral responsibilities attributed to their legal personality. Since the responsibility of corporate directors and managers is derived from the stockholders or shareholders, they should refrain from acting in corporate situations based on moral values. Managers are only responsible for maximizing return on investment for shareholders.[27] Executives of corporations are obliged to

23 Wempe, *Market and Morality*, 100.

24 Friedrich Hayek, *Studies in Philosophy, Politics and Economics* (London: Routlegde, 1967): 229.

25 Hayek, *Studies in Philosophy, Politics and Economics*, 229–233. See also Wempe, *Market and Morality*, 100.

26 Hayek, *Studies in Philosophy, Politics and Economics*, 300–312. See also Kaptein and Wempe, *The Balanced Company*, 112–114.

27 Milton Friedman, "The Social Responsibility of Business is to Increase Its Profits," in *Business Ethics: Readings and Cases in Corporate Morality*, eds. W. Michael Hoffman and

pursue the goal of the owners that is generally profit-maximization, unless the status of the corporation is charitable.[28] "In any case, the key point is that, in his capacity as a corporate executive, a manager is the agent of the individuals who own the corporation or establish the eleemosynary institution, and his primary responsibility is to them."[29]

Contracts are the basis for the responsibility of managers and directors. They have a moral obligation to fulfill the implicit and explicit terms of the contract. Here, Friedman transfers moral responsibility from corporations to the shareholders and executives who issue orders. He proposes the following arguments: (1) Business executives have no moral responsibility to promote the general welfare as a part of corporate responsibility. (2) Since business executives are not democratically elected, they are not accountable to the public. (3) When business executives use company assets or profit for the social welfare, they are violating the rights of the shareholders and in effect, managers are stealing their money.[30] He writes that "If there are social responsibilities, then they are the social responsibilities of individuals and not of business."[31]

Friedman contends that the term "social responsibility" undermines the foundations of a free society and the self-interest of stockholders. If shareholders or stockholders act for the general welfare, then the market system and political system become intertwined. Moreover, the political system would dominate the market system based on collectivist interests. In a free society, business has only one morality and responsibility, that is, to increase profit.[32] He writes that "There is only one social responsibility of business, to use its resources and engage in activities designed to increase its profits as long as it stays within the rules of the game, which is to say, engages in open and free competition without deception or fraud."[33] Collecting profit by fraud or deception is an immoral way for profit

Jennifer Mills Moore (New York: McGraw-Hill, 1990): 153–157. Stockholder is the owner of one or more shares that are issued by the corporation. Stockholders have rights such as voting for directors and auditors, attending annual or special meetings, etc. However, stockholders do not own the company. Cf. Max Clarkson and Michael Deck, "Stockholder," in *Encyclopedic Dictionary of Business Ethics*, eds. Patricia H. Werhane and R. Edward Freeman (Oxford: Blackwell Publishers, 1998): 608.

28 Muhammad Yunus, Bertrand Moingeon, and Laurence Lehmann-Ortega, "Building Social Business Models: Lessons from the Grameen Experience," *Long Range Planning* 43 (2010): 310.

29 Friedman, "The Social Responsibility of Business is to Increase Its Profits," 153.

30 Thomas L. Carson, "Milton Friedman," in *The Blackwell Encyclopedic Dictionary of Business Ethics*, eds. Patricia H. Werhane and Edward Freeman (Oxford: Blackwell Publishers, 1997): 291.

31 Friedman, "The Social Responsibility of Business is to Increase Its Profits," 154.

32 Milton Friedman, *Capitalism and Freedom* (Chicago: Chicago University Press, 1963): 133. See also Kaptein and Wempe, *The Balanced Company*, 113.

33 Friedman, "The Social Responsibility of Business is to Increase Its Profits," 157. See also Friedman, *Capitalism and Freedom*, 133–134.

making. Conflicts of interest are the main ethical problem in the corporate arena and corporate integrity theories attempt to overcome unjustifiable decisions in conflicting situations. Freedman rejects the possibility for making profit through fraud or deception. Therefore, Freedman's view presents some of the main aims of corporate integrity but it needs to go beyond these aims.

2.3 Corporations as Controlled by Society

The basic assumption behind this model is that society forces and expects corporations to act morally.[34] John Kenneth Galbraith criticizes the free enterprise theory that indirectly confirms the amoral corporation and presents clear reasoning on how this happens. According to Galbraith, the free enterprise system leads to multinational corporations that are managed by technocrats and functionaries, who make the actual decision concerning corporations and are not accountable to anyone or controlled by anyone. He concludes that in a free market, neither the government nor the shareholders have any control over a corporation that is exempt from moral criticism.[35]

Galbraith believes that effective control by society is the remedy for amoral corporate activity. This control needs to be applied throughout government instruments and government regulation. If this is implemented, the corporate structure may not run contrary to the general interest. He writes that "the only answer is a strong framework that aligns the exercise of corporate power with the public purpose."[36] Galbraith speaks about effective control of corporations by the government to form an ethical corporate culture. Ethical corporate culture is an important element in the attainment of corporate integrity because it fosters ethical conduct.

2.4 Evaluation of the Amoral Position of Corporations

In an amoral vision, it is nonsensical to speak of corporate moral responsibility. Natural persons are moral agents. They have both reason and freedom to act deliberately and so they have moral responsibility. However, moral responsibility does not apply to corporations; hence corporations can act morally or immorally, according to the boundaries of the law. Corporate responsibility would be an empty concept and it cannot be localized anywhere because the concept of a corporation is understood as

34 Wempe, *Market and Morality*, 106.

35 John Kenneth Galbraith, *The Age of Uncertainty* (Boston: Houghton Mifflin, 1977): 274–278.

36 Galbraith, *The Age of Uncertainty*, 277.

to be nothing more than a collection of self-interested individuals acting as agents under the limits of contractual obligations and duties.[37]

However, if managers were to be given an instrumental status as agents of the owners, then they would no longer be exempt from moral responsibility.[38] The main failure of the amoral model is that it fails to consider the corporate context in which the moral obligation of managers is a result of the job that they currently hold. Since the amoral model of corporations shifts moral problems of businesses to the private arena, the real moral problems of businesses are neither addressed nor accepted. In the business context, most problems are related to a dilemma in the form of choice between two values. Managers are confronted with dilemmas only because they are in a position not to judge whether one decision is right or wrong.[39]

Moreover, the amoral model denies the personal and social moral responsibility of managers and directors in the corporate context. Although the amoral model completely denies the social responsibility of corporations, managers have personal responsibilities toward society as a whole. This personal responsibility of top-level managers limits the amoral conduct of business. Surprisingly, this model is silent on the personal responsibility of the managers at the time when a conflict of interest occurs. The amoral model mistakenly confines personal managerial responsibility to profit maximization when, in fact, since managers, as people, are morally responsible agents, their moral responsibility, within the managerial context extends to societal concerns as well.[40] Therefore, in conflicting situations the amoral model sways in favor of shareholders and denies the interests of stakeholders. As a result, the amoral model violates corporate integrity. At the same time, it must be acknowledged that the amoral model prescribes certain limits for making profits such as the prohibitions against cheating and fraud, and the possibility of societal control of corporations. In this sense, the amoral model contributes to corporate integrity.

3 Association Model of Corporate Moral Agency

Since it is difficult to compromise with the amoral model of corporate responsibility, the question of localizing the moral responsibilities of a corporation remain and the association model of corporate responsibility is an alternative. According to the association model of corporate moral agency, a corporation is defined as "an association of individuals who are

---

37 Peter A. French, "Corporate Moral Agency," in *Encyclopedic Dictionary of Business Ethics*, eds. Patricia H. Werhane and Edward Freeman (Oxford: Blackwell Publishers, 1998): 149.

38 French, "Corporate Moral Agency," 149–151.

39 Kaptein and Wempe, *The Balanced Company*, 177.

40 Wempe, *Market and Morality*, 108–109.

entitled to the same rights and legal protections that apply to all other individuals and organizations."[41] According to this theory, corporations are not separate entities having their own morality; rather, they are collections of individuals who "voluntarily get together for the purpose of doing business in an efficient way."[42]

Corporate actions are the result of the actions of corporate directors; however, the corporation itself does not act. Everything that happens in and through the corporation is a result of the decisions of individuals and as such, corporate action can be traced back to individual decisions, each playing an important role in the formation of the directions of the aggregate. Moreover, a corporation is the sum total of individual actions and interactions that arise between them. This theory neglects the legal basis of corporations and their state licence.[43]

Manuel G. Velasquez defends this view by stating that corporations cannot be held morally responsible because corporations cannot act. He states that moral categories such as emotions, reason, and deliberation are applicable only to human beings and not to corporations. A corporation acts and exists only if the individual exists and acts for it. A "company" is simply an umbrella concept for the many individual acts covered by a legally recognizable personality. Therefore, Velasquez concludes that "a corporate organization lacks the kind of causal powers and intentionality that an entity must possess to be morally responsible for what it does"[44] and the morality of an organization is completely dependent upon the persons who constitute the organization, that is, the people entitled to run it and thereby assume responsibilities toward different parties holding interests in it.[45] However, it is worthwhile to note here the opposite view that "a company, as a moral actor in society, has commitments, values, and responsibilities, such as duties to lenders or contractual obligations to its customers that are distinct from those of its individual members. These

---

[41] Robert Hessen, *In Defence of the Corporation* (Stanford: Hoover Institution Press, 1979): 15. I have cited this quotation from the following book: Wempe, *Market and Morality*, 113.

[42] Patricia H. Werhane, *Persons, Rights and Corporations* (New York: Prentice Hall, 1985): 40.

[43] Hessen, *In Defence of the Corporation*, 46. See also Werhane, *Persons, Rights and Corporations*, 41.

[44] Manuel Velasquez, "Debunking Corporate Moral Responsibility," *Business Ethics Quarterly* 13, no. 4 (2003): 551.

[45] Velasquez, *Business Ethics: Concepts and Cases*, 45. See also Velasquez, "Debunking Corporate Moral Responsibility," 531–562. Some authors state that corporations can act only through the representatives. Cf. R. E. Ewin, "The Moral Status of the Corporation," *Journal of Business Ethics* 10, no. 10 (1991): 749–756. Authors like Corlett state that "collectivism is implausible in regard to punishment because collectives are not moral agents." Cf. Angelo J. Corlett, "Collective Punishment and Public Policy," *Journal of Business Ethics* 11, no. 3 (1992): 207–216.

corporate responsibilities survive even when a company's individual members and agents change."[46]

The association model can be divided into two parts, the management approach and the participants approach. The management approach reduces corporate responsibility to the managers who make decisions, while the participant's approach holds that responsibility lies with all the employees including the managers. In the management approach, a corporation is identified with managers who receive responsibility for the corporation as is delegated by the owners. However, there are authors who hold that managerial moral responsibility is not derived from the owners of corporations, but from a social contract.[47] This view maintains that, "A manager should possess a deep-rooted sense of what the company's policy would be in the case of a particular issue he has to decide. Such a sense can only be instilled by experience, instruction, and personal contact at headquarters or in parts of the organization thoroughly familiar with the policies and style of the corporation."[48]

According to the participants' approach, the employees of a corporation are also included as part of the management of a corporation where the total outcome of the corporations is the total contribution of managers and employees. The causal relationship between labor and final product makes the employees co-responsible. Therefore, all participants share a degree of responsibility for the functioning of the corporation. As such, not only managers but also employees are morally responsible for the actions of corporations.[49]

3.1 The Association Model and Corporate Integrity

Generally corporate cultures and structures are not considered by this model and moral problems are reduced to the individuals who work in corporations as if they were merely aggregations.[50] In this respect, the association model fails to incorporate the role of ethical corporate culture and structure, which is a necessary element of corporate integrity. However, the association model highlights the personal responsibility and integrity of the employees and managers of corporations. As discussed before, my

[46] Lynne Sharp Paine, *Value Shift* (New York: McGraw-Hill, 2003): 145. I have taken this quotation from the following source. Cf. Gibson, "Toward an Intermediate Position on Corporate Moral Personhood," 72.

[47] Wempe, *Market and Morality*, 114–115. Social contract is a theory in business that implies that contract with society gives the legitimacy for the obligations and rights of the corporations. It is a communitarian norm based approach. Cf. Dunfee, "Social Contract Theory," 587.

[48] Pieter Kuin, "Magic of Multinational Management," *Harvard Business Review* 50, no. 6 (1972): 91.

[49] Wempe, *Market and Morality*, 114–116.

[50] Kaptein and Wempe, *The Balanced Company*, 121.

position on this matter is that the personal integrity of managers and employees is also a necessary element to successful corporate integrity.

Kaptein and Wempe propose three main objections to the association model of corporate responsibility: the transfer problem, the dispersion problem, and the complexity problem.[51] The transfer problem raises the question of transferring responsibility throughout time. Certain corporations in the 1950s caused environmental pollution on a large scale due to the negligence of management at the time. The corporate actors were obliged to provide reparation for the damage. In an association or a functional model, however, such responsibility would disappear.[52]

The dispersion problem is concerned with the division of responsibility at any given moment. Organizational decisions are formed as a result of discussions that arise within the organization. Although a manager may not be in favor of a particular decision, in certain situations he/she has to accept it. Regardless of their involvement, managers must be morally responsible for the action. How can individuals be held responsible for collective decisions that they may have personally rejected? Corporate decisions and activities are approved by internal decision making processes in modern complex and large size organizations. The association responsibility model is not applicable to modern complex organizations.[53]

Since corporate policies and structures are made by a board of top managers and even applications and interpretations are entrusted to the managers, they have a greater responsibility when it comes to unethical corporate behavior. However, one cannot neglect the importance of corporate polices and structures along with the personal responsibility of managers and employees. In this regard, my position is that corporate moral agency is to be taken into consideration both for corporations as a whole as well as for the individuals who form the corporations. This will be discussed in detail later in this chapter.

4 Different "Moral Person Theories" of the Corporation

The moral person theory views corporations as independent and responsible social entities. Corporations are not simply tools of the market and thus, corporate responsibility cannot be reduced to the individuals who form and work for corporations. The moral person view attempts to overcome the limitations of both the amoral and the functional models. In this section, I shall elaborate upon three theories of corporate moral persons and analyze them in the light of corporate integrity.

---

51 Wempe, *Market and Morality*, 117.

52 Kaptein and Wempe, *The Balanced Company*, 121.

53 Wempe, *Market and Morality*, 117.

4.1 The Projection Approach

According to Kenneth E. Goodpaster, corporations possess a number of core moral qualities that we also find in people. Based on this analogy, corporations can be viewed as responsible agents just like people. He writes that "it is appropriate not only to describe organizations by analogy with individuals, it is also appropriate normatively to look for and to foster moral attributes in organizations by analogy with those we look for and foster in individuals."[54] For Goodpaster, this analogy justifies the projection of moral responsibility within corporations.[55] This moral projection principle elaborates upon the importance of corporate leaderships because they are "shapers and architects of the conscience of the corporation."[56]

There are different perspectives as to how responsibility applies to individuals. The word "responsibility" is used in different ways such as—causal,[57] rule-following,[58] and decision-making.[59] However, according to Goodpaster and John B. Matthews, the special characteristics of moral responsibility lie in the third sense of the term, decision making.[60] Moreover, moral responsibility is an uncertain concept containing both normative and descriptive realms. In a normative perspective, "moral responsibility lies with respect to the virtues of individual decision-making more than with respect to the rightness or wrongness of specific actions or behaviour."[61] The normative realm refers to the dispositions of the individual. The descriptive realm of moral responsibility, however, is aimed at examining the content of a particular behavior. According to Goodpaster, the

54 Kenneth E. Goodpaster, "Tenacity: The American Pursuit of Corporate Responsibility," *Business and Society Review* 118, no. 4 (2013): 588.

55 Kenneth E. Goodpaster, "The Concept of Corporate Responsibility," *Journal of Business Ethics* 2, no. 1 (1983): 1–22.

56 Goodpaster, "Tenacity: The American Pursuit of Corporate Responsibility," 588.

57 "Causal" means that we speak of holding persons responsible. Here, we are concerned with the role of intentions, free will, and degree of participation in a particular action. Cf. Goodpaster, "The Concept of Corporate Responsibility," 5.

58 Rule-following means that we are concerned with socially expected behavior associated with certain roles. For example, parents have particular roles and responsibilites in society. Cf. Goodpaster, "The Concept of Corporate Responsibility," 5.

59 Third perspective is concerned with the way in which an individual thinks about and responds to different situations. Goodpaster, "The Concept of Corporate Responsibility," 5.

60 Kenneth E. Goodpaster and John B. Matthews, "Can a Corporate Have a Conscience?" in *Business Ethics: Readings and Cases in Corporate Morality*, eds. W. Michael Hoffman and Jennifer Mills Moore (New York: McGraw-Hill, 1998): 185.

61 Goodpaster, "The Concept of Corporate Responsibility," 7.

basic spirits of moral responsibility are "rationality"[62] and "respect."[63] "The principle of moral projection is then advocated as a means of projecting rationality and respect to organizations."[64]

Goodpaster makes a shift from individual moral responsibility to corporate moral responsibility through the principle of *moral projection*. An individual is the primary unit of the analysis of organizations and the corporation plays a significant role in the lives and livelihood of the individual today.[65] The decision-making process is a movement from thought to an action and the above mentioned spirit of rationality and respect is embodied in the decision-making process. There are four main elements that correspond to four stages in an individual's movement from thought to action: perception,[66] reasoning,[67] coordination,[68] and implementation.[69]

Similar to individuals, the shift from thought to action for corporations starts with the collection of data regarding corporate resources, opportunities, risks, and potential impacts. This is a reality within corporate structures even if they do not use the term "perception." Second, in the

---

62 From a moral point of view, "rationality" includes all the rational attributes of decision making including "lack of impulsiveness, care in mapping out alternatives and consequences, clarity about the goals and purposes, and attention given to its implementation." Cf. Kenneth E. Goodpaster, *Conscience and Corporate Culture* (Oxford: Blackwell Publishing, 2007): 66–67.

63 From a moral point of view, "respect" includes a special awareness and concern for the effects of one's decision and policies on others' goals, needs, and interests. Cf. Goodpaster, *Conscience and Corporate Culture*, 67.

64 Rogene A. Buchholz and Sandra B. Rosenthal, "Integrating Ethics All the Way Through: The Issue of Moral Agency Reconsidered," *Journal of Business Ethics* 66, no. 2/3 (2006): 234.

65 Goodpaster and Matthews, "Can a Corporate Have a Conscience?" 187.

66 Decision making begins with an agent's perception of their environment. It is called information gathering. Perception is not entirely a passive process, but rather an active one. Therefore,when we inquire about the moral aspects of perception, we are inquiring about the way in which and the degree to which an agent structures and categorizes the "moral data" available. Cf. Goodpaster, "The Concept of Corporate Responsibility," 8.

67 Moral reasoning is the process by which an individual moves formally or informally from perceptions to conclusions about what and how one ought to do. Different moral theories are to be used in this moral reasoning. Cf. Linda Klebe Trevino, "Moral Reasoning and Business Ethics: Implications for Research, Education, and Management," *Journal of Business Ethics* 11, no. 5 (1992): 445–450. See also, according to a few authors, moral reasoning means "any conscious thought process (about people) that affects moral judgment to count as "moral reasoning." Joseph M. Paxton and Joshua D. Greene, "Moral Reasoning: Hints and Allegations," *Cognitive Science* 2, no. 3 (2010): 515.

68 Coordination is an integration of one's own conclusions with other non-moral disciplines such as politics, sociology, etc. Process of coordination is the capacity to go beyond one's own perception and moral reasoning. Cf. Goodpaster, "The Concept of Corporate Responsibility," 9.

69 It is the final stage of the movement from thought to action. At this stage, the moral responsibility can be manifested. Cf. Goodpaster, "The Concept of Corporate Responsibility," 9.

organizational context, the moral reasoning would take place either formally[70] or informally,[71] based on organizational strategies, policies, and values. Third, the coordination in an organizational context is a moral compromise that a responsible business firm has to make in accordance with the demands of politics, sociology, and the law. Business firms, in accordance with governmental laws and competitive pressure, seek economic objectives like return on investment, market share, and growth. Fourth, "for the individual, implementation consists in the passage from intentions to action through self-monitoring, matching appropriate means to ends, and sustaining motivation and control. For the organization, similar factors come into play."[72] Strong effective organizational response to plans and policies results in management incentive systems, internal control systems, and research agendas. In reference to individuals, these qualities are referred to as self-control, integrity, and conscientiousness. Therefore, Goodpaster concludes that an organization is capable of moral responsibility and has it just like an individual would.[73]

There are several criticisms to this analogy. People share intrinsic values and their survival and existence are prioritized. Corporations, on the other hand, are not natural persons and they, therefore, have no intrinsic value. The "person" analogy appears to conflict with this view because it distracts from the task of motivating people to perform in a morally responsible way.[74] Many authors reject the metaphorical use of words such as moral person, conscience of corporation, corporate feelings, and shame.[75]

4.2 The Secondary Moral Actor Theory

There are situations where a person can act on behalf of another person, for example, when a person grants another power of attorney. In this situation, responsibility rests with the person who has granted power of attorney rather than with the individual who has received it. David Copp calls this action a "secondary action," which means, "an agent's action is a secondary

---

70 Corporate formal moral reasoning is based on corporate strategies and choices, such as the corporate ethical codes. Cf. J. R. C. Kuntz et al., "Characterizing Ethical Cases: A Cross-Cultural Investigation of Individual Differences, Organizational Climate, and Leadership on Ethical Decision-Making," *Journal of Business Ethics* 113 (2013): 317–331.

71 Informal moral reasoning in the organizational context means the moral reasoning based on the unwritten set of values or principles that make up the culture of a corporation. Cf. Sean R. Valentine and Connie R. Bateman, "The Impact of Ethical Ideologies, Moral Intensity, and Social Context on Sales-Based Ethical Reasoning," *Journal of Business Ethics* 102 (2011): 158.

72 Goodpaster, "The Concept of Corporate Responsibility," 10–14.

73 Goodpaster and Matthews, "Can a Corporate Have a Conscience?" 187.

74 Nani L. Ranken, "Corporations as Persons: Objections to Goodpaster's Principle of Moral Projection," *Journal of Business Ethics* 6, no. 8 (1987): 637.

75 Ranken, "Corporations as Persons," 633–637.

action if, and only if, it is correctly attributable to this agent on the basis of either an action of some other agent or action of some other agents."[76] An agent's action is called a "primary action" and the moral responsibility of the primary action lies with that agent. However, the secondary action of an agent is constituted by the actions of other agents. There are similarities between primary actions and secondary actions. Both can be condoned with intended motives: they can either violate obligations or fulfill them. Corporate or collective actions can be placed under the scope of secondary actions. Corporations do not have bodies and are unable to perform bodily actions.[77] Corporations, however, can act through the actions of a person, who forms a part of the corporation. This would mean that when the directors of corporations do something on behalf of the corporation, the corporation acts in the secondary sense. Natural persons act both in the primary and secondary sense whereas corporations always act in the secondary sense.[78]

Werhane describes corporations as secondary moral agents since they depend upon individuals for their capital, property, ownership, contracts, managements, rules, and productivity. Companies function because of human interaction,[79] and corporate actions are based on corporate intentions. An intention is corporative if it fulfills or helps to fulfill corporate objectives that are set by the influences of all stockholders, managers, employees, and external advisors. These constitute the primary intentions of corporations. So, corporate actions are secondary actions made by the corporate directors with the intention to realize superior corporate intentions. Therefore, corporate actions are secondary actions and corporations have moral agency. Werhane always goes back to the moral status of the natural person in the attempt to establish the moral character of the corporations while accepting that corporate secondary moral agency is not the same as ontologizing the corporation. However, natural persons create corporations and corporations function through natural persons because corporations are not above the natural persons who constitute them, in the sense that they cannot act alone. Werhane concludes that corporations have secondary moral agency and are thus morally responsible just like

[76] David Copp, "Collective Actions and Secondary Actions," *American Philosophical Quarterly* 16, no. 3 (1979): 177.

[77] Copp, "Collective Actions and Secondary Actions," 177–179.

[78] Kaptein and Wempe, *The Balanced Company*, 129.

[79] Patrica H. Werhane, "Corporate Social Responsibility/ Corporate Moral Responsibility: Is There a Difference and the Difference It Makes," in *The Debate over Corporate Social Responsibility*, eds. Steve May, George Cheney, and Juliet Roper (Oxford: Oxford University Press, 2007): 462.

individuals.[80] In summary, her approach is a mixture of both "ontological individualism" and "methodological collectivism."[81]

Corporate leadership is important in regard to corporate actions. The unique characteristics of actions are expressed by powerful and meaningful leadership. The corporation expresses its autonomous will when the directors make the decision on behalf of the corporate mission.[82] Moreover, collectives or corporations have particular objectives and collectives can do something for a reason. They can act intentionally, and collective intentionality is the very consciousness of the corporation.[83] Therefore, corporations are moral actors but only in the secondary sense. If a corporation is a moral actor, then its actions can be judged in the moral sense and it has moral responsibility.[84]

4.3 The Corporate Internal Decision Structures Theory

According to Peter A. French, one needs to distinguish between aggregates and conglomerates. Aggregates are unstructured collections of individuals, that can be divided into two parts, that is, coincidental aggregates and statistical aggregates. Coincidental aggregates are coincidental groups of people, for example, seers of a football match, whereas statistical aggregates are collections based upon determinate characteristics, for example, age groups based upon the region in which they all co-habit. An aggregate is described by putting the characteristics of the individual members together. The moral responsibility of the aggregate is equal to that of its members.[85] If we apply the aggregate vision of collectives to corporations,

---

80 Werhane, *Persons, Rights and Corporations*, 76. See also Kaptein and Wempe, *The Balanced Company*, 130–131.

81 Kaptein and Wempe, *The Balanced Company*, 130. According to ontological individualism, corporate responsibility relies upon individuals who act in corporations. It is a claim that the identity of the group is determined by individuals and their properties. However, methodological collectivism asserts that there is corporate collective responsibility independent of individuals. Cf. Brian Epstein, "Ontological Individualism Reconsidered," *Synthese* 166, no. 1 (2009): 188–189. See also Kenneth J. Arrow, "Methodological Individualism and Social Knowledge," *The American Economic Review* 84, no. 2 (1994): 1.

82 Kaptein and Wempe, *The Balanced Company*, 129. Corporate mission is defined as a "tool to articulate the management's beliefs, convictions, perspectives, and approaches in regard to the firm's purpose, social responsibility, and corporate mission and business achievable inspiring goals. Thus, mission statement communicates not merely the future desirable state of a firm. Rather, it explicitly expresses the long embedded corporate identity (CI), corporate purpose (CP), and strategic intent (SI) in a very succinct form." Cf. Shinichi Hirota et al., "Corporate Mission, Corporate Policies and Business Outcomes: Evidence from Japan," *Management Decision* 48, no. 7 (2010): 1135–1136.

83 Copp, "Collective Actions and Secondary Actions," 178–179.

84 Wempe, *Market and Morality*, 128.

85 French, "The Corporation as a Moral Person," 208–215. See also Raymond S. Pfeiffer, "The Central Distinction in the Theory of Corporate Moral Personhood," *Journal of Business Ethics* 9, no. 6 (1990): 473–474.

then "aggregate theorists tend to ignore employees and identify corporations with directors, executives and stockholders."[86] French writes that "a change in an aggregate's membership will always entail a change in the identity of the collection."[87]

On the contrary, a conglomerate is a collection of individuals whose identity is independent of the identity of its members meaning that "the existence of a conglomerate is compatible with a varying membership."[88] The moral responsibility of a conglomerate cannot be distributed among its members. If all the members of the conglomerate were to be replaced by new members, the responsibility of the conglomerate would remain unaltered. French claims that,

> all conglomerates have "three significant characteristics" that "are not found in the case of aggregates." They have, first, internal organizations and decision procedures; second, enforced standards of conduct that are more stringent than standards that apply outside the conglomerate; and third, the presence of defined roles by virtue of which some members of the conglomerates exercise certain power over other members.[89]

French argues that the moral responsibility of a conglomerate does not imply moral responsibility for the individuals associated with it. He calls for the conglomerate to be analogical to moral agents or persons, stating that there are three main characteristics of a conglomerate that reveal the autonomous intentionality of the conglomerate, independent of the intentionality of the members associated with it.[90] He states that "to be the subject to an ascription of moral responsibility, to be a party in responsibility relationships, hence to be a moral person, the subject must be at minimum an intentional actor."[91] Corporations can have intentions that do not coincide with the intentions of their members.

French believes that it is through the Corporate Internal Decision (CID) structure that the actions of an individual can be ascribed to a corporation. Based upon the CID structure, one can draw a distinction between corporate intentions and the intentions of the members who constitute the corporations. The CID structure is the predication of corporate intentionality.[92] The CID structure consists of two elements: the formal decision-making structure and the recognizing rules. The formal

86 French, "The Corporation as a Moral Person," 209.

87 Peter A. French, *Collective and Corporate Responsibility* (New York: Columbia University Press, 1984): 5.

88 French, *Collective and Corporate Responsibility*, 13.

89 French, *Collective and Corporate Responsibility*, 13–14.

90 French, *Collective and Corporate Responsibility*, 38–47.

91 French, *Collective and Corporate Responsibility*, 38.

92 French, "The Corporation as a Moral Person," 211. See also Gibson, "Toward an Intermediate Position on Corporate Moral Personhood," 73.

decision-making structure presents "an organizational or responsibility flow chart that delineates stations and levels within the corporate power structure."[93] It clarifies the responsibility and rank of all its members. It also maps the interconnected lines of responsibility within the corporations. Second, the recognizing rules means that corporate decisions recognize rules or corporate policy.[94] Consequently, in case of immoral or problematic behavior, it is insufficient for individuals to change their behavior because improper behavior is also a matter related to structural adjustment.

Later, Donaldson developed this view by adding two conditions to specify moral personhood of corporations: first, corporations must have the capacity required to make moral reasoning and second, they must have the freedom to develop rules and policies of a corporation free from internal and external coercion. In this respect, corporations are intentional actors capable of being motivated to respond to various upcoming ethical issues effectively and smoothly.[95] He concludes that corporations ought to "be treated in ethics as full-fledged moral persons and not as fictions that disappear completely when questions of moral responsibility are raised with respect to corporate activities."[96]

4.3.1 Later Developments of Corporate Intentionality

As I have explained before, the most outspoken proponent of attributing moral agency to corporations is French. In his early writings, he states that corporations have ontological status leading him to three main conclusions: corporations have intentionality, corporations have rationality for their intentions, and corporations are capable of changing their intentions and behaviors.[97] In his early defence of corporate intentionality, French grounded his arguments in the belief-desire theory of intentionality.[98] He argues that "when the corporate act is consistent with an instantiation or an implementation of established corporate policy, then it is correctly

---

93 Peter A. French, "Corporate Moral Agency," in *Business Ethics: Readings and Cases in Corporate Morality*, eds. W. Michael Hoffman and Jennifer Mills Moore (New York: MCgraw-Hill, 1990): 195. See also Ian Ashman and Diana Winstanley, "For or against Corporate Identity? Personification and the Problem of Moral Agency," *Journal of Business Ethics* 76, no. 1 (2007): 87.

94 French, "Corporate Moral Agency," 195–196.

95 Donaldson, *Corporations and Morality*, 21. See also Gibson, "Toward an Intermediate Position on Corporate Moral Personhood," 72. See also Buchholz and Rosenthal, "Integrating Ethics All the Way Through: The Issue of Moral Agency Reconsidered," 235.

96 Peter A. French, "Corporate Moral Agency," in *Encyclopedic Dictionary of Business Ethics*, eds. Patricia H. Werhane and R. Edward Freeman (Oxford: Blackwell Publishers, 1998): 150–151.

97 Denis G. Arnold, "Corporate Moral Agency," *Midwest Studies In Philosophy* 30, no. 1 (2006): 280.

98 Arnold, "Corporate Moral Agency," 281.

possible to describe it as having been done by a corporate desire coupled with a corporate belief and so, in other words, as corporate intention."[99] Furthermore, he asserts that three notions of personhood are entangled and used interchangeably: metaphysical, moral, and legal.[100] Many critics[101] accuse French of being illegitimately anthropomorphic, arguing that "unlike human persons, corporations are not an end in themselves."[102] French later modified his understanding of corporations as metaphysical person in two manners. First, he changed the concept of corporate moral personhood into corporate moral actors or agents.[103] Second, he abandoned his previous belief-desire theory of intentionality[104] and thereby accepted Michael Bratman's "planning theory of intentionality."[105] Surprisingly, French has only suggested Bratman's account of intentionality as the basis for a theory of corporate intentionality but has not proposed a good argument for that conclusion.[106]

---

[99] French, "The Corporation as a Moral Person," 213.

[100] French, *Collective and Corporate Responsibility*, 84.

[101] Richard De George, "Corporations and Morality," in *Shame, Responsibility and the Corporation*, ed. Hugh Curtler (New York: Haven, 1986): 57–75. See also Thomas Donaldson, "Personalizing Corporate Ontology: The French Way," in *Shame, Responsibility and the Corporation*, ed. Hugh Curtler (New York: Haven, 1986): 99–112. Michael J. Kerlin, "Peter French, Corporate Ethics and the Wizard of Oz," *Journal of Business Ethics* 16 (1997): 1431–1438. John Danley, "Corporate Moral Agency," in *A Companion to Business Ethics*, ed. Robert E. Frederick (Malden: Blackwell Publishers, 1999): 243–256. Rita Manning argues that we do not feel moral wrong when a corporation is "murdered" (taken over) and "divorced" (split into two). However, we feel moral wrong if it happens to human beings. Cf. Rita C. Manning, "Corporate Responsibility and Corporate Personhood," *Journal of Business Ethics* 3 (1984): 77. See also Rita C. Manning, "Dismemberment, Divorce and Hostile Takeovers: A Comment on Corporate Moral Personhood," *Journal of Business Ethics* 7 (1988): 641.

[102] George, "Corporations and Morality," 61.

[103] In 1985, David Ozar mapped the difference between moral personhood and moral agency. A person has moral rights by virtue of one's own ontology or by nature itself. However, corporations have only conventional rights and they do not have moral rights. So, he concluded that ontologically corporation is not a moral agent but conventionally it is. Cf. David T. Ozar, "Do Corporations Have Moral Rights?," *Journal of Business Ethics* 4, no. 4 (1985): 279–280.

[104] A desire-belief model of intentionality refers to "intentional actions as actions that stand in appropriate relations to agent's beliefs and desires." It is the reduction model, wherein intentions are reduced to certain desires and beliefs of the agents. Cf. Michael Bratman, "Two Faces of Intention," *The Philosophical Review* 93, no. 3 (1984): 375.

[105] Peter A. French, "Integrity, Intentions, and Corporations," *American Business Law Journal* 34, no. 2 (1996): 147–148. We are planning creatures. Humans always create plans for the future. Coordination of various plans is necessary for our future activities. Intentions are typically the elements in such coordinating plans. Intentions are distinctive states of mind and cannot be reduced to desires and beliefs. Michael Bratman divided intentions into future-directed intentions (actualizing in future) and present-directed intentions (actualizing now). Since it is already actualized, he rejected the present-directed intention. Cf. Bratman, "Two Faces of Intention," 375–378.

[106] Arnold, "Corporate Moral Agency," 281.

In the "planning theory of intentionality," Bratman writes about shared intentionality, defining shared intentions as "a state of affairs consisting primarily of appropriate attitudes of each individual participant and their interrelations,"[107] and that coordinate our activities.[108] Moreover, as with most of our intentions, shared intentionality consists of a sufficient deliberation and reflection prior to the time of the action.[109]

According to Denis G. Arnold, the above-mentioned shared intentionality extends to corporate intentions. Since corporate intentions are shared, they are neither a set of individual mental states nor the mental state of some super-agent. Rather, "corporate intentions are states of affairs consisting of both the intersecting attitudes of the class of agents comprising the corporation and the internal decision structure of the organization."[110] Arnold takes the CID structure of French and explains that the CID structure serves "as the frame upon which the attitudes of board members, executives, managers, and employers are interwoven to form corporate intentions."[111] How do employees become aware of the corporate intention of a large company? As French puts it, a CID structure is "prescriptive and not just descriptive. It tells the agents of the corporation how they *ought* to act."[112] In order to act properly, employees ought to know what the corporate intentionality is and how they are expected to act by its precise terms. Furthermore, Arnold adds that corporations are capable of evaluating corporate intentions as to whether they should be modified or eliminated.[113]

4.4 The Role of Individual Moral Responsibility in Corporations

Edward Garrett claims that French and Werhane defend the idea that corporate moral responsibility cannot be redistributed. Werhane calls the corporation a secondary collective agent, whereas French calls the corporation a full-fledged moral person.[114]

While Werhane rejects the criticism that she created a radical separation between corporate moral responsibility and individual agency, in her opinion, if we were to accept Garrett's view that corporations are not moral agents, moral responsibility has to be distributed among employees

---

107 Michael Bratman, "Shared Intention," *Ethics* 104, no. 1 (1993): 99.

108 Bratman, "Shared Intention," 99.

109 Michael Bratman, *Intention, Plans, and Practical Reason* (Cambridge: Harvard University Press, 1987): 28.

110 Arnold, "Corporate Moral Agency," 291.

111 Arnold, "Corporate Moral Agency," 291.

112 Peter A. French, *Corporate Ethics* (New York: Harcourt Brace, 1995): 31.

113 Arnold, "Corporate Moral Agency," 291.

114 Jan Edward Garrett, "Unredistributable Corporate Moral Responsibility," *Journal of Business Ethics* 8, no. 7 (1989): 535–536.

accordingly and fairly. In a large corporate context, this is not an easy or cheap task to implement and effectively manage. She writes that "neither French nor I" hold radical separation between corporate moral responsibility and individual agency.[115] She interprets French as follows:

> French argues that because policies and practices that are the source of corporate action are themselves products of corporate intentional activities, the actions that result are not solely distributable to individuals. I underline the word solely here, because French does not preclude individual liability, but wants to extend moral responsibility to the corporation as well. This is because the corporation, as well as individuals, has acted.[116]

According to Werhane, the moral responsibility of a corporate action has to be "attributed both to individuals who created and carried out corporate policy and practices and to the policies and practices themselves."[117] Corporate responsibility is necessary as corporate actions are guided by corporate policies and practices. If we were to punish only individual actors for corporate faults, the possibility of corporate faults being repeated becomes substantial because corporate policies and practices would continue. Furthermore, I think that if managers and employees consciously or deliberately stray from corporate policies and practices in their actions or decision-making, then it is not the corporation but the concerned managers or employees who have responsibility for the unethical corporate behavior. Moreover, in the modern corporate world the responsibility of managers for unethical corporate actions and decisions is substantial since corporate power lies within the spectrum of managerial roles.

4.5 Critical Assessment of Corporate Personhood and Corporate Integrity

According to the law, a "person" includes not only human beings but also entities such as corporations. *Black's Law Dictionary* defines a corporation as an "artificial person" that has a "personality and existence distinct from that of its several members."[118] The court gives personhood to corporations for the purposes of the operation of corporate law.[119] The question is whether we can think of corporations as properly moral persons or merely moral agents.

---

115 Patricia H. Werhane, "Corporate and Individual Moral Responsibility: A Reply to Jan Garrett," *Journal of Business Ethics* 8, no. 10 (1989): 821–822.

116 Werhane, "Corporate and Individual Moral Responsibility: A Reply to Jan Garrett," 822.

117 Werhane, "Corporate and Individual Moral Responsibility: A Reply to Jan Garrett," 822.

118 Henry Campbell Black, "Corporation," in *Black's Law Dictionary* (New York: West Publishing, 1999): 340–343.

119 Arnold, "Corporate Moral Agency," 279.

French's view of corporate moral agency is centered on the intentionality of the corporation through the analysis of the CID structure, which consists of a decision-making structure and corporate policy. This view assumes that anything, which can behave intentionally, is a moral person.[120] The corporate moral person view of Goodpaster and Matthews interpret corporations as persons, just as natural persons would be defined. However, through experience it is clear that entities appear to behave intentionally but do not qualify as moral persons and thereby avoid any substantial responsibility, as seen throughout history.[121] Furthermore, if we were to impose moral agency of corporations on par with human moral agency, then corporations ought to have the same rights as ordinary natural persons. It may be plausible to say that corporations have human privileges such as human rights, the right to own property, the right to vote, the right to live, and so on. A corporation may be considered as a juristic person who receives legal rights from the legislator or courts.[122] However, "they do not appear to be 'moral persons' in any literal sense of that term."[123] Furthermore, corporate intentions differ substantially from individual natural persons' intentions.

Natural persons create corporations, and both intentions and actions of corporations are the collective result of individual acting.[124] If corporation is a moral person then what is the status of employees? Are they lesser moral persons on a hierarchical spectrum?[125] Therefore, a moral person view of corporations undermines the dignity inherent in the ontological priority of human beings. The equalization of artificial person with a human being would be wrong on many levels, particularly with regard to respect for human dignity.

I opt for the secondary moral actor theory for establishing the corporate moral agency, because as Verstraeten observes, "the concept 'secondary collective actor' is more adequate than Peter French's analogy of person and company, because in the 'methodological collectivism' of Werhane, the ontological priority of the human person is still recognized."[126] Furthermore,

---

120 Donaldson, *Corporations and Morality*, 22.

121 A cat behaves intentionally when it crouches to catch a mouse. Although we know that the cat intends to catch the mouse, we do not give moral agency to the cat. A computer also can act intentionally but it is not a moral agent. "Perhaps corporations resemble complicated computers; perhaps they, according to a complicated inner logic, function in an intentional manner but fail altogether to qualify as moral agents. Cf. Donaldson, *Corporations and Morality*, 22.

122 Donaldson, *Corporations and Morality*, 22.

123 Donaldson, *Corporations and Morality*, 23.

124 Werhane, *Persons, Rights and Corporations*, 39–40

125 Werhane, *Persons, Rights and Corporations*, 39–40.

126 Johan Verstraeten, "From Business Ethics to the Vocation of Business Leaders to Humanize the World of Business," *Business Ethics: A European Review* 7, no. 2 (1998): 123.

the secondary collective actor view includes the two elements of French's CID structure of corporations just like the formal decision-making structure and the recognizing rules. Moreover, Arnold's idea of shared corporate intentionality is also more meaningful in the secondary collective actor theory of corporations because secondary moral actor theory does not ontologize corporations and corporate intentionality, rules, and policies that are formed by primary moral agents.

Conclusion

Generally, the above analyzed corporate moral agency theories prioritize methodological collectivism as they attempt to establish autonomous corporate responsibility through the assumption that corporations can act like individuals. If we were to highlight corporations as full-fledged persons, then the individual responsibility and responsibility of top managers and employees would be neglected in corporate integrity theories and corporate social responsibility theories. This is what we can see in corporate integrity theories. Kaptein, Wempe, and Brown also perceive corporations as autonomous moral agents by prioritizing corporate culture and structure. Consequently, they attempt to establish corporate integrity by introducing corporate qualities, communication patterns, and ethical principles in corporate culture and structure. Kaptein and Wempe write that, "the corporation, due to its structured character, is an autonomous party."[127] Moreover, Brown designed his corporate integrity based theory on the view that corporations are civil citizens and thereby, corporate integrity depends upon the communication and behavioral patterns of the corporation in question. Although he states that good people would enhance these communication patterns, he does not include actions of good people (person of integrity) as part of corporate integrity.[128] The problem is that corporate integrity theories based on methodological collectivism, ignore the importance of personal integrity of the individuals who constitute the corporation. Moreover, corporate ethics are a matter of choice among various interests of stakeholders, especially during times of conflict of interest of internal and external stakeholders. The corporate structure and culture can guide the managers and employees; however, it is the individuals who make the real decisions. In such a situation, it is worthwhile to note the position of Larry May that "relations among individuals do have a reality, a distinct ontological status, which is different from the individuals who are so related. However, the reality of these relations is not sufficient

127 Wempe, *Market and Morality*, 153. See also Kaptein and Wempe, *The Balanced Company*, 145–153.

128 Brown, *Corporate Integrity*, 35–36.

to ensure that the groups, which are composed of individuals in relationships, have reality independently of the individuals who compose these groups."[129] Therefore, it is clear from this critical analysis that the integrity of managers and employees, along with corporate structure and culture, is a significant element in corporate decision-making during times fuelled by dilemmas.

[129] Larry May, *The Morality of Groups: Collective Responsibility, Group-Based Harm, and Corporate Rights* (Indiana: University of Notre Dame Press, 1987): 23.

CHAPTER THREE

THEORIES OF CORPORATE SOCIAL RESPONSIBILITY (CSR) AND CORPORATE INTEGRITY

INTRODUCTION

The concept of corporate social responsibility has a long history within business literature.[1] Before the 1950s, the main and only focus was on the obligations of businesses to their owners and shareholders. The modern debate on the topic originated after the publication of Howard R. Bowen's book, *Social Responsibilities of the Businessman* (1953).[2] Until 1970, there was an ambiguity regarding the meaning of corporate social responsibility because of the lack of consensus among business ethicists. The real debate got underway after 1970 when many authors proposed different theories for corporate social responsibility. These theories were often controversial, complex, and unclear. In this chapter, I shall follow the classification of Elisabet Garriga and Domènec Melé as they classify the different corporate social responsibility theories into four classes of theories.[3] There are:

(1) Profit motivated theories in which the corporation is seen as a means for the creation of wealth.

---

[1] Shafiqur Rahman, "Evaluation of Definitions: Ten Dimensions of Corporate Social Responsibility," *World Review of Business Research* 1, no. 1 (2011): 166–176. See also Archie B. Carroll, "Corporate Social Responsibility: Evolution of a Definitional Construct," *Business & Society* 38, no. 3 (1999): 268.

[2] The following part of the dissertation is an elaboration of my own article. Cf. Augustine Joseph, "The Need of Personal Responsibility and Integrity in Corporate Social Responsibility Theories," *International Journal of Recent Advances in Organizational Behaviour and Decision Science* 1, no. 1 (2014): 46.

[3] I have taken this classification of corporate social responsibility theories from the following source. Cf. Elisabet Garriga and Domènec Melé, "Corporate Social Responsibility Theories: Mapping the Territory," *Journal of Business Ethics* 53, no. 1/2 (2004): 51–71. See also Joseph, "The Need of Personal Responsibility," 46.

(2) Power motivated theories that see corporations as the means for exercising power in society.

(3) Socially motivated theories that see corporate social responsibility as the fulfillment of social demands.

(4) Ethically motivated theories that deal with corporate social responsibility based on ethical principles.

1 Profit Motivated Theories

This model perceives corporate social responsibility as a tool for the attainment of corporate economic objectives, whereby self-interest is the basis for the understanding of corporate social responsibility in profit motivated theories.[4] Profit motivated theories can be classified in accordance with the economic objectives they aim to achieve such as, short-term profit motivated theories and long-term profit motivated theories.[5]

1.1 Short-Term Profit Motivated Theories

"Milton Friedman is the main advocate of profit motivated corporate social responsibility theory. His theory concentrates on the identity of the corporation, whereby corporate identity is viewed as an artificial person and social responsibility is related with a human being. He concludes that corporations have no social responsibility, as in a free enterprise, a corporate executive is a worker for the owners of the business. Responsibilities of the business executives are given by the owners of the business so as to do business in accordance with their desires to increase shareholders value."[6] Furthermore, he argues that business executives have no direct responsibility to promote general welfare. Since they are not elected by the public, accordingly they have no responsibility to the public. On this basis, if executives sacrificed profit for the sake of public good, they are violating the rights of shareholders as well as their contractual obligations to them such as the duty to act in good faith for the business.[7] Therefore, there is no space for corporate integrity in this regard.

1.2 Long-Term Profit Motivated Theories Based on Strategies

In this view, corporations are concerned with how to allocate resources for long-term social objectives and attain a competitive advantage. This long-term profit motivation is based on corporate strategies.

4 Andrew Crane and Dirk Matten, *Business Ethics: Managing Corporate Citizenship and Sustainability in the Age of Globalization*, 2 ed. (Oxford: Oxford University Press, 2007): 47.

5 Keith Davis, "The Case for and against Business Assumption of Social Responsibilities," *The Academy of Management Journal* 16, no. 2 (1973): 312–322.

6 Joseph, "The Need of Personal Responsibility," 46–47.

7 Carson, "Milton Friedman," 292.

> Strategy refers to the plans and actions taken to achieve competitive advantage and superior performance. Yet this is not enough. The plans and action taken must also lead to the creation of unique resources and capabilities that leverage organizational routines and that are the source of sustainable competitive advantage and superior performance.[8]

I consider this definition to be better because it contains the views of strategies of both schools of thought, the design school[9] and the resources school.[10]

Recently, philanthropic activities[11] became a part of the strategies of many companies in order to receive a competitive advantage. Through philanthropy, companies can benefit in terms of "improved public relations, increased employee productivity, greater satisfaction of various stakeholders in the community, and an enhanced corporate reputation or image."[12] For most of the firms, corporate social responsibility is a strategy when it creates substantial benefit for the firm, particularly by supporting the firm's effectiveness for achieving its stated goals, whether short-term or long-term. Creating value is the most crucial objective of a corporation. Corporate social responsibility activities have a great role in the formation of values for a corporation.[13] Firms can formulate a number of strategic actions toward social issues that are either created by corporate acts or that emerge as a local issue. The response of corporations toward social issues can be divided into four categories: reaction, defence, accommodation, and pro-action. As part of corporate social responsibility, if a company takes pro-action as a strategy toward social issues, the company receives a

---

8 Bryan W. Husted, "Is It Ethical to Use Ethics as Strategy?" *Journal of Business Ethics* 27, no. 1/2 (2000): 22.

9 There are two schools of thought regarding strategies, namely, the design school and the resources based view of strategies. The design school holds that strategies include long-term programs, specific goals, plan for growth, and resource commitment. This school looks at strategy as intellectual process of determining "what a company might do in terms of environmental opportunity, deciding what can be done in terms of power, what executives of the company want to do and should do." Cf. Henry Mintzberg, "The Design School: Reconsidering the Basic Premises of Strategic Management," *Strategic Management Journal* 11, no. 3 (1990): 173.

10 The Resources based strategy of the firm holds that resources and products of companies are two sides of the same coin. According to this view, a company's success is derived from its ability to assemble, preserve, and use available resources. Cf. Birger Wernerfelt, "A Resource-Based View of the Firm," *Strategic Management Journal* 5, no. 2 (1984): 171–180.

11 Corporate philanthropic activities include monetary contributions, charitable donations, starting of educational, and other charitable non-profitable institutions, etc. Cf. Betty Smith Coffey, "Corporate Philanthropy," in *Encyclopedic Dictionary of Business Ethics*, eds. Patricia H. Werhane and R. Edward Freeman (Oxford: Blackwell Publishers, 1998): 151. Cf. Joseph, "The Need of Personal Responsibility," 47.

12 Coffey, "Corporate Philanthropy," 151.

13 Lee Burke and Jeanne M. Logsdon, "How Corporate Social Responsibility Pays Off," *Long Range Planning* 29, no. 4 (1996): 499.

competitive advantage because "profitability and growth go hand in hand with fair treatment of employees, of direct customers, of consumers, and of the community."[14]

The natural resources view of a business presents the idea that the strategy and competitive advantage of business in the future depends upon the environmentally sustainable economic activity of the business. The attitude of the business toward natural resources determines the sustainability of it. Stuart L. Hart proposes three main strategic behaviors of corporations: pollution prevention, product stewardship, and sustainable development. When waste and emission are minimized by pollution control, it gradually leads to a lower cost of production and as a result, the business enjoys a competitive advantage. Both product stewardship and sustainable development consist of the views of environmental interests and as a result, the business enjoys a greater competitive advantage.[15]

Strategies of the bottom of the economic pyramid are proposed by C.K. Prahalad in the Indian context as India is a country where the majority of the population is poor. Traditionally, national and multinational companies perceive that uplifting the poor is a duty better left to governments or NGOs. On the contrary, strategies of the bottom of the economic pyramid propose producing goods that are priced low and affordable to the poor. The sustainable development and harmonization of the most advanced technologies with local conditions should be included as part of the strategy of companies, which would improve the living conditions of the poor.[16] It is worth noting Clayton M. Christensen's classification of sustainable[17] and disruptive innovation of a company.[18] Although disruptive innovations seem to be part of corporate social responsibility, for a few ethicists, it is better as it enhances the competitive advantage of the company.[19]

[14] Elizabeth Gatewood and Archie B. Carroll, "The Anatomy of Corporate Social Response: The Rely, Firestone 500, and Pinto Cases," *Business Horizons* 24, no. 5 (1981): 9. See also Joseph, "The Need of Personal Responsibility," 46–47.

[15] Stuart L. Hart, "A Natural-Resource-Based View of the Firm," *The Academy of Management Review* 20, no. 4 (1995): 991–992.

[16] C.K. Prahalad, "Strategies for the Bottom of the Economic Pyramid: India as a Source of Innovation," *Reflections* 3, no. 4 (2002): 8.

[17] Sustainable innovation is for the mainstream markets. It implies the innovation of the new and improved products to gain an edge over the completion. It is for short-term profits. Cf. Clayton M. Christensen and Michael Overdorf, "Meeting the Challenge of Disruptive Change," *Harvard Business Review* 78, no. 2 (2000): 71–72.

[18] Disruptive innovation refers to the products that are produced not for the customers of mainstream markets but for the poor customers in society. It is the production of low-cost goods and it can improve the socio-economic life situation of the poor people. For example, the production of the low-cost mobile by a mobile company. Cf. Christensen and Overdorf, "Meeting the Challenge of Disruptive Change," 71–72.

[19] Garriga and Melé, "Corporate Social Responsibility Theories," 55.

Cause-related marketing has emerged as a new way of implementing corporate social responsibility. Cause-related marketing can be defined as "the process of formulating and implementing marketing activities that are characterized by an offer from the firm to contribute a specified amount to a designated cause when customers engage in revenue-providing exchanges that satisfy organizational and individual objectives."[20] This means corporations are particularly socially responsible for indirectly attaining "good corporate image, cultivating a favourable attitude in the minds of consumers, and/or realizing incremental sales gains."[21] These cause-related activities include the classical musical concerts, art exhibitions, golf tournaments or literacy campaigns by which a company gains a strong competitive advantage.[22]

1.3 Profit Motivated Theories and Corporate Integrity

Profit motivated theories state that corporate social responsibility is primarily for attaining profit or mutual advantage. These theories go in line with the amoral corporate moral agency theory, which holds that corporate motivation is only for profit. However, social contract based corporate integrity theories share similarities with profit motivated corporate social responsibility theories, that is, they seek mutual sustainable advantage.[23] The difference lies in the motivation. The main ethical concerns of the corporate world are dilemmas and conflicts of interest. Social contract based corporate integrity theories attempt to create balance between different demands by establishing corporate communication patterns, qualities, and behavioral principles in corporate culture and structure. The designed result of this corporate integrity is the mutual advantage of all the contracting parties, that is, both external and internal stakeholders. The motivation of corporate integrity theories is not only for profit alone but also for societal flourishing.

My criticism of profit motivated theories is that they assume that "corporate social responsibility is not at all corporate social responsibility but merely 'profit maximization under the cloak of social responsibility.' This may be true in the sense that a corporation is for-profit but this largely depends on the primary motivation of the decision makers."[24] "The matter is not whether profit emerges from a particular corporate act or not, but

20 Rajan.P. Varadarajan and Anil Menon, "Cause-Related Marketing: A Coalignment of Marketing Strategy and Corporate Philanthropy," *The Journal of Marketing* 52, no. 3 (1998): 60.

21 Rajan.P. Varadarajan and Menon, "Cause-Related Marketing," 60.

22 Garriga and Melé, "Corporate Social Responsibility Theories," 55.

23 Kaptein and Wempe, *The Balanced Company*, 227.

24 Joseph, "The Need of Personal Responsibility," 57. See also Andrew Crane and Dirk Mattam, *Business Ethics: A European Perspective* (Oxford: Oxford University Press, 2004): 47.

whether profit is the main motivation of corporate acts. Recent studies show that it is difficult to determine corporate motives, and the direct relationship between corporate social responsibility and profitability has been impossible to prove indubitably."[25] However, I think that if a well-performing company indulges in socially responsible activities with the consent of the shareholders, then the intentionality is not for competitive advantage; rather it is a responsible act of a corporate moral agency. I believe that the case has to be judged on a case by case basis in determining whether an altruistic activity is for profit or not. However, a company unintentionally may receive a competitive advantage and in this respect, the company is not responsible. Moreover, the profit motivated model is a reductionist approach and consequently, it absolutizes profit as the only intentionality of a corporation. In this perspective, it is contrary to corporate integrity theories.

2 Power Motivated Theories

"Davis explained corporate responsibility in terms of social power. Since corporations enjoy this social power in society, they have to be responsible to society. These theories stand as the basis for corporate integrity theories. Later this approach developed into two: the integrated social contract theory approach and the corporate citizenship theory approach."[26] Both are integral parts of corporate integrity theories.

2.1 Integrated Social Contract Theory

As explained in chapter one, Donaldson presents the relationship between business and society in terms of a social contract.[27] According to this theory, the implicit contract between corporations and stakeholders is the basis for corporate social responsibility.[28]

In 1994, Donaldson and Dunfee elaborated on this as "integrative social contract theory." They used the term "integrative" to describe this theory as it takes into account the socio-cultural context and to integrate empirical[29]

[25] Joseph, "The Need of Personal Responsibility," 57. See also Crane and Mattam, *Business Ethics: A European Perspective*, 47–48.

[26] Joseph, "The Need of Personal Responsibility," 57–58.

[27] See also Donaldson, *Corporations and Morality*, 35–39.

[28] Cf. Joseph, "The Need of Personal Responsibility," 48–49.

[29] In business ethics, the empirical approach used by social scientists is descriptive. The empirical approach is concerned with what actions are rather than what an action ought to be. The empirical approach is difficult to reconcile with the free will concept, and empiricists hold that human behavior is predictable and explainable. In business ethics, ethical success and ethical failure are complex phenomena and can be explained by causal factors. Cf. Linda Klebe Trevino and Gary R. Weaver, "Business Ethics/Business Ethics: One Field or Two?," *Business Ethics Quarterly* 4, no. 2 (1994): 113–128.

and normative[30] aspects of management. The existing normative theories such as stakeholder, deontology, and utilitarianism give common guidelines for ethical reasoning but they fail to respond to "context-specific complexity of business situations."[31] Therefore, "in summary, rationality in economic ethics is bound in three ways: by a finite human capacity to assess facts, by a limited capacity for ethical theory to capture moral truth, and by the plastic or artificial nature of economic systems and practices."[32] Furthermore, moral norms of socio-economic interaction vary from system to system. The use of the universal concepts of ethics for solving moral dilemmas in business ethics is, however, difficult. The common claim is that, "everybody's doing something can have some moral force in business contexts."[33] From this experience emerged a global attempt to form an agreement concerning business ethics and gradually a hypothetical social contract is derived.

Therefore, Donaldson and Dunfee propose an integrative social contract theory, which contains two kinds of contracts. First is a general contract, which gives a "set of principles regarding economic morality to which contractors would agree to the macrosocial contract."[34] It provides a normative ground for the second type of contract. Macrosocial contracts produce basic rules for all the other social contracts and these rules are known as hyper-norms because they limit the moral free space at the microsocial level. Hyper-norms are fundamental and "are discernible in a convergence of religious, political and philosophical thought."[35] Hyper-norms do not establish the idea that utilitarianism or Kantianism is the absolute moral theory. There is a different criterion for hyper-norms such as core human rights and human dignity.[36]

Microsocial contracts are explicit or implicit agreements that are binding to a specific community such as industries, companies, or economic system. Microsocial contract norms depend upon the consent, attitudes, and behaviors of the norm-generating community members. If microsocial

---

30 The normative approach is rooted in philosophy. This theory includes prescriptive, evaluative, and analytical elements. Normative ethical perspectives create standards by which the actions of the business world can be evaluated. It gives prescriptive moral judgments about the actions of the business world. Cf. Trevino and Weaver, "Business Ethics/Business Ethics: One Field or Two?" 113–128.

31 Joseph, "The Need of Personal Responsibility," 48–49.

32 Thomas Donaldson and Thomas W. Dunfee, "Toward a Unified Conception of Business Ethics: Integrative Social Contracts Theory," *The Academy of Management Review* 19, no. 2 (1994): 258.

33 Donaldson and Dunfee, "Integrative Social Contracts Theory," 258–259.

34 Donaldson and Dunfee, "Integrative Social Contracts Theory," 260.

35 Thomas Donaldson, "Precis for Ties That Bind," *Business and Society Review* 105, no. 4 (2000): 441.

36 Donaldson and Dunfee, "Integrative Social Contracts Theory," 267. See also Joseph, "The Need of Personal Responsibility," 49.

norms are compatible with hyper-norms, then they seem obligatory. In a conflict between microsocial and hyper-norms, and between two existing legitimate norms, priority is to be established in accordance with the consistency between the "spirit and letter of hyper-norms."[37]

Critics of integrative social contract theory state that it depends on other ethical theories for the decision-making and it fails to give an independent basis for moral obligations. Corporate mal-influence on the norm generating community is possible and this may lead to false consent.[38]

2.2 Corporate Citizenship Theory

Corporate social responsibility develops in the imbalance of corporate power; a corporation's irresponsible production of goods creates environmental problems. In this situation, the business world would not be happy with the corresponding stakeholder and corporate social responsibility theories.[39] It reasons that ethics or responsibilities, which are not inherent to business, are opposed to business. "Dirk Matten et al. propose that the metaphor of corporate citizenship is a suitable expression for speaking about corporate social responsibility."[40] The corporate citizenship model highlights the fact that corporations perceive their rightful place in society, next to other citizens. The citizenship model then focuses on the rights and duties of both the corporate citizen and other citizens "which are mutually interlinked and dependent on each other."[41]

Archie B. Carroll presents corporate citizenship as identical with philanthropic responsibility.[42] Based on this view, Duane Windsor observes that corporate citizenship enhances the corporate image and it gives a competitive advantage to the long-term corporate financial performance.[43] Marck C. Bolino et al. observe that social capital, which denotes the relation between employees and other citizens, gives competitive advantage to the corporation. They conclude, "just as the good citizens within a community contribute to the development of the social capital within that community, they are likely to be important for the creation of the social capital within

---

37 Dunfee, "Social Contract Theory," 588.

38 Dunfee, "Social Contract Theory," 588.

39 Drik Mattem, Andrew Crane, and Wendy Chapple, "Behind the Mask: Revealing the True Face of Corporate Citizenship," *Journal of Business Ethics* 45, no. 1/2 (2003): 111.

40 Mattem, Crane, and Chapple, "Behind the Mask," 111–112. See also Joseph, "The Need of Personal Responsibility," 49.

41 Steve Waddell, "New Institutions for the Practice of Corporate Citizenship: Historical, Intersectoral, and Developmental Perspectives," *Business and Society Review* 105, no. 1 (2000): 107–126. See also Joseph, "The Need of Personal Responsibility," 49.

42 Archie B. Carroll, "The Pyramid of Corporate Social Responsibility: Toward the Moral Management of Organizational Stakeholders," *Business Horizons* 34, no. 4 (1991): 42.

43 Duane Windsor, "The Future of Corporate Social Responsibility," *International Journal of Organizational Analysis* 9, no. 3 (2001): 238.

their organizations."[44] This is a type of self-interest view of corporate citizenship. Both philanthropic and competitive advantage views of corporate citizenship show that there is no consensus on corporate citizenship.

However, Jeanne M. Logsdon and Donna J. Wood consider community based activities of corporations as the basis for corporate citizenship. To be a citizen is a privilege and at the same time it demands rights and duties. There are different views of citizenship such as minimalist and communitarian. The minimalist position upholds individual liberties, and such individuals can attain personal goals without interference of others. The communitarian view of citizenship considers human identity based on community memberships. The main characteristic of a minimalist position is self-interest whereas the characteristic of a communitarian view of citizenship is based on the community's well-being. The minimalist position considers the business as a group of freely chosen citizens based on the contract. In a communitarian dimension of citizenship, a corporation is a member of the community and therefore, the corporation is also a citizen."[45] Furthermore, "corporations are not viewed as an autonomous entity, independent of society; rather they are members of society with corresponding rights and duties. Enforcement of these rights and duties are a matter of social control as in the case of an individual."[46]

However, corporate citizenship can accept bad behaviors because of local or communitarian morality such as child labor practices, advertising practices, and so on. This would be the denial of universal ethical principles that require equal treatment for customers, children, and workers in any culture or nation. Logsdon and Wood make a shift from corporate citizenship to business citizenship and suggest that, the business citizenship model can overcome this dilemma. In the field of international business, there are two ways of strategic choices for firms. The first is local responsibility that takes into consideration region-specific products, policies, and practices. Second is the global approach that concentrates on policies, processes, and structures that are valid in all relevant cultures.[47] They conclude,

> Business citizenship perspective is firmly grounded in universal ethical norms, or hyper-norms, that infuse a company's globally integrated strategy of ethics and stakeholder relations. It also takes the crucial next step of

---

44 Mark C. Bolino, William H. Turnley, and James M. Bloodgood, "Citizenship Behaviour and the Creation of Social Capital in Organizations," *The Academy of Management Review* 27, no. 4 (2002): 507.

45 Logsdon and J.Wood, "Business Citizenship," 156. See also Joseph, "The Need of Personal Responsibility," 50.

46 Logsdon and J.Wood, "Business Citizenship," 157–158. See also Joseph, "The Need of Personal Responsibility," 50.

47 Logsdon and J.Wood, "Business Citizenship," 173–174.

> recognizing situations where local values are not in substantive conflict with hyper-norms and thus can take precedence. Distinguishing when hyper-norms apply and when moral free space permits or requires different organizational behaviours is the ultimate challenge for managers.[48]

An extension of the above-mentioned view of corporate citizenship was proposed by Drick Matten et al. First, they elaborate on the liberal tradition of citizenship, which includes civil rights, social rights, and political rights.[49] The state is supposed to protect civil, political, and social rights of its citizens. However, citizenship has a territorial limitation. In the modern world, due to globalization, the state fails to protect different rights of its citizens because the main characteristic of globalization is "deterritorialization of social, political, and economic interaction."[50] This means that there are many social activities taking place beyond the power and influence of state governments.

Matten et al. assert that corporations enter into the realm of citizenship when governments fail to protect citizenship. Many philanthropic activities such as employee volunteering and feeding the homeless are activities where businesses focus on protecting social rights. In developing and undeveloped countries, governments cannot afford a welfare state. In this situation, corporations have taken over governmental functions by improving the living conditions of employees, providing schools, medical centers, and roads among many other things. The best example of the corporative protection of civil rights is found in General Motors and other corporations in South Africa during the apartheid period that pressured the government to resist the violation of civil rights of black South Africans.[51] On this basis, "the corporation is essentially an additional conduit for the exercise of an individual's political rights—hence the corporation primarily assumes a channelling role."[52] Corporations actively take part in the field of politics through lobbying, party funding, and other activities.[53]

The corporate citizenship theory has a tendency to equate corporations with human beings. I consider that the term "corporate citizenship" is misleading and degrading to the individual citizens because corporations are

48 Logsdon and J.Wood, "Business Citizenship," 173.

49 Civil rights consist of freedom from abuses and interference by third parties. Social rights mean the freedom to participate in various welfare activities of society. Political rights guarantee an individual's right to take part in the process of collective will formation. Cf. Mattem, Crane, and Chapple, "Behind the Mask," 114.

50 Mattem, Crane, and Chapple, "Behind the Mask," 115.

51 A. Crane and D. Matten, *Business Ethics*, 3 ed. (Oxford: Oxford University Press, 2004): 75.

52 Crane and Matten, *Business Ethics*, 77–78.

53 Mattem, Crane, and Chapple, "Behind the Mask," 116–117.

artificial persons. As a solution, it seems better to use the term secondary corporate citizenship.

2.3 Power Motivated Theories and Corporate Integrity

I have classified two types of corporate integrity theories: the social contract and corporate civic citizenship based theories. It is clear that these are based on power motivated corporate social responsibility theories. From the explanation of the link between corporate moral agency debate and corporate integrity, it is clear that both corporate integrity theories consider corporation as a moral person within society. Therefore, the question is, since a corporation is a collective moral person, can corporate social responsibility be achieved? The proposed solution is social contract and corporate (business) citizenship theories. I think that Kaptein and Wempe transform the social contract based corporate social responsibility theory into a corporate integrity theory by integrating corporate behavioral principles and qualities into corporate culture and structure. Behavioral principles help contracting parties to overcome various barriers such as opportunism or bounded rationality, whereas corporate qualities help the contracting parties to overcome various dilemmas that can vitiate the contract.[54] Kaptein and Wempe conclude that all contracting parties will receive the advantage mutually. Similarly, Brown transforms corporate citizenship theory along with stakeholder theory into a corporate integrity theory by adding certain communication and behavioral patterns into corporate relationships.

However, my criticism that follows is that these authors go in the direction of methodological collectivism while neglecting the ontological priority of the individual; hence they are neglecting the personal integrity and personal responsibility of managers and employees, for the attainment of corporate social responsibility. As stated earlier, although Brown has accepted that the "integrity of business leaders depends on how they represent or signify the integrity of corporations to which they belong,"[55] he does not include the personal integrity of managers and employees as part of corporate integrity. However, I think that the success of corporate communication patterns depend greatly upon the personal integrity of employees and managers along with corporate structure and culture. As I have explained earlier, the culture and structure of corporations can contribute to creating guidelines in the presence of conflicts of interest. The real decision makers are individuals; therefore, personal integrity is also important along with corporate culture and structure for the maintenance of contracts and communication patterns.

54 Kaptein and Wempe, *The Balanced Company*, 234–251.

55 Brown, *Corporate Integrity*, 225.

3 Socially Motivated Theories

Since the existence, continuity, and growth of business depends directly upon the society it serves, businesses must consider and fulfill the social demands. There is no specific responsibility for the managers throughout time. Therefore, "the theories of this group are focused on the detection and scanning of, and response to, the social demands that achieve social legitimacy, greater social acceptance, and prestige."[56]

3.1 Social Responsiveness Theories

Corporate social responsiveness is a managerial concept that can be defined as the "capacity of a corporation to respond to various social pressures."[57] The social responsiveness of a company depends upon the ability of a company to manage its relation with various social groups.[58] There are three characteristics of a socially responsible firm: (a) "it monitors and assesses environmental conditions, (b) it attends to many stakeholder demands placed on it, and (c) it designs and plans policies to respond to changing conditions."[59] According to Steven L. Wartick and Philip L. Cochran, companies attain corporate social responsiveness through three stages. First, companies should have corporate policies giving importance to local social issues. Second, companies must have an organizational structure to solve social issues, and finally, companies should make a commitment to meet social demands.[60] However, there are three obstacles, which one has to overcome in order to reach the stage of social responsiveness: decentralized managerial authority in corporate structure that is good for attaining economic goals but insufficient for the attainment of social responsiveness; an accounting system that is perfect for collecting financial data but insufficient for detecting social factors; and organizational incentives system that encourages economic performance but is insufficient for rewarding social performance.[61]

It is worthwhile to note that Edwin M. Epstein distinguishes corporate social responsiveness from corporate social policy process. The notion of

---

56 Mattem, Crane, and Chapple, "Behind the Mask," 58.

57 Gweneth Norrisa and Brendan O'Dwyer, "Motivating Socially Responsive Decision Making: The Operation of Management Controls in a Socially Responsive Organisation," *The British Accounting Review* 36, no. 2 (2004): 175.

58 William C. Frederick, "From CSR1 to CSR2: The Maturing of Business and Society Thought," *Business & Society* 33, no. 2 (1994): 154.

59 Norrisa and O'Dwyer, "Motivating Socially Responsive Decision Making," 175.

60 Joseph, "The Need of Personal Responsibility," 51. Norrisa and O'Dwyer, "Motivating Socially Responsive Decision Making," 175.

61 Cf. Joseph, "The Need of Personal Responsibility," 51. See also Norrisa and O'Dwyer, "Motivating Socially Responsive Decision Making," 176.

corporate social policy process integrates various key elements[62] of business ethics, corporate social responsibility, and corporate social responsiveness.[63] He defines the corporate social policy process as "the institutionalization within the corporation of process facilitating value-based individual and organizational reflection and choice regarding the moral significance of personal and corporate action on identifiable stakeholders in specific situations."[64]

In discussing the social responsiveness of companies, one has to give sufficient importance to the ethical decision making process of organizations. An individual[65] and the environmental factors[66] of the organization can influence an ethical decision making process of an organization.[67] The corporate decision making processes include the following steps: "setting managerial objectives; searching for alternatives; evaluating alternatives; choosing an alternative; implementing the decision; and monitoring and controlling the results."[68] Corporate decision-making process is influenced by both corporate values and personal values; these may be in conflict. Therefore, importance is given to the process as opposed to principles in the discussion of corporate social responsibility.[69] I am of the opinion that personal integrity of managers plays an important role in this process.

---

62 Corporate social policy process includes eight interrelated, analytical elements such as relationship amongst various stakeholders, issues, problems, criteria, goals, decisional process, implementation, and evaluation, which are potentially useful for corporate managers and employees in determining appropriateness of specific corporate actions. Cf. Edwin M. Epstein, "Business Ethics, Corporate Social Citizenship and the Corporate Social Policy Process: A View from the United States," *Journal of Business Ethics* 8, no. 8 (1989): 587.

63 Epstein, "Business Ethics, Corporate Social Citizenship and the Corporate Social Policy Process," 586–587.

64 Epstein, "Business Ethics, Corporate Social Citizenship and the Corporate Social Policy Process," 587.

65 Individual factors include personal goals, motivational mechanisms, position/status, self-concept, life experience, etc., since individual is the real acting agent of corporation, the personal realm of individual can influence the decision making process. Cf. Michael Bommer et al., "A Behavioral Model of Ethical and Unethical Decision Making," *Journal of Business Ethics* 6, no. 4 (1987): 273–274.

66 There are many environmental factors that determine the decision making process of a company. First of all, social environment refers to the humanistic, religious, cultural and social values that influence the social decision making process and are shared by the members of the society or sub-groups like companies. It is known as the value based view of corporate social responsibility. The legal and professional environment can influence the decision making process of a manager. Professional codes of conduct for managers can establish the ethical standards for the actions of managers. Furthermore, the work environment includes corporate goals, policies, and corporate culture. Cf. Bommer et al., "A Behavioral Model of Ethical and Unethical Decision Making," 268–273. See also Joseph, "The Need of Personal Responsibility," 51.

67 Bommer et al., "A Behavioral Model of Ethical and Unethical Decision Making," 267.

68 Bommer et al., "A Behavioral Model of Ethical and Unethical Decision Making," 274.

69 Thomas M. Jones, "Corporate Social Responsibility Revisited, Redefined," *California Management Review* 22, no. 2 (1980): 59–67.

It is very difficult to define corporate social responsibility in light of particular decisions. Jones views "corporate social responsibility as means not as to an end." Therefore, corporate social responsibility is to be judged not based on the outcome but on the process through which the outcome is reached. This would mean that corporations need to understand the social consequences of their decisions before they put them into practice. He makes an analogy between political, legal, and judicial systems with corporate social responsibility. In a political system, very few rights are held absolutely and most basic rights are "expressed in terms of rights to a fair process."[70] He writes that "the law cannot guarantee that an innocent person will be found innocent, but promises a fair trial. Life, liberty, and property can be denied, but only through due process of law."[71] He gives more importance to the implementation of corporate social responsibility than the process of conceptualization.[72]

Few authors have severely criticized both the responsiveness approach and pure process approach and have suggested the "principle of public responsibility approach." According to this view, guidelines for managerial behavior can be seen in public policy of corporations. Public policy contains not only law but also "the broad pattern of social direction reflected in public opinion, emerging issues, formal legal requirements, and enforcement or implementation practices."[73] This view perceives managerial responsibility in terms of primary and secondary involvement of the business in social situations. Primary involvement includes production, marketing of production, locating and establishing of the production, and legal obligation such as registration and tax obligation. Secondary obligations are the result of the primary obligations such as "selection and advancement of employees, a primary activity that generates career and earning opportunities for some types of individuals."[74]

3.2 Corporate Social Performance Theory

Carroll presents the corporate social performance theory as a global concept for corporate social responsibility. He states that the sum total of social performance of a corporation is indeed corporate social responsibility.[75]

He proposes a pyramid of corporate social responsibility. The most important social responsibility of a business is economic in nature. However,

70 Jones, "Corporate Social Responsibility Revisited, Redefined," 64–65. See also Joseph, "The Need of Personal Responsibility," 51.

71 Jones, "Corporate Social Responsibility Revisited, Redefined," 65.

72 Jones, "Corporate Social Responsibility Revisited, Redefined," 65.

73 Lee E. Preston and James E. Post, "Private Management and Public Policy," *California Management Review* 23, no. 3 (1981): 57.

74 Preston and Post, "Private Management and Public Policy," 57.

75 Cf. Joseph, "The Need of Personal Responsibility," 52.

at the same time it is the economic duty of the business to be as profitable as it can be. Businesses have to maintain a competitive position and a high level of operative efficiency.[76] Second, firms have to abide by the legal responsibilities that are sanctioned by society. Society lays down certain rules and regulations by which businesses are to operate. Businesses have to provide goods and services to society in accordance with legal requirements and a business can be successful only if it fulfills legal obligations.[77] Third, corporations have ethical obligations, which imply that corporations have to do certain activities in addition to law, which the social members expect of them. Ethical obligations are defined as society's expectation of business beyond all legal requirements. Fourth, there are certain discretionary responsibilities for corporations, which are the activities left to a corporation's choices and judgments.[78] "These responsibilities are purely voluntary, and the decision to assume them is guided only by business's desire to engage in social roles not mandated, not required by law and not even generally expected of business in an ethical sense."[79]

Carroll states that total corporate social responsibility is the simultaneous fulfillment of a business's legal, ethical, social, and discretional responsibilities. It includes the requirements that businesses have to make profit, fulfill the law, be ethical, and be good corporate citizens. He defines corporate social responsibility as follows: "The social responsibility of business encompasses the economic, legal, ethical, and discretionary expectations that society has of organizations at a given point of time."[80]

It is surprising to see why Carroll presents the pyramid of corporate social responsibility and places economic responsibility at the bottom. Corporations depend upon society and the laws of society to facilitate their very existence. As such, it is rational to place the legal responsibilities at the bottom. Furthermore, other authors state that "Carroll's pyramid of corporate social responsibility is also very simplistic and static; failing to capture the complexity of corporate social responsibility in practice."[81] For example, Crane and Matten argue that the main limitation of this model

---

76 Joseph, "The Need of Personal Responsibility," 52. Archie B. Carroll, "A Three-Dimensional Conceptual Model of Corporate Performance." The Academy of Management Review 4, no. 4 (1979): 497–505.

77 Joseph, "The Need of Personal Responsibility," 52.

78 Joseph, "The Need of Personal Responsibility," 52. Carroll, "The Pyramid of Corporate Social Responsibility," 41–43.

79 Carroll, "A Three-Dimensional Conceptual Model of Corporate Performance," 500.

80 Carroll, "A Three-Dimensional Conceptual Model of Corporate Performance," 500.

81 Wayne Visser, "Revisiting Carroll's Pyramid: An African Perspective," 1–8, accessed February 18, 2012, http://www.waynevisser.com/wp-content/uploads/2012/07/article_africa_pyramid_wvisser.pdf.

is that it "does not adequately address the problem of what should happen when two or more responsibilities are in conflict."[82]

3.3 Socially Motivated Theories and Corporate Integrity

The social responsiveness theory of corporate social responsibility advocates for a better relationship between businesses and society. The view proposes that social responsibility can be achieved by corporate policies, structures and decision-making processes, which fulfill the economic, legal, ethical, and discretionary expectations of society in regard to corporations.

Corporate integrity theories are really empowering the ethical culture and structure of corporations, which are essential to move in the direction of socially motivated corporate social responsibility theories.[83] Corporate behavioral principles, corporate qualities, and communication patterns within corporate structure and culture are important elements of corporate integrity theories, which would enable the business to overcome conflicts of interests in the process of decision making and become more socially responsible. However, my objection is that just like corporate integrity theories, social performance corporate social responsibility theories also neglect individual responsibilities and integrity of managers and employees in the establishment of corporate social responsibility.

4 Ethically Motivated Theories

Ethically motivated corporate social responsibility theories concentrate on the ethical principles, which determine the link between businesses and society.[84] These theories stand as the background for corporate integrity theories. Ethically motivated theories can be divided into two: normative stakeholder theory and sustainable corporate vision theory.

4.1 Normative Stakeholder Theory

Some authors use stakeholder theory to integrate social demands toward the people who are subjected to corporate policies and its practices. There are two basic principles in stakeholder management: to achieve overall cooperation between various stakeholder groups and to use the most efficient strategies for keeping stakeholder relationships.[85] Max B. E. Clarkson defines stakeholders as essential "without whose continuing participation

---

82 Crane and Matten, *Business Ethics*, 44.

83 Joseph, "The Need of Personal Responsibility," 58.

84 Joseph, "The Need of Personal Responsibility," 52.

85 Garriga and Melé, "Corporate Social Responsibility Theories," 59.

the corporation cannot survive as a going concern."[86] According to R. Edward Freeman and William M. Evan, the term "stakeholder" refers to "the various groups that provide critical support to a business firm."[87] These definitions reveal that the relationships between corporations and stakeholders are interdependent.

Stakeholders are interdependent and can affect each other either by harmful activities or by beneficial activities. Corporations have different stakeholders such as owners, employees, suppliers, customers, and local communities. Owners have a financial stake in the firm in the form of money or bonds, and they hope for it to be returned and additionally make profits. Employees have to do their job in the firm and the firm is obliged to pay them for it. Since the raw materials are important for the existence and function of the firm, suppliers are vital to the firm. If the supplier is a member of the stakeholder network, then the supplier would respond positively when the firm is in need. Customers pay for the product and receive the benefits of the products. The local community is vital in the stakeholder network because local communities provide all facilities for the functioning of corporations.[88]

"Management plays an important role in the practice of the stakeholder theory. Since stakeholders are equally important in corporations, there is the possibility for conflicting interests among stakeholders and the duty to keep the relationship among the stakeholders in balance falls on the managers. However, if this balance is lost, the firm's survival falls in jeopardy."[89]

Donaldson and Lee E. Preston propose two criteria for determining the normative sphere of stakeholder theory. First, stakeholders are people or a group with legitimate interests[90] and second, the stakeholder interest has an intrinsic value.[91] Later, Donaldson and Preston expanded the theory of stakeholder and presented different interpretations of it. According to them, stakeholder theory can be divided into three parts: instrumental stakeholder theory, which holds that if managers want to

---

86 Max B. E. Clarkson, "A Stakeholder Framework for Analyzing and Evaluating Corporate Social Performance," *The Academy of Management Review* 20, no. 1 (1995): 107.

87 Freeman and Evan, "A Stakeholder Theory of the Modern Corporation," 311.

88 Cf. Joseph, "The Need of Personal Responsibility," 53. See also Freeman and Evan, "A Stakeholder Theory of the Modern Corporation," 312–313.

89 Joseph, "The Need of Personal Responsibility," 53.

90 It is controversial to determine who is a legitimate stakeholder. The contract view of the firm holds that those who have contract with stakeholders are legitimate stakeholders. Donaldson and Preston are of the opinion that this explanation is incomplete because of the vagueness of the position of communities in the contract. These authors state that "stakeholders are identified through actual and potential harms and benefits that they experience or anticipate to experience as a result of a firm's action." Cf. Thomas Donaldson and Lee E. Preston, "The Stakeholder Theory of the Corporation: Concepts, Evidence, and Implications," *The Academy of Management Review* 20, no. 1 (1995): 85.

91 Donaldson and Preston, "The Stakeholder Theory of the Corporation," 67.

achieve traditional corporative objectives (such as profitability or growth), then managers have to take into account stakeholder's interest; descriptive stakeholder theory which states how managers and stakeholder properly interact; and normative stakeholder theory, that holds how managers and stakeholders ought to act. They propose that these three aspects of stakeholder theory are nested with one another.[92]

However, in 1994, Freeman made a fourth division to stakeholder theory in addition to Donaldson and Preston's metaphorical division of stakeholder theory. It shows the narrative aspects of corporate life.[93] This narrative approach shows various stakeholder theories, each of which has a "normative core" consisting of the "way corporations should be governed and the way managers should act."[94] Since the "normative core" cannot be reduced to strict fundamental rules, there are many possibilities and alternatives to the "normative core." The "normative core of a stakeholder theory might be a feminist standpoint, rethinking how we would restructure value-creating activity along with the principle of caring and connection."[95] "In an ecological normative core, corporations and managers ought to act in accordance with the rule of caring for earth."[96]

Both stakeholder and shareholder theories are in contrast to one another on the maximization of values, namely, stakeholder value and shareholder value. In the final analysis, the most difficult thing is to find out the normative justificatory framework for stakeholder theory and to fix stakeholder identity.[97] According to Freeman, those whom the corporation affects, will affect the corporation back. Therefore, it is good to take into account stakeholders in order to increase benefit to the firm in the long-term. He qualifies this view as "prudential stakeholder model."[98] This leaves open the question of "how the business would treat the stakeholder group who are affected by the business but do not affect it in any way. Robert A. Phillips with the help of John Rawls proposes the principle of fairness as the normative basis for the prudential stakeholder model. There are six characteristics for the principles of fairness: mutual benefit, justice, cooperation, sacrifice, free rider possibility, and voluntary acceptance of

---

92 Donaldson and Preston, "The Stakeholder Theory of the Corporation," 70–73. See also Joseph, "The Need of Personal Responsibility," 53–54.

93 R. Edward Freeman, "The Politics of Stakeholder Theory: Some Future Directions," *Business Ethics Quarterly* 4, no. 4 (1994): 413.

94 Freeman, "The Politics of Stakeholder Theory," 413. Joseph, "The Need of Personal Responsibility," 54.

95 Freeman, "The Politics of Stakeholder Theory," 414. Joseph, "The Need of Personal Responsibility," 54.

96 Joseph, "The Need of Personal Responsibility," 54.

97 Robert A. Phillips, "Stakeholder Theory and a Principle of Fairness," *Business Ethics Quarterly* 7, no. 1 (1997): 53–54.

98 R. Edward Freeman, *Strategic Management: A Stakeholder Approach* (Boston: Pitman Publishing, 1984): 25.

benefit of cooperative schemes."[99] He concludes that "obligations of fairness are created among the participants in the cooperative scheme in proportion to the benefit accepted."[100]

Clarkson proposes seven principles for normative stakeholder management. First, managers should accept and seriously keep an eye on the demands of the stakeholders and consider their demands in the decision making processes. Second, managers should have an open mind in order to dialogue with stakeholders regarding their demands and the risk that they undergo because of their active participation with corporations. Third, since stakeholder groups are different in their demands and concerns, managers should plan for a special way of dealing with each stakeholder group. Fourth, managers should keep in mind the interdependence of different groups of stakeholders and do a fair distribution of the benefits. Fifth, managers should maintain a cooperative mentality with stakeholders and avoid harm as far as possible and if this is not possible, they must provide compensation. Sixth, managers must be careful to avoid violating the rights of the stakeholders. Finally, managers must minimize potential conflicts of interest by communication and third party review.[101]

Contrary to the stakeholder view, many ethicists hold the critical view that the primary objective of corporations is to maximize the wealth of shareholders, as based on agency theory.[102] Advocates of the stakeholder theory state that managers and directors are the agents of corporation and not the agents of shareholders.[103] Corporations are only artificial persons; moreover, according to many ethicists, the corporation has only a secondary moral agency. I would state that directors and managers are the agents of corporations; this implies that managers and directors are the agents of shareholders who are the real causes of the formation of the businesses in question. This theory, however, lacks clear guidelines on how to achieve its aim. According to the stakeholder theory, managers have to take into account the demands of stakeholder groups and normally, there is a

[99] Joseph, "The Need of Personal Responsibility," 54. Phillips takes the principle of fairness from Johan Rawls. The first characteristic of the principle of fairness is mutual benefit that is received either by corporations or by stakeholders. In economic interactions, justice means giving each one their due. Cooperation in corporative matters is another condition for fairness. Sacrifice means the limitation of freedom in economic interactions, for example, requiring that a worker should arrive at the exact work time. Lastly, fairness also includes the voluntary acceptance of the benefit that is created and received either by corporation or by stakeholders. Cf. Phillips, "Stakeholder Theory and a Principle of Fairness," 53–63.

[100] Phillips, "Stakeholder Theory and a Principle of Fairness," 57.

[101] Max Clarkson, *Principles of Stakeholder Management* (Toronto: The Clarkson Centre for Business Ethics, 1999): 3–8. See also Joseph, "The Need of Personal Responsibility," 55.

[102] Barry M. Mitnick, "Agency Theory," in *Encyclopedic Dictionary of Business Ethics*, eds. Patricia H. Werhane and Edward Freeman (Oxford: Blackwell Publishers, 1998): 14–15.

[103] R. Phillips Robert, Edward Freeman, and Andrew C. Wicks, "What Stakeholder Theory Is Not," *Business Ethics Quarterly* 13, no. 4 (2003): 483.

possibility for conflicting interests of stakeholder groups to occur. It is not clear how managers can make decisions in such a situation or prioritize the demands of equally valuable conflicting interests.

Clarkson suggests different methods to overcome conflicts of interests. These include open communication, reporting and incentive systems, third party review, and dialogue.[104] "The methods are applied by managers; however, they are not adequate to solve the dilemmas themselves."[105] The contribution of the moral personality of managers and directors in this situation is the real substantive element, and cannot be neglected. "An alignment of personal and organizational values is typically seen as an ideal basis for developing good working relations, and for retaining and motivating staff."[106]

4.2 Sustainable Corporate Vision

There are various definitions for the theory of sustainable development.[107] David Wheeler et al. define sustainable corporate vision "as an ideal toward which society and business can continually strive, the way we strive is by creating value, i.e. creating outcomes that are consistent with the *ideal* of sustainability along social, environmental, and economic distensions."[108] Furthermore, corporate level sustainable development can be viewed as short-term and long term sustainability. Short-term sustainability indicates economic sustainability. Long-term sustainability needs three dimensions of sustainability: the economic, environmental, and the social.[109] Precisely, corporate sustainability can be defined as "meeting the needs of a firm's direct and indirect stakeholders without compromising its ability to meet the needs of future stakeholders as well."[110] Similarly, the

---

104 Clarkson, *Principles of Stakeholder Management*, 4. See also Joseph, "The Need of Personal Responsibility," 55.

105 Joseph, "The Need of Personal Responsibility," 55.

106 Crane and Matten, *Business Ethics*, 145.

107 Cf. Joseph, "The Need of Personal Responsibility," 55. Thomas N. Gladwin, James J. Kennelly, and Tara-Shelomith Krause, "Shifting Paradigms for Sustainable Development: Implications for Management Theory and Research," *The Academy of Management Review* 20, no. 4 (1995): 877.

108 David Wheeler, Barry Colbert, and R. Edward Freeman, "Focusing on Value: Reconciling Corporate Social Responsibility, Sustainability and a Stakeholder Approach in a Network World," *Journal of General Management* 28, no. 3 (2003): 17.

109 Economically sustainable companies guarantee the cash flow in the market. Ecologically sustainable companies use natural resources in a responsible manner. They try not to create environmental damage and engage in any activity that will degrade the eco-system. Socially sustainable companies always take care of the stakeholder in the activities and decisions of the company. Cf. Thomas Dyllick and Kai Hockerts, "Beyond the Business Case for Corporate Sustainability," *Business Strategy and the Environment* 11, no. 2 (2002): 132–133. See also Joseph, "The Need of Personal Responsibility," 56.

110 Dyllick and Hockerts, "Beyond the Business Case for Corporate Sustainability," 131.

desired outcome of corporate integrity theories is the mutual sustainable advantage of all contracting parties.[111]

A sustainable corporate vision depends upon different organizational cultures. First, the compliance culture gives importance to rules for maintaining the relationships between organizations and stakeholders. Second, a relationship management culture uses instrumental mentality to uphold the relationship between corporation and stakeholder.[112] Finally, a "sustainable organization culture which recognizes the interdependencies and synergies among the firm, its stakeholders, society, seeks to *maximize the creation of value* simultaneously in economic, social, and ecological terms."[113] According to Paul Shrivastava, avoiding negative ecological impact is a method to attain an ecologically sustainable corporation. In this attempt, corporations face many obstacles such as environmental disasters through pollution, waste, consumer's unsustainable consumption, and selfish interests of businesses. System of inputs, throughputs, and outputs are used by organizations to achieve their vision. Legal regulations and corporate vision determine a company's relationship with its surrounding environment. Input is related to the use of natural resources for the corporate production of goods. The production system and output can affect nature in either way.[114] "These inputs, throughputs, and outputs have systematic interconnections among them and with environmental, economic, social, and organizational variables. Corporations can become ecologically sustainable only by simultaneously directing these variables and interconnections toward ecologically performance."[115] Moreover, the dominant value system in corporations determines the possibility for corporate sustainability within each corporation.[116]

4.3 Ethically Motivated Theories and Corporate Integrity

As explained previously, ethically motivated theories attempt to create an efficient atmosphere to maintain stakeholder relationships. Stakeholders are important in corporate life and there is a possibility for conflicts of interest to arise. By introducing a normative and value-based framework, ethically motivated theories attempt to maintain a balance between the

111 Kaptein and Wempe, *The Balanced Company*, 227–228.

112 Joseph, "The Need of Personal Responsibility," 56.

113 Wheeler, Colbert, and Freeman, "Focusing on Value," 11.

114 Paul Shrivastava, "The Role of Corporations in Achieving Ecological Sustainability," *Academy of Management Review* 20, no. 4 (1995): 941–942. See also Joseph, "The Need of Personal Responsibility," 56.

115 Shrivastava, "The Role of Corporations in Achieving Ecological Sustainability," 942.

116 Marcel van Marrewijk and Marco Werre. "Multiple Levels of Corporate Sustainability." *Journal of Business Ethics* 44, no. 2 (2003): 112. See also Joseph, "The Need of Personal Responsibility," 56.

various interests of stakeholders.[117] The same efforts can be seen in corporate integrity theories but the difference is that corporate integrity theories present this normative and value based framework more clearly and systematically by introducing ethical corporate culture, structure, and communication patterns.

How can a multinational company sincerely do justice to the stakeholders in the host country? Corporate sustainable vision is a proposed solution and it includes nature, but the real executors of this vision, in conflicting situations, are corporate managers and their employees. The feeling, personal integrity, belongingness, and nationalistic feelings of managers and directors of the multinational firms have a significant role in rightly dealing with the stakeholders' rights. The personal values and principles of managers and employees are neglected in stakeholder theory as well as in corporate integrity theory. In this context, I argue for a shift from corporate perspective social responsibility and corporate integrity theories to a corporate and individual centered corporate social responsibility and corporate integrity theories.[118]

Conclusion

There are different theories regarding corporate social responsibility. These theories are generally divided into four groups, namely, profit motivated theories, power motivated theories, socially motivated theories, and ethical theories. Profit motivated theories hold that corporate social responsibility is to increase shareholder value. Power motivated theories perceive that since corporations enjoy social power in society, they have to be responsible to society. Socially motivated theories say that since the existence, continuity, and growth of business depend on society, business must consider and fulfill social demands. Ethically motivated corporate social responsibility theories concentrate on ethical principles that determine the link between business and society. I conclude this section with a suggestion that we need more powerful individual and corporate centered corporate socially responsible theories rather than corporate centered socially responsible theories.

---

117 Marrewijk and Werre, "Multiple Levels of Corporate Sustainability," 112. See also Freeman, *Strategic Management: A Stakeholder Approach*, 25.

118 Whatever one says, the real actors and decision makers of corporations are individuals or top managers, and managers are to a certain extent guided by governmental rules and customs. I think that corporate social responsibility is the right of stakeholders. Moreover, the actualization of these rights is dependent upon the top managers of corporations and governmental rules. More than a theory we need the formation of trust of managers. Furthermore, I think what we need today is not only excellent managers but also good managers and right governmental rules that support the rights of stakeholders.

CHAPTER FOUR

CORPORATE REPUTATION AND CORPORATE INTEGRITY

Introduction

Corporate reputation is a multidimensional concept and includes multiple definitions, conceptualizations, and operationalizations that have emerged across studies.[1] According to various literature, there are three different dimensions of organizational reputation: "being known," "being known for something," and "generalized favorability."[2] "Being known" refers to the "generalized awareness or visibility of the firm; prominence of the firm in the collective perception."[3] Reputation as prominence refers to "the extent to which an organization is widely recognized amongst stakeholders in its organizational field, and the extent to which it stands out relative to competitors."[4] Corporate reputation as awareness "encompasses those definitions that referred to a term or used language indicating that observers or stakeholders had a general awareness of a firm but did not make judgments about it."[5] The commonly used term to denote corporate reputation in this perspective is perception. Perception entails "an aggregation of perceptions, latent perceptions, net perceptions, global perceptions,

[1] Donald Lange and Peggy M. Lee, "Organizational Reputation: A Review," *Journal of Management* 37, no. 1 (2011): 154.

[2] Lange and Lee, "Organizational Reputation: A Review," 155.

[3] Lange and Lee, "Organizational Reputation: A Review," 155.

[4] Violina P. Rindova et al., "Being Good or Being Known: An Empirical Examination of the Dimensions, Antecedents, and Consequences of Organizational Reputation," *The Academy of Management Journal* 48, no. 6 (2005): 1035.

[5] Michael L. Barnett, John M. Jermier, and Barbara A. Lafferty, "Corporate Reputation: The Definitional Landscape," *Corporate Reputation Review Volume* 9, no. 1 (2006): 32.

perceptual representations and collective representations."[6] However, many authors do not commonly accept prominence as part of reputation.[7]

The second conceptualization of corporate reputation is "being known for something," that refers to the "perceived predictability of organizational outcomes and behaviour relevant to specific audience interests."[8] In this dimension, corporate reputation is based on perceived quality.[9] Contrary to the conceptualization of "being known," judgment of the stakeholders is the central feature of this conceptualization,[10] and therefore, corporate reputation, from this perspective, indicates that "stakeholder impressions of the firm's disposition to behave in a certain manner, incorporate information about how a firm compares to its competitors."[11] However, since there are multiple stakeholder groups within a given corporation, there will be diverse interests and goals that would lead to multiple reputational assessments.[12]

The third conceptualization of corporate reputation, "generalized favorability" refers to "the perceptions or judgments of the overall organization as good, attractive, and appropriate."[13] From this perspective, corporate reputation is defined as "the collective judgments of a corporation based on assessments of the financial, social, and environmental impacts attributed to the corporation over time."[14]

1 Critical Assessment of Corporate Reputation Conceptualizations

The "being known" dimension of corporate reputation shows the non-evaluative image of corporations. The problem is that "the depth and content of this collectively held mental image of the organization will be different depending on which social group is sampled."[15] "Being known for something," a dimension of corporate reputation, is the result of evaluation by stakeholders, as to whether the company meets specific stakeholders'

6 Barnett, Jermier, and Lafferty, "Corporate Reputation," 32.

7 Brian K. Boyd, Donald D. Bergh, and David J. Ketchen, "Reconsidering the Reputation–Performance Relationship: A Resource-Based View," *Journal of Management* 36, no. 3 (2010): 508–609.

8 Lange and Lee, "Organizational Reputation: A Review," 155.

9 Rindova et al., "Being Good or Being Known," 1035.

10 Lange and Lee, "Organizational Reputation: A Review," 158.

11 Dax K. Basdeo et al., "The Impact of Market Actions on Firm Reputation," *Strategic Management Journal* 27, no. 12 (2006): 1206.

12 Lange and Lee, "Organizational Reputation: A Review," 159.

13 Lange and Lee, "Organizational Reputation: A Review," 155.

14 Barnett, Jermier, and Lafferty, "Corporate Reputation," 34. See also Scott Highhouse, Margaret E. Brooks, and Gary Gregarus, "An Organizational Impression Management Perspective on the Formation of Corporate Reputations," *Journal of Management* 35, no. 6 (2009): 1481–1493.

15 Lange and Lee, "Organizational Reputation: A Review," 164.

interests. On the other hand, the "generalized favorability" dimension of corporate reputation is the result of the evaluations of corporation as an aggregate whole. This evaluation is universal in nature.[16]

The question here is whether corporate reputation can be evaluated locally by a specific group of stakeholders (financial investors or environmental activists) or whether it must be evaluated from a universal stakeholder perspective. Both "being known" and "generalized favorability" dimensions of corporate reputation have universal dimensions, but the difference is that the latter includes critical evaluations. Although "being known" speaks of universal corporate image, it is not evaluated, and fake perceptions can be created with the use of the media and advertisement techniques. Therefore, I promote the universal stakeholder evaluation because it includes a particular specific group of stakeholders and it has the potential to be objective. Therefore, "a corporate reputation is a stakeholder's overall evaluation of a company over time. This evaluation is based on the stakeholder's direct experiences with the company, any other form of communication and symbolism that provides information about the firm's actions."[17] In other words, corporate reputation is a "net reaction of customers, investors, employees, and the general public to the company's name."[18]

2 Advantages of Corporate Reputation

The concept of corporate reputation has a significant role in corporate performance and in the recent studies of the management literature. Corporate reputation has both tangible[19] and intangible[20] benefits.[21] Corporate reputation allows the corporation to have good stakeholder relationships and stability when experiencing difficulties. Moreover, corporations with a favorable corporate reputation "attract more and better candidates for employment, pay less for supplies, gain essentially free press coverage that is worth as much if not more than advertising, and accrue other benefits that

16 Lange and Lee, "Organizational Reputation: A Review," 165.

17 Manto Gotsi and Alan M. Wilson, "Corporate Reputation: Seeking a Definition," *Corporate Communications: An International Journal* 6, no. 1 (2001): 29.

18 Highhouse, Brooks, and Gregarus, "An Organizational Impression," 1483.

19 Tangible assets include "financial resources and other capital-based resources that are controlled by the firm." Cf. Verna Allee, "Value Network Analysis and Value Conversion of Tangible and Intangible Assets," *Journal of Intellectual Capital* 9, no. 1 (2008): 6.

20 Intangible corporate assets "include relationships, employee know-how and competency, the effectiveness of the organisation's work groups and structure, the efficiency of the organisation's production and service processes, and the level of trust between the people or organisations forming the relationships." Cf. Allee, "Value Network Analysis and Value Conversion of Tangible and Intangible Assets," 6.

21 John Doorley and Helio Fred Garcia, *Reputation Management: The Key to Successful Public Relations and Corporate Communication*, 2 ed. (New York: Routledge, 2011): 4.

actually contribute to profits. Reputation adds value to the actual worth of a company that is, market capitalization."[22]

In a globalized world, a company with a strong reputation receives "preference in doing business with a company when several companies' products or services are similar in quality and in price."[23] A strong corporate reputation supports the business in times of corporate controversies. Moreover, a corporation's value in the financial market will be higher if the company enjoys a positive and strong reputation.[24] Corporate reputation enhances corporate performance.[25]

3 Attainment of Corporate Reputation

Corporate reputation is connected with corporate ethical culture and structure. It is possible to attain corporate reputation "by adopting various popular management practices (e.g., total quality management, employee empowerment, and teams)."[26] Reputation is connected with tangible organizational output. If the organizations attain efficient and quality productions, then it influences their reputation.[27]

Innovation, quality of management, leadership, corporate culture and structure, financial performance, social responsibility, product quality, communicativeness, governance, and corporate integrity are considered the key factors for the attainment of a corporate reputation.[28] Moreover, corporate communication with stakeholders is a decisive element of reputation management.[29]

4 Link between Corporate Reputation and Corporate Integrity

Corporate reputation is the reaction of both external and internal stakeholders regarding the company's name. Corporate social responsibility,

---

[22] Doorley and Garcia, *Reputation Management*, 4–5.

[23] Stephen A. Greyser, "Advancing and Enhancing Corporate Reputation," *Corporate Communications: An International Journal* 4, no. 4 (1999): 178.

[24] Greyser, "Advancing and Enhancing Corporate Reputation," 178.

[25] Kristin B. Backhaus, "Organizational Identity, Corporate Social Performance and Corporate Reputation: Their Roles in Creating Organizational Attractiveness," in *Corporate Reputation: Managing Opportunities and Threats*, eds. Ronald J. Burke, Graeme Martin, and Cary L. Cooper (Burlington: Ashgate Publishing company, 2011): 119.

[26] E. Geoffrey Love and Mathew Kraatz, "Character, Conformity, or the Bottom Line? How and Why Downsizing Affected Corporate Reputation," *Academy of Management Journal* 52, no. 2 (2009): 317.

[27] Love and Kraatz, "Character, Conformity, or the Bottom Line?," 317.

[28] Doorley and Garcia, *Reputation Management*, 13. See also Greyser, "Advancing and Enhancing Corporate Reputation," 179.

[29] James G. Hutton et al., "Reputation Management: The New Face of Corporate Public Relations?," *Public Relations Review* 25 (2001): 247–261.

corporate communication, and corporate stakeholder relationships are important elements of corporate reputation. Corporate integrity theories aim to improve stakeholder relationships, communication, and mutual advantage.[30] In order to achieve a better stakeholder relationship, the corporate integrity theories propose ethical corporate structures and culture with behavioral principles, corporate qualities, and certain communication patterns.[31] If corporate integrity is designed within the corporation, then to a certain extent, one can conclude that corporate integrity can improve corporate reputation as both are linked.

However, corporate integrity is not a full-fledged theory for corporate reputation because it supports only methodological collectivism and neglects ontological priority, an important element of corporate reputation. Because individual managers who enjoy good reputations and public image can create good corporate reputations,[32] managers with good reputations or personal integrity, therefore, become the very image and reputation of the company "through having integrity, communicating, team building, planning of the long haul, and possessing a vision."[33] However, individuals can have a negative reputation, that in turn can cause damage to corporate reputation. Often, corporate corruption and crime are the effects of the decision-making of top managers with damaged reputations.[34] Moreover, effective leadership is an essential element of the creation of corporate reputation, which depends upon the personal integrity of leaders. Similarly, unethical behavior by managers of companies is a very big threat to corporate reputation.[35] Since corporate integrity theories do not incorporate the personal integrity and reputation of top managers as an element of corporate integrity, it is insufficient for corporate reputation.

Conclusion

Corporate reputation is the perception of the company's name by both external and internal stakeholders. Corporate integrity theories attempt to safeguard better stakeholder relationships with the corporation and thereby, the personal integrity of top managers is crucial for a successful corporate reputation because they are the real acting persons in a corporation.

30 Kaptein and Wempe, *The Balanced Company*, 227–228.

31 Kaptein and Wempe, *The Balanced Company*, 227–294. See also Brown, *Corporate Integrity*, 2222–234.

32 Ronald J. Burke, "Corporate Reputations: Development, Maintenance, Change and Repair," in *Corporate Reputation: Managing Opportunities and Threats*, eds. Ronald J. Burke, Graeme Martin, and Cary L. Cooper (Burlington: Ashgate Publishing Company, 2011): 12–13.

33 Burke, "Corporate Reputations," 12.

34 Burke, "Corporate Reputations," 12–14.

35 Burke, "Corporate Reputations," 32.

PART II

THE ROLE OF PERSONAL INTEGRITY IN CORPORATE ETHICS

CHAPTER FIVE

WORKING DEFINITION OF PERSONAL INTEGRITY

Introduction

Personal integrity is a multidimensional ideal and considered as a prerequisite for trust between different levels of relationships in management. However, there is little agreement as to the meaning and scope of personal integrity and, moreover, it is defined in numerous ways. Since many of the existing descriptions and definitions are narrow in scope and focus only upon particular aspects, the descriptions and definitions, therefore, create confusion. This calls for a more comprehensive and clear view of personal integrity. In this chapter, I examine the various descriptions of personal integrity and form a working definition.

1 Diverse Descriptions of personal Integrity

Integrity is a dynamic ideal that can be applied to both animate and inanimate objects. The integrity of inanimate objects such as ecosystems, art works, and music is determined by their completeness, uncorrupted state, and wholeness.[1] However, Webster's *Third New International Dictionary* defines human integrity as "firm adherence to a code of especially moral or artistic values, that is incorruptibility; an unimpaired condition, that is soundness; the quality or state of being complete or undivided, that is completeness."[2] In a discussion of human integrity, few authors make

[1] Cora Diamond, "Integrity," in *Encyclopedia of Ethics*, eds. Lawrence C. Becker and Charlotte B. Becke (New York: Garland Publishing, 1992): 618. See also Marguerite La Caze, Damian Cox, and Michael Levine, "Integrity," eds. Uri Nodelman Edward N. Zalta, and Colin Allen (Stanford: Stanford University, 2008), "Integrity," *Stanford Encyclopedia of Philosophy*, accessed September 18, 2008, 25, https://plato.stanford.edu/entries/integrity/.

[2] Philip Babcock Gove, ed., *Webster's Third New International Dictionary* (Massachusetts: Merriam-Webster Publishers, 1993): 1174.

a distinction between personal integrity and moral integrity,[3] and there are those who do perceive personal integrity as being entirely separate from social morality.[4] The idea of a person with integrity refers to various qualities of the character of a person, namely, integration of self, authenticity, word/action consistency, and virtue.[5] None of these descriptions can portray a clear picture of the ideal concept of integrity. Nevertheless, they underline the various dimensions of personal integrity. In this context, Stephen Carter writes that "integrity is a lot like the weather: everyone talks about it, but no one knows what to do about it."[6] In the following section, I discuss the various descriptions of integrity and their limitations.

1.1 Integrity as Integrated Self

Integrity is the integration of various realms of one's personality into a harmonious whole, or keeping one's self integral or uncorrupted. This definition of integrity focuses on "a unified agency that makes the individual a 'whole' person."[7] It refers to the serenity of a person to follow ethical principles, especially in the face of adversities, dilemmas, or temptations that occur in life; a person of integrity is not concerned with immediate

---

3 On a personal level, integrity is viewed as internal consistency and coherence between a person's beliefs and convictions, and external consistency and coherence between what someone professes and does. This is an agent-centered view of integrity. However, the 'moral integrity of a person is a behavior-centered view of integrity. This means that in moral integrity, we check whether someone does what is expected. As Musschenga states, "in this view, moral integrity is intimately linked with the social side of morality." Although moral integrity shares the features of personal integrity such as internal and external coherence and consistency, it refers to the core of someone's self, that is, whether one's core self conforms to social morale. Cf. Albert W. Musschenga, "Integrity—Personal, Moral, and Professional," in *Personal and Moral Identity*, eds. Albert W. Musschenga et al., (London: Kluwer Academic Publishers, 2001): 188. See also Albert W. Musschenga, "Education for Moral Integrity," *Journal of Philosophy of Education* 35, no. 2 (2001): 221–235.

4 Musschenga, "Personal," 222.

5 D. Koehn, "Integrity," 134. See also Linda Klebe Trevino, Laura Pincus Hartman, and Michael Brown, "Moral Person and Moral Manager: How Executives Develop a Reputation for Ethical Leadership," *California Management Review* 42, no. 4 (2000): 130. See also Skip Worden, "The Role of Integrity as a Mediator in Strategic Leadership: A Recipe for Reputational Capital," *Journal of Business Ethics* 46, no. 1 (2003): 33. See also Michael E Palanski and Francis J. Yammarino, "Integrity and Leadership: A Multi-Level Conceptual Framework," *The Leadership Quarterly* 20 (2009): 405. See also Mark Gosling and Heh Jason Huang, "The Fit between Integrity and Integrative Social Contracts Theory," *Journal of Business Ethics* 90, no. 3 (2009): 410–411. See also Rosa Nelly Trevinyo-Rodrı´guez, "Integrity: A Systems Theory Classification," *Journal of Management History* 13, no. 1 (2007): 80–85.

6 Stephen Carter, *Integrity* (New York: Harpercollins, 1996): 6.

7 Peter Verhezen, "The (Ir)Relevance of Integrity in Organizations," *Public Integrity* 10, no. 2 (2008): 134. See also Andrew Edgar and Stephen Pattison, "Integrity and the Moral Complexity of Professional Practice," *Nursing Philosophy* 12, no. 2 (2011): 97. Tim Dare, "Detachment, Distance and Integrity," in *Personal Ethics and Integrity*, eds. Tim Dare and W. Bradley Wendel (Newcastle upon Tyne: Cambridge Scholars Publishing, 2010): 101.

gratification.[8] Moreover, stability and self-integration involve a deeper level of character that enables an individual to overcome external and internal pressures, temptations, and constraints.[9] Strength of will[10] is an important quality or disposition of the integrated self. The strength of will makes the correspondence between a person's desire or intention and actions because actions are the very manifestation of the person's desires or intentions, as results from the exercises of the strength of will.[11]

A more developed idea of the integrated self is proposed by Harry Frankfurt.[12] Frankfurt believes that human beings have two types of desires: "first order desires" and "second order desires."[13] A first order desire is common to all animals and humans, and is simply the desire to do or not do something. The reflective evaluation of the first order desire paves a way for the emergence of second order desires, which can be either the conscious selection of one of the first order desires, or the emergence of a new desire due to the volition of a first order desire. Through this reflective evaluation or volition, one attains the highest level of desire. Thus an integrated person shows/possesses harmony between desire and volition at various levels of the latter category. Therefore, self-integration is created through the unity of the acts of ordering, rejecting, or integrating and separating desires or the conflicting desires.[14]

8 Lynne McFall, "Integrity," *Ethics* 98, no. 1 (1987): 7–8. See also Worden, "The Role of Integrity as a Mediator in Strategic Leadership: A Recipe for Reputational Capital," 34–35. Michael E. Palanski and Francis J. Yammarino, "Integrity and Leadership: Clearing the Conceptual Confusion," *European Management Journal* 25, no. 3 (2007): 174. Matthew Pianalto, "Integrity and Struggle," *Philosophia* 40 (2012): 329. See also Joseph, "The Conceptual Link between Personal Integrity and Positive Fundamental Option," 109.

9 Muel Kaptein, *The 6 Principles of Managing with Integrity: A Practical Guide for Leaders* (Trowbridge: The Cromwell Press, 2008): 36. See also Muel Kaptein and Johan Wempe, *The Balanced Company*, 91.

10 Strength of will is the controlling force of one's own behavior or intentions. It is an act of volition and strong exercise of the power of will. Cf. Richard Holton, "How is Strength of Will Possible?" in *Weakness of Will and Practical Irrationality*, eds. Sarah Stroud and Christine Tappolet (Oxford: Oxford University Press, 2003): 40.

11 Caze, Cox, and Levine, "Integrity," accessed September 18, 2013, http://plato.stanford.edu/archives/spr2013/entries/integrity.

12 Harry Frankfurt is an American philosopher of mind, morality, and action. He was an advocator of rationalism. His books include '*Demons, Dreamers, and Madmen: The Defense of Reason in Descartes's Meditations*', '*Necessity, Volition, and Love*', '*The Reason of Love*' etc., Cf. Harry G. Frankfurt, "Taking Ourselves Seriously: Getting It Right," in *Taking Ourselves Seriously: Getting It Right*, ed. Debra Satz (California: Stanford University Press, 2006): 7.

13 Harry G. Frankfurt, "Freedom of the Will and the Concept of a Person," *The Journal of Philosophy* 68, no. 1 (1971): Musschenga, "Personal," 7.

14 Harry G. Frankfurt, "Identification and Wholeheartedness," in *Responsibility, Character, and the Emotions: New Essays in Moral Psychology*, ed. Ferdinand Schoeman (New York: Cambridge University Press, 1987): 39. See also Frankfurt, "Freedom of the Will," 7–13. Later, however, there is a change in his position when he maintained that "one cannot make himself wholehearted or integrated just by a psychic movement [...] Will is

There are many criticisms of Frankfurt's integrated self-view and its application to integrity. Cheshire Calhoun argues that the integrated self-concept of integrity does not elucidate the criteria for using reason in the act of volition. That is, using one's own reason at will is not sufficient to form integrity.[15] The view of integrity as an integrated self reduces the ideal integrity as unified agency. Albert W. Musschenga states that "although there is substantial overlap between having unified agency and having personal integrity, there are significant differences."[16] Transparency, honesty, and sincerity are to be present in personal integrity, whereas unified agency does not presuppose them all.[17] Moreover, integrity is more than simply unifying one's will, which according to Frankfurt, would involve attempting to control and change one's will, but is a matter of finding and acting in accordance with one's will.[18] Marguerite La Caze, Damian Cox, and Michael Levine criticized the integrity theory of Frankfurt when they observe that an integrated person should never experience temptation because temptation is an abandoned or a bad desire. According to Frankfurt, if abandoned desire enters the mind, it is subordinated by the wholeheartedly endorsed desires through the volition of the will. However, since human beings experience the abandoned desire, this situation is contrary to Frankfurt's notion of integrity as an integrated self.[19]

Many authors consider integrity as "wholeness."[20] Kaptein and Wempe propose that such wholeness includes integration of the self into two

---

not fully under his immediate voluntary control." Cf. Harry G. Frankfurt, "The Faintest Passion," *Proceedings and Addresses of the American Philosophical Association* 66, no. 3 (1992): 10. Robert Audi and Patrick E. Murphy, "The Many Faces of Integrity," *Business Ethics Quarterly* 16, no. 1 (2006): 9.

[15] Cheshire Calhoun, "Standing for Something," *The Journal of Philosophy* 92, no. 5 (1995): 241. In the integrated self view, integrity rests upon the individual's claim of the rightness of a principle as a criterion for volition. In the integrated self view, "you define yourself by saying that I did what I thought right and effectively can and need say nothing more than that." Edgar and Pattison, "Integrity and the Moral Complexity," 98. See also Calhoun, "Standing for Something," 251. On the contrary, some authors propose objective integrity. Elizabeth Ashford, "Utilitarianism, Integrity, and Partiality," *The Journal of Philosophy* 97, no. 8 (2000): 425. See also Joseph, "The Conceptual Link between Personal Integrity and Positive Fundamental Option," 109.

[16] Musschenga, "Personal," 185.

[17] Musschenga, "Personal," 185–186.

[18] Damian Cox, Marguerite La Caze, and Michael P. Levine, *Integrity and the Fragile Self* (Burlington: Ashgate Publishing Company, 2003): 24.

[19] Caze, Cox, and Levine, "Integrity," accessed September 18, 2013, http://plato.stanford.edu/archives/spr2013/entries/integrity. Similar thoughts can be seen in Gabriele Taylor and Raimond Gaita's article. Cf. Gabriele Taylor and Raimond Gaita, "Integrity," *Proceedings of the Aristotelian Society, Supplimentary Volumes* 55 (1981): 151.

[20] Integrity is derived from the Latin word *integer* that means "wholeness" or "completeness." Integrity as wholeness is used by authors to describe those who uphold integrity as a multi-faceted reality. Integrity as wholeness is considered both locally and globally. In global integrity, all parts of the life of an individual are to be coherent, but in

spheres: the personal and social level. "Integrity concerns the degree to which people are integrated both on a personal level and in relation to society (toward others)."[21] Kaptein believes that "integrity is particularly concerned with integration and harmony: seeking an optimal solution to the situations where values and interests are mutually exclusive."[22] The optimal solution is based on right reason, mutual dialogue as well as compromise.[23] Integrated managers know how to select from different intentions of the self and they are aware of what they do and what they gain.[24] I doubt whether an immediate compromise is always possible regarding conflicts of interest or values.

It is worthwhile to note further developments in this area of thought. A substantial number of authors divide the understandings of integrity into two categories: integrity A and integrity B.[25] Integrity A is related to one's own personal integrated self, where integrity "becomes the personification of your most dearly held moral principles."[26] A positive aspect of integrity A is that people with this sort of integrity always stand for their values and principles. However, it prevents the individual from considering new evidence and facts that might be relevant for moral discussions.[27] Integrity B holds that no one can stand outside the society in which they live, and therefore "integrity B implies flexibility and compromise in conflicting

local integrity, integrity is referred to (as) one's jobs or professional roles etc. Cf. Verhezen, "The (Ir) Relevance of Integrity in Organizations," 134. See also Gosling and Huang, "The Fit between Integrity and Integrative Social Contracts Theory," 410. Palanski and Yammarino, "Integrity and Leadership," 173. Maximilian de Gaynesford, "Integrity over Time: Korsgaard and the Unity Criterion," *The Harvard Review of Philosophy* 18, no. 1 (2012): 50.

21 Kaptein and Wempe, *The Balanced Company*, 87. See also Gerhold K. Becker, "Integrity as a Moral Ideal and Business Benchmark," *Journal of International Business Ethics* 2, no. 2 (2009): 77.

22 Muel Kaptein, "Integrity Management," *European Management Journal* 17, no. 6 (1999): 101.

23 Kaptein and Wempe, *The Balanced Company,* 96. Compromise is defined as "a mode of conflict resolution or prevention in which the parties agree to withdraw or to reduce some of their initial demands." Cf. Mohamed Nachi, "The Morality in/of Compromise: Some Theoretical Reflections," *Social Science Information* 43, no. 2 (2004): 293. The person of integrity can make neither a simple choice between conflicting equal values nor avoid both conflicting values, and partial fulfillment of conflicting values. What can the person of integrity do in the situation of conflicting values? Wempe and Kaptein suggest that a person of integrity always seeks a maximal solution as a compromise in conflicting values and obligations. They take both obligations very seriously and there is no negation from the heart level. They will be ready to dialogue with others and reach a richer solution. The person of integrity would give justice to all conflicting values. Dialogues and discussions will never diminish one's integrity. Cf. Kaptein and Wempe, *The Balanced Company*, 96.

24 Kaptein, "Integrity Management," 101.

25 Integrity A is basically the personal experience of integrity whereas integrity B is more a social and reflective experience of integrity. Cf. Edgar and Pattison, "Integrity and the Moral Complexity," 100.

26 Edgar and Pattison, "Integrity and the Moral Complexity," 101.

27 Edgar and Pattison, "Integrity and the Moral Complexity," 101.

situations. People with integrity B would weigh their values and perspectives in balance with a wide variety of other perceptions and factors before arriving at a definitive moral stance."[28] Although integrity B is desirable in an organizational context, people can be either of these two. In accordance with this context,[29] both integrity A and B people are described as people with integrity.[30]

One could argue that a real matter to integrity is the core of the self. Volition, choice, and mutual dialogue are a part of the integrated self, dependent on the core of a person. Therefore, it follows that integrity is the status or condition of the core of the self and the expression of the self. Through volition, choice, and mutual dialogue, integration is the normal outcome of the wholeness of a person and determines whether the core of the self has a positive or negative status toward society.

1.2 Integrity as Authenticity

Integrity as authenticity refers to the condition of a person who stands for something or attempts to attain something while remaining true to their internal ideals. According to this view, a person of integrity knows what he/she wants or does not want, and his/her conduct streams from his/her inner self. An authentic person is aware of the reasons for his/her actions and consequences of his/her actions. An authentic person is, therefore, better able to handle temptations, external pressures and dilemmas in life.[31] In short, "authenticity can be characterized as reflecting the unobstructed operation of one's true, or core, self in one's daily enterprise."[32] The above mentioned definition shows that in human life, authenticity functions at two levels; personal and behavioral. Personal level authenticity is defined

---

28 Edgar and Pattison, "Integrity and the Moral Complexity," 102–103.

29 The complete integration of values and moral principles is unattainable. This is because people's different social and personal backgrounds lead to unavoidable conflicts between values. Therefore, integrity as integrated self creates more confusion about the evaluation of personal integrity. The argument of the narrative theory of the self has to be used in each context in order to find whether one person has integrity or not. Cf. Alasdair Maclntyre, *After Virtue: A Study of Moral Theory* (Notre Dame: University of Notre Dame Press, 1981): 203.

30 Edgar and Pattison, "Integrity and the Moral Complexity," 105.

31 Kaptein, *The 6 Principles of Managing with Integrity*, 60. See also Kaptein and Wempe, *The Balanced Company*, 90. See also Thomas R. Flynn, "Authenticity," in *The Blackwell Encyclopedic Dictionary of Business Ethics*, eds. Patricia H. Werhane and Edward Freeman (Malden: Blackwell Publishers Ltd, 1997): 30. Marisal L. Miller and Barry R. Schlenker, "Integrity and Identity: Moral Identity Differences and Preferred Interpersonal Reactions," *European Journal of Personality* 25 (2011): 3. See also Joseph, "The Conceptual Link between Personal Integrity and Positive Fundamental Option," 110.

32 Hannes Leroy, Michael E. Palanski, and Tony Simons, "Authentic Leadership and Behavioral Integrity as Drivers of Follower Commitment and Performance," *Journal of Business Ethics* 107 (2012): 256. See also Michael H Kernis, "Toward a Conceptualization of Optimal Self-Esteem," *Psychological Inquiry* 14, no. 1 (2003): 13.

as a personality "that is fully self-endorsed, volitionally enacted, and personally meaningful to the individual,"[33] whereas on the behavioral level, authenticity is the acting in accordance with one's own true self and being genuine to one's interactions and relations.[34] The culture of authenticity is reduced to remain true to oneself. In order to cultivate authenticity, "business students, employees, and corporate leaders should all be encouraged to launch their own inquiry into sources of bad faith organization, conventional business practices, etc., and reflect on how they choose to live their professional lives in the midst of them."[35]

Similar to integrity as with authenticity, integrity of a person presents as an identity of the person.[36] Generally, the identity of a person can be perceived from different perspectives such as personal identity, moral identity, and social identity. Personal identity is defined as "a sense of self built up over time as the person embarks on and pursues projects or goals that are not thought of as those of a community, but as the property of the person. Personal identity thus emphasizes a sense of individual autonomy rather than of communal involvement."[37] In short, the identity of a person is explained as the core of one's being.[38] However, according to Charles Taylor, the identity of a person is constituted "dialogically" through interaction with others. Thus, he emphasizes the importance of the communitarian dimension of personal identity.[39] The social identity of a person consists of the person's "knowledge that he [or she] belongs to certain groups together with some emotional and value significance to him [or her] of the group membership."[40] Individuals attempt to maintain their social identity by performing acts that enhance the "positive distinctiveness of the group

---

33 Julie Menard and Luc Brunet, "Authenticity and Well-Being in the Workplace: A Mediation Model," *Journal of Managerial Psychology* 26, no. 4 (2011): 332.

34 Menard and Brunet, "Authenticity and Well-Being in the Workplace," 332.

35 Kevin T Jackson, "Towards Authenticity: A Sartrean Perspective on Business Ethics," *Journal of Business Ethics* 58, no. 4 (2005): 321.

36 Verhezen, "The (Ir)Relevance of Integrity in Organizations," 135. See also Caze, Cox, and Levine, "Integrity," accessed September 19, 2013, http://plato.stanford.edu/archives/spr2013/ entries/integrity.

37 John Hewitt, *Self and Society: A Symbolic Interactionist Social Psychology* (Boston: Allyn and Bacon, 1997): 93.

38 Karl Aquino and Americus Reed, "The Self-Importance of Moral Identity," *Journal of Personality and Social Psychology* 83, no. 6 (2002): 1424.

39 Charles Taylor, "The Politics of Recognition," in *Multiculturalism: Examining the Politics of Recognition*, ed. Amy Gutmann (New Jersey: Princeton University Press, 1994): 32–35.

40 Henri Tajfel, "La CatéGorisation Sociale," in *Introduction a` La Psychologie Sociale*, ed. S. Moscovici (Paris: Larouse, 1972): 31. I have taken this quotation from the following sources. Cf. S. Alexander Haslam, Rachael A. Eggins, and Katherine J. Reynolds, "The Aspire Model: Actualizing Social and Personal Identity Resources to Enhance Organizational Outcomes," *Journal of Occupational and Organizational Psychology* 76 (2003): 84.

with which that identity is associated."[41] Moral identity can be explained as "one kind of self-regulating mechanism that motivates moral action."[42] Moral identity, therefore, is the self-conception that is organized around certain moral traits.[43] There is a link between these different dimensions of the identity of the person, especially the social and moral identity of the person because, "although moral identity is rooted in a trait-based conceptualization, it is presumed that a person's moral identity may have a social referent that could be a real membership group."[44] Although the link between the different dimensions of identity of a person is debatable,[45] I do not intend to elaborate on this as it is beyond the scope of this book.

According to the identity view, "integrity means fidelity to those projects and principles that are constitutive of one's core identity."[46] Thus, integrity means also the keeping of the elements of one's core identity. While dealing with identity, Robert Noggle made a distinction between ontological identity[47] and psychological identity,[48] though they are related. A change in ontological identity does not affect the integrity of a person, but if there are radical changes[49] to the psychological identity, then it will diminish or increase integrity of the person.[50] The transformation of Saul, on the way to Damascus, is the best example for the change of psychological identity and integrity.[51] However, Calhoun holds an opposite view of psychological identity and integrity. She believes that integrity means fidelity to one's endorsements rather than mere psychologically deep identifications. An act, without deep reflection, would simply be based upon our psychological impulses. In this situation, one cannot say that she/he is a person of integrity.[52]

Similarly, the identity view of integrity is also related to one's commitments.[53] Nancy Schauber makes a distinction between active commitments

41 Haslam, Eggins, and Reynolds, "The Aspire Model," 84.

42 Aquino and Reed, "The Self-Importance of Moral Identity," 1423.

43 Aquino and Reed, "The Self-Importance of Moral Identity," 1424.

44 Aquino and Reed, "The Self-Importance of Moral Identity," 1424.

45 Steven Hitlin, "Values as the Core of Personal Identity: Drawing Links between Two Theories of Self," *Social Psychology Quarterly* 66, no. 2 (2003): 118–137.

46 Calhoun, "Standing for Something," 235.

47 This is the descriptive information of an entity.

48 Psychological identity can be described as reflective human features developed differently in each human being.

49 Radical change means change in one person's convictions, values, and character.

50 Robert Noggle, "Integrity, the Self, and Desire-Based Accounts of the Good," *Philosophical Studies* 96, no. 3 (1999): 315. See also Cox, Caze, and Levine, *Integrity and the Fragile Self*, 30.

51 Eileen Hanson, "Integrity and Identity," *Macalester Journal of Philosophy* 6, no. 1 (2011): 25.

52 Calhoun, "Standing for Something," 244.

53 Commitment implies that person of integrity is ready to bear the consequences of their convictions and actions even when the consequences are unpleasant. In other words,

and passive commitments. Active commitments are commitments based on special obligations and responsibilities, but active commitments are not merely an intention to do something, rather others have a right to get it. Promises are the best example of such types of commitments. Since active commitments are performative, even though there is a lack of motivation, the person has to do what she/he said or promised and he/she has less choice in the matter. Passive commitments are based on one's virtue or concerns. A person is passively committed because he/she has specific beliefs, concerns and projects.[54] Integrity of the person manifests not in active commitments but in passive commitments.[55] However, philosophers such as Damian Cox, M.L. Caze and M.P. Levine severely criticize the dichotomy of passive and active commitments. They believe that the division of commitments is false as well as confusing, as they introduce the notion of having several transactional and conventional commitments. According to them, these commitments are either passive or active and an exact division is impossible. For example, when one finds himself/herself committed to helping the poor, it can be seen from both active and passive perspectives, so the division of commitments is confusing.[56]

Some authors contend that the contribution of authenticity to integrity is ambiguous.[57] Gosling et al. suggest that if the behavior of an individual is authentic when he/she does not act contrary to existing hyper norms,[58] then he/she does not lack integrity. Moreover, if the individual demonstrates the same behavior over a long period of time, then that individual acts with integrity. "In the same manner for an individual who acts contrary to socially acceptable authentic norms so as to obey a hyper norm, an individual who acts to obey legitimate norms, despite his/her personal

commitments are those principles and actions that are part of one's core self, and a person of integrity acts in compliance with these principles. Cf. McFall, "Integrity," 9–11. See also, Thomas Maak, "Undivided Corporate Responsibility: Towards a Theory of Corporate Integrity," *Journal of Business Ethics* 82 (2009): 353. Calhoun, "Standing for Something," 245–246.

54 Nancy Schauber, "Integrity, Commitment and Concept of a Person," *American Philosophical Quarterly* 33, no. 1 (1996): 122.

55 Schauber, "Integrity, Commitment and Concept of a Person," 122.

56 Cox, Caze, and Levine, *Integrity and the Fragile Self*, 48.

57 Mark Gosling and Heh Jason Huang, "The Fit between Integrity and Integrative Social Contracts Theory," *Journal of Business Ethics* 90 (2009): 414. See also Cox, Caze, and Levine, *Integrity and the Fragile Self*, 31. John Cottingham, "Integrity and Fragmentation," *Journal of Applied Philosophy* 27, no. 1 (2010): 12–13.

58 Hyper norms are defined as "fundamental moral precepts for all human beings [...] that express principles so fundamental to human existence that one would expect them to be reflected in a convergence of religious, political, and philosophical thought." Cf. Thomas Donaldson and Thomas W. Dunfee, "Integrative Social Contract Theory," *Economics and Philosophy* 11 (1995): 95–96

notion, is in fact acting with integrity."[59] Therefore, in order to have authenticity, one's actions have to be consistent with the true nature of the actor. However, since lies and deception are always possible, how can authenticity be ascertained? Can integrity be merely a matter of who we are? Or, as I have explained before, is integrity related to whether or not the status of the core of one's self is in conformity with the social morale? In this context, the contribution of Taylor is remarkable.

Taylor proposes a distinctive view of authenticity that contains both a personal and a communitarian dimension. According to him, from an ideal point of view, authenticity refers to an attitude of being true to one's originality or true self.[60] This ideal concept of authenticity derives from the fact that there is something distinctive within each person, where "there is a certain way of being human that is my way"[61] and by being faithful to one's own originality, each person achieves self-fulfillment and self-realization.[62] In this understanding, authenticity means being true to one's own inner voice, which indicates what kind of person one is and what kind of life one ought to live.[63] Taylor's personal dimension of authenticity requires individual freedom and demands that each must discover their own inner voice and true self. He writes,

> Being true to myself means being true to my own originality, and that is something only I can articulate and discover. In articulating it, I am also defining myself. I am realizing a potentiality that is properly my own. This is the background understanding to the modern ideal of authenticity, and to the goals of self-fulfillment or self-realization in which it is usually couched. This is the background that gives moral force to the culture of authenticity, including its most degraded, absurd, or trivialized forms. It is what gives sense to the idea of "doing your own thing" or "finding your own fulfillment."[64]

However, at the same time, Taylor argues that the ideal of authenticity does not make us free from our obligations in relation to others (communal dimension). Taylor objects to contemporary perspectives of a purely self-centered view of authenticity and suggests that human authenticity is created dialogically through interaction with others. Thus, to be an authentic person, one need not only be true to oneself but also to exist

---

59 Gosling and Huang, "The Fit between Integrity and Integrative Social Contracts Theory," 414.

60 Charles Taylor, *The Ethics of Authenticity* (Cambridge: Harvard University Press, 1991): 25–29. See also Taylor, "The Politics of Recognition," 29–32. See also Charles Taylor, *A Secular Age* (Cambridge: The Belknap Press, 2007): 475. See also Joseph, "The Conceptual Link between Personal Integrity and Positive Fundamental Option," 110.

61 Taylor, *The Ethics of Authenticity*, 28–29.

62 Taylor, "The Politics of Recognition," 31.

63 Taylor, *The Ethics of Authenticity*, 26 and 29.

64 Taylor, *The Ethics of Authenticity*, 29.

actively in the "horizons of significance"[65] and one needs "recognition" for being the particular kind of individual that one is.[66]

The two conditions, "horizons of significance" and "recognition," are crucial because, according to Taylor, being true to oneself or one's originality involves acknowledging the plural sources of one's moral self.[67] Indeed, the identity of a person is constituted "dialogically" through interactions with others.[68] He, therefore, believes that authenticity presupposes some horizons of significance determined by the community and tradition in which one participates. Such horizons are needed because no one can make authentic action simply by willing it so. Taylor writes that "even the sense that the significance of my life comes from its being chosen—the case where authenticity is actually grounded on self-determining freedom—depends on the understanding that independent of my will, there is something noble, courageous, and hence significant in giving shape to my own life."[69] It is clear that if the way of self-expression obscures the "horizons," then it is self-defeating. This means "we must not close ourselves off to the moral horizons that make meaningful identity possible: accepting the ideal of authenticity entails resisting the slide to subjectivism."[70]

The need for recognition becomes apparent when Taylor argues that "the ideal of authenticity incorporates some notions of society or at least of how people ought to live."[71] Two social principles are important in this regard: (1) "fairness" or "universal right," that is, "everyone should have the right and capacity to be themselves,"[72] and (2) intimate love relationships. Recognition is a reciprocal activity. We are satisfied by the need to be recognized only insofar as it is given by someone whose judgment and esteem we value.[73] In order to have mutual recognition in a community, we need some common moral standard. Taylor writes that "to come together on a mutual recognition of difference—that is, of the equal value of different identities—requires that we share more than a belief in this principle; we

---

65 Taylor, *The Ethics of Authenticity*, 39. A "horizon of significance" is a technical term used by Taylor in order to denote that authenticity is closely related with moral standards of community and nature.

66 Taylor, *The Ethics of Authenticity*, 35–48.

67 Charles Taylor, *Sources of the Self: The Making of Modern Identity* (Cambridge: Harvard University Press, 1989): 495–496; 28–29. See also Brenda Lyshaug, "Authenticity and the Politics of Identity: A Critique of Charles Taylor's Politics of Recognition," *Contemporary Political Theory* 3 (2004): 302.

68 Taylor, "The Politics of Recognition," 32–35.

69 Taylor, *The Ethics of Authenticity*, 39.

70 Joseph R. Reisert, "Authenticity, Justice, and Virtue in Taylor and Rousseau," *Polity* 33, no. 2 (2000): 310.

71 Taylor, *The Ethics of Authenticity*, 44.

72 Taylor, *The Ethics of Authenticity*, 45.

73 Taylor, "The Politics of Recognition," 50.

have to share also some standards of value on which the identities concerned check out as equal."[74]

Although Taylor does not deny that innate characteristics are necessary for human development, he rejects the idea that humans develop their authenticity or identity in accordance with built-in programs that originate from within that person. According to Taylor, "we achieve our own distinctive identities in large part through our interactions with others—who not only introduce us to our native language but who also teach us the 'languages' of art, of gesture, of love, and the like."[75] We not only learn cultural languages from others but also "the contribution of significant others, even when it occurs at the beginning of our lives, continues throughout."[76]

Taylor believes that to have authenticity, we must give "expression in our speech and action to what is original in us."[77] In order to have an authentic expression in our speech and action, it is not only enough to depend upon our inner voice but also, we have to take into account the consideration of the community, because the ideal of authenticity itself has certain limits on how it is actualized in actions. The limits correspond to our dependence on others or the community for our moral development, and our experience of emotional dependency on others, as for the road to demanding recognition.[78] Taylor writes that "only if I live in a world in which history, or the demands of nature, or the needs of my fellow human beings, or the call of God, or something else of this order matters crucially, can I define an identity for myself that is not trivial. Authenticity is not the enemy of demands that emanate from beyond the self; it presupposes such demands."[79]

The backdrop of Taylor's view of authenticity, in both the personal and communitarian dimension, goes back to his distinctive view of human identity or self. Taylor affirms multiple sources of the moral self: God, disengaged reason, nature, and authenticity.[80] He argues that "our identities, as defined by whatever gives us our fundamental orientation, are in fact complex and many-tiered."[81] Brenda Lyshaug interprets Taylor, stating that

---

74 Taylor, *The Ethics of Authenticity*, 52. See also Taylor, "The Politics of Recognition," 69.

75 Taylor, *The Ethics of Authenticity*, 33. See also Reisert, "Authenticity, Justice, and Virtue in Taylor and Rousseau," 308–309.

76 Taylor, *The Ethics of Authenticity*, 34.

77 Taylor, *The Ethics of Authenticity*, 61.

78 Taylor, *The Ethics of Authenticity*, 35–48. See also Reisert, "Authenticity, Justice, and Virtue in Taylor and Rousseau," 309.

79 Taylor, *The Ethics of Authenticity*, 40–41.

80 Taylor, *Sources of the Self: The Making of Modern Identity*, 495–496. See also Peter Digeser, *Our Politics, Our Selves? Liberalism, Identity, and Harm* (New Jersey: Princeton University Press, 1995): 76.

81 Taylor, *Sources of the Self: The Making of Modern Identity*, 28–29.

"being true to ourselves in the fullest sense, involves acknowledging and attending to this plurality."[82] This means authenticity as being true to oneself includes both personal and communal dimensions, since one's identity or moral self includes multiple sources of morality. Moreover, when Taylor writes about authenticity, he upholds the "rejection both of anthropocentrism—the idea that there are no sources of value beyond the self, and of self-determining freedom—the idea that all is permitted."[83]

Taylor develops a view of authenticity that is both communal (objective) and personal (subjective). He formulates this view by admitting two realities: (1) he writes that our identity or self is constituted by different moral sources. (In *Ethics of Authenticity,* he uses terms such as "'inner voice and horizons of significance"). (2) He accepts the "importance of dialogical action in human life [...]. It places us in some social space"[84] and so, human identity or self is constituted by dialogical interaction with others. Although authenticity exists by virtue of being true to one's true self, it presupposes the moral standards of the community in which a person lives because no self or identity formed without community and authenticity is the expression of one's self in an action. Similarly, Raymond T. Sparrowe observes that "authenticity is not only achieved by self-awareness of one's inner values or purpose, but also instead is emergent from the narrative process in which others play a constitutive role in the self."[85]

1.3 Integrity as Word/Action Consistency or Honesty

Often, integrity is identified with honesty or word/action consistency, and this remains true in the business world, particularly regarding leadership, employee selection, and moral judgments. While elaborating on the qualities of leadership, Gray A. Yukl and David D. Van Fleet define integrity to mean "that a person's behaviour is consistent with espoused values and that the person is honest and trustworthy."[86] In addition, John K. Butler views integrity as one of nine basic elements of trust. He uses the concept of integrity as a character of honesty and a moral quality.[87] However,

[82] Lyshaug, "Authenticity and the Politics of Identity: A Critique of Charles Taylor's Politics of Recognition," 302.

[83] Reisert, "Authenticity, Justice, and Virtue in Taylor and Rousseau," 310. See also Taylor, *The Ethics of Authenticity*, 68–69.

[84] Charles Taylor, "The Dialogical Self," in *The Interpretive Turn: Philosophy, Science, Culture*, eds. David R. Hiley, James F. Bohman, and Richard Shusterman (London: Cornell University Press, 1991): 311.

[85] Raymond T. Sparrowe, "Authentic Leadership and the Narrative Self," *The Leadership Quarterly* 16 (2005): 419.

[86] Gray A Yukl and David D. Van Fleet, "Theory and Research on Leadership in Organizations," in *Handbook of Industrial and Organizational Psychologists*, eds. M. D. Dunnette and L. M. Hough. Palo (Alto: Consulting Psychologists Press, 1992): 151.

[87] John K Butler, "Toward Understanding and Measuring Conditions of Trust: Evolution of Conditions of Trust Inventory," *Journal of Management History* 17, no. 3 (1991): 646.

according to Thomas E. Becker, although honesty and integrity are related in some ways, they are conceptually distinct because integrity is beyond honesty.[88]

A deeper understanding of the concept of integrity based on word/action consistency would imply that persons of integrity must have some specific qualities, namely, they do not cheat others and they also stick to their principles. People of integrity must be honest to themselves.[89] However, in this conception of integrity, there is a problem of moral relativism.[90] To tackle this problem, the distinction between personal integrity and moral integrity is helpful. Personal integrity refers to a personal dimension of morality, whereas moral integrity refers to a communitarian dimension of morality.[91] However, from this perspective, even Hitler could be considered a person of integrity because he acted according to his personal moral principles and convictions in his promotion of a master race, and a communitarian moral principle, that is, love of one's own race. Therefore, an application of the concept of integrity in this sense is not always very helpful.[92]

Becker views integrity differently. He understands integrity as a loyalty to rational principles and values. He observes that "integrity is the principle of being principled, practicing what one preaches regardless of emotional or social pressure, and not allowing any irrational consideration to overwhelm one's rational convictions."[93] Integrity is not only a matter of keeping consistency between words and actions but also acting in accordance with rational values. A person of integrity can also change convictions in accordance with an increase in his/her knowledge and over time as he/she develops different opinions. Leonard Peikoff supports this view that persons with integrity can change their views if they find that some of their ideas were wrong.[94]

Behavioral integrity is viewed as behavioral consistency between an agent's words and actions. There are two theoretical components to behavioral integrity: explicit promise keeping and consistency between

---

88 Thomas E. Becker, "Integrity in Organizations: Beyond Honesty and Conscientiousness," *Academy of Management Review* 23, no. 1 (1998): 155.

89 Taylor and Gaita, "Integrity," 143.

90 Moral Relativism is a theory holding that all ethical principles are subjectively valid i.e. only in relation to individual choices or cultural norms. This view implies that moral principles are relative and there are no universal moral principles. Cf. Gilbert Harman. Cf. Gilbert Harman, "Moral Relativism Defended,"*The Philosophical Review* 84, no. 1 (1975): 1. See also Becker, "Integrity in Organizations," 155.

91 McFall, "Integrity," 6. See also Becker, "Integrity in Organizations," 155.

92 Becker, "Integrity in Organizations," 155.

93 Becker, "Integrity in Organizations," 157.

94 Leonard Peikoff, *Objectivism, the Philosophy of Ayn Rand* (New York: Meridiam, 1991): 260.

espoused values and actually displayed values.[95] It is quite natural to ask whether behavioral integrity can remain stable across time and situations. Tony Simon argues that word/action inconsistency is inevitable in behavioral integrity, since the manager has to satisfy diverse constituencies and diverse role expectations. Many authors suggest that although there is an inconsistency between the manager's words/actions, they can maintain behavioral integrity by accepting personal responsibility for inconsistency and being transparent about different situations and the reasons behind their decisions.[96] Moreover, whether "a person can be considered to have acted with integrity depends upon the specific situation, place or time," writes Kaptein.[97] He goes on to argue that "today's acceptable behavior may be considered objectionable tomorrow."[98] Thus, a person of integrity would be able to understand the signs of the day and change his/her convictions accordingly with an increase of knowledge.

Integrity is considered as word/action consistency in adversity, temptation, or challenge. A person's reactions to adverse situations are considered to be the necessary conditions for measuring the integrity of the person. A situation of adversity, dilemmas, temptations, and challenges offer the possibility of a choice. Although unethical, some choices may be more profitable than others. The choices made depend upon the priority of values of the person, determining their behavioral integrity.[99]

1.4 Integrity as a Virtue

According to Hayden Ramsay, a person of integrity is a virtuous[100] person in whom integrity can be divided into two parts: formalist and *aretaic* integrity. Formalist integrity is characterized by the principle of coherence and individual freedom that is used to articulate and follow principles.

[95] Tony Simons, "Behavioral Integrity: The Perceived Alignment between Managers' Words and Deeds as a Research Focus," *Organizational Science* 13, no. 1 (2002): 19. See also Palanski and Yammarino, "Integrity and Leadership," 174. See also Rangapriya Kannan-Narasimhan and Barbara S. Lawrence, "Behavioral Integrity: How Leader Referents and Trust Matter to Workplace Outcomes," *Journal of Business Ethics* 111 (2012): 167.

[96] Simons, "Behavioral Integrity," 27. See also Leroy, Palanski, and Simons, "Authentic Leadership," 257.

[97] Kaptein, "Integrity Management," 2.

[98] Kaptein, "Integrity Management," 2.

[99] Worden, "The Role of Integrity as a Mediator in Strategic Leadership: A Recipe for Reputational Capital," 34. See also McFall, "Integrity," 9. Palanski and Yammarino, "Integrity and Leadership," 406. Michael E. Palanski and Francis J. Yammarino, "Impact of Behavioral Integrity on Follower Job Performance: A Three-Study Examination," *The Leadership Quarterly* 22 (2011): 767. See also Cottingham, "Integrity and Fragmentation," 6.

[100] Hayden Ramsay explains: "Virtue is to be explained dynamically as good habits of an activity at first practiced without being fully understood, then gradually understood through increasingly refined practice, eventually ingrained as excellent practices characteristic of the individual." Cf. Hayden Ramsay, *Beyond Virtue: Integrity and Morality* (London: Macmillan Press, 1997): 24.

In formalist integrity, a person can decide his/her principles and actions. *Aretaic* integrity includes all virtues, and within this model, integrity builds up character. Furthermore, formalistic integrity is descriptive, whereas *aretaic* integrity is normative. *Aretaic* integrity is the unified expression of virtues.[101]

One can move to *areteic* integrity from formalist integrity, that is, the character or habits formed in formalist integrity that reach perfection in *areteic* integrity. In formalist integrity, there is a unified self and a real identity, whereas in *areteic* integrity, there is a harmonious relationship between disposition, belief, and action. Formalist integrity is centered on practical reasoning, whereas *areteic* integrity is centered on prudence. Practical reasoning guides the application of our moral principles in integrity that is formalist, but prudence helps us to judge whether our judgments are right or not in integrity that is referred to as *areteic*. In the life of a person with *areteic* integrity, moral norms are internalized and exemplified in behavior, which helps one to lead a more virtuous life.[102] Unlike deontology and utilitarianism, which concentrate on the morality of particular actions, with respect to integrity, virtue is "much more than coherence and consistency, […] it concerns what it takes to be a whole, a complete moral person."[103]

For many authors, the definition of integrity as a virtue gives a clear solution for the complex and diverse explanations of integrity.[104] There are two categories of virtues: substantive and adjunctive. Substantive virtues are morally good in themselves and include honesty and fairness, while adjunctive virtues are neither morally good nor bad in themselves and include courage and steadfastness, but are necessary for moral personhood. The existing definitions of integrity have been included both in the substantive and adjunctive categories of virtues. Every explanation of integrity belongs to either substantive or adjunctive category of virtue. For example, integrity as being true to oneself and consistent in adversity comes under the category of adjunctive virtues such as authenticity and courage.[105]

If integrity is considered as an adjunctive virtue (consistency of action and words), then it logically follows that integrity is maintained when the

---

101 Ramsay, *Beyond Virtue: Integrity and Morality*, 3. See also Denise M. Dudzinski, "Integrity: Practical Coherence, Virtue, or Both?"*The Journal of Value Inquiry* 38 (2004): 299–300. See also Joseph, "The Conceptual Link between Personal Integrity and Positive Fundamental Option," 112.

102 Dudzinski, "Integrity: Practical Coherence, Virtue, or Both?" 309.

103 Musschenga, "Education for Moral Integrity," 227. See also Craig P. Dunn, "Integrity Matters," *International Journal of Leadership Studies* 5, no. 1 (2009): 117–118.

104 Palanski and Yammarino, "Integrity and Leadership," 177. See also Audi and Murphy, "The Many Faces of Integrity," 12.

105 Audi and Murphy, "The Many Faces of Integrity," 12. See also Palanski and Yammarino, "Integrity and Leadership," 177–178.

person promises to do harm and keeps the promise. Michael Palanski and Francis J. Yammarino, referring to Alasdair Maclntyre's work on virtue, state that the virtue of integrity would be accompanied by smaller virtues, because character is made up of a set of virtues. Therefore, integrity as a virtue can be considered to be the character of a person. The boundary condition for integrity is determined not by one virtue, but by virtues (both adjunctive and substantive).[106]

1.5 Dichotomy in Different Explanations of Personal Integrity

The above mentioned descriptions or definitions of integrity can be classified into two views: narrow and broader.[107] The narrow view considers personal integrity as "one or a collection of personality traits."[108] Yukl and Van Fleet state that "integrity means that a person's behaviour is consistent with espoused values and that the person is honest and trustworthy."[109] This definition shows that integrity and honesty or trustworthiness are synonymous. This narrow view of personal integrity is not concerned with the issue of the moral justifiability of the principles to which the person of integrity is committed.[110] Similarly, Calhoun observes that "no theory of moral justification is inherently hospitable to integrity."[111] On the contrary, a broader view holds that "a moral standard is an essential part of a reputation for integrity."[112] On the basis of the narrow and broad view of integrity, however, Musschenga makes a distinction between personal integrity and moral integrity.[113] Although he makes the distinction between personal and moral views of integrity, I prefer to hold the moral integrity view because I use the term "person of integrity" to denote the moral self of the person and its expression rather than personality traits.

The deep-rooted problem of different descriptions of integrity is found within the question of whether personal integrity is totally subjective (narrow sense), or does it have an objective realm (boarder sense) that defines the moral wholeness or core of the person.[114] Integrity as integrated

[106] Palanski and Yammarino, "Integrity and Leadership," 178.

[107] Gosling and Huang, "The Fit between Integrity and Integrative Social Contracts Theory," 409–410.

[108] Gosling and Huang, "The Fit between Integrity and Integrative Social Contracts Theory," 410.

[109] Yukl and Fleet, "Theory and Research on Leadership in Organizations," 151.

[110] Becker, "Integrity in Organizations," 155.

[111] Calhoun, "Standing for Something," 248.

[112] Gosling and Huang, "The Fit between Integrity and Integrative Social Contracts Theory," 409.

[113] Musschenga, "Education for Moral Integrity," 222. Moral standard means that certain moral principles are characterized by impartiality and universality. Moral integrity is excepted to meet the conditions of these principles. Cf. McFall, "Integrity," 15.

[114] Palanski and Yammarino, "Integrity and Leadership," 178. See also Joseph, "The Conceptual Link between Personal Integrity and Positive Fundamental Option," 113.

self means integration of self with one's own values, moral principles, and deeds; that is, to act with one's convictions. How can a person of integrity overcome dilemmas and conflict situations? A proposed solution for overcoming dilemmas is volition,[115] which lies within the subjective realm of integrity. The question is whether one's own values and principles are objective or merely personal. Are there any objective criteria for volition? What is the role of local and global society in the exercise of one's own integrity? Since the integrated-self approach is silent regarding these issues, I believe that this approach is insufficient to have a comprehensive vision of personal integrity.

Integrity as authenticity means to be true to oneself or true to one's own originality. In this case, importance is given to a personal or subjective dimension. This definition is silent about the content of one's own originality. Taylor, on the contrary, creates a view of authenticity that is both subjective and objective.[116] Mark Gosling et al. suggest that sometimes a person of integrity can become untrue to himself in order to follow hyper norms.[117]

Integrity is widely defined as a person's word/action consistency. A person of integrity can expose inconsistency of word/action on the basis of reasonable grounds. The core points of discussion in the above mentioned definitions, integrity as authenticity and word/action consistency, are whether integrity is only objective, only subjective, or both objective and subjective.[118] The definition of integrity as virtue does not limit integrity to one personal virtue, but defines integrity as a mixture of adjunctive and substantive virtues. In this instance, there is a perfect combination of subjective and objective dimensions of integrity because the boundaries

---

115 Volition means the self-judgment and decision a person makes when they face moral dilemmas.

116 Taylor, *The Ethics of Authenticity*, 40–44.

117 Gosling and Huang, "The Fit between Integrity and Integrative Social Contracts Theory," 413–414.

118 The role of local and global levels of society, in the exercise of personal integrity, bears a similarity to macro and micro social contracts of integrative social contract theory. According to the integrative social contract theory, if a norm or moral standard is not contradicted to the hyper norms (Global level), then it is authentic in a given community (Local level). So, the content of word/action consistency and authenticity must be in accordance with the legitimate moral standard of the community. If the individual is a member of multiple significant communities, then it is possible to face the conflicts between different authentic norms of different communities; then to keep integrity, individuals can follow the hyper norms. Cf. Gosling and Huang, "The Fit between Integrity and Integrative Social Contracts Theory," 413. See also Andrew Spicer and Wendy J. Bailey, "When Does National Identity Matter? Convergence and Divergence in International Business Ethics," *The Academy of Management Journal* 50, no. 6 (2007): 1465. Thomas Donaldson and Thomas W. Dunfee, "Toward a Unified Conception of Business Ethics: Integrative Social Contracts Theory," *The Academy of Management Review* 19, no. 2 (1994): 253–254.

and objective reasonable grounds of integrity are determined by substantive moral virtues.[119]

Conclusion

It seems that the conceptual confusion and diverse descriptions and definitions are caused by the lack of integration of subjective and objective dimensions of integrity in one description or definition. However, it is clear that authors hold either the subjective or objective realm for all descriptions of integrity, and few authors like Taylor hold both subjective and objective realms. Volition, choice, mutual dialogue, and one's core self or originality are part of the integrated self and authenticity, and depend upon the core or moral stance of a person that is formed by different sources. Word/action consistency and virtue are the normal outcomes of the wholeness of the person, that is, whether the core of the self has positive or negative implications toward oneself and society.

In summary, personal integrity is the core of self or moral identity, which is the guiding force for the actions and decisions of a person. The core of the self or moral identity is both personal and objective, because, as Taylor observes, no self or identity is formed without the influence of different sources that are both personal and communal.[120] Moreover, the integrity of the person works as a moral motivation in the decision-making process and in our actions, especially when we face dilemmas and temptations in private and public capacities of our existence,[121] because integrity is the moral core of the self of a person, and a person of integrity attempts to be true to one's core. Therefore, it logically follows that personal integrity is the moral core of the self or conscientiousness of the person that works as a stimulus or motivation or practical wisdom to do what is right or to make a justifiable decision in conflicting situations.[122] In short, personal integrity is an expression of the moral self of a person.

---

119 Palanski and Yammarino, "Integrity and Leadership," 178.

120 Taylor, *Sources of the Self: The Making of Modern Identity*, 495–496.

121 McFall, "Integrity," 5–20. See also Worden, "The Role of Integrity as a Mediator in Strategic Leadership: A Recipe for Reputational Capital," 34.

122 The following author connects integrity with the moral conscientiousness and practical wisdom of a person. Cf. Lynn Sharp Paine, "Integrity," in *Encyclopedic Dictionary of Business Ethics*, eds. Patricia H. Werhane and R. Edward Freeman (Oxford: Blackwell Publishers, 1998): 335. See also Johan Verstraeten, "Non e solo questione di applicare de principi," in *L'etica Negli Ambiti Di Vita*, ed. Simone Morandini (Padova: Proget Edizioni, 2010): 37–61. I have used the English translation of the article that I received from the author.

CHAPTER SIX

ROLE OF PERSONAL INTEGRITY IN ORGANIZATIONAL CONTEXTS

Introduction

In organizational contexts, personal integrity is connected with the problems of corporate dilemmas. As explained earlier, the quest for an ethical understanding of corporate dilemma is also connected to the discussion about corporations as moral agents, as well as to the distinction between the three types of relationships within a corporation. Conflicts can arise between various relationships if the company fails to take care of the interests, expectations, and responsibilities of employees and stakeholders at each level in a harmonious manner. Although corporations are moral agents, individuals are the real constitutive elements of corporations, and corporations cannot make decisions—individuals make decisions within corporations.[1] So, the individual decisions are crucial to corporate dilemmas. On the basis of the conflicts of interest, we can divide corporate dilemmas into three: conflicts of interest between corporation and stakeholders, conflicts of interest between corporation and employees, and conflicts of interest between employees.[2] In this chapter, I explain how personal integrity helps managers and employees to overcome the above-mentioned conflicts of interest.

1 Conflicts of Interest between Corporation and Stakeholders

Since corporations do not exist by themselves, they are dependent upon employees and other external stakeholders. The most efficient way for corporations to survive is by attracting both collective and individual

[1] Johan Verstraeten, "From Business Ethics to the Vocation of Business Leaders to Humanize the World of Business," *Business Ethics: A European Review* 7, no. 2 (1998): 120.

[2] A similar division can be seen in the following source. Cf. Kaptein and Wempe, *The Balanced Company*, 174.

stakeholders. In order to gain stakeholder trust, a corporation must be able to share an advantage with individual stakeholders[3] because "those stakeholder(s) that are necessary for the functioning of the corporation and who only receive compensation for this at a later time must be convinced of the corporation's importance as a long-term partner. Only then can these parties be prepared to contribute to its continued existence."[4]

The production and supply of goods in the market at a lesser cost is a legitimate demand from the common stakeholders and a corporation has to be mindful of this. Therefore, on the one hand, a corporation has to safeguard both the interests and rights of common stakeholders, and on the other hand to honor the rights of individual shareholders as far as possible.[5] Due to the pressure of competition and need for survival and increased profits, corporations may ignore those stakeholders' interests that are not immediately necessary for the realization of their competitive objectives. The need to produce goods and services and to gain profit may be considered to be a justification for neglecting common stakeholder interest.[6] This conflict can be summarized as follows:

> In order to safeguard the continuity of the corporation and, thereby, the rights and interests of the collective stakeholders, these rights and interests must be honoured as minimally as possible. Running a business requires dirtying one's hands. Here, the corporation encroaches upon legitimate stakeholder interests and expectations in order to realize other legitimate interests and expectations that are seen as more important in keeping the corporation afloat.[7]

There are plenty of examples of the negation of external stakeholder interests from Indian business contexts. Coca-Cola started a bottling plant in Plachimada in the Palakad district of the state of Kerala, India, in 2000. This part of Kerala is known as the "rice bowl" because 35 percent of the rice production of the state came from this area, and the majority of the people in the district depend on agriculture and natural resources for their livelihood. Over the course of time, the company decided to over-extract groundwater from more borewells than were permitted by the state. They also discharged toxic waste back to the groundwater.[8] The managers of

[3] An example of an individual stakeholder is an employee. Employees are ready to contribute to the corporation only if they are convinced that they will profit from this. Cf. Kaptein and Wempe, *The Balanced Company*, 167.

[4] Kaptein and Wempe, *The Balanced Company*, 167.

[5] Muel Kaptein, "The Ethics Thermometer: An Audit-Tool for Improving the Corporate Moral Reputation," *Corporate Reputation Review* 2, no. 1 (1998): 11–12.

[6] Muel Kaptein, *Ethics Management: Auditing and Developing the Ethical Content of Organizations* (Boston: Kluwer Academic Publishers, 1998): 107.

[7] Kaptein and Wempe, *The Balanced Company*, 168.

[8] C. R. Bijoy, "Kerala's Plachimada Struggle: A Narrative on Water and Governance Rights," *Economic and Political Weekly* 41, no. 41 (2006): 4332–4339.

the company made selfish decisions in this dilemma because they had to increase their profits at any cost and thus, they ignored the rights and justifiable interests of the local people.[9] Although the locals complained about the shortage of water in wells, foul smell of the water, and health-related problems, the company continued nevertheless to pursue its own interest.[10] It is obvious that the managers made an unfair decision in favor of the company by disregarding the rules and permissions of the local government. After many battles in court, the company was held responsible "for the permanent closure of the Coca-Cola bottling plant and compensation, the campaign was also demanding that the Coca-Cola Company be held criminally liable for its actions in Plachimada."[11]

2 Conflicts of Interest between Employees and Corporation

Corporations act through managers and employees, and because of this, employees are able to access the corporation's wealth, goods, equipment, and time. Employees are both stakeholders and agents who fulfill the expectations of the employees and stakeholders; thus, employees function in both roles: as an individual person and as a stakeholder.[12] Since in corporate life, employees have multiple identities, they sometimes favor their own interests and values over those of the corporation. It is possible that a conflict may arise between the personal interests of the employees and the interests of the corporation and its stakeholders.[13]

The dedication and commitment of employees are important for a corporation to function well. At the same time, although employees and managers constitute corporate assets, they are not like inanimate corporate assets. They are human beings with their own interests and limitations. It is also important to realize that corporations must create a corporate environment to attain corporate objectives.[14] Thus, corporations must define certain limits or boundaries for corporate behavior. Verstraeten states that "morally responsible behaviour begins with the realization that no society

[9] Mahesh Menon, "Lessons from Plachimada for Water Law: Who Should Own the Groundwater," accessed June 27, 2014, http://www2.lwr.kth.se/Publikationer/PDF_Files/LWR_EX_13_44.pdf, 5–6.

[10] The selfish interest of the company is clear from the High Court judgment. Cf. Coca Cola Case, 2003, Judgement of the High Court of Kerala in *Perumatty Grama Panchayat vs State of Kerala*. Cf. http://www.indiankanoon.org/doc/1161084/[accessed July 26, 2014].

[11] Tineke Lambooy, "Corporate Social Responsibility: Sustainable Water Use," *Journal of Cleaner Production* 19 (2011): 855.

[12] Kaptein and Wempe, *The Balanced Company*, 170.

[13] Laura L. Nash, *Good Intentions Aside: A Manager's Guide to Resolving Ethical Problems* (Boston: Harvard Business School Press, 1990): 7.

[14] Muel Kaptein and Jan Van Dalen, "The Empirical Assessment of Corporate Ethics: A Case Study," *Journal of Business Ethics* 24 (2000): 99.

is possible, and hence no market or business, without a number of commonly recognized fundamental norms."[15]

Even though there are norms, codes of conduct, and other guidelines in corporations, there is always a possibility for conflicts between the individual and corporate interests to arise. Employee's interests include "career, personal development, power, influence, standing, pleasure, comfort, and pleasant working conditions."[16] As Kaptein observes,

> This dilemma would not exist, if employees had no interests at heart other than those of the corporation: employees would then have no motive for misusing the corporation's assets. Some of the dilemmas that can occur are concerned with the extent to which employees are allowed to make use of the corporation's assets, to hold other jobs that are incompatible with the interests of the organization, to accept promotional gifts, to have business relationships with family members, and to make private purchases from the corporation's suppliers.[17]

In the Indian business world, especially in family owned businesses, the exploitation of shareholders' resources for personal gain becomes very wide (corruption).[18] The Satyam Computers Limited scandal represents this. In 2009, Mr. Ramalinga Raju (the top manager and major shareholder of the company) reported to the Satyam Computers' Limited Board of Directors that "he had been manipulating the computer's accounting numbers for years."[19] The motivation behind Raju is that "greed for money, power, competition, success, and prestige compelled Mr. Raju to 'ride the tiger,' which led to violation of all duties imposed on them as fiduciaries—the duty of care, the duty of negligence, the duty of loyalty, the duty of disclosure toward the stakeholders."[20]

3 Conflicts of Interest between Employees

Internal coordination, cooperation, and perfect division of labor reveal the efficiency of corporate functioning. The internal stakeholder is considered to be a representative agent of a large corporation.[21] The duties and responsibilities of each internal stakeholder must be clear; if they are unclear to

15 Verstraeten, "Business Leaders to Humanize the World of Business," 144.

16 Kaptein, *Ethics Management*, 76.

17 Kaptein, "Integrity Management," 627.

18 Pratip Kar, "Fighting Abusive Related Party Transactions in Asia: Workshop on Implementation," *Background Document, OECD-Asian Roundtable on Corporate Governance*, Cf. http://www.oecd.org/daf/ca/corporategovernanceprinciples/46435512.pdf [accessed June 28, 2014].

19 Madan Lal Bhasin, "Corporate Accounting Fraud: A Case Study of Satyam Computers Limited," *Open Journal of Accounting* 2 (2013): 30.

20 Bhasin, "Corporate Accounting Fraud," 30.

21 John Ladd, "Morality and the Ideal of Rationality in Formal Organizations," *The Monist* 54, no. 4 (1970): 493.

employees, then they will not feel accountable for a particular misdeed or negligent act. However, since corporate actions are the effects of collective endeavors, it is difficult to assign individual responsibility for the activities undertaken by corporations.[22]

Conflicts between employees arise in corporations in many ways. If corporate missions and aims are not well coordinated and employees are ill informed, then each would interpret the corporate aim and mission differently where there is space for ambiguity. This may negatively influence the handling of individual responsibilities. Furthermore, due to lack of coordination, employees may show an unwillingness to undertake certain tasks together with others and to concentrate only on their authorized responsibilities. This tendency focuses on fulfilling one's own tasks at maximum level while at the same time losing the feeling that the corporation is a corporative body.[23]

These conflicts include corporate problems such as the emergence of a "department within an organization that often provides others with information that is incorrect [...] unhealthy competition among the departments [...]. There are all sorts of ways of allocating one's own mistakes to other departments and for claiming other department's success for oneself."[24] Therefore, it is not easy to handle these dilemmas as part of corporate life, but it is necessary to present a possible solution for this kind of corporate situation.

Although conflicts of interest are normal within corporate existence at various levels, the most important elements are the decisions of managers and employees in such situations. What is needed are justifiable decisions that would consider the interests of different parties that is sometimes beyond codes of conduct. To have a justifiable decision at the time of conflict of interest, business ethicists suggest an integrity approach.[25] In the following section, I shall deal with the integrity approach and the role of personal integrity in this approach.

4 Integrity Approach in Business Ethics

The organizational moral decision making process follows an integrity approach[26] that takes every situation as a whole, namely, input, context, outcome, personal values, and the whole life of the decision-maker, the individuals involved in each case or stakeholders, and different ethical

22 Kaptein and Dalen, "The Empirical Assessment of Corporate Ethics," 99.

23 Kaptein and Wempe, *The Balanced Company*, 169.

24 Kaptein, *Ethics Management*, 94.

25 Kaptein and Wempe, *The Balanced Company*, 97.

26 Integrity approach indicates how a person with integrity takes decisions in an organizational context. Cf. Kaptein and Wempe, *The Balanced Company*, 97.

theories.[27] The advantage of this approach is that it takes into account the situation of the conflict as a whole and the decision would, therefore, always be justifiable.[28] Normally, we use different ethical theories for decision making. Although there are different ethical theories in the literature of business ethics,[29] I shall focus on three categories of ethical theories; namely, consequentialism, deontology, and virtue ethics. Each ethical theory has its own role in the integrity approach; however, one theory alone is insufficient to undertake this approach.

4.1 Consequentialism and the Integrity Approach

The key features of utilitarianism make it appealing for an integrity approach in the business context. The main feature of the utilitarian theory is the utility or general welfare, and how these are used as criteria for decision-making. Since conflicts of interest are the main ethical problems in the business context, general welfare can be used as an objective criterion for solving the conflicts of interest among other contextual factors.[30] Although business is primarily concerned with shareholders and profit, nevertheless "utilitarianism recognizes the four primary claimant groups in organizational activity: owners, employees, customers, and society"[31] due to the application of the principle of utility which aims at the greatest happiness for the greatest number of people. This is that link between utilitarianism and the integrity approach.

Utilitarianism alone is insufficient for the promotion of integrity in the business context. Utilitarian ethics are outcome-oriented, that is,

27 Kaptein and Wempe, *The Balanced Company*, 96–97.

28 Kaptein and Wempe, *The Balanced Company*, 98.

29 In business ethics, ethical theories are divided into two categories: traditional theories and contemporary theories. Traditional ethical theories are divided into two groups:consequentialist, namely, egoism and utilitarianism and non-consequentialist, namely, ethics of duties. Intended outcomes, the aims and goals of certain actions, are the basis for moral judgment of an action in consequentialist theories. However, non-consequentialist theories stand for some universal rules and principles that are the basis for the rightness and wrongness of an action. Contemporary ethical theories have been brought into prominence in the business ethics field over the past decade. There are four main contemporary ethical theories; these are virtue ethics, feminist ethics, discourse ethics, and postmodern ethics. Virtue ethics focuses on the formation of good persons because good actions come from good persons. Feminist ethics prioritizes empathy, care for others; healthy social relationships etc. are the basis for the morality of an action. According to discourse ethics, business ethics ought to prioritize the peaceful settlement of conflicts through rational reflection on the life experiences of all relevant participants. Post modern ethics says that morality is beyond the sphere of rationality. It promotes the individuals to question the everyday practices and rules in business and follow their emotions, convictions, and good feelings. Cf. Andrew Crane and Dirk Matten, *Business Ethics: Managing Corporate Citizenship and Sustainability in the Age of Globalization*, 2 ed. (Oxford: Oxford University Press, 2007): 90–121. See also John R. Boatright, *Ehics and the Conduct of Business* (New Jersey: Prentice Hall, 1993): 27–127.

30 Kaptein and Wempe, *The Balanced Company*, 58–60.

31 Vincent Barry, *Moral Issues in Business* (Belmont: Wadsworth, 1986): 49–50.

whether an action is ethical or not is directly dependent upon how effectively the action "created the greatest net social good or reduced the net social harm."[32] This means that "actions are not identified as ethical in and of themselves; only the outcomes of actions are deemed ethical or not."[33] However, in the globalized world it is very difficult to predict the outcomes of an action because "outcomes are usually the result of many, unpredictable factors and so is it reasonable to judge an act in terms that the actor could not have foreseen the result?"[34] It is not so easy to make an ethical decision on the basis of the consequences of an action alone. On the contrary, an integrity approach considers not only the end of an action but also the context, means, and ethical principles in the process of ethical decision-making. There is also a problem of injustice in utilitarian ethics because "utilitarianism tries to maximize the greatest good for the greatest number and thereby risks injustice for the minority."[35] As a result, according to this view, slavery could be perhaps justified for the prosperity of society. In such an instance, the benefit of one person is weighed against the general utilitarian good. Moreover, since the utility principle determines what the agent must do, it constitutes an attack on the agent's integrity "because it undermines the way his actions and his decisions have to be seen as flowing from the projects and attitudes with which he is most closely identified."[36] Therefore, utilitarianism alone is insufficient for the holistic view of the integrity approach.

4.2 Deontology and the Integrity Approach

Deontological ethical theories are an integral part of the integrity approach. No morally responsible behavior is possible without the realization of a society or business with some fundamental moral principles.[37] Universal fundamental moral principles can be either positive or negative. The prohibition created by a negative fundamental moral principle "opens a field of human possibilities because it sets only a minimum level to human dignity without normatively fixating and defining the humanly

[32] Marshall Schminke, Maureen L. Ambrose, and Jeffrey A. Miles, "The Impact of Gender and Setting on Perceptions of Others' Ethics," *Sex Roles* 48, no. 7/8 (2003): 362.

[33] Schminke, Ambrose, and Miles, "The Impact of Gender and Setting on Perceptions of Others' Ethics," 362.

[34] John Mingers and Geoff Walsham, "Toward Ethical Information Systems: The Contribution of Discourse Ethics," *MIS Quarterly* 34, no. 4 (2010): 835.

[35] Mingers and Walsham, "Toward Ethical Information Systems: The Contribution of Discourse Ethics," 835.

[36] This quotation is originally from Bernard Williams and since I could not find the original source, I have taken it from the following article. Cf. Barbara Herman, "Integrity and Impartiality," *The Monist* 66, no. 2 (1983): 233.

[37] Johan Verstraeten, "Business Ethics and Personal Moral Responsibility," in *Business Ethics: Broadening the Perspectives*, ed. Johan Verstraeten (Leuven: Peeters, 2000): 98.

dignified and meaningful."[38] Positive fundamental norms give certain "attitudes and dispositions, without determining the concrete content of what should be done."[39] Therefore, moral control of an action imposed by prohibition leaves sufficient space for individual creativity and the realization of higher values.[40] Moreover, the Kantian articulation of categorical imperatives does not place any obstacles on the integrity approach in business ethics because they do not suggest concrete patterns of actions.[41] As explained previously, the second formulation of the categorical imperative states: "act so that you use humanity, as much in your own person as in the person of every other, always at the same time as an end and never merely as means."[42] Kant states that ethical decisions must treat human beings as an end in themselves and not as means to an end. This would mean that human beings have an inherent inner worth.[43] Therefore, deontology has a positive influence on the integrity approach in business ethics. It is clear from the statement of Shannon A. Bowen that according to the deontological model, in "ethical issues, management is to consider decision alternatives through the categorical imperative."[44]

In the integrity approach of business ethics, however, the deontological model alone is insufficient. The common way of incorporating deontology in a business context is done through the implementation of codes of conduct. Although codes of conduct are necessary to the integrity approach, overemphasis of codes of conduct reduces the integrity approach to role integrity or compliance with codes of conduct.[45] The integrity approach is more than mere role integrity because, first, it requires not only that you make the right choice based upon an existing duty, but also circumstances and consequences play a role here.[46] Second, role integrity neglects the narrative unity of the person and the integrity approach gives significant

38 Roger Burggraeve, "Prohibition and Taste: The Bipolarity in Christian Ethics," *Ethical Perspectives* 1, no. 3 (1994): 135.

39 Verstraeten, "Business Ethics," 98.

40 Verstraeten, "Business Ethics," 99.

41 The same idea is expressed by Johan Verstraeten. Verstraeten, "Business Ethics," 99.

42 Immanuel Kant, "Groundwork of the Metaphysics of Morals," in *Rethinking the Western Tradition*, ed. Allen. W. Wood (New Haven: Yale University Press, 2002): 46–47.

43 Kant, "Groundwork of the Metaphysics of Morals," 45.

44 Shannon A. Bowen, "Expansion of Ethics as the Tenth Generic Principle of Public Relations Excellence: A Kantian Theory and Model for Managing Ethical Issues," *Journal of Public Relations Research* 16, no. 1 (2004): 81.

45 Robert Solomon, "Corporate Roles, Personal Virtues: An Aristotelian Approach to Business Ethics," in *Virtue Ethics: A Critical Reader*, ed. Daniel Stratman (Edinburgh: Edinburgh University Press, 1997): 215.

46 Johan Verstraeten, "Institutionalised Corruption and Integrity: A Theological-Ethical Clarification of the Issue," in *Financial Crimes: Psychological, Technological, and Ethical Issues*, eds. Michel Dion, David Weisstub, and Jean-Loup Richet (Basel: Springer, 2016): 236–239. See also Johan Verstraeten, "Integriteit in een context," in *Witboek over Corruptie En Integritiet*, eds. Roger Burggraeve et al. (Leuven: Davidsfonds, 2008): 111–131.

attention to the wholeness of an acting person in the process of decision making. Third, the overemphasized role of integrity can promote hypocrisy in business ethical choices because codes of conduct can be used as a means for avoiding moral liability and thus, further responsibility.[47] Fourth, role integrity neglects various organizational contexts that are more important in the integrity approach.[48]

4.3 Virtue Ethics and the Integrity Approach

Robert C. Solomon introduces a strong virtue ethics approach in business. After giving a critique to the principle-based approach in business, he spells out a series of business virtues such as "honesty, loyalty, sincerity, courage, reliability, trustworthiness, benevolence, sensitivity, helpfulness, cooperativeness, civility, decency, modesty, openness, cheerfulness, amiability, tolerance, integrity."[49] According to business ethicists, these virtues would enable managers to act or make decisions in a morally correct manner while facing moral dilemmas and pressures.[50] Moreover, virtue ethics has certain dimensions that distinguish it from other ethical theories in business: it is personal, contextual, and based on the motivation of the actor.[51] Because of this, it contributes to the core of the integrity approach. Indeed, the integrity approach highlights an individual's role in the process of decision-making. Although there are various theories, the real interpretation and decision of each context is made by the person.

However, virtue ethics is not a full-fledged ethical theory without shortcomings, and by itself it is insufficient to the integrity approach. In virtue ethics, there are no necessary rules, guidelines, or principles that would amount to conditions for arriving at practical conclusions in conflicting and contradicting ethical situations.[52] Structural features are important

---

47 Many companies include anti-corruption laws in their codes of conduct but they continue to bribe politicians. Cf. Johan Verstraeten, "Integriteit in een context van geïnstitutionaliseerde corruptie," 238.

48 Verstraeten, "Integriteit in een context van geïnstitutionaliseerde corruptie," 238–239.

49 Solomon, "Corporate Roles, Personal Virtues: An Aristotelian Approach to Business Ethics," 330. See also Robert Solomon, *Ethics and Excellence: Cooperation and Integrity in Business* (Oxford: Oxford University Press, 1992): 225–230.

50 Solomon, *Ethics and Excellence*, 145–179. See also Barbro Froding, *Virtue Ethics and Human Enhancement* (London: Spiringer, 2013): 4. See also Chris Provis, "Virtuous Decision Making for Business Ethics," *Journal of Business Ethics* 91 (2010): 3–16. Daryl Koehn, "A Role for Virtue Ethics in the Analysis of Business Practice," *Business Ethics Quarterly* 5, no. 3 (1995): 533–539.

51 J. Thomas Whetstone, "How Virtue Fits within Business Ethics," *Journal of Business Ethics* 33 (2001): 104.

52 Whetstone, "How Virtue Fits within Business Ethics," 105. See also Russ Shafer Landau, *The Fundamentals of Ethics* (Oxford: Oxford University Press, 2010): 249–258. Daniel Statman, "Introduction to Virtue Ethics," in *Virtue Ethics*, ed. Daniel Statman (Edinburgh: Edinburgh University Press, 1997): 20–21.

in corporate life because many ethical problems in business are not the result of personal failures, but the result of the pathological corporate environment. John R. Boatright observes that "policy and strategy matters are important to business ethics, and no course would be complete and no book directed to senior managers and executives would be very useful if it did not address them."[53] According to business ethicists, what is needed are comprehensive ethical frameworks that include both theories of moral worth and of moral obligations.[54] This is because of the existence of limitations, complementarities, and tensions between different ethical theories. Moreover, the existence of various ethical theories causes dilemmas in moral reasoning for decision.

4.4 Moral Dilemmas and Ethical Theories

Although the above-mentioned major ethical theories are silent about pluralism of values, they have their own interpretations by way of moral reasoning. Therefore, each theory has its own distinctive understanding of value in question. The greatest good is the highest value in consequentialist ethical theories. Rules and principles are of great value in deontological-based moral reasoning. Virtues are of the highest value in virtue ethics. These values are irreducible to each other and are independent.[55] It may lead to the possibility of different behaviors in similar situations, ethical conflicting situations or dilemmas.[56]

---

53 John R. Boatright, "Aristotle Meets Wall Street: The Case for Virtue Ethics in Business Ethics and Excellence: Cooperation and Integrity in Business by Robert C. Solomon," *Business Ethics Quarterly* 5, no. 2 (1995): 359.

54 Robert Audi, "Virtue Ethics as a Resource in Business,"*Business Ethics Quarterly* 22, no. 2 (2012): 289.

55 Joseph, "The Need of Personal Responsibility," 59. There are five types of values that give rise to basic conflicts. These values play an important role in the process of decision making. They create conflict in their interaction with each other and this influences our decision making process. This five-fold distinction was introduced by Thomas Nagel. The first value is obligation. We have various obligations, such as obligations to parents, family, institutions etc. The basis for this obligation is the relationship. Obligations create some situations in which we cannot avoid certain demands. Second, rights—every individual has certain rights either to do certain actions, or to enjoy the effect of certain actions, or the right to be treated in a special way. Rights give certain duties too and they are divided into specific duty and general duty. A doctor has a specific duty to treat his own patient and at the same time a general duty to care for all patients. Rights and duties usually come into our moral reasoning. Third, we are concerned with the utility principle. Which action is fitting to the welfare of all people or an individual? The utility principle implies that the concern is not only the benefit and harm of an action or decision for the people with whom the agent has special relation, but also to the entire human community. Perfectionist ends or values are the fourth category. Thomas Nagel asserted the intrinsic value of certain achievements or creations apart from their utility to individuals who have achieved it, such as space exploration and artistic creation. Finally, one's own projects and undertakings have value. Cf. Thomas Nagel, *Mortal Questions* (New York: Cambridge University Press, 1979): 129–130.

56 Kathleen A. Getz, "International Codes of Conduct: An Analysis of Ethical

However, a monistic approach of different ethical theories is possible: this is the case when one believes that there is only one ultimate value. According to this view, values are reducible to one supreme value and ethical monists deny the plurality of values. Monist utilitarianism holds that pleasure or happiness is the ultimate value and all other values are reducible to this ultimate value. Monist deontologists state that categorical imperative is the ultimate value.[57] Similarly, there is a school of thought called the rationalist ethics, which denies the possibility of moral dilemmas. It holds that true judgments are the outcome of sound reasoning, and universal principles are employed in such reasoning. So in every conflicting situation, the individual has to use deductive reasoning to reach an apt conclusion. If there are inconsistencies in ethical reasoning, the mistake is committed by the reasoner rather than the ethical system. The disposition of an agent would be the cause of a failure in ethical reasoning. Reason never fails by ethical reasoning and so monists reject the possibility of dilemmas in ethical reasoning.[58] Similarly, according to Mary Mothersill, the concepts of duty and obligation lead us to a necessity of action, and whenever there are two conflicting rules, the actualization of these two rules is not necessary. Take one rule and act accordingly. The opposite rule is not our duty and it is not contrary to our duty.[59]

Henry Sidgwick maintains that valid reasoning cannot lead to conflicting situations. If a conflicting situation occurs, then this would imply that the norm/rule/principle must be modified or rejected. With regard to such dilemmas, John S. Mill holds that dilemmas are caused by the absence of one fundamental moral principle. If we do have such a fundamental moral principle, we can determine the relativity of an important action. The fundamental moral principle will be a way out of the moral dilemmas.[60] The non-cognitivist traditions hold arguments against moral dilemmas. Ethics is a practical science that helps the conscientious agent to make a moral decision on a particular action as right or wrong by the use of principles. One may not find an answer to all complex situations from ethical norms and in this way, they reject the possibility of dilemmas and suggest that we examine the data and use apt principles to overcome all conflicting situations.[61]

Reasoning," *Journal of Business Ethics* 9, no. 7 (1990): 565. See also Harvey S. James, "On Finding Solutions to Ethical Problems in Agriculture," *Journal of Agricultural and Environmental Ethics* 16 (2003): 441. Cf. Joseph, "The Need of Personal Responsibility," 59.

57 Kaptein and Wempe, *The Balanced Company*, 85–86.

58 Alasdair Macintyre, "Moral Dilemmas", available at http://www.justor.org/stable/2108048, accessed December 4, 2010.

59 Mary Mothersill, "The Moral Dilemmas Debate," in *Moral Dilemmas and Moral Theory*, ed. H.E. Manson (Oxford: Oxford University Press, 1996): 69–71.

60 Mothersill, "The Moral Dilemmas Debate," 72–74.

61 Mothersill, "The Moral Dilemmas Debate," 71.

On the contrary, Kaptein and Wempe suggest that there are certain situations that lead to moral dilemmas, situations such as "scarcity of resources, lack of knowledge, and insight to make responsible choice, incomparable values, norms, and ideals that are mutually exclusive are at stake."[62] The existence of different values and norms create ethical dilemmas because they are mutually exclusive.[63]

5 Relevance of the Integrity Approach and the Role of Personal Integrity

Generally speaking, dilemmas can be solved in numerous ways. First, we can select one value, interest, or obligation against the other. Second, we can consciously neglect all values, interests, and obligations. Third, a compromise as a partial realization of both values or interests or obligations can be reached. Fourth, we can reach a compromise as an optimal solution for the conflicting situation.[64]

Business ethics must take into consideration the tensions between a moral duty and an ethical ideal. Moral duties and the interests of different stakeholders can be in conflict, and norms are never absolutely applicable to an entire complex situation in an organizational context. In this context, the most important elements of a moral judgment are the practical wisdom and prudence of a person.[65]

Different ethical theories are interrelated. We cannot reduce ethical theories into one theory or value. Since there is no comprehensive moral theory, we cannot form absolute ethical conclusions.[66] However, some ethicists such as Vincent Barry have suggested a selection of the most important obligation among the more important obligations. Finally, Barry admits that the selection of obligations is a "matter of values and valuation."[67] The selection would be in accordance with the personal values or internalized values. If these obligations are equally valuable to a person, then this proposal is problematic and the selection of obligation depends on the integrity of the acting person.[68] Indeed, it is worthwhile to note the reduction of the causes of Indian corporate corruption into two, namely low moral quality of managers, employees, and structural reasons.

---

62 Kaptein and Wempe, *The Balanced Company*, 85.

63 J. Philip Wogaman, *Moral Dilemma: An Introduction to Christian Ethics* (Kentucky: Westminister John Knox Press, 2009): 10.

64 Kaptein and Wempe, *The Balanced Company*, 93–94.

65 Originally, this view is from Alain Thomasset and I have taken it from the following source. Cf. Verstraeten, "Business Ethics," 118.

66 Verstraeten, "Non e solo questione di applicare de principi," 38. I have made use of the original English text of this article that I got from the author.

67 Barry, *Moral Issues in Business*, 67.

68 Barry, *Moral Issues in Business*, 67. See also Joseph, "The Need of Personal Responsibility," 60.

Conclusion

Integrity approach is the proposed solution to overcome conflicts of interest. The success of the integrity approach depends on the integrity of the acting persons to consider different theories, circumstances, values, stakeholders, and obligations for making a justifiable decision while they make a decision in the presence of a conflict of interest. This leads to the valuing of personal integrity (and hence virtue), and the ability to assess conflicting values, obligations, or interests in such a way as to allow one to take account of the specificity of the context and different theories, and select one that makes the best possible justifiable decision in conflicting situations. This is because, as I have mentioned earlier, personal integrity is the core of the moral self or conscientiousness of the person that then works as an impetus or motivation or practical wisdom to do what is right. However, the integrity approach is silent on personal integrity and how personal integrity works in corporate ethical decision-making processes. Qualities of personal integrity, such as moral imagination, inner freedom, dialogue, and moral courage, help the person to make a justifiable ethical decision.

CHAPTER SEVEN

THEORY OF THE FUNDAMENTAL OPTION AND PERSONAL INTEGRITY

INTRODUCTION

The theory of the fundamental option became very popular in the 1960s. Existentialist[1] and personalist[2] analyses gave insight to moral theologians regarding the inadequacy of any atomistic way of determining whether a particular action is good or bad. The main aim of the theory of the

[1] Although it is very difficult to define and describe, existentialism is very influential in Western philosophy. Existentialism is opposed to rationalism, romanticism, idealism, and psychologism. It is generally agreed that with Søren Kierkegaard, contemporary existentialism begins. According to existentialism, the way to truth has to be found through human subjectivity. Existential theology is based on the existential philosophy. Karl Rahner had the most influence in bringing existentialism into theology. Cf. Kenan B. Osborne, "Existentialism," in *The New Dictionary of Theology*, eds. Joseph A. Komonchak, Mary Collins, and Dermot A. Lane (Dublin: Gill and Macmillan): 366–367. See also Alasdair MacIntyre, "Existentialism," in *The Encyclopedia of Philosophy*, ed. Paul Edwards (New York: Macmillan Publishing 1967): 150–151.

[2] Under "personalist" morality, person is considered as the most fundamental norm of morality. According to personalist thinking, good and evil are determined in relation to the human person adequately considered. According to Louis Janssen, the human person adequately considered means that the human person is a totality. He introduced eight dimensions of the human person. First, the person is a subject. That means he is an autonomous being. Second, a person is a body. The human body is more than an objective body, but it is a subjective body. A human body is a means of relationship and love. Third, a person is a part of the material world. Persons are corporeal and therefore since they are corporeal, they are part of the world. Fourth, the person is substantively related with other persons. Referring to Martin Bubber, he argued that a human being becomes a person only in relation with other human beings. Fifth, the person is part of the larger social world. Persons develop as persons only in relation with a community. Sixthly, a person is in relation to God. Human beings are created in the image of God; God is Trinity and the Trinity is a relationship. Hence, a human being has a special call to share this relationality to all other beings and God. Seventh, a person is a historical being. Human beings are evolving beings. Lastly, every individual/ person are equal and at the same time unique. Cf. Louis Janssens, "Artificial Insemination: Ethical Considerations," *Louvain Studies* 8, no. 1 (1980): 3–11. See also Joseph A. Selling, "Introduction," in *Personalist Morals: Essays in Honor of Professor Louis Janssens*, ed. Joseph A. Selling (Leuven: Leuven University Press, 1988): 1–7.

fundamental option is to show that "moral life is a continuous process with definitive moral direction," rather than as a result of a single action.[3] The emphasis of morality shifts from the particular actions to the living person as the "holder of morality."[4] The first use of the concept of the fundamental option can be traced back as early as the work of Piet Fransen and Dietrich von Hildebrand.[5] Moreover, theologians such as Louis Janssens, Karl Rahner, Bernard Häring, and Josef Fuchs were also considered as some of the earliest ones to use the theory of the fundamental option in their theological ethical discourse.[6] In this chapter, I try to demonstrate the link between fundamental option theory and personal integrity conceptualizations.

1 Theory of the Fundamental Option

From the Christian point of view, the theory of the fundamental option "refers to a person's basic moral orientation in life toward or away from God. It is the underlying and recurrent response to God of either a 'yes' or a 'no' that shapes an individual's course throughout life."[7] For non-religious persons, the fundamental option is the basic life direction or fundamental stance, "seen in a holistic vision of growth and or regression, there is a kind of transcendental experience of bringing one's own existence into conformity with the reign of good or making oneself a part of evil."[8]

The theory of the fundamental option is to be "understood within the transcendental dimension of the human being, rather than the categorical dimension of an action."[9] Although the fundamental option is a transcendental category, it does not reduce the presence of the fundamental option

3 E. McDonagh, "Fundamental Option," in *New Catholic Encyclopedia*, eds. Bernard L. Marthaler et al. (New York: Gale Group, 2003): 26.

4 McDonagh, "Fundamental Option," 26.

5 Dietrich von Hildebrand, "Sittlichkeit und sittliche werterkentnis," *Jahrbuch für Philosophie und Phänomenologische Forschung* 5 (1992): 463–502. I have taken this reference from the following source. Cf. Timothy E O'Connell, *Principles for a Catholic Morality* (New York: The Seabury Press, 1978): 216.

6 Michael Fahey, "Janssens, Louis, 1908–2001," *Theological Studies* 63 (2002): 2. See also James F. Keenan, *A History of Catholic Moral Theology in the Twentieth Century: From Confessing Sins to Liberating Consciences* (New York: Continuum International Publishing Group, 2010): 186.

7 Kent Wallace, "Fundamental Option," in *Encyclopedia of Catholic Social Thought, Social Science, and Social Policy*, eds. Michael L. Coulter et al. (Toronto: The Scarecrow Press, 2007): 456.

8 Bernhard Häring, "Sin in Post-Vatican Ii Theology," in *Personalist Morals: Essays in Honor of Professor Louis Janssens*, ed. Joseph Selling (Leuven: Leuven University Press 1988): 93. See also Bernhard Häring, *Free and Faithful in Christ: Moral Theology for Priests and Laity*, vol. 1 (London: Billing and Sons Ltd, 1978): 164–222.

9 Wallace, "Fundamental Option," 456.

to individual decisions and actions,[10] because the fundamental option gives "integrated consistency between an individual's whole personal existence and one's daily actions and major life decisions."[11] Every individual decision and action will be sustained by the fundamental option, and every decision and action will be substantiated by the fundamental option.[12] Indeed, the fundamental option can be either positive or negative because it depends upon the fundamental orientation of a person. Therefore, Häring observes that "the healthy fundamental option is openness to the 'Other' and the others. It includes the cooperative relationship in trust and self-transcending love. Otherwise, it is a wrong or an abortive fundamental option."[13]

According to many authors, the axiom—"grace presupposes and perfects nature"—is behind the Christian view of the theory of the fundamental option.[14] The instinct of grace leads us toward God as our ultimate end. The theory of the fundamental option indicates that "the root of the moral life is singularly built on grace that finds its expression in the life of virtue."[15] The theory of the fundamental option developed as a reaction to the neo-scholastic emphasis of the transcendence of grace and its discontinuity with nature. According to the personalist understanding of grace, "the gracious and salvific initiative of God presupposes a receptive potential on our part, and our inclination for union with God is perfected by God's free and gratuitous offer of himself."[16] The theory of the fundamental option has a strong basis in Scripture and the traditions of the Church.

1.1 Theory of the Fundamental Option and Scripture

The backdrop of the ethical notion of the fundamental option goes back to the Old Testament. The prophet Ezekiel speaks of the fundamental choices that one has to make, which determine the stance of the person.[17] The prophet writes that "if a wicked man turns away from all his sins that he has committed and keeps all my statutes and does what is lawful and right,

10 Thomas Kopfensteiner, "The Theory of Fundamental Option," in *Christian Ethics: An Introduction*, ed. Bernard Hoose (London: Cassell, 1998): 124–125.

11 Wallace, "Fundamental Option," 457.

12 Kopfensteiner, "The Theory of Fundamental Option," 124.

13 Häring, *Free and Faithful in Christ*, 167.

14 Kopfensteiner, "The Theory of Fundamental Option," 124. See also Eugene J. Cooper, "The Fundamental Option," *Irish Theological Quarterly*, no. 39 (1972): 383–392. Paul Qureshi, "Sin, Fundamental Option and Conversion," *Irish Theological Quarterly* 71 (2006): 272–284. Jean Porter, "Moral Language and the Language of Grace: The Fundamental Option and the Virtue of Charity," *Philosophy and Theology* 10 (1997): 171–182.

15 James F. Keenan, "Virtue, Grace and the Early Revisionists of the Twentieth Century," *Studies in Christian Ethics* 23, no. 4 (2010): 366.

16 Kopfensteiner, "The Theory of Fundamental Option," 124.

17 Ezra 18:21.

he shall surely live; he shall not die."[18] On the basis of the fundamental choices of the person, the righteous person can become wicked and the wicked person righteous. Here, the prophet writes about salvation in accordance with the core choice of the person. Jesus makes it clear that no one can serve both God and Mammon at the same time; it implies that we have to make a fundamental choice that determines our own destiny.[19] Similarly "a tree is known by its fruits."[20]

The biblical understanding of the fundamental option is closely related to the biblical usage of "the heart" of a human person.[21] A person with a "heart" does not refer to a person withdrawn to interiority; the heart of a person refers to the innermost core, which is opened by the person to the other in an "I-Thou" relationship and the person commits with wholeness to the other in an integrated manner.[22] It can also be the core of a person where he/she is gradually becoming blind and wicked without a proper "I-Thou" relationship. In short, according to Häring, when people lose the capacity to love, then, they lose the best part of their heart.[23] Similarly, according to Rahner, the biblical concept of "heart" is intimately connected with the capacity to love in freedom and wholeness. He writes that "freedom is always the self-realization of man making his choice with regard to this whole accomplishment before God. It is thus the capacity of the "heart," the capacity for love."[24]

The "heart" of a person is determined by the values he/she upholds. It is obvious from the Gospel of Matthew that "where your treasure is, there will be your heart also."[25] Yahweh did not correct so much the perverted

---

18 Ezra 18:21.

19 Matt 6:24.

20 Wallace, "Fundamental Option," 456. See also, Matt 12:33.

21 The word "heart" is often used in the Bible to refer to one's personality and intellect, memory, emotions, desires, and will. "Heart" as personality means "heart" is used to describe those dynamic forces that make a person as a unique individual. Cf. Leland Ryken, James C. Wilhoit, and Tremper Longman, eds., *Dictionary of Biblical Imagery: An Encyclopedic Exploration of the Images, Symbols, Motifs, Metaphors, Figures of Speech and Literary Patterns of the Bible*, 1998 (Illinois: Inter Varsity Press, 1998): 368–369; Ps 31:1; 2 Chr 32:26; 1 Sam 17:28; Isa 44:20; Jer 17:9. In the Bible, the functions of memory and intellect are associated with the idiom "heart." Cf. Ps 77:6; Gen 6:5; 1 Sam 1:13; Luke 2:19. According to biblical usage, "heart" is the source from which emotions and desires flow. Cf. Exod 4:14; Deut 1:28; Ps 27:3; Gen 34:3–8. Many Biblical passages tell that the "heart" chooses an action. Jesus says that out of the heart comes evil thoughts and good one. Cf. Matt 15:19; Deut 2:20; Exod 4:14; Exod 8:15. In short, many of the biblical usages of "heart" refer to the core of a person from which good and bad deeds come. Cf. Häring, *Free and Faithful in Christ*, 90–94.

22 Häring, *Free and Faithful in Christ*, 185. See also Thomas Palelil, "Conversion a Positive Fundamental Option: A Critical Developmental Interpretation" (KU: Leuven, 1997): 119.

23 Häring, *Free and Faithful in Christ*, 185.

24 Karl Rahner, *Grace in Freedom* (London: Burns & Oates, 1968): 214.

25 Matt 6:21.

actions of Israelites but he strongly complained against their "hardened hearts" and their perverted dispositions[26] because all evil actions flow from an "evil heart."[27] The nutshell of great messianic prophecies is found in God's promise and repeated assurance to give a "new heart" to the people of God.[28] It is obvious from the writings of Ezekiel that "I will give them a new heart and will put a new spirit in their innermost being; I will take away the stony heart out of their flesh and will give them a sensitive heart."[29] Essentially, to have a conversion in the context of God's promises is to have a new heart. The essence of this new heart is the total self-surrender to God's ways, and all our actions would be marked by this fundamental disposition, which transcends the boundaries of fulfilling merely one's duty or being merely submissive to the laws.[30]

If the ethical sphere is reduced to a bare "must," it can form a duty-bound citizen but it cannot form a creative, responsive person. According to Häring, ethics must give the foundation for responsive and creative persons. They must give great importance to "emotions, affectivity, and the whole realm of sensitivity to values that lie deep in man's being."[31] Moreover, it is well established that "emotions function as a central motivational mechanism for taking moral action."[32] Emotions create the real "heart of a man" from which come both good actions and evil actions. Here, Häring refers to the "emotional mindset of that affectivity that expresses the person's basic relationship to the 'Other,' the others, and to one's self"[33] and not to the scattered emotions or biological moods. Moreover, it is well examined that "emotions play a crucial role in the initiation, the development, and the sustenance of relationships over time."[34]

If focus is centered on the formation of dispositions, then that will make people ready for purposive action, but there is a danger that the purpose may serve the fulfillment of the selfish purposes of individuals and groups. However, if one seeks to form an altruistic, creative, and purposive person then "we have to give attention to those *Gesinnungen*[35] or

---

26 Häring, *Free and Faithful in Christ*, 186. Mark 6:52; Isa 6:9.

27 Häring, *Free and Faithful in Christ*, 186.

28 Jer 32:40; Ezra 36:26.

29 Ezra 11:19.

30 Häring, *Free and Faithful in Christ*, 187.

31 Häring, *Free and Faithful in Christ*, 90.

32 Weichun Zhu et al., "The Effect of Authentic Transformational Leadership on Follower and Group Ethics," *The Leadership Quarterly* 22 (2011): 801.

33 Häring, *Free and Faithful in Christ*, 92.

34 Poul Houman Andersen and Rajesh Kumar, "Emotions, Trust and Relationship Development in Business Relationships: A Conceptual Model for Buyer–Seller Dyads," *Industrial Marketing Management* 35 (2006): 523.

35 Gesinnungen is a German word used by the German school of ethics of value. "Gesinnungen are the emotions that express the inner and profound capacity of a person to value, to discern, to respond beyond biological pressure." Cf. Häring, *Free and Faithful*

value responses that re-echo in the heart of a man beyond any particular purpose."[36] According to Häring, "heart points to the person in his or her wholeness, building bridges to others, grasping the unique value of each one as a person, and the manifold values embodied by persons, and thus calling for an ever new embodiment of these values in one's own life."[37]

The wholeness, creativity, responsiveness, and the right action of a person depends on the positive and negative emotions that prevail within the person.[38] The prophets are the best examples of the creative and responsive persons. Their wrath is a negative emotion but it is deeply integrated into their positive value response that they acquired from their relationships with God.[39] However, it is obvious that "when negative emotions and reactions in one's heart are not integrated into a positive commitment and disposition, they are sign of emotional starvation, a sign of one's loss of responsiveness to positive values."[40] Disintegrated negative emotions lead to evil actions.[41]

In short, from the biblical perspective, a heart stands for the wholeness of the person or the fundamental life direction of the person. As Eugene Cooper observes, this "fundamental option" or "basic life's direction" that so many theologians speak of and that has been described above, has its source and center in what the Old and New Testaments described as the "heart" of the person. It is in the "heart" where basic decisions regarding life and the moral-religious sphere flow and upon which all concrete, particular choices and actions depend. Personalistic anthropology and modern depth psychology have named "the heart" as the core and center of the person or the self that moral theology calls as the faculty of conscience.[42] Moreover, the New Testament shows the interior dimension of morality, that is pure conscience, as the basic option for God and good.[43]

---

in Christ, 92. It entails "emotions and sentiments as part of the value responses, especially when it is a matter of relations to persons [...]. It is the sentiments enlightened by a kind of intuition." Cf. Häring, *Free and Faithful in Christ*, 90.

36 Häring, *Free and Faithful in Christ*, 91.

37 Häring, *Free and Faithful in Christ*, 90.

38 Susan Michie and Janaki Gooty, "Values, Emotions, and Authenticity: Will the Real Leader Please Stand Up?," *The Leadership Quarterly* 16 (2005): 445.

39 Häring, *Free and Faithful in Christ*, 92.

40 Häring, *Free and Faithful in Christ*, 92.

41 Häring, *Free and Faithful in Christ*, 92.

42 Cooper, "The Fundamental Option," 392. Conscience is a person's most secret core and their sanctuary. It is the place where law is inscribed by God. There they are alone with God; whose voice guides the actions of the person. Through loyalty to conscience, Christians are joined with others in search of truths and for the right solution to so many moral problems in day to day life and social situations. Cf. Timothy E. O'Connell, "An Understanding of Conscience," in *Conscience*, ed. Charles E. Curran (New York: Paulist Press, 2004): 32–33.

43 Rom 1:5.

According to the Pauline understanding, total conversion is expressed by a new life in Christ.[44]

1.2 Theory of the Fundamental Option and the Christian Tradition

The notion of the fundamental option is rooted in various realms of Christian tradition. As explained earlier, evidence for the root of the fundamental option is in the Bible. For Augustine, the firm and whole hearted commitment of self will lead to a good action. He writes, "change your heart and then your work will be changed."[45] According to Häring, for Augustine the fundamental option is either self-giving love or selfish love. Self-giving love is the positive fundamental option, whereas selfish love is the negative fundamental option.[46]

References to the fundamental option can be found in the writings of Aquinas. According to him, life in the new law (Jesus Christ) is a perfect state of existence.[47] While elaborating on mortal sin that is totally against God, Aquinas argues that no little child can make a basic self-disposition against God. He writes that "before a man comes to the age of discretion, the lack of years hinders the use of reason and excuses him from mortal sin, [...]. But when he begins to have the use of reason, he is not entirely excused from the guilt of venial or mortal sin."[48] Häring interprets and connects Aquinas to the fundamental option as follows: "from all this, it becomes clear that freedom in its "basic depth" is not just a matter of saying "yes" or "no" to a specific decision; it is the power to mould and create ourselves."[49] Although encyclical *Veritatis Splendor* refers to the importance of fundamental choice in life that influences the moral life of a person,[50] it does not accept the principal ideas of fundamental option.

Fuchs is of the opinion that the fundamental option is a fundamental or basic freedom t is the basis for a mature act of self-determination or basic self-commitment.[51] Häring, referring to Scripture and contemporary psychology,[52] defines the fundamental option with the biblical heart

44 Phil 2:5; Rom 13:4.

45 Jacques-Paul Migne, *Patrologia Latina*, vol. 72 (Paris: 1844): 468–469. I took this quotation from the following reference. Cf. Häring, *Free and Faithful in Christ*, 187.

46 Häring, *Free and Faithful in Christ*, 187.

47 Thomas Aquinas, "Summa Theologica," ed. Fathers of English Dominican Province (New York: Benziger Brothers, 1947): 1. II, q. 106.art. 4.

48 Aquinas, "Summa Theologica," 1–II, q. 89.art. 6.

49 Häring, *Free and Faithful in Christ*, 188.

50 John Paul II, "Veritatis Splendor," 66, accessed February 1, 2017, http://w2.vatican.va/content/john-paul-ii/en/encyclicals/documents/hf_jp-ii_enc_06081993_veritatis-splendor.html.

51 Josef Fuchs, *Human Values and Christian Morality* (Dublin: Cahill & Co. Limited, 1970): 90–111.

52 Bernard Häring explains that modern anthropology and depth psychology paved way for the development of the ethical notion of the fundamental option. Existential

image "as the deepest core of a person where conversion and an authentic relationship with God develop."[53] He writes about the "basic intention," the "fundamental option," and "fundamental attitude."[54] Janssens uses the term as "fundamental choice" for the expression of his view regarding the fundamental option.[55] According to Cooper, Janssens insists on the importance of the fundamental choice because all other concrete particular choices depend upon it. Moreover, "particular choices are thus a realization, concretization, and incarnation of the fundamental choice."[56] Rahner makes a distinction between the freedom at the categorical and transcendental level. He is of the opinion that the fundamental option is a total self-understanding and the radical self-expression of the person, that is, the fundamental choice of the person for or against God[57] that is based on the transcendental freedom of the person.

1.3 Theory of the Fundamental Option and Human Freedom

Traditionally, human freedom is divided into two categories: negative and positive. Negative freedom is the absence of obstacles or constraints, whereas positive freedom is the acting and realizing of one's fundamental aims. The division of freedom takes place within the context of political and social philosophy.[58]

---

philosophy holds that human beings are capable of creating their future self through free decisions. Through their free choices, human beings determine their life patterns. S. A. Kierkegaards's (1967) "*Stages on Life's Way*" emphasizes the internal tendency of human beings for integration and dynamic harmony. Edward Spranger (1928) describes the influence of the cultural climate in the formation of the fundamental orientation of a person. Eric Erikson (1969) describes the different stages of the development of the life of a person. Each stage strengthens the basic life direction of the person. By elaborating on Erikson's different stages of the development of the life of a person, Haring concludes that "at the end the unfolding of identity comes very close to what theologians call fundamental option or basic intention" and "I know of no better word for it than integrity." Häring again connects moral theological understanding of the fundamental option with Abraham Maslow's description of peak experience and Viktor Frankl's "search for meaning." Cf. Häring, *Free and Faithful in Christ*, 168–181.

[53] Mark O'Keefe, "Social Sin and Fundamental Option," *Irish Theological Quarterly* 58 (1992): 86.

[54] Häring, *Free and Faithful in Christ*, 164–221.

[55] Louis Janssens, "Personalist Morals," *Louvain Studies* 3 (1970): 9.

[56] Cooper, "The Fundamental Option," 389.

[57] Karl Rahner, *Foundations of Christian Faith: An Introduction to the Idea of Christianity*, trans. William V. Dych (New York: Seabury Press, 1978): 90–115. See also Rahner, *Grace in Freedom*, 213. See also O'Keefe, "Social Sin and Fundamental Option," 86–87. Brian F. Linnane, "Rahner's Fundamental Option and Virtue Ethics," *Philosophy & Theology* 15, no. 1 (2003): 231. This is important to note that Rahner's view of fundamental option does not give enough attention to the objectivity and the connection of the fundamental option with nature.

[58] Ronald H. Nash, *Freedom, Justice and the State* (Washington: University Press of America, 1980): 83–86.

1.3.1 Positive and Negative Freedom

This division of freedom goes back to Isaiah Berlin's famous essay in 1958, *Two Concepts of Liberty*. Negative freedom refers to the absence of something, while positive freedom refers to the presence of something. According to Berlin, the negative concept of freedom is an attempt to make up an answer to the question, "What is the area within which the subject—a person or group of persons—is or should be left to do or be what he is able to do or be, without interference by other persons?"[59] Similarly, the positive concept of freedom is an answer to the question, "What, or who, is the source of control or interference that can determine someone to do, or be, this rather than that?"[60] Succinctly, negative freedom is freedom from obstacles or constraints and positive freedom is the freedom to become something greater.[61]

This division of freedom is based on factors that are both internal and external to the agent.

> While theorists of negative freedom are primarily interested in the degree to which individuals or groups suffer interference from external bodies, theorists of positive freedom are more attentive to the internal factors affecting the degree to which individuals or groups act autonomously. Given this difference, one might be tempted to think that a political philosopher should concentrate exclusively on negative freedom, a concern with positive freedom being more relevant to psychology or individual morality than to political and social institutions.[62]

However, several objections have been raised against this division of freedom. The division between freedom from and freedom to, is unclear because a careful analysis will remove the significant differences between these two notions.[63] For example, a lack of education can be interpreted as a lack of positive freedom because if education is available, then the person acquires the freedom to have education. However, the person's lack of education might be explained as the result of certain conditions prevalent in the social system. In this situation, positive freedom turns out

---

59 Isaiah Berlin, "Two Concepts of Liberty," in *Four Essays on Liberty*, ed. Isaiah Berlin (London: Oxford University Press, 1969): 121–122.

60 Berlin, "Two Concepts of Liberty," 121–122.

61 Nash, Freedom, *Justice and the State*, 82.

62 Ian Carter, "Positive and Negative Liberty," in *The Stanford Encyclopedia of Philosophy* ed. Edward N. Zalta (2012), accessed September 18, 2013, http://plato.stanford.edu/archives/spr2013/entries/integrity. This position rises to deep debate in political philosophy. Is positive freedom a political concept? Would political action provide positive freedom to individuals? Is the state able to provide positive freedom? Among political philosophers there are both yes and no answers to these questions. Cf. Carter, "Positive and Negative Liberty."

63 Gerald C. MacCallum, "Negative and Positive Freedom," *The Philosophical Review* 76, no. 3 (1967): 312–334.

to be indistinguishable from the negative freedom.[64] Joel Feinberg states that the distinction between positive and negative freedom is based on an "artificially limited idea of constraint."[65] Generally, positive freedom is not supposed to contain elements of restraint. However, in reality, people are affected by not only external but also internal constraints such as depression, illness, or any other circumstances over which one has no control but that influences them in a detrimental manner. According to Feinberg, the complete freedom from constraints is impossible. Therefore, he states that "freedom from and freedom to are logically linked and there can be no special positive freedom."[66]

Gerald C. MacCallum has made an attempt to provide the core concept to freedom based on his "triadic Schema,"[67] that contains three elements: "an agent, certain preventing conditions, and certain doings or becoming of the agent."[68] This is a perfect combination of both the positive and negative dimensions of freedom, which means that freedom is freedom from something and freedom to do or become something.

Gradually, freedom is understood as a monadic property of agents. According to this view, "a free agent is one who possesses the appropriate personality—is self-realized, self-actualized, in a stage of harmony, rational, autonomous in any one of a number of senses of these notions."[69]

The contribution of Rahner to the above mentioned debate is remarkable. A more comprehensive and reasonable division and harmonization of different dimensions of freedom can be seen in Rahner's division of basic and categorical freedom, and it serves as the basis for his view of the fundamental option.

1.3.2 The Basic and Categorical Freedom of the Human Being

The ethical notion of the fundamental option is based on the division of human freedom as basic or transcendental, and categorical. In this section, I discuss these two notions to clarify the ethical notion of the fundamental option.

Since human beings are agents, they are also able to be analyzed and as such, they are an object of knowledge. Categorical freedom is used by humans at the level of human acts. It is the freedom exercised in the selection among different options and alternatives. It is categorical only because it is related to "doing." However, humans as persons are subjects.

64 Nash, *Freedom, Justice and the State*, 84–85.

65 Joel Feinberg, *Social Philosophy* (New Jersey: Prentice Hall, 1973): 12.

66 Feinberg, *Social Philosophy*, 13.

67 MacCallum, "Negative and Positive Freedom," 318.

68 Carter, "Positive and Negative Liberty."

69 Christine Swanton, *Freedom: A Coherence Theory* (Cambridge: Hackett Publishing Company, 1990): 9.

This non-objective status makes human beings unique. At the deeper level of our being, since we are not objects, there is no possibility of the use of categorical freedom. Our being is perceived as a whole and not as one category of objects or another.[70] At the level of persons as beings, we can make the decision only to be or not to be, a yes or a no. Suppose that the central core of a person finds an "Other" (God) that transcends all categories, the person can reject or accept the "Other." In this situation, the freedom of a human being is not categorical; moreover, it is the freedom, which transcends all categories and it is transcendental freedom that is the freedom of being.[71]

According to Rahner, basic or transcendental freedom is the capacity of a subject to decide about oneself in single totality, and he clearly differentiates it from the categorical freedom as a capacity to do this or that arbitrarily.[72] Basic freedom exists at the level of the person as a person or as a moral being. A human being can be a certain kind of person, that is, either good or evil. Here, the person is becoming through the course of life, either a good or an evil person. In our day-to-day life experience, we understand that there are people who are predominantly either good or bad. This is the fundamental stance of a person, which is the result of the use of basic freedom because it affects and shapes a person's whole being, outlook, and manner of living.[73] As Fuchs observes,

> Basic freedom, on the other hand, denotes a still more fundamental, deeper-rooted freedom, not immediately accessible to psychological investigation. This is the freedom that enables us not only to decide freely on particular acts and aims but also, by means of these, to determine ourselves totally as persons and not merely in any particular area of behaviour. [...]. A man can, in one and the same act, choose the object of his choice (freedom of choice) and by so doing determine himself as a person (basic freedom).[74]

2 Attainment and Functions of the Fundamental Option

Before explaining the attainment of the fundamental option, it is worthwhile to mention the distinction between a human being as a "being" and as an "agent." As I have already explained, categorical freedom and transcendental freedom stand as the basis for the distinction between the human being as an agent and as a being, because human agency is a result

70 Rahner, *Foundations of Christian Faith: An Introduction to the Idea of Christianity*, 93–95.

71 Karl Rahner, *Theology of Freedom*, Theological Investigations, vol. 6 (New York: The Seabury Press, 1974): 184. See also O'Connell, *Principles for a Catholic Morality*, 60–62.

72 Rahner, *Foundations of Christian Faith: An Introduction to the Idea of Christianity*, 94.

73 William Cosgrave, "Basic Choice and Basic Stance: Explaining the Fundamental Option," *The Furrow* 35, no. 8 (1984): 509–510.

74 Fuchs, *Human Values and Christian Morality*, 93.

of categorical freedom, whereas the human person or being is the result of use of transcendental freedom.[75] Charles E. Curran observes that one's being and one's agency is closely related because "by my actions I make myself as the person I am; and by my action I do things for good or for ill in this world. I am both subject and agent."[76]

In the personalist approach to morality, we give importance to the human person (moral subject), which refers to the person acting in relation to others. Here, we take into consideration the person as a whole and not their individual actions, but at the same time, every isolated act of a being has to be integrated into the meaning of the totality of human life. Every act may be physically good but "in order to be morally good, it has to be, next to its aptitude to fulfill our being in one of its aspects and in one of its needs, objectively suited to our personal totality, completely considered in itself and in its relations."[77] This means that "at the deepest level of the person, in the core of his being, he has adopted a fundamental moral stance or direction or orientation to reality, to life itself, to people, and to God; he has decided to become a fundamentally good person or a fundamentally evil one."[78] Moreover, according to Aquinas, the primary good, (the ultimate end) is the fundamental criterion for living a moral life.[79]

The fundamental option is the basic life orientation or basic choice of a person that is transcendental and based on transcendental freedom,[80] but that is never apart from ordinary life.[81] "When the individual experiences his existence as a meaningful totality and accepts the responsibility for the task of directing his life to its final goal, he forms a fundamental option for his life direction that is on the moral level."[82] It is totally different from the specific life choices of a person such as to go for a walk, go to see a play, and so on. Specific choices are made at the peripheral level of the person and do not engage at the deepest level of the person. The fundamental option is not limited by specific values and choices. In short, the fundamental

---

75 Mary Jo Iozzio, *Self Determination and the Moral Act* (Leuven: Peeters, 1995): 42–43. See also Charles E. Curran, *The Catholic Moral Tradition Today: A Synthesis* (Washington: Georgetown University Press, 1999): 42–43. See also Janssens, "Personalist Morals," 10–11.

76 Curran, *The Catholic Moral Tradition Today: A Synthesis*, 88.

77 Louis Janssens, "Time and Space in Morals," in *Personalist Morals: Essays in Honor of Professor Louis Janssens*, ed. Joseph A. Selling (Leuven: Leuven University Press, 1988): 13.

78 Cosgrave, "Basic Choice and Basic Stance: Explaining the Fundamental Option," 509.

79 Aquinas, "Summa Theologica," I–II, q. 1, a. 4; I–II, q.88, a. 1.

80 Transcendental freedom is the capacity of an individual to decide about oneself in one's single totality. Cf. Rahner, *Foundations of Christian Faith: An Introduction to the Idea of Christianity*, 94–99.

81 Häring, "Sin in Post-Vatican II Theology," 93. See also Linnane, "Rahner's Fundamental Option and Virtue Ethics," 231. David Coffey, "Rahner's Theology of Fundamental Option," *Philosophy and Theology* 10, no. 1 (1997): 257.

82 Cooper, "The Fundamental Option," 388.

option is the basic stance of a person in which one exists as either a good or an evil person, or is predominantly oriented toward goodness.[83]

At the same time, basic choice and peripheral choices are related. When individuals experience and accept their existence as a meaningful totality and decide to direct their life to its final goal, then they form their fundamental option.[84] The particular actions of a person can strengthen and deepen one's basic options in life. Once individuals have reached the fundamental stance of their life then their particular actions will be the expression of this basic stance. The particular choice demands a judgment of consciousness in each situation. However, it does not mean that every act of categorical freedom necessarily corresponds to one's fundamental option. Moreover, the acts, which do not correspond to the fundamental option, are not moral in the real and full sense but only by way of an analogy. The fundamental option remains as the primary criterion for the moral evaluation of any particular action. Since human beings are autonomous beings, they are responsible for having conformity between their basic stance and free acts, or they are accountable for not only free acts but also for the entire course of their life.[85]

Fuchs observes that "the free choices and realization of good or bad acts and the creation by free choice of good or bad tendencies may decide or occasion the intensification or diminution of the basic intention arising out of basic freedom, and even indeed the reversal into its opposite—always according to whether they correspond to or contradict the basic intention."[86] Since the fundamental option is a result of the choice by way of the exercise of the basic freedoms of a person, it can be rejected or radically changed into a new one or even opposite to the present fundamental option. Such change from one fundamental option to a new fundamental option can take place gradually,[87] "a person does not become fundamentally good or bad either easily or quickly; it takes time and effort and in fact, it may be only later that the subject adverts to it and recognizes that he has in fact made a basic choice."[88]

The overall account of the fundamental option follows from the individual's transcendental freedom and the fundamental self-disposition before God. The fundamental option determines the link between an individual's

[83] Cosgrave, "Basic Choice and Basic Stance: Explaining the Fundamental Option," 510.

[84] Cooper, "The Fundamental Option," 388. See also Fuchs, *Human Values and Christian Morality*, 102.

[85] Cooper, "The Fundamental Option," 390. See also Qureshi, "Sin, Fundamental Option and Conversion," 279.

[86] Fuchs, *Human Values and Christian Morality*, 104.

[87] Cooper, "The Fundamental Option," 389. See also Fuchs, *Human Values and Christian Morality*, 104.

[88] Cosgrave, "Basic Choice and Basic Stance: Explaining the Fundamental Option," 513.

fundamental stance before God and the moral life of the individual.[89] However, "it is possible to acknowledge that a person might be fundamentally united with God, even while engaged in morally reprehensible behaviour, and this in turn provides a way of acknowledging the complexity and brokenness that are to be found in even the most admirable lives."[90] Although the fundamental option theory permits the division of sins between mortal and venial sins, it contradicts the spirit of the traditional division of sins. When individuals have a positive fundamental option and act in accordance with their fundamental stance, their actions are morally right. However, if their actions are the expression of a negative fundamental option, then they commit a mortal sin. If one person commits grave sin with a positive fundamental option, then that action is mortal sin.[91]

3 The Subjective and Objective Dimensions of the Fundamental Option

As already seen, the fundamental option is the result of the exercise of the transcendental and categorical freedom of a human being. It can be either the positive or negative orientation of the person, which represents their longing for or against God or good. Both categorical and transcendental freedoms direct certain values. As Mark O'Keefe observes, "categorical freedom is directed at individual, discrete values that are present in particular situations and that serve human flourishing. Transcendental freedom, on the other hand, is directed at the transcendental level of value itself, which is God and in which all other values participate and have their end."[92] O'Keefe concludes that by choosing or negating particular values in a particular situation, the person implicitly either accepts God in whom all these values participate, or rejects God.[93]

Freedom never exists in a vacuum, however. The exercise of freedom has both a personal and a social realm, and this is clear at the categorical level of freedom in which the person chooses certain values, which exist in social matrix. This means that freedom is exercised not only "within the limits of physical and biological boundaries but also within the cultural, social, economic, and religious environment in which the person develops."[94] One person receives knowledge of value through social interaction, and in such a way that knowledge and freedom are interrelated. Although the social nature of value and freedom exists at the categorical level, it has profound implications for the transcendental freedom and fundamental

89 Porter, "Moral Language and the Language of Grace," 174.
90 Porter, "Moral Language and the Language of Grace," 175.
91 Porter, "Moral Language and the Language of Grace," 172–173.
92 O'Keefe, "Social Sin and Fundamental Option," 86.
93 O'Keefe, "Social Sin and Fundamental Option," 86–87.
94 O'Keefe, "Social Sin and Fundamental Option," 87.

option. O'Keefe observes that "the exercise of transcendental freedom cannot be isolated from the social interrelationships in which the person finds himself or herself."[95] The fundamental option of a person is formed in accordance with the ability of that person to recognize and act upon authentic values in the social world. Categorical freedom and the choice of values from the society, in which one lives, are the medium by which one reaches one's fundamental option.[96]

It is not possible to examine a person's fundamental orientation at once so as to establish whether the person's fundamental stance is good or evil. At this level, the fundamental option is purely subjective reality. However, the fundamental option is expressed through the day-to-day actions and decisions made by that person. Therefore, the fundamental option is objective because we can know the good and evil stance of people through evaluating their actions and decisions, and the narrative approach to the self can be useful at this point.[97] As Fuchs writes, "we can also to some extent conclude by a conjecture based on our actions whether we really are as persons good or evil: that is, whether we are bound firmly in God's grace and love or not."[98] Moreover, the basis for determining good and evil actions is founded upon "the shared, interpreted experiences of human community through time."[99] Therefore, by objectively evaluating the series of different actions and decisions of a person,[100] that is, whether the series

---

95 O'Keefe, "Social Sin and Fundamental Option," 88.

96 O'Keefe, "Social Sin and Fundamental Option," 92.

97 The narrative self explains the character of a being or individual as being. This narrative approach includes the evaluation of the person as a whole rather than the particular action itself. Here, the self becomes both subject and object. Character and self-consistency are two important elements of the integrity of a person. The narrative self is a connecting link between character and self consistency. Narrative self is not static self. It experiences change, reversal, and surprise. In the narrative approach we begin with the events that have occurred in a person's life, and without narrative, such events are contingents. In order to make sense of these events, we recognize them as an outcome of intention or contextual factors. The analyses of intention and contextual factors in relation with life as a whole lead to the formulation of narrative self. Cf. Sparrowe, "Authentic Leadership and the Narrative Self," 426–430.

98 Josef Fuchs, "Good Acts and Good Persons," in *Understanding Veritatis Splendor: The Encyclical Letter of Pope John Paul 2 on the Church's Moral Teaching*, ed. John Wilkins (Melksham: The Cromwell Press, 1994): 31.

99 Joseph A. Selling, "The Human Person," in *Christian Ethics: An Introduction*, ed. Bernard Hoose (New York: The Liturgical Press, 2003): 96.

100 On what basis do we label human actions as good or evil? There are several answers to this, such as pleasure, pain, commandments, etc. I prefer here to hold the personalist morality. According to personalist morality, the ultimate good is that which enhances the human person and evil is that which harms the human person adequately considered. Cf. Janssens, "Artificial Insemination: Ethical Considerations," 3–29. See also Louis Janssens, "Ontic Evil and Moral Evil," *Louvain Studies* 4 (1972): 115–156. Joseph A. Selling observes that the goodness and badness of a set of actions are determined by the observation and interpreted experience of the community through time. Selling, "The Human Person," 96–97.

of our actions are bound with the goodness and truth of God,[101] we can ascertain what the person's fundamental orientation or stance is.[102]

4 Conceptual Link between the Fundamental Option and Integrity

Although there are diverse definitions of integrity, all describe integrity as the moral core of the person, which works as a willingness or practical wisdom or motivation to do what is right. There are diverse descriptions of integrity due to the lack of integration of subjective and objective dimensions of integrity. However, Christian views of the fundamental option also describe fundamental orientation or the fundamental stance of the person for or against God or good. Since the fundamental option is either for or against God or good, it can be either positive or negative. Although one cannot equate Christian views of the fundamental option with personal integrity, one can use the connective link as well as what is conceptually common between these two concepts.[103]

Since both personal integrity and the fundamental option are dynamic concepts that contain both subjective and objective dimensions, I shall argue against the reduction of these concepts to individualistic realm. Although these concepts have a personal condition or state, a human being is not an isolated subject, but rather a social being with intrinsic relationships and an interdependent existence. As noted earlier, personalist morality suggests that a person has to be considered adequately and integrally in moral discourse because the person is always in relation to the "totality of reality."[104]

However at the same time, human beings maintain their autonomy and freedom and are solely responsible for their actions.[105] This is why Joseph Selling observes that "if one opts for a personalist kind of morality, then the notion of the person functions not only on the subjective pole but also on the objective pole as well, forming the reference point for the determination of good and evil, and subsequently right(ness) and wrong(ness)."[106] In the same vein, Robert Solomon speaks about integrity stating that "it means wholeness of virtue, wholeness as a person, wholeness in the sense of being part of something larger than the person—the community, the

---

101 Wallace, "Fundamental Option," 456.

102 Fuchs, "Understanding Veritatis Splendor," 23.

103 Joseph, "The Conceptual Link between Personal Integrity and Positive Fundamental Option," 116–118.

104 Selling, "The Human Person," 96–97.

105 Domènec Melé, "Integrating Personalism into Virtue-Based Business Ethics: The Personalist and the Common Good Principles," *Journal of Business Ethics* 88 (2009): 229.

106 Selling, "The Human Person," 96.

corporation, society, humanity, and the cosmos."[107] The fundamental option refers to the fundamental orientation of the person for or against God, and since each human person is both free and a relational being, the fundamental option cannot be conceptualized as separate from the social and subjective realm.

Both the person of integrity and one with a positive fundamental option have a self, which is linked with society's positive morality[108] because personal integrity is the expression of moral self or motivation to do what is right, whereas positive fundamental option is the fundamental stance of the person for God, who is the embodiment of all values. For non-believers the positive fundamental option is a fundamental stance of a person for good. This does not mean that they unreflectively follow social moral rules and convictions. A person of integrity or a person with positive fundamental option can interpret and apply society's moral rules and values, and therefore sometimes deviates from what is usual in the community.

The integrity of the person will help us to reach and maintain the positive fundamental option because integrity is the expression of the moral self or motivation or practical wisdom to do what is right and good. The integrity of the person works on a categorical level. As I have explained earlier, when the person of integrity is faced with moral challenges or dilemmas and makes a justifiable decision, this will normally be in favor of good. So, on the categorical level, it is integrity that enables the person to make right choices. These series of right choices will lead the person to have a positive fundamental option. However, the fundamental option is not the same as right choices. Once individuals reach the fundamental option, then normally their individual choices will be an incarnation of the fundamental option. Since human beings are free in categorical choices, the fundamental option can be changed from positive to negative, based on the use of categorical freedom. Here, the integrity of individuals will help them to maintain their positive fundamental option, but integrity will never block their freedom.

Conclusion

The fundamental option is neither an act nor a process. It is a state or fundamental orientation of the person for or against God; for a non-believer it is the fundamental orientation from within for or against good. The theory of the fundamental option is rooted in Scripture, Christian tradition, and it is particularly based on the distinction between categorical

107 Robert C. Solomon, *A Better Way to Think About Business: How Personal Integrity Leads to Corporate Success* (Oxford: Oxford University Press, 1999): 38.

108 Musschenga, "Education for Moral Integrity," 226. Cosgrave, "Basic Choice and Basic Stance: Explaining the Fundamental Option," 510.

and transcendental freedom. Categorical freedom is the freedom of day to day choices, therefore it is in the realm of "doing," whereas transcendental freedom is in the realm of one's "being." The fundamental option of a person is gradually developed by the manner in which one uses one's categorical freedom in the process of arriving at the level of transcendental freedom. Once individuals reach a level of transcendental freedom, then their actions will be the manifestations of their fundamental option. Change in the fundamental option is also possible, but it happens gradually in accordance with the use of one's categorical freedom.

Although one cannot equate the Christian interpretation of the fundamental option with personal integrity, one can see and understand their connective links or the similar features conceptually shared by the positive fundamental option and the integrity of a person. Both the person of integrity and the person with a positive fundamental option have a self, which identifies with society's positive morality. This does not mean that individuals unreflectively follow the conventional moral rules and convictions of a society. Persons of integrity or persons with a positive fundamental option can interpret and use their society's moral rules and values in their decision-making process, being sensitive to their specific contexts, and therefore sometimes they may even deviate from what is accepted in their communities as "normal," "natural," or "morally right." Both personal integrity and the fundamental option are dynamic concepts that contain subjective and objective dimensions, given that human beings are relational beings. Furthermore, both integrity and the fundamental option are formed and developed within the community. However, personal integrity helps one to make right choices and conduct right actions. This in turn reaffirms the fundamental option. Moreover, the integrity of a person will help the person to maintain a positive fundamental option since integrity is the moral self that works as motivation or practical wisdom to do what is right and good in corporate conflicts of interests.

PART III

PERSONALIST APPROACH TO CORPORATE INTEGRITY THEORIES

CHAPTER EIGHT

ETHICAL REASONS AND FOUNDATIONS FOR PERSONALIST APPROACH TO CORPORATE INTEGRITY

Introduction

As seen earlier, corporate integrity theories ignore personal integrity. I have already demonstrated that personal integrity is crucial when managers and employees deal with conflicts of interests. Moreover, individuals, particularly those in leadership roles, are the real constitutive elements of corporations and thus play decisive roles in the performance of corporations. In this chapter, I articulate the reasons and foundations for personalist corporate integrity approach, which includes personal integrity of managers and employees along with ethical corporate structure and culture.

1 Ethical Reasons for the Personalist Approach to Corporate Integrity

I think that there is more to ethics, especially in the business context, than simply having rules, regulations, monitoring, and sanctions. I therefore propose a shift from the compliance-based idea of corporate integrity to a person-centered view of corporate integrity. In the following section, I shall establish ethical arguments for the above-mentioned shift.

1.1 Argument for a Good Life

The concept of a good life is not widely discussed in business ethics literature. Although welfare economics deals with the good life, "it is mostly concerned with the distribution of costs and benefits of various economic choices wherein the benefits are measured in terms of utility and costs in terms of disutility or utility foregone."[1] However, I consider the good life as a fundamental argument for placing personal integrity among the corporate ethical decision-making processes.

1.1.1 The View of Theory of the Good Life According to Aristotle

In *Nicomachean Ethics,* Aristotle writes about *eudaimonia,*[2] that is the "good life," or "living well" or "faring well," or "doing well."[3] Aristotle lists five qualities of a good life. First, a good life is a part of our own activities. It is neither the life of idleness nor the things that happen to us by luck:[4] "For excellence consists in doing good rather than in having good done to me, and in performing noble actions rather than in not performing base ones."[5] Moreover, according to Aristotle, in order to have a good life it is insufficient to acquire certain potentialities, abilities, or excellence but one must have an act and a result. *Eudaimonia* is an activity as much as it is a state of being, "for a characteristic may exist without producing any good result, for example, in a man who is asleep or incapacitated in some other respect. An activity on the other hand, must produce a result."[6]

Second, activities that lead to good life should be "the best activities open to us, activities of what is best in us, performed well."[7] What differentiates human beings from other animals is our rational capacity.[8] According to Roger J. Sullivan, Aristotle considers reason as the "best part of us," "our most sovereign part," and "divine element."[9] Aristotle divided reason into two parts: "theoretical (concerning the contemplation of unchangeable truths) and practical (to do with choosing wisely in the sphere of what can be changed)."[10] Aristotle defines the "good life as a life consisting of

---

1 Donald G. Richards, "Eudaimonia, Economics and the Environment: What Do the Hellenistic Thinkers Have to Teach Economists About 'the Good Life'?," *Ethics & the Environment* 18, no. 2 (2013): 33.

2 It is also translated as happiness. However, Aristotle's view of happiness points toward the good life. He writes, "also the view that a happy man lives well and fares well fits in with our definition: for we have all but defined happiness as a kind of good life and well being." Cf. Aristotle, *The Nicomachean Ethics*, trans. Martin Ostwald (New Jersey: Prentice Hall, 1999); Roger J. Sullivan, *Morality and the Good Life: A Commentary on Aristotle's Nicomachean Ethics* (Memphis: Memphis State University Press, 1980): 1.4. 1095a 17–19; 1.8. 1098b 20–21.

3 Aristotle, *The Nicomachean Ethics*, 1.4. 1095 a 17–19; 1.8. 1098b 20–21. See also Sullivan, *Morality and the Good Life*, 160.

4 Sullivan, *Morality and the Good Life*, 161.

5 Aristotle, *The Nicomachean Ethics*, 4.1. 1120a 12–13.

6 Aristotle, *The Nicomachean Ethics*, 8.1. 1098b 30–31.

7 Sullivan, *Morality and the Good Life*, 161.

8 Aristotle, *The Nicomachean Ethics*, 1.7. 1098a 1–5.

9 Sullivan, *Morality and the Good Life*, 161.

10 Antonia Macaro, "Aristotle and the Good Life," *Practical Philosophy* 7, no. 2 (2005): 5.

rational activities.'[11] Moreover, he writes that "the good of man is an activity of the soul in conformity with excellence or virtue, and if there are several virtues, in conformity with the best and most complete."[12]

Third, finality is another quality of the good life,[13] but is not something distinct from our activities; rather it is what we achieve by way of conducting our activities. Aristotle writes, "Only the goal of action is an end in the unqualified sense: for the good life is an end, and desire is directed toward this. Therefore, a choice is either intelligence motivated by desire or desire operating through thought, and it is as a combination of these two that man is a starting point of action."[14]

Fourth, activities that constitute a good life must be pleasurable. Indeed, Aristotle accepts that not all pleasures are good and equal.[15] According to the interpretation of Antonia Macaro, the best kind of pleasure "is that deriving from being involved in some worthwhile activity."[16] Finally, the activities that create good life must have an inherent permanence throughout one's life.[17]

In short, good life in the writings of Aristotle refers to the "maximum realization of the function that was unique to humans."[18] This means that a good life is an activity made by the soul in accordance with virtue.[19] There are three elements of the soul that are directly relevant to any human action: perception, desire, and intellect. The vital part of human actions is "the intellect presiding over the process of deliberation."[20] Therefore, "The candidate for the good life, besides having the opportunity to act on the virtues, must have known what he was doing; chosen to act the way he did and chose it for its own sake; and the act must come from a firm and unchangeable character."[21] In order to achieve good life, "we should adopt appropriate ideals, learn to identify the appropriate course of action

---

11 Aristotle, *The Nicomachean Ethics*, 1.7. 1098a 5–15. See also Sullivan, *Morality and the Good Life*, 161.

12 Aristotle, *The Nicomachean Ethics*, 1.7. 1098a 15–18.

13 Sullivan, *Morality and the Good Life*, 162.

14 Aristotle, *The Nicomachean Ethics*, 6.2. 1139b 1–4.

15 Aristotle, *The Nicomachean Ethics*, 7.11. 1152b 20.

16 Macaro, "Aristotle and the Good Life," 5.

17 Sullivan, *Morality and the Good Life*, 163.

18 Susan Haslip, "Aristotle's Theory of the Good Life: A Consideration of the Role of Luck in the Good Life and the Concept of Self-Sufficiency," *Quodlibet Journal* 5, no. 1 (January 2003): 1.

19 Aristotle, *The Nicomachean Ethics*, 1.7. 1098a 15–18.

20 Francis H. Eterovich, *Aristotle's Nichomachean Ethics: Commentary and Analysis* (Washington: University Press of America, 1980): 114.

21 Haslip, "Aristotle's Theory of the Good Life," 1. This author made use of the following source for this idea. Cf. Abraham Edel, Elizabeth Flower, and Finbarr W. O'Connor, eds., *Morality, Philosophy, and Practice: Historical and Contemporary Readings and Studies* (New York: Random House, 1989): 45.

through rational deliberation, and train ourselves to feel and act accordingly."[22] Thus, for Aristotle, the good life is possible only by way of making virtuous decisions and performing virtuous actions in one's daily life.

1.1.2 The Good Life According to Paul Ricoeur

Paul Ricoeur's view of a good life parallels Aristotle's contention. He wants to exemplify the primacy of teleology over deontology or the primacy of ethical aims over ethical obligation.[23] However, an aim of a good life has to undergo "the test of moral obligation."[24] Ricoeur clearly declares the above-mentioned aim of his ethical study in *Oneself as Another*. He proposes to establish "(1) the primacy of ethics over morality,[25] (2) the necessity for the ethical aim to pass through the sieve of the norm, (3) the legitimacy of recourse by the norm to the aim whenever the norm leads to impasses in practice."[26]

He defines the ethical aim as "the good life with and for others in just institutions."[27] The definition has three constituents with equal importance. The good life is not based on the commandment of others to seek but "is something that someone is concerned about either for oneself or for another."[28] Self-esteem is the basis for the good life for oneself. A self becomes worthy of esteem based on two abilities: the "capacity to choose" with reason and the "capacity to act effectively." The "capacity to choose" refers to one's ability to "act purposefully."[29] The "capacity to act effectively" means the ability "to interpret the causal flow of nature and to introduce changes into the course of things, indeed to begin something new in this world."[30] Self-esteem is a reflective result of one's actions or self-interpretation leading to self-esteem in ethics.[31] Eftichis Pirovolakis observes that unlike Aristotle, Ricoeur holds that "the content of the good life remains

22 Macaro, "Aristotle and the Good Life," 5.

23 Paul Ricoeur, *Oneself as Another*, trans. Kathleen Blarney (Chicago: The University of Chicago Press, 1992): 170.

24 Ricoeur, *Oneself as Another*, 218.

25 Ethics is concerned with understanding and examining the moral life in different ways. Reason is the source of ethics. Contrarily, morality refers to the norms about the right and wrong of human conduct. However, both are related. Cf. Tom L. Beauchamp and James F. Childress, *Principles of Biomedical Ethics* (New York: Oxford University Press, 2009): 1–3.

26 Ricoeur, *Oneself as Another*, 170.

27 Ricoeur, *Oneself as Another*, 180.

28 Bernard P. Dauenhauer, "Response to Rawls," in *Ricoeur as Another: The Ethics of Subjectivity*, eds. Richard A. Cohen and James L. Marsh (New York: State University of New York Press, 2002): 210.

29 Dauenhauer, "Response to Rawls," 210–211.

30 Dauenhauer, "Response to Rawls," 210.

31 James L. Marsh, "The Right and the Good: A Solution to the Communicative Ethics Controversy," in *Ricoeur as Another: The Ethics of Subjectivity*, eds. Richard A. Cohen and James L. Marsh (New York: State University of New York Press, 2002): 225.

a nebulous ideal and an infinite and ever changing aim—one has to interpret and reinterpret ceaselessly one's finite choices."[32] On the other hand, Ricoeur does not deny the narrative unity of the person. Narrative unity of life is used to evaluate particular actions. According to Ricoeur, under the idea of good life, there is a "hermeneutical circle" between one's life as a whole and one's own particular choices.[33] In self-esteem, human beings feel that they are not instruments but they live to have an ultimate aim, the aim of a good life.[34]

While the concept of a good life is not an aim for oneself alone, it requires that we also "live well with others and for others."[35] Ricoeur understands specific actions in accordance with our ideals that always "involve an exercise of judgment which, at best, can aspire to plausibility in the eyes of others."[36] Thus, self-esteem is connected with solicitude for others.[37] According to Ricoeur, "Solicitude is not added to self-esteem from the outside. Rather, it unfolds the dialogical dimension that is implicit in self-esteem. Self-esteem and solicitude can neither be lived nor thought without each other [...]. Self implies the other than self, so that one can say of someone that he esteems himself as another."[38] As I have explained earlier, Ricoeur defines self-esteem in terms of the reflective evaluation of one's actions. Therefore, he intends to include others also in the concept of good life as they also convey the evaluations of the agent's actions.[39] Moreover, the relation between self and the other is characterized by reciprocity: the exchange of giving and receiving.[40] It is opposite to a moral injection from the other, for example, "Thou shall not kill." In short, a good life is also linked with living together in the experience of equality.[41] Ricoeur writes,

> It is the fruit of the exchange between esteem for oneself and solicitude for others. This exchange authorizes us to say that I cannot myself have self-esteem unless I esteem others as myself. 'As myself' means that you

[32] Eftichis Pirovolakis, *Reading Derrida and Ricoeur: Improbable Encounters between Deconstruction and Hermeneutics* (New York: State University of New York Press, 2010): 99.

[33] Ricoeur, *Oneself as Another*, 179. See also Charles E. Reagan, "Personal Identity," in *Ricoeur as Another: The Ethics of Subjectivity*, eds. Richard A. Cohen and James L. Marsh (New York: State University of New York Press, 2002): 17.

[34] Dauenhauer, "Response to Rawls," 210.

[35] Dauenhauer, "Response to Rawls," 210.

[36] Ricoeur, *Oneself as Another*, 180.

[37] Dauenhauer, "Response to Rawls," 210.

[38] Paul Ricoeur, "Ethique Et Morale: Visee Theologique Et Perspective Deontologique," in *Ragione Pratica Liberta Normativita*, ed. Marcello Sanchez Sorondo (Roma: Universita Lateranense, 1991): 355. I have taken this quotation from the following source. Cf. Dauenhauer, "Response to Rawls," 211.

[39] David Pellauer, "At the Limit of Practical Wisdom," in *Ricoeur as Another: The Ethics of Subjectivity*, eds. Richard A. Cohen and James L. Marsh (New York: State University of New York Press, 2002): 191.

[40] Reagan, "Personal Identity," 18.

[41] Reagan, "Personal Identity," 18.

> are capable of starting something in the world, of acting for a reason, of hierarchizing your priorities, of evaluating the ends of your actions, and having done this, of holding yourself in esteem as I hold myself in esteem.[42]

Finally, Ricoeur incorporates just institutions in his ethical interpretation of the good life because "Whom we may encounter face to face is itself incomplete if we do not take into account the existence of our relations to others constituted through and mediated by institutions."[43] Institution is a community structure of living together and it has the "function of distribution of roles, responsibilities, privileges, goods, and rewards."[44] The quality of an institution is just and not oppressed or unjust. A just institution would assist another person to flourish in interpersonal relationships.[45] For Ricoeur, the mediation of the other for a good life exists "not only in the dialogical and in the intimate, but also in the anonymity of the third person. Interpersonal relations do not exhaust the whole gamut of living together that will include communities, societies, and nations."[46]

Thus, Ricoeur thinks that a good life is an aim of ethical approach. Self-interpretation leads to self-esteem in ethics. Good life is based on one's self-esteem, which contains one's capacity to choose and act. However, good life is not an isolated project. While in this line of argument a clear priority has been given to the ethical aim over morality, it is important that Ricoeur incorporates others and just institutions in his project.

1.1.3 The Good Life as an Ethical Aim of Business Ethics

Business ethics is more than compliance-based ethics.[47] As already explained, along with many authors including Aristotle and Ricoeur, I hold that the good life or entire happiness is the primary concern of actions in the business context. In order to have a good life, managers and employees require not only codes of conduct but also the possibility to exercise their own values and ends in organizational life, which makes their work meaningful and fosters an appreciation of the spectrum of their own choices. This is possible by "giving individuals opportunities to thoughtfully participate in the management of their company's affairs and contemplate the

---

42 Ricoeur, *Oneself as Another*, 193.

43 Pellauer, "At the Limit of Practical Wisdom," 191.

44 Reagan, "Personal Identity," 19.

45 Boyd Blundell, "Refiguring Virtue," in *A Passion for the Possible: Thinking with Paul Ricoeur*, eds. Brian Treanor and Henry Isaac Venema (New York: Fordham University Press, 2010): 168–169.

46 Ranhilio Callangan Aquino, "The Dialectics of Power, Rights, and Responsibility," *Kritike* 3, no. 1 (2009): 4–5. See also Paul Ricoeur, *The Just* (Chicago: The University of Chicago Press, 2000): 5.

47 This section is an elaborated version of my own article. Cf. Augustine Joseph, "The Relevance of Personal Integrity in Corporate Ethics: A Study Based on Indian Scenario," *Indian Theological Studies* 52, no. 1 (2015): 77–90.

ultimate meaning of things."[48] Furthermore, a "meaningful work is that which actualizes certain human potentials including creativity, autonomy, abilities, talents, identity, and sociality."[49] Verstraeten observes that these personal involvements at the core of organizational life transform managers and employees from a passive mentality to being motivated members of a meaningful organization.[50]

Personal integrity would aid managers and employees to use their own moral-self while being involved in the organization's daily functioning. Personal ethics and organizational ethics are not identical, however. Further, there is a possibility of conflicts arising "between individual values and company values, and between family or social role demands and the specific role demands within the company."[51] As discussed earlier, the integrity approach is a solution whereby managers and employees consider all the circumstances and all stakeholders' interests before finalizing a decision. The personal integrity of managers and employees plays a vital role in this. Moreover, the written values of each department may conflict with one another.[52] Ethical auditing is proposed as the way to improve the functioning of organizational values and codes. It is the process of evaluating a company's policies, procedures, and the way by which decisions are made from an ethical viewpoint.[53] This is a matter of interpretation and reinterpretation of organizational cultures and traditions. In this process, businesses should receive insight from their personal experiences and moral integrity of managers and employees.[54] It is clear from the observation of Verstraeten that managers and employees experience the good life in so far as both company and personnel inspire each other. The experience of the good life in a business is a mutual-party process of movement between managers and their employees.[55]

It is clear from the above discussion that an exercise of codes of conduct alone is insufficient to attain the aim of business ethics of a good life. The personal involvement of managers and employees in the daily functioning of an organization is essential to having a meaningful life. How is this possible in a corporate context? George Bragues proposes that first,

---

48 George Bragues, "Seek the Good Life, Not Money: The Aristotelian Approach to Business Ethics," *Journal of Business Ethics* 67, no. 4 (2006): 343.

49 Ferdinand Tablan, "Catholic Social Teachings: Toward a Meaningful Work," *Journal of Business Ethics* 128, no. 2 (2015): 292.

50 Johan Verstraeten, "From Business Ethics to the Vocation of Business Leaders to Humanize the World of Business," *Business Ethics: A European Review* 7, no. 2 (1998): 115.

51 Verstraeten, "Business Leaders to Humanize the World of Business," 115.

52 Verstraeten, "Business Leaders to Humanize the World of Business," 116.

53 Paul B. Hofmann, "Performing an Ethics Audit," *Healthcare Executive* 10, no. 6 (1995): 47.

54 Verstraeten, "Business Leaders to Humanize the World of Business," 116–117.

55 Verstraeten, "Business Leaders to Humanize the World of Business," 116–117.

in corporate structure there should be a participatory decision-making process rather than a centralized one.[56] The attitudes of a company toward employees and managers are crucial, and the company should allow its members to participate in the decision-making processes. "Employees are given enough autonomy to make decisions concerning how they can produce the required outcome. That is, they are not micromanaged. Their supervisor is not scrutinizing their every move."[57]

Second, it is worthwhile to have a shared responsibility structure in organizations. Such a structure would provide employees and managers with an opportunity to exercise and develop their virtues and capacities respectively.[58] It helps "for contributing to the good of others through sustaining a healthy economy and providing people with goods and services that are needed for living a good life."[59]

Third, acceptance and "respect for employee rationality by ensuring that management liberally discloses information pertaining to the firm's condition and prospects and provides reasons for company policies,"[60] is needed.

Fourth, there should be ample leisure time for managers and employees to engage in activities such as reading, personal reflection, and fulfilling the demands of one's own life.[61] Work/life balance[62] is essential for the creative involvement of managers and employees within corporate life. Stress at work is one of the main causes of failure in achieving the desired balance. As a result, the involvement and performance of managers and employees in corporate life may be weakened.[63] According to Bragues, implementing the above-mentioned steps in corporate life creates opportunities for better employee involvement and consequently, they will make use of their own values and ends in their life at the corporation; this then gives meaning to their work or good life.

Corporate integrity theories tend to limit corporate integrity to the realm of corporate structure and culture along with codes of conduct.

---

56 Bragues, "Seek the Good Life, Not Money," 354.

57 M. Joseph Sirgy, "Employee Well-Being: An Integrative Perspective," in *Work and Quality of Life: Ethical Practices in Organizations*, eds. Nora P. Reilly, M. Joseph Sirgy, and C. Allen Gorman (Dordrecht: Springer, 2012): 51.

58 David McPherson, "Vocational Virtue Ethics: Prospects for a Virtue Ethic Approach to Business," *Journal of Business Ethics* 116, no. 2 (2013): 290.

59 McPherson, "Vocational Virtue Ethics," 290.

60 Bragues, "Seek the Good Life, Not Money," 354.

61 Bragues, "Seek the Good Life, Not Money," 355.

62 Work/life balance can be defined as "the ability to accomplish the goals or meet the demands of one's work and personal life and achieve satisfaction in all life domains." Cf. Carrie A. Bulger and Gwenith G. Fisher, "Ethical Imperatives of Work/Life Balance," in *Work and Quality of Life: Ethical Practices in Organizations*, eds. Nora P. Reilly, M. Joseph Sirgy, and C. Allen Gorman (Dordrecht: Springer, 2012): 182.

63 Bulger and Fisher, "Ethical Imperatives of Work/Life Balance," 181–203.

The perspective of the good life goes a step further, however, and paves a reasonable ground by incorporating personal integrity into corporate integrity theories.

1.2 To Overcome Instrumentalization

The corporate integrity theories combine corporate codes of conduct, structure, and culture. Through this combination, corporate managers in consultation with the owners of the corporation develop a compliance-based approach and aim to prevent, find, and punish unethical corporate conduct.[64] As I have stated previously, I do not want to underestimate the value of such a compliance-based approach. However, I believe that since it neglects the personal integrity of managers and employees, it may in turn lead to an instrumentalization of ethics for the maximization of profit, which can lead to corporate corruption. A balanced view of both the compliance-based and a personal integrity-based approach is needed to reduce or eliminate corruption.

Business ethics can be viewed from an instrumental and non-instrumental perspective. According to Bouckaert, "The instrumental use of ethics involves the introduction of ethics to external goals, such as better reputation, lower transaction cost, less regulation, and, most of all, higher profitability. On the other hand, an intrinsic or spiritual approach to ethics is characterized by its openness to its non-instrumental motivations."[65] There is no doubt that profit and good reputation are desirable. However, if corporate codes of conduct, structure, and culture are merely designed for profit and good reputation, corporate ethics instrumentalizes employees and managers for the benefit of the company and moreover, instrumentalize the business ethics itself. Thus, the reflections and study regarding business ethics is reduced to a matter of utility maximization.[66]

From an instrumental perspective, corporate ethics can be a tool for an efficient means of the production of problematic goods or for the realization of purposes that are ultimately unethical.[67] For example, a company can make very dangerous agricultural pesticides in an efficient way. Hence, business ethics require more than mere efficiency or obedience to codes of conduct. From a non-instrumental perspective, business ethics has to

64 Lynn Sharp Paine, "Managing for Organizational Integrity," *Harvard Business Review* 72, no. 3/4 (1994): 106.

65 Luk Bouckaert, "Spirituality and Rationality," in *The Palgrave Handbook of Spirituality and Business*, eds. Luk Bouckaert and Laszlo Zsolnai (Basingstoke: Palgrave Macmillan, 2011): 20.

66 John Hooker, "The Case against Business Ethics Education: A Study in Bad Arguments," *Journal of Business Ethics Education* 1, no. 1 (2004): 77.

67 Muel Kaptein and Johan Wempe, *The Balanced Company: A Theory of Corporate Integrity* (Oxford: Oxford University Press, 2002): 165.

consider employees and managers as subjects with moral responsibility and not as means to an end.

It cannot, however, be denied that there is a tension between instrumental and non-instrumental motivations of corporations, particularly when owners, managers, and employees use ethics for the realization of a business's selfish interests. This tension requires the keeping of a right order. The negligence of non-instrumental perspective is destructive because it may lead to a selective moral blindness.[68]

Moreover, Bouckaert shows the weakness of compliance-based corporate ethics, which do not incorporate the personal integrity of managers and employees. Compliance-based ethical programs contain values and principles as part of corporate codes of conduct, structure, and culture. However, when corporations are confronted with a deep financial crisis, for example, history has shown that they act as if ethics never existed in the first place, as their overarching priorities lie with the resolution of the crisis instead.[69] For instance, Bouckaert draws our attention to the closing of Renault Plant in Brussels in 1997.[70] The reason for the decision to close was long-term profitability, which was in doubt, undoubtedly a significant issue for the operation of any business. Bouckaert indicates that prior non-communication to employees regarding the closing of a corporate plant was not seen as a moral problem for managers and shareholders in this instance.[71] This action completely neglected the stakeholder relationship and treated employees in an instrumental way.

"Business is not only an instrumental action in function of economic goals, but also an intrinsically economic/ethical practice."[72] Business ethics is for both profit and for the creation of a good or meaningful life through the relationship of cooperation.[73] Both prioritization and the exclusion of either instrumental or non-instrumental motivations of corporate life is not appropriate. However, Bouckaert considers non-instrumental motivation as primary, and instrumental motivation as secondary.[74] Moreover,

68 Bouckaert, "Spirituality and Rationality," 20–23.

69 Bouckaert, "Spirituality and Rationality," 20.

70 Renault was a French car company. This company has very good ethical programs for the participation and decision-making process. However, when it was confronted with the crisis of long-term profitability, it forgot about ethics and decided to close this firm without considering the thousands of employees who work in the firm. Here, we see how business ethics is sub-ordinated to the profit-maximization interests of shareholders. Cf. Bouckaert, "Spirituality and Rationality," 20. See also Luk Bouckaert, "Spirituality in Economics," in *Spirituality as a Public Good*, eds. Luk Bouckaert and Laszlo Zsolnai (Antwerp: Garant, 2007): 18.

71 Bouckaert, "Spirituality and Rationality," 20.

72 Verstraeten, "Business Leaders to Humanize the World of Business," 112.

73 Verstraeten, "Business Leaders to Humanize the World of Business," 112.

74 Bouckaert, "Spirituality and Rationality," 21.

according to some studies,[75] rational or instrumental and non-instrumental motivations are complementary. If a company has a strong ethical atmosphere, then it generally helps to have a good reputation and profit. Therefore, the ethical significance becomes considerate. The critical remark of Verstraeten is an important observation. "The authors of these optimistic studies do not show to what extent the link can be interpreted as a causal link. It is often unclear to what extent other factors may play a part."[76] Similarly, Bouckaert states that the instrumental use of business ethics converts our aims from good ethics to good business. Gradually, we begin to equate good ethics with good business; the result is that "business ethics loses its intrinsic stance and its potential to criticize opportunistic tendencies within business."[77]

Furthermore, the institutionalization of ethics[78] in the corporate world underestimates the importance of the personal integrity of managers and employees in corporate ethics. Through institutionalization of ethics, sometimes a company may construct an ethical mask for its own selfish interests.[79] That is why I already mentioned that the motivation of the implementation of ethics is crucial within the corporate world. Moreover, the fundamental thinking patterns of managers and employees contribute to maintaining legitimate activity in the midst of tension between ethics and economics.[80]

The instrumentalization and institutionalization of business ethics prevents the possibility of a personalist approach in business ethics that would include personal integrity and moral imagination of managers and employees. The possibility of instrumentalization is high within corporate integrity theories because it rests upon corporate codes, structures, and cultures. The observation of Madhumita Chatterji is important in this regard. She states that "all rules, codes, systems, and processes can only achieve the basic minimum and not excellence. Therefore, an effort should be to move beyond the norms in a positive direction toward excellence

75 Shigehisa Tsuchiya, "Utility Deregulation and Business Ethics: More Openness through Gaming/Simulation," *Simulation & Gaming* 36, no. 1 (2005): 114–133.

76 Verstraeten, "Business Leaders to Humanize the World of Business," 112.

77 Luk Bouckaert, "Doing Business Ethics in Europe: Before and after the Financial Crisis," in *Imagine Europe: The Search for European Identity and Spirituality*, eds. Luk Bouckaert and Jochanan Eynikel (Antwerpen: Garant, 2009): 82.

78 The term "institutionalizing ethics" denotes incorporating ethics in firms' day-to-day functioning through formal codes, policies, mission, etc. Cf. John Tsalikis and David Fritzsche, "Business Ethics: A Literature Review with a Focus on Marketing Ethics," *Journal of Business Ethics* 8, no. 9 (1989): 701.

79 Verstraeten, "Business Leaders to Humanize the World of Business," 112.

80 Peter Ulrich and Ulrich Thielemann, "How Do Managers Think About Market Economies and Morality? Empirical Enquiries into Business-Ethical Thinking Patterns," *Journal of Business Ethics* 12, no. 11 (1993): 880.

and perfection."[81] In order to move toward a perfect business conduct and overcome the possibility of instrumentalization, I, therefore, propose the inclusion of the personal integrity of managers and employees along with corporate integrity theories.

1.3 The Holistic Christian Perspective of Business Ethics

The compliance-based approach to business ethics reduces business ethics to role integrity but business ethics requires something more. Focusing unilaterally on role integrity neglects issues of business such as conflicts between different roles of conduct and complex institutional contexts. In order to have a holistic perspective of business ethics, one must see the work of managers and employees as a vocation or calling[82] and not as an automatic role performance. However, taken alone, this is insufficient since referring to "engaging business activities as a morally justifiable vocation"[83] can be misleading in so far as managerial rationality may make use of the concept of vocation from an instrumental perspective.[84]

The terms "calling" or "vocation" have a religious root.[85] The word vocation comes from the Latin word *vocare,* meaning to call. Vocation always shows the relationship between one who calls and one who is being called. From a biblical perspective, God is the caller. Each calling demands a response.[86] The word *beruf* in German refers to calling as well as profession. The Lutheran tradition sees profession as a means to praise God.[87] Business people including managers and employees, have a specific vocation or

[81] Madhumita Chatterji, "Humanizing the Economic Man," in *Spiritual Humanism and Economic Wisdom*, eds. Hendrik Opdebeeck and Laszlo Zsolnai (Antwerpen: Garant, 2011): 97.

[82] Work fulfills three basic needs of human beings such as "surviving and fulfilling economic needs, cultural, and artistic creation associated with psychological activities and finally cooperation that characterizes social and political relations. As result, in any way that it can be considered, the category of labour represents a vast and complex field of investigation." Cf. Agamenon R. E. Oliveira, *A History of the Work Concept: From Physics to Economics* (Dordrecht: Springer, 2014): 10–11. In this section, we try to present a holistic view of work from a Christian point of view.

[83] Michael Novak, *Business as a Calling: Work and the Examined Life* (New York: The Free Press, 1996): 34–40. See also Gregory Wolcott, "The New (Old) Case for the Ethics of Business," *Journal of Business Ethics* 132, no. 1 (2015): 130.

[84] Johan Verstraeten, "How Faith Makes a Difference: Business as a Calling or the Calling of Christians in Business," *Estudios Empresariales* 113, no. 3 (2003): 58.

[85] In the Bible, we can see the term 'calling' means to ensure the special mission to the people. It is clear from the interpretation of Max Weber. He states, "The only way of living acceptably to God was not to surpass worldly morality in monastic asceticism, but solely through the fulfillment of the obligations imposed upon the individual by his position in the world. That was his calling." Cf. Max Weber, *The Protestant Ethic and the Spirit of Capitalism* (London: Taylor & Francis e-Library, 2005): 40.

[86] Shirley J. Roels, "The Christian Calling to Business Life," *Theology Today* 60, no. 3 (2003): 358.

[87] Verstraeten, "Business as a Calling," 56–60.

calling. This vocation is not only for profit making. It is evident that "many businesses have already brought forth marvellous innovations that have cured disease, brought people closer together through technology and created prosperity in countless ways."[88] However, it is a fact that "this century has also brought business scandals and serious economic disturbances, and an erosion of trust in business organisations and in free-market institutions generally."[89] Therefore, from a Christian perspective, it is important to analyze vocation or calling of business leaders, with the use of which a holistic view of business ethics shall be presented.

Bryan J. Dik and Ryan D. Duffy formulate a clear difference for both calling and vocation. Both calling and vocation indicate an approach to one's particular life role with a sense to demonstrate the purpose and meaningfulness of one's life role. Moreover, both the "calling" and "vocation" approach to one's life role give differently focused values and goals as the core source of the motivation to do something. However, the inspiration to approach work is different in "calling" and "vocation."[90] According to Dik and Duffy, "Individuals with callings and vocations connect their work to an overall sense of purpose and meaningfulness toward other-oriented ends, but only individuals with callings perceive the impetus to approach work in this manner as originating from a source external to the self."[91] This external source can be God, a family legacy, or a pressing societal need, world peace, environmentalism, education, or public health. This means that the external source can be religious or secular.[92] However, vocation is inspired by purely personal internal reasons.[93] The action and mission orientation of the calling and vocation is important.[94] Therefore, A.R. Elangovan et al. define calling as "a course of action in pursuit of pro-social intentions embodying the convergence of an individual's sense of what he or she would like to do, should do, and actually does."[95]

Calling and vocation encompass all areas of legitimate work. Moreover, every person has the potential to have a calling or vocation. Human

88 Pontifical Council for Justice and Peace, "Vocation of the Business Leader: A Reflection," 4, accessed December 10, 2015, http://www.pcgp.it/dati/2012-05/04-999999/Vocation%20ENG2.pdf.

89 Peace, "Vocation of the Business Leader: A Reflection," 4.

90 Bryan J. Dik and Ryan D. Duffy, "Calling and Vocation at Work: Definitions and Prospects for Research and Practice," *The Counseling Psychologist* 37, no. 3 (2009): 426–428. See also Bryan J. Dik and Ryan D. Duffy, "Calling and Vocation in Career Counseling: Recommendations for Promoting Meaningful Work," *Professional Psychology: Research and Practice* 40, no. 6 (2009): 625.

91 Dik and Duffy, "Calling and Vocation at Work," 428.

92 A. R. Elangovan, Craig C. Pinder, and Murdith McLean, "Callings and Organizational Behavior," *Journal of Vocational Behavior* 76, no. 3 (2010): 430.

93 Dik and Duffy, "Calling and Vocation in Career Counseling," 625.

94 Elangovan, Pinder, and McLean, "Callings and Organizational Behavior," 430.

95 Elangovan, Pinder, and McLean, "Callings and Organizational Behavior," 430.

beings are "meaning-making organisms" and they contrast meaning for every life experience.[96] Furthermore, "Calling and vocation can be seen as encompassing a process that can include making a career choice but extends beyond choice behavior to include the question of how a career, once chosen, might be pursued in a manner that connects work activities to one's overall sense of purpose and meaningfulness toward 'other-oriented' or pro-social ends."[97] It is important to examine how it is possible for people to be different from other than capitalist managerial rationality in the contexts of business. When we consider business, it is generally not a field dominated by rationality but collective human interactions leading to business. These interactions are between individuals and business structures.[98] Furthermore, the innovative interaction of individuals reshapes business structures and contexts.[99] Prof. Verstreten rightly observes that through the interaction of individual people in business, they can reinterpret the story of business and thus give it meaning.[100]

Religious communities have access to different interpretations, which are older than the horizon of managerial instrumental rationality. The religious horizon of interpretation helps managers and employees to "discover ethical and meta-ethical perspectives" that can go beyond the narrow instrumental rationality and problem solving. A religious horizon of interpretation brings "innovative new perspectives."[101] This horizon of interpretation can also be understood from the perspective of narrative ethics as it is obvious that "narrative can link the past with the future by giving a sense of continuity to an ever-changing story of the self."[102]

With regard to Christian members of the business community, Verstraeten proposes a "narrative" aspect of Christian calling in business. Christian morality is not about abstract principles but needs to be understood in concrete narrative contexts. A clear example is the commandment of love in the narrative context of the parable of the Good Samaritan whereby the narrative of the story and the way by which action gives new insights to the reader and listener were important.[103] Moreover, biblical passages, stories, and messages of the Christian community lead to a change in the reader, that is, a new way of being and acting that they

96 Dik and Duffy, "Calling and Vocation at Work," 428–430.

97 Dik and Duffy, "Calling and Vocation at Work," 429.

98 Robert Bellah, *The Good Society* (New York: Knopf, 1992): 11–12. I have taken this view of the author from the following source. Cf. Verstraeten, "Business as a Calling," 3.

99 Verstraeten, "Business as a Calling," 3.

100 Verstraeten, "Business as a Calling," 4.

101 Verstraeten, "Business as a Calling," 4.

102 David Rasmussen, "Rethinking Subjectivity: Narrative Identity and the Self," in *Ricoeur as Another: The Ethics of Subjectivity*, eds. Richard A. Cohen and James L. Marsh (Albany: State University of New York, 2002): 62.

103 Verstraeten, "Business as a Calling," 9–10.

develop. A biblical exhortation can give fundamental life direction to the reader.[104] Furthermore, "Reading stories creates the possibility for developing an imaginative space for experiments of thought in which one's moral judgment can exercise itself in a hypothetical way."[105] Through the process of moral imagination,[106] we get an integration of a person's life as a whole (one's being) and his/her decisions in particular contexts, which they can later make with the influence of the read materials. Therefore, the imaginative solutions and possibilities of particular businesses will be the reflection of one's core being, which is formed by biblical texts or stories. At the same time, each decision has to be examined from the narrative whole of the person and the business community because the business community has different narratives, which give the possibility to look at business life in a completely new and better way as it goes beyond instrumental rationality.

In narrative ethics, there is no contradiction between one's being and doing. The alignment between one's being, values, and corporate decisions, means that actions provide meaning to one's life.[107] This perspective brings the person to work more prepared and focused because of the imaginative impact of stories and moreover, there is a connection between the moral self and the consequences of a person's professional activities. Indeed, "this integration of the body, mind, heart, and spirit promotes wholeness rather than fragmentation of self so often experienced by dispirited employees."[108]

Fragmentation of the self in the workplace is one of the challenges that come from the absolutization of the compliance-based approach in corporate ethics. Due to fragmentation in work life, "Even people with excellent professional or technical educations can find themselves driven by an ethic of self-interest that ignores the meaningful and rich concept of vocation and focuses solely on the limited and ultimately meaningless concept of career."[109] MacIntyre states that modern society fails to confront the challenges of compartmentalization, instead we encourage this to happen.[110] A corporate integrity theory, which is going in the line of absolutization

104 Verstraeten, "Business as a Calling," 9–14.

105 Verstraeten, "Business as a Calling," 15.

106 A detailed analysis of the role of moral imagination in business ethics will be given at the end of this chapter.

107 Susan Cartwright and Nicola Holmes, "The Meaning of Work: The Challenge of Regaining Employee Engagement and Reducing Cynicism," *Human Resource Management Review* 16 (2006): 16, no. 2 (2006): 204.

108 Val M. Kinjerski and Berna J. Skrypnek, "Defining Spirit at Work: Finding Common Ground," *Journal of Organizational Change Management* 17, no. 1 (2004): 32–33.

109 Michael J. Naughton, "Business as a Calling: Overcoming the Divided Life," 2, accessed December 10, 2015, http://www.stthomas.edu/media/catholicstudies/center/ryan/publications/publicationpdfs/businessasacallingpdf/I.pdf.

110 Alasdiar MacIntyre, *Whose Justice Which Rationality* (Notre Dame: University of Notre Dame Press, 1998): 397–398.

of the compliance-based approach, encourages the fragmentation of self in corporate life because of the negligence of personal integrity of managers and employees in corporate life. As a result, "our working lives spawn inner division and conflict, our search for happiness beyond the transitory satisfactions of 'success' must fail."[111] Moreover, ethics is not only a simple obedience to moral norms but also "the result of a more spontaneous and creative process in which people are moved by a re-productive and productive imagination."[112] Therefore, it is necessary to incorporate personal integrity in corporate integrity theories in order to have a comprehensive business ethics based on the hypothesis of a personalist approach to corporate integrity.

1.4 Lack of an Absolute Moral Theory

As elaborated earlier, three corporate ethics are related to three types of relationships and interactions in corporations. There are situations that create conflicts of interest between employees and the corporation and stakeholders. The compliance-based approach is not an absolute and perfect solution to solve this. Moreover, there is no absolute moral theory or codes of conduct to apply to each conflicting situation of corporate life. Indeed, a code of conduct alone is insufficient because codes of conduct are not able to incorporate different contexts and circumstances in which corporate interactions take place.[113] As articulated earlier, it is evident that corporate integrity should incorporate the personal integrity of managers and employees along with codes of conduct.

2 Foundation for a Personalist Approach to Corporate Integrity

In this section, I deal with the personalistic economics view of Luk Bouckaert in a concrete way. I do not intend to give a detailed description of the history of personalism[114] but I shall elaborate on the personalistic

111 Naughton, "Business as a Calling," 4.

112 Verstraeten, "Business as a Calling," 15.

113 Mollie Painter-Morland, "Triple Bottom-Line Reporting as Social Grammar: Integrating Corporate Social Responsibility and Corporate Codes of Conduct," *Business Ethics: A European Review* 15, no. 4 (2006): 353.

114 The origin of personalism can be traced back to philosophers like Plato and Plotinus. Based on the study of Albert C. Knudson (Boston University), Johan De Tavernier states that "significant for personalism is Plato's presentation of the logical, the ideal, and the self-active as the true being." Cf. Johan De Tavernier, "The Historical Roots of Personalism: From Renouvier's Le Personnalisme, Mounier's Manifeste Au Service Du Personnalisme and Maritain's Humanisme Integral to Janssens' Personne Et Societe.," *Ethical Perspectives* 16, no. 3 (2009): 362. Plotinus stressed the "unique nature of self-conscious being" against immaterial views. Later it was developed through St. Thomas, St. Augustine and other philosophers. There are various schools of thought regarding the personalist view based on how we consider persons, that is, as a subject, as an individual or as a person. According to Alma Acevedo,

economics of Bouckaert. I demonstrate how his views on the economics of personalism stand as the basis for a personalist approach to corporate integrity theory.

"thinkers who consider human beings as subjects (e.g., René Descartes, Immanuel Kant), or as individuals (e.g., Adam Smith, Friedrich von Hayek, Abraham Maslow), espouse what may be referred to as a non-personalistic humanism; those who consider them as persons, a personalistic humanism." Cf. Alma Acevedo, "Personalist Business Ethics and Humanistic Management: Insights from Jacques Maritain," *Journal of Business Ethics* 105, no. 2 (2012): 198. St. Augustine is considered as the first personalist. He presented "a more highly developed conception of the unity of the mental life, (2) a new insight into the significance of the will in the life both of God and man, (3) the earliest clear formulation of the great truth that self certainty is more immediate than our knowledge of external world [...], (4) the first clear grasp of the fact that a valid metaphysics must be based on the self-knowledge of the finite personality." Cf. Albert C. Knudson, *The Philosophy of Personalism: A Study in the Metaphysics of Religion* (New York: Kraus Reprint, 1969): 429–430. St. Thomas Aquinas established personal immortality of human beings. He considered person as the unity of mental life and will. He defines person as an "individual substance of rational nature." Cf. Thomas Aquinas, "Summa Theologica," ed. Fathers of English Dominican Province (New York: Benziger Brothers, 1947): 1, 29.4. The contributions of René Descartes and Immanuel Kant for personalism are remarkable. Cf. Knudson, *The Philosophy of Personalism: A Study in the Metaphysics of Religion*, 430–432.

The Personalist movement of the nineteenth century is a reaction to the materialistic and absolutistic views of the eighteenth century regarding life. Against the materialistic views of life, the personalist stressed the value of man as a person, a moral self, with freedom, dignity, and responsibility. In short, personalism is a reaction to the social and intellectual tendencies to treat human as a means and not as an end in itself. Cf. J.A. Mann, "Personalism," in *New Catholic Encyclopedia*, eds. Berard L. Marthaler et al. (New York: Gale, 2003): 152. French philosopher Charles Renouvier (1815–1903) proposed personalism for the first time as a new philosophical system in his book, *Le Personnalism*. His original contribution toward personalism is that the primacy of the individual must be the basis of any community. During the same period, the contribution of Borden Parker Bowne (1847–1910) is also remarkable. His view of personalism is known as Boston Personalism. As far as economic personalism is concerned, the contribution of Emmanuel Mounier (1905–1950) comes first. He blames the primacy of economics, which ignores the person and concentrates only on profit. Personalistic economics gives primacy of persons over economics. Mounier's contribution to personalistic economics is that labor is the center of business activities and not the capital. Jacques Maritain (1882–1973) moves in line with St. Thomas and formulated a view of personalism based on two principles, namely the spiritual value of the human person and the common good. Later, Louis Janssens (1901–2001) propagated personalism. He considered the human person adequately and integrally for moral evaluations. According to Roger Burggraeve, Janssens resolutely affirms "the dignity of the human person." Cf. Tavernier, "The Historical Roots of Personalism," 365. See also Kevin M. Dirksen and Paul Schotsmans, "The Historical Roots of Personalism: Borden Parker Bowne and the Boston Tradition on Personal Identity and the Moral Life," Bijdragen, *International Journal in Philosophy and Theology* 73, no. 4 (2012): 388–400. See also Louis Janssens, "Particular Good and Personalistic Morals," *Ethical Perspectives* 6, no. 1 (1999): 55–59. See also Roger Burggraeve, "The Holistic Personalism of Professor Magister Louis Janssens," *Louvain Studies* 27, no. 1 (2002): 30.

2.1 The Personalistic Economics of Luk Bouckaert

The term personalistic economics "refers to a style of doing economics that does not simply reconstruct the problem of efficient allocation as an individual or collective problem of utility, but initially as a problem of human dignity and social justice."[115] The premises of personalistic economics are different from the premises of mainstream economics. Traditional mainstream economics has four vital premises: (1) The individuals are the core unit of the economy, (2) they act freely in accordance with the interest of the self-regulated economy, (3) they will have a mathematically and principally fixed economic behavior, and (4) they have only instrumental worth. However, the premises of personalistic economics are: (1) The person is the basic unit of the economy, (2) a person acts freely within certain limits and concerns for the common good, (3) although a person's economic behavior is based on reason, sometimes it goes beyond codes of conduct, and (4) a person has a worth beyond instrumentality.[116]

The concepts of a person and of an individual are different. Both persons and individuals reflect the notion of self but the difference lies in how the self is understood and functions within society. In the concept of person, self and reflection are joined while in the concept of individual, both are distinct. A person exists in relation to a community and the world while the use of the concept of an individual presupposes some kind of independence from the entire world.[117] The use of the concept of an individual in economics refers to the dominance of self-interest in economics while the use of the concept of a person denotes an-other centered economics.

Economic agency is crucial in economic affairs. As stated earlier, the economic agency debate goes back to the period of Smith. Although in *The Wealth of Nations,* Smith introduced the individual with self-interest as an economic agent, in his earlier work, *The Theory of Moral Sentiments,* he presents different economic agents who are benevolent, generous, and sympathetic.[118] According to Edward J. O'Boyle and Patrick J. Welch, classical economics goes in line with *The Wealth of Nations* focusing on self-interest and self-advantage and it rejects the benevolent

[115] Luk Bouckaert, "Personalism," in *The Palgrave Handbook of Spirituality and Business,* eds. Luk Bouckaert and Laszlo Zsolnai (Basingstoke: Palgrave Macmillan, 2011): 158.

[116] William. R. Waters, "Social Economics: A Solidarist Perspective," *Review of Social Economy* 46, no. 2 (1998): 115–117. See also Edward J. O'Boyle, "Personalist Economics: Unorthodox and Countercultural," *Review of Social Economy* 59, no. 4 (2001): 368.

[117] Roland Breuer, "Individualism and Personalism," *Ethical Perspectives* 6, no. 1 (1999): 67–69. See also Pavel Chalupnicek, "From an Individual to a Person: What Economy Can Learn from Theology About Human Beings," *Econ Journal Watch* 11, no. 2 (2014): 122.

[118] Adam Smith, *The Wealth of Nations,* vol. 2 (London: J. M. Dent and Sons Ltd., 1964): 13–14. See also Adam Smith, *The Theory of Moral Sentiments* (New York: Arlington House, 1969): 354.

views of *The Theory of Moral Sentiments.*[119] The fundamental difference between traditional mainstream economics and personalistic economics lies in their focus on economic actions. Traditionalist mainstream economics is a narrow and deterministic science, whereas personalistic economics is a "liberal morally based science." According to mainstream economics, economic activities are seen "in terms of the decision-making process and the utility- and profit-maximizing behaviour of the individual. Personalist economists think about economic affairs principally in terms of human material well-being, integral human development, and human perfection."[120]

The system theory[121] of economics is different from personalistic economics in its focus. The ultimate aim of the system theory of economics is the system equilibrium and sustainable growth, which is important from personalist perspective of fair economy and society. System theory places people as external but for personalist persons, they are internal and they also constitute the meaning of the functionality of systems. System theory of economics conceptualizes persons as utility-maximizing actors. Proponents of the personalistic perspective reject this conceptualization.[122]

2.1.1 Background of the Personalistic Economics View of Bouckaert

It is difficult to accurately describe the notions of the personalistic school of economics as it is, like personalism, a broad concept. Bouckaert is considered a strong representative of the approach of personalistic economics.[123] Bouckaert states that, "There is a wide gulf between the economic *philosophy* of the personalists and the mathematical contexts of economic science."[124] He believes that from 1930 onwards, philosophers such as Jacques Maritan and Emmanual Mounier attempted to make a "third way between individualistic capitalism and statist socialism,"[125] based on the personalist view of the human being, an approach seldom

119 Edward J. O'Boyle and Patrick J. Welch, "Tracing the Origins of Personalist Economics to Aristotle and Aquinas," *Forum for Social Economics* (2015): 3, accessed January 8, 2016, http://www.tandfonline.com/doi/pdf/10.1080/07360932.2015.1016083.

120 O'Boyle and Welch, "Tracing the Origins of Personalist Economics to Aristotle and Aquinas," 5.

121 "A system may be defined as any set of two or more interdependent parts that has a relatively high degree of closure, connectivity, and stability." Cf. Allan G. Feldt, "General System Theory," (1986), accessed January 9, 2016, http://www.holisticwisdom.org/hwpages/chapt%202%20-%20GST.htm.

122 Luk Bouckaert, "The Project of a Personalistic Economics," *Ethical Perspectives* 6, no. 1 (1999): 21.

123 Chalupnicek, "From an Individual to a Person," 123.

124 Bouckaert, "The Project of a Personalistic Economics," 20.

125 Individualistic capitalism can be defined as "plain old textbook free enterprise capitalism, featuring individual values, competition between firms in an industry, and little or no government intervention." Cf. Edward M. Gramlich, "A Natural Experiment in Styles

employed by scientific economists.[126] There are attempts to overcome the gap between the personalistic view of human beings and economic rationality.[127] These influenced Bouckaert's thinking. They include the areas of humanistic economics, socio-economics, and moral economics. He interprets these attempts as a movement in line with personalistic economics.[128] Furthermore, by introducing a personalistic economics, he wants to develop a better theory than the above-mentioned attempts and formulate a deeper personalistic economics so that he can overcome the gap between the personalistic view of human beings and economic rationality. In order to understand the implications of Bouckaert's personalistic economics approach, I first distinguish his approach from some similar approaches such as humanistic economics, moral economics, and socio economics.

2.1.1.1 Humanistic Economics

Humanistic economics developed out of the background of humanistic psychology, which advocates considering the behavior of human beings in its totality. According to Abraham H. Maslow, "A human being is simultaneously that which he is and that which he yearns to be."[129] As a result, humans have two types of needs, namely basic needs and self-actualization or growth needs.[130] Maslow's hierarchy of needs points out two types of motivation that make up what he calls the material pole (deficiency needs) and the spiritual pole (growth needs).[131] Similarly, corresponding to the two types of needs and motivational makeup, human beings have two selves, a lower self and a higher self, although both are related to each other.[132] The instinct of the lower self seeks one's own advantage and it is the rationale of capitalist free trade where the "higher self identifies with a common humanity and seeks rationality in objectivity, fairness and

---

of Capitalism: Professional Sports," *Quarterly Review of Economics and Finance* 34, no. 2 (1994): 122. Static socialism refers to an absolute socialistic society.

126 Bouckaert, "The Project of a Personalistic Economics," 20. See also Jacques Maritain and John J. FitzGerald, "The Person and the Common Good," *The Review of Politics* 8, no. 4 (1946): 419–445.

127 Economic rationality refers to the "maximization of exclusively materialist objectives, namely profit by producers and utility by consumers." Milan Zafirovski, "Human Rational Behavior and Economic Rationality," *Electronic Journal of Sociology* (2003), accessed February 18, 2016, http://www.sociology.org/content/vol7.2/02_zafirovski.html.

128 Bouckaert, "The Project of a Personalistic Economics," 20.

129 Abraham H. Maslow, *Toward a Psychology of Being* (New York: Van Nostrand Reinhold, 1968): 160, 176.

130 Maslow, *Toward a Psychology of Being*, 26.

131 Abraham Harold Maslow, *Motivation and Personality* (New York: Harper & Row, 1954): 97–101. See also Mark A. Lutz and Kenneth Lux, *Humanistic Economics: The New Chellenge* (New York: The Bootstrap Press, 1988): 16.

132 Lutz and Lux, *Humanistic Economics*, 17.

truth."[133] The dual self-concept of humanistic psychology helps to break down the narrow and distorted image of economic rationality regarding human beings.[134]

Traditional economic rationality reduces the whole person to self-interest motives. On the contrary, humanistic economics attempts to understand a person entirely in their economic activities by considering the other classes of motives. Humanistic economics seeks to incorporate a complete image of the person in economics. Therefore, humanistic economics puts "the existence of the truth or fairness seeking side" of a human person along with their self-interests side.[135] Mark A. Lutz proposes four prepositions for humanistic welfare economics. First, there is no possibility for a value free welfare economics. Moreover, humanistic economics rejects the possibility of a value reductionist or a value neutral position. Second, there should be a possibility of the existence of objective and absolute social values, which are independent of individual self-interest. Third, the goal of an economy is to achieve the basic needs and dignity of all. The need of satisfaction includes basic needs as well as the higher needs such as self-actualization. Fourth, there should be a possibility for meaningful work in humanistic economics.[136]

Humanistic management is the outcome of humanistic economics. In a broader sense, humanistic management can be explained as a management that is concerned with humanity and its characteristics. According to Domènec Melé, "Humanistic management is understood as management that emphasizes the human condition and is oriented to the development of human virtue, in all its forms, to its fullest extent."[137] Humanistic management holds the individualistic perspective of human beings. The perspective of this management focuses "on the individual or on intra individual properties (e.g., motivations, needs, drives)—and does not address what the human being is or ought to be."[138]

There are three types of approaches to humanistic management. First, the human motivation approach that concentrates on higher productivity. It is not concerned with human beings in their totality. In this approach, economic rationality is purely work focused and management does not concern "investigating what a human being actually is both as an individual and as a social being."[139] The second approach is

[133] Shahbaz Ahmad, "Humanistic Economics Needed to Sustain Society," *Indian Journal of Economics and Development* 1, no. 4 (2013): 98.

[134] Lutz and Lux, *Humanistic Economics*, 18.

[135] Lutz and Lux, *Humanistic Economics*, 18–19.

[136] Lutz and Lux, *Humanistic Economics*, 147–150.

[137] Domènec Melé, "The Challenge of Humanistic Management," *Journal of Business Ethics* 44, no. 1 (2003): 79.

[138] Acevedo, "Personalist Business Ethics," 199.

[139] Melé, "The Challenge of Humanistic Management," 80.

the organizational cultural approach. It is true that organizational culture influences the behavior of employees and managers. This approach of management is attempting to build an ethical organizational culture through vision, mission, codes of conduct, and regulating the behaviors of its members. Although it is an important approach, it nevertheless neglects the importance of the personal integrity and character of employees and managers in the organizational context for an ethical conduct.[140] The third approach is "centered on building up a community of persons embedded with an organizational culture that fosters the character."[141] Based on this approach, human beings are persons. This approach can be called personalistic humanistic management. It allocates equal importance to productivity, community, relationality, and virtues of managers and employees.[142] I believe that Bouckaert lines up with this approach; moreover, his theory of personalistic economics is a guideline for practicing personalistic humanistic management.

2.1.1.2 Socio-Economics

There are various paradigms in the social sciences. The individual is considered as the center of one paradigm and is viewed as an agent and choice maker.[143] This goes in line with the neoclassical paradigm of utilitarianism, rationalism, and individualism. Maximizing individual utility is the primary concern of this paradigm. The above-mentioned utilitarian assumptions are the roots of neoclassical economics.[144] Neoclassical economics accepts methodological individualism.[145]

Socio-economics develops as a reaction to neoclassical economic assumptions. As a reaction to the neoclassical assumption of maximizing one of the individual utilities such as pleasure, happiness, or consumption, socio-economics suggests that people seek two irreducible utilities or sources of valuation, such as pleasure and moral obligation. Neoclassical economists suggest that people make decisions only on a rational basis. Socio-economics states that decisions of people are based on their values, emotions, and reasons. Neoclassical economists hold that the individuals are the first decision-making units, whereas socio-economics holds that "social collectivises are the prime decision-making units." Individual

---

140 Melé, "The Challenge of Humanistic Management," 80–82. See also Acevedo, "Personalist Business Ethics," 199–200.

141 Melé, "The Challenge of Humanistic Management," 82.

142 Melé, "The Challenge of Humanistic Management," 82–85.

143 Amitai Etzioni, "Toward a New Socio-Economic Paradigm," *Socio-Economic Review* 1, no. 1 (2003): 107.

144 Amitai Etzioni, *The Moral Dimension: Toward a New Economics* (New York: Free Press, 1998): 1–21.

145 David Colander, "The Death of Neoclassical Economics," *Journal of the History of Economic Thought* 22, no. 2 (2000): 134–135.

decisions always occur within social contexts. Neoclassical economists treat market as a separate system; a "self-containing system." This is suitable for a perfect competition model.[146] However, socio-economic thinking states that the "economy is a subsystem of a more encompassing society, polity, and culture."[147] It is obvious that the economy or a market system cannot be studied without taking into consideration social, political, and cultural factors. Moreover, social contexts are an integral part of an individual's existence.[148]

Socio-economic thinking perceives the economy as a part of the society. Hence, "The starting point of socio-economic analysis is that the economy is a subsystem of the societal system. Much of what is occurring within the economy is best explained by attributes and processes that occur outside of it."[149] According to socio-economics, no business or economy can neglect its moral obligation to society.[150] Economics or businesses cannot be reduced only to the social realm and what we therefore require is a mixture of social and neoclassical views of business. The practical side of individual and social dimensions of economic activities is well explained in the personalistic economics of Bouckaert.

2.1.1.3 Moral Economics

The concept of moral economics is broad. It was popularized by Edward Palmer Thompson's (1924–1993) research on the eighteenth century England food riots.[151] According to Thompson, food riots of England in the eighteenth century were "grounded upon a consistent traditional view of social norms and obligations, of the proper economic functions of several parties within the community, which, taken together, can be said to constitute the moral economy of the poor."[152] Following Thompson, various researchers studied the concerns of the moral economy, that is, the interplay between the traditional capitalist economic perspectives and various "protest movements or alternative economic traditions."[153] In general, the concept of moral economy consists of: "(a) A set of moral or values-based attitudes or beliefs concerning economic agents, practices, or structures

---

146 Etzioni, *The Moral Dimension: Toward a New Economics*, 4–5. See also Milan Zafirovski, "Reconsidering Equilibrium: A Socio-Economic Perspective," *Journal of Socio-Economics* 31 (2002): 559–579.

147 Etzioni, *The Moral Dimension: Toward a New Economics*, 4–5.

148 Etzioni, *The Moral Dimension: Toward a New Economics*, 5.

149 Etzioni, "Toward a New Socio-Economic Paradigm," 110.

150 Etzioni, "Toward a New Socio-Economic Paradigm," 111.

151 Edward Palmer Thompson, "The Moral Economy of the English Crowd in the Eighteenth Century," *Past & Present* 50, no. 2 (1971): 76–136. See also Joakim Sandberg, "Moral Economy and Normative Ethics," *Journal of Global Ethics* 11, no. 2 (2015): 176.

152 Thompson, "The Moral Economy of the English Crowd," 79.

153 Sandberg, "Moral Economy and Normative Ethics," 176.

that are shared by a certain population or group, and (b) the actualization or institutionalization of these attitudes in a certain social practice or structure, common tradition, or general 'way of life' of the population."[154]

The moral economics tradition upholds certain fundamental criteria for economic activities, such as the "enhancement of human life, human dignity, and human rights."[155] Moral economics criticizes the neoclassical economic position of the maximization of wealth as the aim of economic activity. It holds that a good society and the well-being of the other must also have a space in economic activities.[156] According to a moral economic perspective, "a business must in its decisions actively address the issue of the wealth effects of its actions. The firm may not ethically rely only on its wealth creating effects to satisfy its moral imperative. It is not enough, for example, for a business firm to pay minimum wages to its workers if the minimum wage does not constitute a living wage."[157] Moral economic thinking rejects instrumental economic rationality. Moral economy fails to respond accurately to how one can engage in an economic activity in accordance with its fundamental criteria. The personalistic economics of Bouckaert goes further by including practical steps that can be used in the implementation of moral economy.

2.2 The Basic Personalistic Economics Assumptions of Bouckaert

Traditionally, personalistic economics does not have a standard recognized set of assumptions because it is not a school. Most of the personalistic assumptions are vague and intuitive. Therefore, Bouckaert proposes four basic assumptions for a personalistic economics view. At least two of the basic assumptions must be fulfilled in order to represent personalistic economics. The fundamental aim of the basic assumptions is to defend a human being against all kinds of unreasonable economic instrumentalizations. In other words, personalistic economics as a normative economics attempts to reconstruct the problem of human dignity and social justice in economic life.[158] According to Bouckaert, the basic assumptions must have two bases: (1) Basic assumptions must go in line with the categorical imperative of Immanuel Kant; and (2) Assumptions must be the "expression of recognizable and effective historical dynamics."[159] In the following

[154] Sandberg, "Moral Economy and Normative Ethics," 177.

[155] John Kohls and Sandra L. Christensen, "The Business Responsibility for Wealth Distribution in a Globalized Political-Economy: Merging Moral Economics and Catholic Social Teaching," *Journal of Business Ethics* 35, no. 3 (2002): 225. See also H.M. Burdenski and D.H. Dunson, "Acquiring Economic Justice for All: An Ongoing Struggle," *Journal of Business Ethics* 20, no. 2 (1999): 94.

[156] Kohls and Christensen, "The Business Responsibility for Wealth Distribution," 225.

[157] Kohls and Christensen, "The Business Responsibility for Wealth Distribution," 225.

[158] Bouckaert, "The Project of a Personalistic Economics," 21.

[159] Bouckaert, "The Project of a Personalistic Economics," 22.

section, I shall present the four basic personalistic economics assumptions of Bouckaert.

2.2.1 Priority of Basic Needs Over Subjective Preferences

Basic needs and subjective preferences are different. Basic needs can be defined as the "necessary preconditions for humane functioning in a historically and culturally determined community."[160] Basic needs can also be explained as one's fundamental rights based on one's human dignity.[161] It is worthwhile to note that according to Amartya Sen, rights can be seen as an aim of the economic deals.[162]

Subjective preferences can be explained as person-specific wants, these are determined by personality and social situations. Moreover, "Wants are assumed to be instrumentally rather than intrinsically valuable; if they are not fulfilled, they are not associated with serious impairment, as they are either not linked to a universal need, or to one of many possible ways to fulfill that need."[163] Moreover, preferences are individual-based and sometimes they can transform, intensify, suppress, or obstruct basic needs.[164]

The controversy regarding the basic need approach is that "there is no consensus regarding the content of basic needs."[165] It is obvious that the experience of basic needs depends upon a person's subjective preferences. Although it is true to a certain extent, it does not mean therefore that both basic needs and subjective preferences are equal.[166] There is a tension in neoclassical economics to reduce basic needs to individual preferences: there is no question of needs or wants and everything is a question of desires, which are infinite because there is no end to human desires. However, basic needs are finite and necessary for one's own sustainability. Moreover, basic needs have a natural basis.[167] As Bouckaert states, "They are embedded in human nature and human history and go beyond individual preferences, similar to the way that human rights transcend particular interests."[168]

---

160 Bouckaert, "Personalism," 159.

161 Bouckaert, "The Project of a Personalistic Economics," 23.

162 Amartya Sen, *Resources, Values and Development* (Oxford: Basil Blackwell, 1984): 310–315. See also Amartya Sen, *On Ethics and Economics* (Oxford: Basil Blackwell, 1990): 47–51.

163 Laura Camfield and Monica Guillen-Royo, "Wants, Needs and Satisfaction: A Comparative Study in Thailand and Bangladesh," *Social Indicators Research* 96, no. 2 (2010): 187.

164 Bouckaert, "Personalism," 159.

165 Bouckaert, "Personalism," 159.

166 Bouckaert, "The Project of a Personalistic Economics," 23. See also Bouckaert, "Personalism," 159.

167 Lutz and Lux, *Humanistic Economics*, 21–23.

168 Bouckaert, "Personalism," 159.

Furthermore, Bouckaert points out that, traditionally, personalistic economics encompasses two economic sectors: the publicly organized sector and the free sector. In the publicly organized sector, people have to do some common service and subsequently are guaranteed a minimum income. Their basic needs are therefore satisfied. In the free sector, production and marketing would be based on free associations and it would satisfy the subjective preference of individuals. This division in economy goes in line with the division of work as labor and as self-expression. Indeed, Bouckaert acknowledges that this proposal never works in its pure form.[169] Moreover, it is worthwhile to note that the credibility and success of the public sector depends upon the personal moral quality of the bureaucrats.

Bouckaert suggests that in the capability approach of Sen, we can see a middle way between subjective preference and objective necessity.[170] While discussing the "evaluative framework of individual welfare," Sen depicts the difference between "functioning" and "capability." According to Sen, "functioning is an achievement of a person: what he or she manages to do or to be. It reflects, as it were, a part of the state of that person."[171] It is indeed different from having goods (commodities) and utility. For example, driving a car has to be different from having a car and being happy regarding the doing of the activity of driving.[172] In short, functioning includes an individual's state of being or activities such as being in good health, being educated, or cycling.[173]

According to Sen, capabilities can be defined as the "various combinations of functioning (beings and doings) he or she can achieve."[174] It is the beings and doings that a person can potentially achieve.[175] It indicates the freedom of a person to choose between various "ways of living."[176] In short, the capability approach has two levels: the realized level (functioning) and the potential or feasible level (capabilities).[177] According to Bouckaert, "capabilities express a person's capacity to fulfill his/her basic needs."[178] In

169 Bouckaert, "The Project of a Personalistic Economics," 24.

170 Bouckaert, "Personalism," 159.

171 Amartya Sen, *Commodities and Capabilities* (Oxford: Elsevier Science Publishers, 1985): 10.

172 Sen, *Commodities and Capabilities*, 10–11.

173 Wiebke Kuklys and Ingrid Robeyns, "Sen's Capability Approach to Welfare Economics," in *Amartya Sen's Capability Approach: Theoretical Insights and Empirical Applications*, ed. Wiebke Kuklys (Berlin: Springer, 2005): 10.

174 Sen, *Commodities and Capabilities*, 14.

175 Kuklys and Robeyns, "Sen's Capability Approach to Welfare Economics," 10.

176 Amartya Sen, "Development as Capability Expansion," in *Readings in Human Development. Concepts, Measures and Policies for a Development Paradigm*, eds. Sakiko Fukuda-Parr and A.K. Shiva Kumar (Oxford: Oxford University Press, 2003): 5.

177 Kuklys and Robeyns, "Sen's Capability Approach to Welfare Economics," 12.

178 Bouckaert, "The Project of a Personalistic Economics," 23.

this context, the most important thing is not only the possibility to live freely and autonomously, but also to have the resources and opportunities to achieve one's capabilities. Moreover, quality of life or merit of the economic activity should not be measured in accordance with the satisfaction of subjective preferences or happiness. It must be measured in accordance with the achievement of capabilities.[179]

Furthermore, like other personalists, Bouckaert states that desire for transcendental value is unique to human beings. According to Bouckaert, the total "development of a human person presupposes a balanced ordering of material, social, and metaphysical needs."[180] As seen before, it is based upon Maslow's distinction between lower needs and higher needs.[181] The main criticism regarding Maslow's distinction between lower and higher needs is that the internal dialectic between such needs is not mapped well.[182] Although personalistic economics gives priority to basic needs, the aim of personalistic economics is the "overall development of a human person." Moreover, material and social needs are the first precondition to go beyond.[183]

2.2.2 Priority of Commitment and Meaning over Self-interest

Commitment and meaning in economic activities and decisions are prominent assumptions in the personalistic economic thinking of Bouckaert. They are different from narrowly focused economic assumptions based on self-interest.[184] As we have already seen, thinking in terms of meaning in economic activity is much more powerful than calculative economic thinking. Calculative rationality of economic behavior is restricted to efficiency. If the efficiency is the criterion for economic behavior, then there is no room for meaningful creation. According to Bouckaert, the reflection of meaning in economics is always related to the formation of the identity of the person or a company. Since the formation of an identity is a future oriented event, there should be sufficient room for moral imagination and individual creativity in economic decisions and activities. Moreover, meaningful creation in economic activities is always confronted with conflicts between material and immaterial values. In such situations, the making of a decision is a matter of prioritizing preferences, which depends

---

179 M.A Verkerk, J. J. V. Busschbach, and E. D. Karssing, "Health-Related Quality of Life Research and the Capability Approach of Amartya Sen," *Quality of Life Research* 10, no. 1 (2001): 52.

180 Bouckaert, "The Project of a Personalistic Economics," 24.

181 Maslow, *Motivation and Personality*, 97–104.

182 Bouckaert, "The Project of a Personalistic Economics," 25.

183 Bouckaert, "The Project of a Personalistic Economics," 25.

184 Bouckaert, "Personalism," 159–160.

upon the value system of the decision makers. Such choice is not based on cost-benefit analysis but on commitment to one's core values.[185]

Generally, commitment is explained as "a state in which a person has passed some 'point of no return' in some course of action and must go forward due to the costs of backing out, even when going forward no longer seems like the best choice."[186] There are two types of approaches to commitment: attitudinal and behavioral. In the attitudinal approach, commitment is the result of some experience and personal characteristics that create positive feelings and as a result, a person decides to make a commitment. Similarly, the behavioral approach to commitment indicates that "a person attains a state or position of commitment as a result of engaging in committing behaviors—behaviors that, in effect, make it costly to subsequently reverse a position or disengage from some line of activity."[187]

Commitment is different from sympathy, however. Sen makes this clear by the following example: "If the knowledge of torture of others makes you sick, it is a case of sympathy; if it does not make you feel personally worse off, but you think it is wrong and you are ready to do something to stop it, it is a case of commitment."[188] It is important to note that action based on sympathy moves toward the fulfillment and satisfaction of one's own self-interests or utility. For instance, suppose the welfare of a person is psychologically dependent upon another's welfare, then it is a matter of sympathy or if the person feels pain with another's pain and happiness with another's happiness, then it becomes a matter of sympathy.[189] Rational choice also parallels sympathy. The possibility of the influence of instrumental motivation is high within the framework of rational choices.[190] In the case of commitment, there is no instrumental motivation as such because "commitment is in terms of a person choosing an act that he/she believes will yield a lower level of personal welfare to him/her than an alternative that is also available to him/her."[191]

Experimental economics and economic psychology indicate that social motivation has a vital role to play in economic behavior. Social motivations are based on inequity aversion, reciprocal fairness, and pure

---

185 Bouckaert, "The Project of a Personalistic Economics," 25–26.

186 Randall B. Brown, "Organizational Commitment: Clarifying the Concept and Simplifying the Existing Construct Typology," *Journal of Vocational Behavior* 49, no. 3 (1996): 233.

187 Brown, "Organizational Commitment," 230–231.

188 Amartya K. Sen, "Rational Fools: A Critique of the Behavioral Foundations of Economic Theory," *Philosophy & Public Affairs* 6, no. 4 (1977): 326.

189 Sen, "Rational Fools," 326–328. See also Bouckaert, "The Project of a Personalistic Economics," 26.

190 Bouckaert, "The Project of a Personalistic Economics," 26.

191 Sen, "Rational Fools," 327.

altruism.[192] Inequity aversion indicates that "people are willing to give up some material payoff to move in the direction of more equitable outcomes."[193] Therefore, people are altruistic regarding other persons and they want to increase the material resources of others, when it is below an equitable benchmark. On the contrary, the behavior of people is different if the material resources of others are above the equitable level.[194] Reciprocal fairness indicates that people respond to actions in the same manner as the actions are perceived. It is therefore not based on future benefit. Nevertheless, justice is an underlying principle of both inequity aversion and reciprocal fairness. Pure altruism is unconditional kindness in action.[195] The empirical study of Ernst Fehr and Urs Fischbacher shows that "fairness and reciprocity are important for economics in bilateral negotiations for the functioning of markets and incentives, for the structure of property rights and contracts, and for the laws governing collective action and cooperation."[196] This is because people always care for the well-being of others and it has its relevant consequences exhibited in economics.[197] Based on these insights, Bouckaert states that in economics, "social commitment has a moral priority over selfish behaviour."[198]

The motivation behind a social commitment is not instrumental. Bouckaert writes, "commitment arises through a non-instrumental attachment to something that appears as intrinsically meaningful."[199] A true artist creates work not for the satisfaction of personal preferences, but for the sake of artistic work itself. In this context, we do not find any possibility for instrumental motivation. The order of preferences and choices of an artist, non-artist, and a mystic will be different.[200] It is clear that our attachments and who we are, what we want, and what we value also determine our preferences or choices.[201] Therefore, according to Bouckaert, the distinctiveness of the commitment lies in the fact that it is an action based on non-instrumental attachment. Moreover, it is a way of being and expressing of one's own identity in a selfless manner.[202]

---

192 Ernst Fehr and Urs Fischbacher, "Why Social Preferences Matter—the Impact of Non-Selfish Motives on Competition, Cooperation and Incentives," *The Economic Journal* 112, no. 478 (2002): C2–C5. See also Bouckaert, "Personalism," 160.

193 Ernst Fehr and Klaus M. Schmidt, "A Theory of Fairness, Competition, and Cooperation," *The Quarterly Journal of Economics* 114, no. 3 (1999): 819.

194 Fehr and Fischbacher, "Why Social Preferences Matter," C3.

195 Fehr and Fischbacher, "Why Social Preferences Matter," C3–C4.

196 Fehr and Fischbacher, "Why Social Preferences Matter," C30.

197 Fehr and Fischbacher, "Why Social Preferences Matter," C31.

198 Bouckaert, "Personalism," 160.

199 Bouckaert, "The Project of a Personalistic Economics," 26.

200 Bouckaert, "Personalism," 160.

201 Robert Cooter and Melvin A. Eisenberg, "Fairness, Character, and Efficiency in Firms," *University of Pennsylvania Law Review* 149, no. 6 (2001): 1730.

202 Bouckaert, "The Project of a Personalistic Economics," 26.

2.2.2.1 Moral Commitment and the Ethical Paradox of Management

The need for moral commitment in business can be explained by the analysis of the ethical paradox of management in business. Opportunism is prevalent in modern economic activity and is based on rational behavior "by which someone tries to turn every opportunity to its own advantage (or to the advantage of his own group), even if this may be costly to other people or harm the common interests."[203]

There are various economic approaches to reduce the tension between individual rationality and public interests. First, economic incentives are the means for making businesses act ethically. It can be in the "form of taxes, subsidies, rewards, and penalties, as economic incentives to induce businesses to behave ethically."[204] For example, pollution taxes would reduce the level of pollution produced by the business activity.[205] Second, governments can regulate on all varieties of subordinate aspects. Third, businesses can have moral self-regulation by codes of conduct or covenants. The underlying question is, whether such regulations are implemented and practiced by businesses in a freely motivated sense of social responsibility or the motivation of an economic advantage or removal of punishment.[206]

Economic rationality may lead managers to use ethics as a managerial tool rather than a moral commitment. If businesses make ethics a managerial tool, then "business ethics become an instrument to manipulate emotions of the people as a means"[207] for attaining organizational materialistic objectives. Bouckaert has rightly pointed out that economic rationality does not formulate a moral commitment in business, rather it boosts opportunistic activities in business. As a result, although some firms have ethics in an organizational context, they are not ethical due to the economic and rational interests in ethics. The theories of efficient

203 Luk Bouckaert, "Reducing Opportunism through Moral Commitment: The Ethical Paradox of Management," in *Moral Leadership in Action*, ed. Heidi von Weltzein Hoivik (Cheltenham: Edward Elgar, 2002): 84.

204 Praveen Kulshreshtha, "Business Ethics Versus Economic Incentives: Contemporary Issues and Dilemmas," *Journal of Business Ethics* 60, no. 4 (2005): 396.

205 Kulshreshtha, "Business Ethics Versus Economic Incentives," 396.

206 Bouckaert, "Reducing Opportunism," 84–85.

207 Bouckaert, "Reducing Opportunism," 84–86. See also Francis Sejersted, "Managers and Consultants as Manipulators: Reflections on the Suspension of Ethics," *Business Ethics Quarterly* 6, no. 1 (1996): 67–86.

contracting,[208] game theory,[209] transaction cost theory,[210] and human resource management theory[211] can cure the symptoms of opportunistic behavior. However, these theories automatically strengthen the root cause of it, i.e. the economic rationality because these theories have economic rationality as their basis. As a result, opportunism would return in economic dealings even when organizational ethics are in place, and that is the ethical paradox of management.[212]

As already explained above, if economic rationality is the basis of ethics, then it may lead to the instrumentalization of ethics. Highlighting the instrumental side of ethics is the basis for the ethical paradox of management. As Bouckaert observes, if the prime motivation of ethics in economics is the instrumental side of ethics, it is never acceptable as a primary motive but only as a secondary motive. The primary motive of ethics in business is

---

208 Efficient contract theory indicates that in a competitive market, contracts will help to have an efficient and moderate economic transaction. Although economic rationality can be the prime concern, it can help businesses to be more ethical. Cf. David Emanuel, Jilnaught Wong, and Norman Wong, "Efficient Contracting and Accounting," *Accounting and Finance* 43, no. 2 (2003): 149–166.

209 Game theory is a science, which explains the conflict and cooperation between intelligent rational decision makers. There are two types of game theory namely corporative and non-corporative game theory. Both branches of game theory deal with how individuals interact with each other intelligently to achieve their own goals in corporate and non-corporate ways. Cf. Roger A. McCain, "Commitment and Weakness of Will in Game Theory and Neo-Classical Economics," *The Journal of Socio-Economics* 38, no. 4 (2009): 549–556. See also Alexandre Ziegler, *A Game Theory Analysis of Options: Contributions to the Theory of Financial Intermediation in Continuous Time* (Heidelberg: Springer, 1999): 1–140. The spirit of game theory can reduce the instrumentalization of others because there is a corporative way of decision-making.

210 According to transaction cost theory, firms have to select an organizational structure with the lowest transaction cost for protecting against partner opportunism and to have a better fulfillment of contractual obligations, moreover, "institutional structure leads to higher transactions efficiency." Cf. Chenlung Yanga, John G. Wackerb, and Chwen Sheuc, "What Makes Outsourcing Effective? A Transaction-Cost Economics Analysis," *International Journal of Production Research* 50, no. 16 (2012): 4462–4476.

211 Human resources management theories analyze how to manage people effectively within organizations through policies, strategies, and systems. Human resource practices help managers to make decisions regarding the human capital of the business in a justifiable manner. Cf. Dirk Buyens and Jasmijn Verbrigghe, "Adding Value and HRM Practice: Evidence-Based HR," in *Human Resource Management Practices: Assessing Added Value*, eds. Maike Andresen and Christian Nowak (Heidelberg: Springer, 2015): 15–31. Equality based distributive justice is considered as one of the principles of human resource practices. Such practices would help to reduce the instrumentalization of people within organizations. Cf. David A. Morand and Kimberly K. Merriman, "'Equality Theory' As a Counterbalance to Equity Theory in Human Resource Management," *Journal of Business Ethics* 111, no. 1 (2012): 133–144.

212 Bouckaert, "Reducing Opportunism," 84–96.

"to inspire people by means of an intrinsic moral drive."[213] He suggests that what we require in economic dealings is a moral commitment that is based on the internal relation with oneself and other people, which seems to be a solution to the ethical paradox. In moral commitment, ethics is operative on a relational level and is more intuitive.[214]

Bouckaert used Robert H. Frank's indicators of the moral commitment to move toward the sources of the moral commitment. According to Frank, honesty and long-term reputation are the indicators of a moral commitment.[215] An opportunist attempts to be honest in front of others while using every opportunity to maximize personal gain. However, this is not possible because opportunism itself is dishonest. Frank writes that "in order to appear honest, it may be necessary, or at least very helpful, to be honest."[216] Reputation and opportunistic behavior are not compatible because reputation is the consequence of a person's actions in accordance with ethics or moral sentiments.[217] It is worthwhile to note the observation of Bouckaert that if we just show the indicators, managers can misunderstand moral commitment for honesty or good reputation. He ascertains that although these indicators are important, what we must stress is the sources of inner moral commitment.[218]

2.2.2.2 Sources of Inner Moral Commitment

To move toward sources of moral commitment, Bouckaert made use of the arguments advocated by Henri Bergson regarding the sources of ethics.[219] Bergeson points to social pressure as the first source of ethics. No society or collective can function well without limits on the individual behavior and opportunism of its members. Bergson writes, "It is society that draws up for the individual the program of his daily routine."[220] Social control of individual behavior is through social taboos, collective rules, customs, and so on. Religion reinforces societal ethical perceptions by religious elements such as reward or punishments. He states that "religion does little

---

213 Luk Bouckaert, "From Business Ethics to Business Spirituality: The Socratic Model of Leadership," in *Spirituality and Business: Exploring Possibilities for a New Management Paradigm*, eds. Sharda S. Nandram and Margot Esther Borden (Heidelberg: Springer, 2010): 77.

214 Bouckaert, "Reducing Opportunism," 84–96.

215 Robert H. Frank, *Passions within Reasons: The Strategic Role of the Emotions* (New York: Norton and Company, 1988): 1–93.

216 Frank, *Passions within Reasons*, 18.

217 Frank, *Passions within Reasons*, 91.

218 Bouckaert, "Reducing Opportunism," 86–88.

219 Bouckaert, "Spirituality and Rationality," 21.

220 Henri Bergson, *The Two Sources of Morality and Religion*, trans. R. Ashley Audra and Cloudesley Brereton (Garden: Doubleday and Company, 1956): 19. See also Bouckaert, "Spirituality and Rationality," 21.

more than promise an extension and rectification of human justice by divine justice."[221]

According to Bergson, mysticism is a second source of ethics. Mystics "feel within them something better than themselves, they prove to be great men of action, to the surprise of those for whom mysticism is nothing but visions, and raptures and ecstasies."[222] These mystics have a super-rational power and they show creative moral and religious leadership. They are not satisfied with the existing status quo, so they attempt to have new practices in spiritual and social life.[223] Mystics experience a creative movement, this leads to appropriate attitudes in spiritual and social life. The reality is always mobile, however. Time is the emergence of something new or openness toward something new and not repletion of moments. This mystical movement is related to God or it has an ontological meaning. This relationship with God or inner motion reveals the sharing of the love of God to all humanity. However, it is important to realize that the second source of morality is not religion but mysticism. Moreover, it is not emerging from reason but from an inner self.[224] Greek philosophers, Buddhist monks, and Christian saints are good examples of this notion. Based on Bergson, Bouckaert concludes that rational theory and practices are not the root of moral commitment, rather it is rooted in the dynamic and creative inner movement of the self (mysticism), and this is based on an openness and relatedness toward others.[225] I think this points to the relevance of spirituality for the attainment of moral commitment in the business world.

2.2.2.3 Spirituality and Moral Commitment

The second source of ethics (mysticism) is the root of moral commitment and overlaps with spirituality. Adaptation to new situations and circumstances is a necessity in business because it works in different circumstances and countries. Static ethical rules and values would hinder adaptation. Moreover, conflicting situations and crisis are also part of business. In this situation, we require dynamic ethics rather than static ethics. Along with Bergson, Bouckaert presents spirituality as the root of dynamic ethics.[226] How this is possible shall be explored later. According to Bouckaert, "spirituality is the search for inner identity, connectedness,

221 Bergson, *The Two Sources of Morality and Religion*, 98.

222 Bergson, *The Two Sources of Morality and Religion*, 99.

223 Bouckaert, "Reducing Opportunism," 84–96.

224 Bergson, *The Two Sources of Morality and Religion*, 209–266. See also Bouckaert, "Reducing Opportunism," 90–96.

225 Bouckaert, "Reducing Opportunism," 90–96.

226 Bouckaert, "From Business Ethics to Business Spirituality," 79. See also Bergson, *The Two Sources of Morality and Religion*, 209–266.

and transcendence."[227] More accurately, spirituality is a "personal quest for a transcendent, self-revealing meaning in one's life."[228] The richness of spirituality has to be revealed if we study the masters of human spirituality, that is, "those human beings who have discovered new ways of being connected with their deeper self, with all living beings, and with the sources of life."[229] Based on Bergson, Bouckaert states that it is "moral and religious geniuses/leaders/pioneers, who succeed in developing a new way of life and lifestyle in response to a profound crisis. People then mobilize around this new way of life and, in turn, spread and refine it."[230]

There are different approaches to spirituality. A market approach of spirituality considers it as a private matter and a private good. In this approach, there is a strong separation of state and religion known as liberal pluralism. However, spirituality is also considered a public affair, going beyond liberal pluralism. Spirituality can also be seen as a public affair based on active pluralism, dialogue, and inclusion of others.[231] From an economic perspective, spirituality is an attempt to combine both maximum utility of economic rationality and the relational existence of each human being. The essence of human existence is the relationship to the other. This relational dimension of self cannot be neglected for the sake of shared group interests. Bouckaert writes that, "This spiritual self-understanding is not a matter of abstract philosophical thinking but is instead a feeling of universal love and compassion that gives our lives and actions an inner purpose and drive. It transforms our active and rational ego into a responsible and compassionate self."[232]

Spirituality in business is related to "innovative leadership and entrepreneurship."[233] Innovative behavior is a multifaceted reality. Innovative behavior is related to creativity, which in turn is the formation of ideas, whereas innovation is its implementation. This would mean that innovative behavior includes "idea generation, idea promotion, and idea realization."[234] Both creativity and innovativeness depend upon one's own attachments and dispositions. As seen previously, moral commitments exist when one acts with one's own attachment in relation to others; this must be beyond economic rationality. The role of spirituality is significant

---

227 Bouckaert, "Spirituality in Economics," 14.

228 Luk Bouckaert, "Spirituality as a Public Affair," *Ethical Perspectives* 10, no. 2 (2003): 107.

229 Bouckaert, "Spirituality in Economics," 14.

230 Bouckaert, "From Business Ethics to Business Spirituality," 79.

231 Bouckaert, "Spirituality in Economics," 14–15.

232 Bouckaert, "Spirituality and Rationality," 24.

233 Bouckaert, "From Business Ethics to Business Spirituality," 79.

234 Mark Reuvers et al., "Transformational Leadership and Innovative Work Behaviour: Exploring the Relevance of Gender Differences," *Creativity and Innovation Management* 17, no. 3 (2008): 229.

here in the exercise of the moral commitments. The question is, how does spirituality help in the exercise of innovative behavior and moral commitment? Invoking Socrates, Bouckaert states that there are three stages in attaining a right and creative intuition and decision. First, one should be aware of one's own ignorance. Second, one should "turn inwards; i.e., learning to listen to one's own deeper intuitions, to the deeper layer of one's consciousness that is concerned with the quest for meaning."[235] Third, we should have a Socratic dialogue. Socratic dialogue is more than a transparent communication skill. It is indeed "a learning process in which the participants seek to find an answer to a specific question by asking questions with each other. Both question and answer need to be consistent with the inner convictions and experience of the participants in the dialogue."[236]

The spiritual elements of Socratic dialogue are the participant's openness to each other, mutual willingness to listen, and honesty to ignore one's own interests. Contrary to the instrumental or rational nature of ethics, the "intrinsic or spiritual approach to ethics is characterized by its openness for the 'Other,' be it the otherness of nature or the self-expression of the other people or the transcendence of Ultimate Reality."[237] The intrinsic approach to ethics is always linked with "relationality." However, Bouckaert does not argue that the spiritual approach to ethics would completely make obsolete the instrumental side of ethics. He, however, argues that what we need is an awareness of the tension between instrumental and spiritual motivation of ethics and that we should maintain a balance. He criticizes the current ethics management practices that give primary importance to instrumental motivations and, as a result, substitute economic rationality for true moral commitment. Therefore, he offers "spirituality in economics" as a means to keep a balance between economic rationality and moral commitment, and consequently, help to have a moral commitment in economics.[238]

Van Luijk, however, criticizes these arguments for giving primary importance to spirituality in economics by stating that, doing so is the same as giving primacy to subjective and personal feelings. Consequently, it neglects the importance of social and corporate structure, culture, and other conditions.[239] However, according to Bouckaert, "We already have a very elaborative list of standards of social accountability and an impressive

---

235 Bouckaert, "From Business Ethics to Business Spirituality," 81.

236 Bouckaert, "From Business Ethics to Business Spirituality," 82.

237 Bouckaert, "Spirituality in Economics," 19.

238 Bouckaert, "Spirituality in Economics," 19. It is worthwhile to note that he does not use economics of spirituality but he uses spirituality in economics. Economics of spirituality gives values like trust, loyalty, and connectedness. However, in the end, "it results in the economics as usual, missing the genuine meaning of non-rational, spiritual commitment." Bouckaert, "Spirituality and Rationality," 19.

239 Henk Van Luijk, "Facing the Ethics Management Paradox," in *Interdisciplinary Yearbook for Business Ethics*, ed. László Zsolnai (Oxford: Peter Lang, 2006): 202–204.

body of institutional regulations. Yet, the problem is that we see that all these regulations have a natural drive to develop a strong culture of instrumental rationality. [...] the end is a loss of moral inspiration and imagination or even worse, in a loss of social integrity."[240]

2.2.2.4 Section Summary

Ethical commitment is a personal conviction to act without instrumental motivation. It is the expression of one's own identity or being. In management ethics, we see an ethical paradox; ethics tends to increase the occurrence of managerial economic rationality. More accurately, managers use ethics as a tool for attaining economic rationality. As a result, the harder a company tries to promote non-instrumental ethics, the less likely they are to achieve it. Therefore, we need a moral commitment in economics beyond rules and regulations. Based on Bergson, Bouckaert states that moral commitment is rooted in mysticism, a creative movement of the self in relation to the entire universe, including others. Spirituality in economics has a vital role in the creative movement of the self because it creates relational beings. Moreover, primacy of spirituality in economics helps to maintain a balance between instrumental rationality and non-instrumental rationality in economics or it forms a prime motivation for moral commitment in economics.

2.2.3 Priority of Mutual Trust over Mutual Advantage in the Market

A market can be defined as "any forum, having a minimum stability, where people exchange their goods and services for money on mutually agreed terms."[241] According to the conventional economic approach, the "market is the meeting point of an anonymous group of consumers and providers, where the price mechanism leads to the most efficient production and the distribution of goods and services."[242] There are different views regarding the market in accordance with various ideologies. Libertarians consider the market as "efficient and good," while communists consider it "inefficient and bad." European social democrats view market as "efficient but bad." However, economists John Maynard Keynes and his followers view the market as good but not efficient. According to Keynes, state intervention is necessary for the well-functioning of the markets, otherwise the market will destroy itself. Neoliberalism upholds that the state has to

240 Bouckaert, "Spirituality in Economics," 19. See also Luk Bouckaert, "When More Ethics Create Less Ethics—Some Fruther Clarifications on the Ethics Management Paradox," in *Interdisciplinary Yearbook for Business Ethics*, ed. László Zsolnai (Oxford: Peter Lang, 2006): 215–218.

241 Mathew Illathuparambil, *Business Ethics* (Tiruvalla: Macfast Publications, 2005): 104.

242 Bouckaert, "The Project of a Personalistic Economics," 27.

ensure the primacy of the market force. At the same time, neoliberalism has little to say about what a market is and how it works.[243]

In the late nineteenth century, there was a gradual development in the idea of the market i.e. the emergence of a neoclassical economic view of the market. Accordingly, "The market was understood primarily as a price mechanism, or a way to determine prices through the interplay of demand and supply. In addition, the idea of the market became excessively abstract. The demand-supply schedule includes no legal system, no state, no people, and no social relations. It is truly a hypothetical market."[244] The free market is the basic quality of neoclassical economics. As an attempt to extend the neoclassical economics view, a new institutional economics perspective originated. It was an attempt to insert the institutional content into mainstream economics. According to new institutional economics, "The information available to individuals is incomplete, their mental capacity to process information is limited, their motivation is more complicated and their preferences subjective and less stable than assumed in neoclassical theory."[245] Therefore, the new institutional economics suggests including transaction costs and institutional aspects[246] such as search and information costs, bargaining costs, and cost for enforcing the contract, into the economic analysis of neoclassical economics.[247] Furthermore, in the nineteenth century, markets were viewed as a price mechanism that means that the efficient production of goods and services increase the wealth of nations. Production, distribution, and consumption are major elements constituting a market. According to this view, consumption creates profit and profit again leads to investment, which is the basis for economic growth.[248]

The political view of markets focuses on the observation "that a market can only function when property rights, free competition, and respect for contract are legally regulated and protected."[249]According to Bouckaert,

---

243 John Maynard Keynes, *The General Theory of Employment, Interest and Money* (London: Macmillan, 1967): 340–367. See also Richard Swedberg, "The Market," *Contexts* 6, no. 4 (2007): 64–66. See also Mark Skousen, *The Big Three in Economics: Adam Smith, Karl Marx, and John Maynard Keynes* (New York: M.E.Sharpe, 2007): 133.

244 Swedberg, "The Market," 65.

245 Alirat Olayinka Agboola, "Neoclassical Economics and New Institutional Economics," *Property Management* 33, no. 5 (2015): 417.

246 It is defined as "the rules of the game in a society, or the humanly devised constraints both formal and informal, that shape human interactions. Formal rules [...] comprise written constitutions, statute, common laws, property rights, specific bylaws, etc., while informal constraints are unwritten traditions, customs, taboos, conventions, norms, codes of behaviour, etc., that are put in place to coordinate human interactions." Cf. Agboola, "Neoclassical Economics," 420.

247 Swedberg, "The Market," 65. See also Agboola, "Neoclassical Economics,"

248 Swedberg, "The Market," 65–66.

249 Bouckaert, "The Project of a Personalistic Economics," 27.

one of the main contributions of game theory is that due to the uncertainty of a competitive market, it does not always lead to the best ethically justifiable results and an efficient market. Although the market produces freedom, it is possible that the "market instrumentalizes and individualizes all values in order to maximize an individual's subjective welfare."[250] If everyone determines what each person wants without moral cohesion, as a result, the market can promote opportunistic behaviors.[251] The fundamental question here is, what makes a market efficient? According to Bouckaert, in personalistic economics, cooperation, and mutual trust make a market efficient.[252] Distrust has negative impacts on the political, social, and economic life of people. As far as economic life is concerned, distrust causes the least efficient economic transactions.

In this context, it is worthwhile to note the sociologist James Coleman's use of "social capital," which is necessary for having a good society and efficient economy. Social capital is the ability of the people to work together based on a general aim in a group or within a community order.[253] This ability is crucial in economics as well as in the social life. As Fukuyama observes, "The ability to associate depends, in turn, on the degree to which communities share norms and values and are able to subordinate individual interests to those of large groups. Out of such shared values come trust, and trust as we will see, has a large and measurable economic value."[254] According to Bouckaert, economic institutions can win trust by keeping social reputation and the personal integrity of their members. Both personal integrity of the members and the social reputation of an economic institution would help economic institutions to be more trustworthy in a societal order because these elements create a strong social relationship with all stakeholders.[255]

As seen above, a moral economy is a "system of transactions that are defined as socially desirable (moral) because through them social ties are recognized, and balanced social relationships are maintained."[256] In a moral economy, trust is achieved by sharing a common way of life; this consists of the commitments to fulfill obligations to others. As a result, trust and cooperation among members of the society is achieved. According to

---

250 Bouckaert, "Personalism," 161.

251 Bouckaert, "Personalism," 161.

252 Bouckaert, "The Project of a Personalistic Economics," 27. In the first chapter, I have given the definition and other explanations of the concept of trust.

253 James S. Coleman, "Social Capital in the Creation of Human Capital," *American Journal of Sociology* 94 (1988): S95–S120. See also Francis Fukuyama, *Trust: The Social Virtues and the Creation of Prosperity* (New York: The Free Press, 1995): 10.

254 Fukuyama, *Trust*, 10.

255 Bouckaert, "The Project of a Personalistic Economics," 28.

256 David Cheal, *The Gift Economy* (London: Routledge, 1988): 15.

David Cheal, the primary aim of gifts in business or day-to-day life is to create social relationships and thus promote mutual trust.[257]

Furthermore, the quality of goods and services in the market is determined by the context where the goods and services are produced. If people noticed that the products in the market are the result of exploitation or the destruction of nature, then for many, those products and services would become unattractive and morally objectionable. The context of products and services, therefore, has the potential to determine their value within the marketplace. Therefore, social capital should be free from exploitation in the market. The market is not, as such, against the higher values of social, moral, and spiritual life. However, the freedom that we enjoy in the market would increase the chance of the instrumentalization of all values in the market for subjective preferences.[258] Therefore, trust in market transactions is dependent upon the meaning of the product and services that the market provides.

In personalistic economics, Bouckaert proposes a prime motivational emphasis in market transactions, such as trust and social relationships. Traditionally, a mutually sustainable advantage is considered as the prime motivation in market transactions; this can be applied also to corporate integrity theories.[259] Mutual advantage is a cooperative motivation based on reciprocity. The motivation of mutual advantage is aligned with ongoing cooperative practices.[260] In a mutual advantage scenario, priority is given to the subjective preference of all parties. Bouckaert states that, "When everyone determines his values himself, a lack of moral cohesion can open the way to far reaching opportunistic behavior, which is the threat to a good functioning of a market. Hence, the plea nowadays is for greater moral self-regulation in the market."[261] Therefore, Bouckaert holds the priority of mutual trust over mutual advantage in market functioning.

2.2.4 The Priority of Economic Democracy over Shareholder Capitalism

Personalist economists cannot agree with the shareholder capitalist view that the only aim of a business is to increase shareholder value. Bouckaert states that socially oriented business ethics theories, social contract, and stakeholder views of business[262] help to move the basic orientation of

---

257 Cheal, *The Gift Economy*, 14–16; 121–142.

258 Bouckaert, "The Project of a Personalistic Economics," 28.

259 Kaptein and Wempe, *The Balanced Company*, 258.

260 Robert Sugden, "Mutual Advantage, Conventions and Team Reasoning," *International Review of Economics* 58, no. 1 (2011): 14–20.

261 Bouckaert, "The Project of a Personalistic Economics," 28.

262 We have already given a detailed explanation of social contract and stakeholder views of firms in the second chapter. Therefore, we are not dealing with it in detail in this chapter.

business from the shareholder to a stakeholder perspective. As presented earlier, the view of a company as a social contract helps not only to increase the efficiency of the company but also to incorporate the interests of all stakeholders. However, according to Bouckaert, the contractual agreement does not give an inner motivation to all stakeholders to engage each other and to take the initiative for incorporating the interests of all. The aim of each stakeholder would be to secure their own position, although the company exists as the result of a contract.[263]

Stakeholder management has a vital role in today's capitalist management. There are two different views of stakeholder management: strong and weak. According to the weak stakeholder view, stakeholder interests are taken into consideration by the board of directors of the company without democratic representation of the stakeholders. According to the strong stakeholder theory, stakeholders are full partners of the business. Accordingly, they have the rights and claims of partners. A company is seen as a "community of co-responsible persons."[264] Considering a company as a community would give it the advantage not only to protect and increase the motivation of people to work together in various situations, but also to achieve the economic objectives of the company. Bouckaert critically observes that in this perspective, business ethics can be reduced to a technique for securing human motivation or as a chance to redefine the goals and nature of the firm. According to the personalistic view, business ethics is aligned with the second option. The key idea of the personalistic view of the company becomes highly relevant here, that is, economic democracy.[265]

Generally, democracy is defined as a "form of government in which people (through representatives) govern themselves and freely express their opinions and wishes."[266] This definition shows that there are two main characteristics of democracy. First, in a democracy, people govern themselves; this is exercised by the right to vote. Second, people can express themselves freely. This is possible through public debates and the quality, openness, and accessibility of public debates, which determines the democratic level within a given state. Although the above-mentioned characteristics have a place in democracy, it might nevertheless happen that the people who constitute the minority within a given state become discriminated against or engaged in inhumane activities. In order to overcome this situation, Bouckaert suggests that a democracy has to link with a

---

263 Bouckaert, "The Project of a Personalistic Economics," 29.

264 Bouckaert, "Personalism," 161.

265 Bouckaert, "The Project of a Personalistic Economics," 29–30.

266 Luk Bouckaert, "Economic Democracy as a Social and Spiritual Utopia," in *Respect and Economic Democracy*, eds. Luk Bouckaert and Pasquale Arena (Antwerp: Grant Publishers, 2010): 14.

third principle, adequate "norms about human dignity and human rights." Although the meaning of human dignity does not have a fixed content, respect for people is vital for the successful functioning of a democracy.[267]

The fundamental question is, how can we apply the democratic view to economics or to a company? Applying a democratic view to a business is far from usual business practice, particularly in a capitalist economy. Moreover, there is a gap between economy and democracy. A person who governs employees and workers is not appointed or selected by them, this is usually decided by the board of shareholders. Usually, employees are used to share their expertise and they are not directly involved in the decision-making process. Furthermore, corporate decisions are not the result of a democratic debate. Usually, companies pay attention to human rights and human dignity only when the governing state laws or trade unions, or, more rarely, the public compel them to do so, but this generally occurs following some sort of a tragedy. The market stands for profit and the purchasing power of consumers, and not for individual rights. Moreover, according to some economists, democratic principles are a concern for politics and not for business or economics. From the economic perspective, democratic debates and processes result in higher costs, delays and loss of creativity.[268] According to the scientific view, "The knowledge produced by natural sciences, by hard sciences, can be subjected to two types of discussion only: one concerning the validity of its formulation, resulting from the application of scientific rationality, and another, the consequences of its implementation."[269] As a result, economics can navigate to come up with a solution to economic problems and society has to accept its implementation for its well-being.[270]

According to Bouckaert, however, the fundamental matter in economics is the well-being of humans or human flourishing. Human flourishing cannot be based on material well-being alone, however, but rather calls for a balance between material and spiritual well-being or needs. Spiritual well-being includes the "respect for democratic values such as true freedom for everyone, personal responsibility, and respect for human dignity. If an increase in the satisfaction of material needs lead to a decrease in spiritual well-being, then it is difficult to speak of an improvement in the person's well-being."[271] Bouckaert thinks that when the competency of

---

267 Bouckaert, "Economic Democracy," 14–15.

268 Bouckaert, "Economic Democracy," 15–16.

269 Manuel Couret Branco, "Economics against Democracy," *Review of Radical Political Economics* 44, no. 1 (2012): 28.

270 Branco, "Economics against Democracy," 28.

271 Bouckaert, "Economic Democracy," 16.

stakeholders improves through knowledge, then their involvement in the company would also increase.[272]

It is worthwhile to note that an economic democracy is not a worker's democracy, but rather a balanced participation between all stakeholders in corporate life. However, as part of the wish to move toward economic democracy, "a lot of democratic experiments have been set up, mostly in the form of cooperative associations."[273] Mondragon (Spanish Worker Cooperative Company) is a good example of a worker's democracy.[274] It is a cooperative company established in 1956. Since it is a workers-owned firm, it has advantages over the investment-owned firm. Workers-owned businesses face fewer conflicts between the interests of the workers and the business purposes because the interests of both are aligned.[275] A democratic self-governed company organizes the "principle of delegation, hierarchy, participation, and cooperation" in a different way from a classical shareholder company. The above-mentioned democratic self-governed company operates by virtue of the use of two basic principles; these are the democratic principle and the principle of ownership. Democratic principles work by worker-owners' right to vote and control rights in general meetings. The system, therefore, works similarly with a political democracy. This means that the governed control their governors. The principle of ownership gives each member the right to have a part of the company's share of capital by way of an "individualized internal capital account."[276]

A worker's democracy is in line with the personalistic view of labor, which denotes that the people have more value than the resources. In his Encyclical *Laborem Exercens* (Human Work), Pope John Paul II addresses the priority of labor over capital and its instrumentalization. He states that "excessive bureaucratic centralization, makes the worker feel that he/she is just a cog in a huge machine moved from above, that he/she is a mere production instrument rather than a true subject of work with an initiative of his/her own."[277] Furthermore, while explaining the personalistic view of Mounier, Tavernier states that, "It is not capital but labour that is central to the market economy. The primacy of labour over capital rests on the fact that human work is the one and only agent that is productive in economic

---

272 Bouckaert, "Personalism," 161. See also Bouckaert, "Economic Democracy," 16.

273 Bouckaert, "Personalism," 161.

274 Bouckaert, "Personalism," 161. See also Bouckaert, "Economic Democracy," 20.

275 Henry Hansmann, "When Does Worker Ownership Work? ESOPs, Law Firms, Codetermination, and Economic Democracy," *The Yale Law Journal* 99, no. 8 (1990): 1749–1816.

276 Bouckaert, "Economic Democracy," 21–22.

277 John Paul II, "Laborem Exercens," (1981), accessed 9 March, 2015, http://w2.vatican.va/content/john-paul-ii/en/encyclicals/documents/hf_jp-ii_enc_14091981_laborem-exercens.html.

activity."[278] A worker's democracy legitimizes the central view of the personalist; that labor should not be instrumentalized by capital.[279]

However, Bouckaert's view of the economic democracy of a company must go beyond the worker's democracy. According to him, economic democracy has "many different degrees varying from supervision, voting rights, profit sharing, and co-participation to full self-government."[280] Economic democracy is the active participation of all stakeholders in the day-to-day functioning of a company. In other words, the purpose of an economic democracy is to have "structural and existential participation of all parties involved in determining and attaining the company's goal."[281] However, economic democracy is a multidimensional concept. As explained earlier, democracy has three basic elements; these consist of self-government, open debate, and respect for human rights. Each of these elements is crucial in an economic democracy of a company. Some companies follow some of these basic elements of economic democracy and keep a partial form of economic democracy. Many companies have adopted codes of conduct that protect human rights. This, however, does not mean that they have a democratic economic view in the full sense.[282] That is why Bouckaert presents the view that the Mondragon Company is far from a perfect economic democracy because "not all stakeholders have a voice. Consumers, the local community and the common good have no direct say in the internal decision-making process."[283] Although, as a theory, economic democracy seems to be ideal, the fundamental question is how practical it is.

2.2.4.1 Economic Democracy and Spirituality

Economic democracy is commonly seen as an alternative to Marxist collectivism and bourgeois capitalism. As seen above, there are certain experiments in line with the possibility of economic democracy by the establishment of cooperative associations. Although some like Mondragon survived, most of them failed to serve the purpose. Why did this happen? Bouckaert states that there is a historical resistance to economic democracy.[284]

The presence and absence of resistance to economic democracy is related "to trust or distrust in the human person as a source of creativity and

278 Tavernier, "The Historical Roots of Personalism," 371.

279 Bouckaert, "The Project of a Personalistic Economics," 30.

280 Bouckaert, "The Project of a Personalistic Economics," 30.

281 Bouckaert, "The Project of a Personalistic Economics," 30.

282 Bouckaert, "Economic Democracy," 24.

283 Bouckaert, "Economic Democracy," 24.

284 Luk Bouckaert, "Spirituality and Economic Democracy," in *Spirituality and Ethics in Management*, ed. Laszlo Zsolnai (London: Springer, 2011): 46–47.

otherness. Those who trust the person will see in economic democracy a tool to disclose this unique source. Those who distrust the human being will strive to control the person within the confinements of instrumental rationality and bureaucracy."[285] According to the view of economic democracy, a company is not only a place where goods are bought and sold, but also a place where democratic principles are implemented. Therefore, "the governed appoint and supervise the governors. Mergers are then only possible on the basis of a democratically controlled decision-making process."[286] It is obvious that these democratic principles can be implemented in a company only based on trust and openness.

Trust and openness are fundamental spiritual attitudes based on respect for freedom and otherness because "spirituality is people's multiform search for a deep meaning of life interconnecting them to all living beings and to God or an Ultimate Reality."[287] Since spirituality is other oriented, it is opposite to control and manipulation, and is based on trust and openness. Therefore, traditional management is not much concerned with spirituality because spirituality is a meta-rational and non-manipulative way of dealing with uncertainty and other corporate problems while traditional management is a rational and manipulative way of controlling and dealing with corporate problems. However, modern management theories attempt to incorporate trust, value driven leadership, and the democratic stakeholder in management discourse.[288] As Bouckaert indicates, this trend can have a paradoxical nature as, "The more economic democracy can be sustained by a rational and economic discourse, the more it risks losing its inner spiritual force and driving out the moral attention of the stakeholder as a person."[289]

The movement from a capitalist shareholder to a democratic stakeholder indicates the redistribution of power and income. The fundamental question is, how is this possible or how practical it is. For Marx and many other social reformers, redistribution of power and income cannot be done through spirituality and ethics. Moreover, they believe that it is a new drug or opium for manipulating power conflicts. Bouckaert suggests that there is a new way of using spirituality for the change or establishment of economic democracy. This new way is based on two facts of spirituality. First, spirituality is a non-violent tool and it can be used as a means for the emancipation of the person. Second, spirituality and ethics direct toward

---

285 Bouckaert, "Spirituality and Economic Democracy," 47.

286 Bouckaert, "The Project of a Personalistic Economics," 30.

287 Luk Bouckaert and Laszlo Zsolnai, "Spirituality and Business," in *The Palgrave Handbook of Spirituality and Business*, eds. Luk Bouckaert and Laszlo Zsolnai (Basingstoke: Palgrave Macmillan, 2011): 7.

288 Bouckaert, "Spirituality and Economic Democracy," 47.

289 Bouckaert, "Spirituality and Economic Democracy," 47.

the other with openness and it paves the way for the possibility of moral imagination. If people really have a mystical experience of spirituality in their lives and implement spirituality in business with the right motivation, the transition from capitalist shareholder to a democratic stakeholder is possible.[290]

2.2.5 Personalistic Economics as the Basis for the Personalist Approach to Corporate Integrity

Bouckaert presents four assumptions as a sign of personalistic economics: "The recognition of basic needs, the necessity of commitment, mutual trust as a foundation of the market, and economic democracy as a touchstone for business ethics."[291] These assumptions can be seen and used from different perspectives, however. First, they can be seen as ethical principles, which highlight the intrinsic value of people. On the other hand, they can be used for the instrumental purpose of economics. For instance, more efficient allocation of resources can be attained by satisfying the basic needs of the people. If ethical meaning suppresses economic meaning, moralization of economics would occur. Similarly, presupposing economic meaning suppresses the ethical meaning of economics, and then the instrumentalization of economics would be the outcome. An equal importance has to be given to both economic rationality and ethics. Avoiding one leads to either the loss of ethical meaning of economics or the economic loss of efficiency. A balance between these two is required, however. If we could attain such a balance, this would help to have personalistic economics assumptions in economic decisions and activities. In order to attain a balance between ethical meaning and economic efficiency, Bouckaert suggests that imagination, creativity, and moral initiative are needed. This balance is the rationale of personalistic economics.[292]

The capacity to attain the balance or the use of imagination, creativity, and moral initiative depends upon one's self or fundamental life stance. That is why Bouckaert suggests the necessity of spirituality for the attainment of various personalistic assumptions.[293] For Bouckaert, spirituality refers to "the awareness of being related to other."[294] A spiritual person has the relatedness to the other from the level of being. He writes that, "This spiritual self-understanding is not a matter of abstract philosophical thinking but is instead a feeling of universal love and compassion that gives our lives and actions an inner purpose and drive. It transforms our active and

290 Bouckaert, "Spirituality and Economic Democracy," 47–48.
291 Bouckaert, "The Project of a Personalistic Economics," 30–31.
292 Bouckaert, "The Project of a Personalistic Economics," 31.
293 Bouckaert, "Spirituality and Economic Democracy," 46–47.
294 Bouckaert, "Spirituality and Rationality," 24.

rational ego into a responsible and compassionate self."[295] Spirituality indicates the fundamental stance or core of a person, whether one has a self that is related to the other from the level of being. Therefore, spirituality as openness to others is a source of imagination, creativity, and moral initiative.[296] The role of moral imagination, creativity, and moral initiative shall be discussed in the sections that follow.

Keeping a balance between ethics and economic rationality depends upon the disposition of the person (Being) who deals with it. Bouckaert indicates this idea through the introduction of spirituality in ethics and two sources of ethics. He also believes that ethics does not just follow rules and regulations but rather can create "[...] and inspire ideals for future generations."[297]I have already discussed that conflict of interests such as that between employees and corporations, between corporation and stakeholders, and among employees, is the real problem in business structures. In this context, the decision depends upon the moral integrity of the person who deals with it because sometimes conflicting interests can be equally important. Similarly, I think that keeping a balance between the ethical meaning of economics and economic rationality depends on the moral integrity of the individuals who truly make the decisions. In other words, the spirituality of the person or moral imagination or creativity and moral initiative of a person would help to balance ethics and economic rationality.

However, the corporate integrity approach is predominantly in line with economic rationality because it is interpreted as the sum total of the corporate culture and structure along with the codes of conduct. In this case, the possibility of the instrumentalization of ethics and people is high because there is no sufficient space for moral imagination or creativity and the moral initiative of a person in corporate integrity theories. Furthermore, I pointed out that corporate integrity theories neglect the individual integrity of managers and employees who are really the acting persons within corporations. Therefore, the possibility of instrumentalization of managers and employees by the business is relatively high. On the contrary, the ethics and various contextual factors of each company can be used by managers and employees from an instrumental purpose, that is, to satisfy one's selfish interests. Moral imagination, personal creativity, and moral initiative of a person depend on the personal integrity of the person. Therefore, based on the personalistic economics view, I propose a personalist approach to corporate integrity theories, which gives sufficient space for the personal integrity of managers and employees in corporate life. By introducing a personalist approach to corporate integrity theories,

295 Bouckaert, "Spirituality and Rationality," 24.

296 Bouckaert, "Spirituality and Economic Democracy," 48.

297 Bouckaert, "Economic Democracy," 27.

I hope to achieve more personalistic economics assumptions in corporate decisions and activities.

Conclusion

In this chapter, I proposed the reasons and foundations for a personalist approach to corporate integrity. There are five ethical reasons for a personalist approach to corporate integrity theory: (1) Ethics promotes the good life or human happiness, therefore, in order to have a good life, managers and employees require not only codes of conduct but also their own values and ends in organizational life, which in turn gives more meaning to their work; (2) The real problem in business is the conflict of interests that arise. When conflicts of interest arise, corporate rules and behavioral principles are insufficient for moral reasoning because a code of conduct cannot cover all issues within the business arena. Therefore, managers have to take into account each context, different ethical theories, and codes of corporations in order to arrive at a right decision in conflicting situations; (3) Although there are different moral theories, their application does not lead ethicists to an absolutely certain conclusion because there is no comprehensive moral theory, which determines or outweighs all others; (4) If we do not attribute enough importance to a person who is an actor in economic activity, the codes of conduct of companies can instrumentalize employees and managers for the benefit of the company; (5) Finally, if corporate integrity does not allow sufficient room for personal integrity, then it consequently neglects the link between the moral acts of managers and employees and the moral quality of their lives.

Due to the above-mentioned ethical reasons, I have argued for a person centered view of corporate ethical life based on the personalistic economics view of Bouckaert. According to Bouckaert, "the 'personalistic economics' refers to a normative economics […], which is based on human dignity and social justice."[298] He proposes four basic assumptions for economic activities, which can be read as ethical imperatives emerging from the moral intuition that the person has a value greater than any form of instrumental action. From the personalist perspective, ethical business conduct must give priority to the meaningful development of all stakeholders, including managers and employees. By using the intuition of a personalistic economics view, I propose a personalist approach to corporate integrity theories.

[298] Bouckaert, "The Project of a Personalistic Economics," 21.

CHAPTER NINE

A PERSONALIST APPROACH TO CORPORATE INTEGRITY THEORIES

Introduction

The personalist approach to corporate integrity attempts to give equal importance to corporate structure, culture, codes, and the personal integrity of managers and employees. This is particularly relevant to entrepreneurship, which is not only an efficient means for profit making but also to create new meanings and practices.[1] Innovation cannot be reduced to a rational allocation of resources for the making of profit. Although profit making is an aim of entrepreneurship, it is not its core meaning.[2] Peter Drucker defines the practice of entrepreneurship as the attempt to "create something new, something different; change or transmute values."[3] An entrepreneur can be successful if one can mobilize the creative potential of stakeholders. Mobilizing human resources can be done differently. According to the rational manager, it is the use of certain tools and incentives for motivating people to reach for the aim of the business. For an ethical manager, it is the starting of a new relationship between people based on trust and dialogue.[4] Bouckaert states that "employees will become responsible for themselves and care for the common good if management is capable of creating an environment promoting trust and autonomy."[5] In this environment, there will be no tendency for corporate unethical conduct. I think this is possible by having managers and employees with

1 Luk Bouckaert, "Humanity in Business," in *Sustaining Humanity: An Ethics Agenda for European Leaders Today*, eds. Johan Verstraeten and Maria Duffy (Leuven: Bibliotheek Faculteit Godgeleerdheid with European Ethics Network Co-Ordination Centre, 2004): 104.

2 Bouckaert, "Humanity in Business," 104.

3 Peter F. Drucker, *Innovation and Entrepreneurship* (New York: Harper and Row, 1985): 22. I have taken this quotation from the following sources: Charles Spinosa, Fernando Flores, and Hubert L. Dreyfus, *Disclosing New Worlds* (Cambridge: The MIT Press, 1997): 35.

4 Bouckaert, "Humanity in Business," 105.

5 Bouckaert, "Humanity in Business," 105.

personal integrity because the use of freedom with responsibility depends on how a person acts /what values a person has. Therefore, in this chapter I argue that in order to have an ideal entrepreneurship, we need to incorporate the personal integrity of managers and employees in corporate integrity theories.

1 Main Elements of Personalist Approach to Corporate Integrity

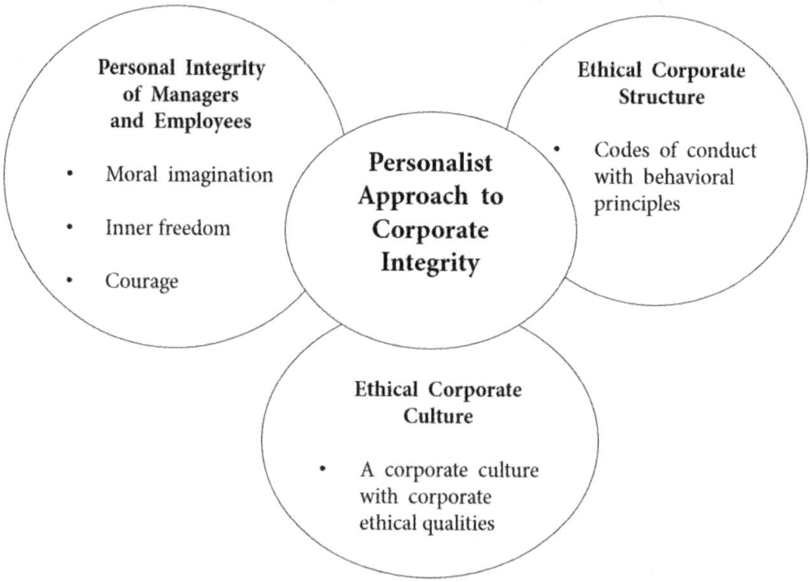

The corporate structure and culture are the same as in corporate integrity theories. The additional element of the personalist approach to corporate integrity theories is the personal integrity of managers and employees. The question is, how would personal integrity help to fulfill the personalistic economics vision in corporate life or to balance ethics and economic rationality, or to overcome conflicts of interest and corporate unethical conduct in the day-to-day functioning of corporations.

1.1 Moral Imagination

It is not so easy to define moral imagination. It is a fluid concept. Moreover, it can be viewed from different perspectives. Traditionally, morality understood as a matter of reason and a moral decision is made by applying rules to particular situations. On the other hand, moral imagination is subjective and is not governed by reason and rules. Therefore, it is generally taken for granted that morality and moral imagination are not compatible.[6] Patricia H. Werhane introduced the dynamic concept of moral imagination into the field of business ethics.[7] She defines moral imagination as "the ability in particular circumstances to discover and evaluate possibilities not merely determined by that circumstance, or limited by its operative mental models, or merely framed by a set of rules or rule-governed concerns."[8] It is clear from this definition that the moral imagination helps us to have a cognitive aptitude, which in turn helps the agents to make a responsible moral judgment based on an objective moral standard.[9] Werhane writes that "only through imagination one can project alternative ways to frame experience and thus broaden, evaluate, and even change one's moral point of view."[10] It is worthwhile to note the qualification of imagination as moral. The qualifier, moral, is intended to limit the concept to a "morally motivated imaginative thought."[11]

In the following section, I shall explain influential factors of moral imagination, the dynamic nature of moral imagination, and how moral imagination works out in corporate contexts to have a personalistic economics view in corporate life. Moreover, I demonstrate how moral imagination would help to overcome corporate unethical conduct, while not giving a historical narration of the development of the concept of moral imagination.

1.1.1 Dynamic Nature of Moral Imagination

Moral imagination is explained variously as: "(a) subsumed under moral perception, (b) a precondition or aspect of moral judgment, (c) the radical revision of moral understandings, and (d) the capacity to generate new possibilities for realizing moral ends."[12] The various explanations of moral imagination indicate that it is an integral part of moral deliberation. It is very clear that "moral knowledge is not simply intellectual grasp of propositions; it is not even simply intellectual grasp of particular facts; it is perception. It is seeing a complex, concrete reality in a highly lucid and

6 Mathew Illathuparampil, *Technology and Ethical Ambiguity* (New Delhi: Global Vision Publishing, 2009): 163.

7 Jianfeng Yang, "Linking Proactive Personality to Moral Imagination: Moral Identity as a Moderator," *Social Behavior and Personality* 41, no. 1 (2013): 165.

8 Patricia H. Werhane, *Moral Imagination and Management Decision Making* (New York: Oxford University Press, 1999): 93. See also Patricia H. Werhane, "Moral Imagination and Systems Thinking," *Journal of Business Ethics* 38 (2002): 33.

9 Mavis Biss, "Moral Imagination, Perception, and Judgment," *The Southern Journal of Philosophy* 52, no. 1 (2014): 2.

10 Werhane, *Moral Imagination and Management Decision Making*, 90.

11 Biss, "Moral Imagination, Perception, and Judgment," 2.

12 Biss, "Moral Imagination, Perception, and Judgment," 3.

richly responsive way; it is taking in what is there, with imagination and feeling."[13]

Imagination is the ability to form and activate various mental images and rearrange these various mental images. Imagination is active, creative, and artistic. Imagination is a potential tool for moral knowledge.[14] Moreover, according to Mathew Illathuparampil, there is imaginative input in the formation of moral concepts. He proposes two arguments for this. First, moral concepts are formed in a prototypical way, and second, there is a metaphorical nature for moral concepts.[15] He credited Mark Johnson and George Lakoff for making these claims. According to Johnson, "most categories used by people are not actually definable by a list of features. Instead, people tend to define categories (e.g., bird) by identifying certain prototypical members of the category (e.g., robin) and they recognize other non-prototypical members (e.g., chicken) that differ from the prototypical ones."[16] In a classical theory, a concept or a category is normally defined by a set of necessary and sufficient features.[17] A general ethical concept cannot contain a list of inevitable conditions for specific situations. The extension of an ethical concept causes dispute, debate, and ambiguity if we accept the traditional view.[18] Johnson gives the instance of a lie, a concept of which we tend to have a prototypical idea. However, there are different types of lies such as white lies, social lies or even jokes. The fundamental question is, how far can we extend the concept of a lie.[19] According to Illathuparambil, "Moral concepts are often structured around prototypical cases and frequently, moral debates are concerned about the question of whether or how far we could extend moral concepts to problematic and non-prototypical instances. [...]. The extension of prototypical cases to non-prototypical cases involves imagination rather than discursive reasoning."[20]

Moral concepts and theories are metaphorical in nature. Metaphors are the core modes of human understanding. A metaphor can be defined as follows:

---

13 Martha C. Nussbaum, *Love's Knowledge: Essays on Philosophy and Literature* (New York: Oxford University Press, 1990): 152. I have taken this quotation from the following source. Cf. Illathuparampil, *Technology and Ethical Ambiguity*, 166.

14 Cécile Rozuel, "Moral Imagination and Active Imagination: Searching in the Depths of the Psyche," *Journal of Management Development* 31, no. 5 (2012): 489–490.

15 Illathuparampil, *Technology and Ethical Ambiguity*, 166.

16 Mark Johnson, *Moral Imagination: Implications of Cognitive Science for Ethics* (Chicago: The University of Chicago Press, 1993): 8.

17 Johnson, *Moral Imagination*, 8.

18 Illathuparampil, *Technology and Ethical Ambiguity*, 166–168.

19 Johnson, *Moral Imagination*, 92.

20 Illathuparampil, *Technology and Ethical Ambiguity*, 169.

> The cognitive mechanism whereby one experiential domain is partially 'mapped,' i.e. projected, onto a different experiential domain, so that the second domain is partially understood in terms of the first one. The domain that is mapped is called the source or donor domain, and the domain onto which the source is mapped is called the target or recipient domain. Both domains have to belong to different super ordinate domains.[21]

The nature of metaphors helps us to derive the rich and wide meaning of a moral concept and theory. In this process, we are both free and constrained because the "reader has to connect the metaphor to the meaning he/she already possesses. At the same time, he/she will have to forgo certain of her/his preconceived notions."[22] According to Johnson and Lakoff, the ethical concept of love has very little to communicate in a literal sense. If we imagine the concept of love without the metaphors of union, madness, giving of oneself, closeness or journeys, then what we have is a skeleton of the concept of love, that is, a lover, beloved, or feelings of love.[23] Moreover, Johnson shows the basis of metaphors in the formation of Kant's categorical imperatives. Metaphors make it clear what is meant by a categorical imperative. Kant writes, "Act so that you use humanity, as much in your own person as in the person of every other, always at the same time as end and never merely as means."[24] The literal meaning of end is something that we produce with our actions. What does "an end in itself" actually mean? According to Johnson, it is more than a literal meaning of end and it is a metaphorical extension of our literary meaning of end. Johnson writes, "Instead of being something we produce or realize through actions, an end in itself is a rational creature who we respect by our action. In other words, we must take care to insure that our acts do not violate the integrity of other people as moral beings."[25]

The moral concept of action is deeply understood by the event structure of a metaphorical system, and includes the concept of action, purpose, cause, state, change, and means. It means that every moral concept that is connected to action becomes metaphorical. This also means that our conceptions of a free will, rights, duties, and obligations are metaphorical in nature. Conceptions of a will, rights, duties, and obligations can be understood properly by the social accounting metaphor (social well-being), that

[21] Antonio Barcelona, "Introduction: Cognitive Theory of Metaphor and Metonymy," in *Metaphor and Metonymy at the Crossroads: A Cognitive Perspective*, eds. Antonio Barcelona (Berlin & New York: Mouton/ de Gruyter, 2003): 3.

[22] Illathuparampil, *Technology and Ethical Ambiguity*, 169.

[23] George Lakoff and Mark Johnson, *Philosohy in the Flesh: The Embodied Mind and Its Challenge to Western Thought* (New York: Basic Books, 1999): 72.

[24] Immanuel Kant, "Groundwork of the Metaphysics of Morals," in *Rethinking the Western Tradition*, ed. Allen. W. Wood (New Haven: Yale University Press, 2002): 46–47.

[25] Johnson, *Moral Imagination*, 73.

is connected to the event structure metaphor.[26] However, Johnson does not claim that all our moral concepts are metaphoric. Concepts are based on our bodily experience and have no metaphorical nature, for instance "containment, up-down, inside-outside, or balance."[27]

The metaphoric nature of moral concepts and theories allows for the possibility for interpretative ventures in morality. This generates sufficient room for creativity and imagination in morality because "metaphor is one of the principal mechanisms of imaginative cognition."[28]

Although we have already seen the importance of the narrative context of life in Christian ethics, it is also important to note that the narrative context of morality is crucial to the functioning of moral imagination. According to Johnson, "Narrative is the most comprehensive means we have for constructing temporal synthesis that bind together and unify our past, present, and future into more or less meaningful patterns."[29] As Verstraeten observes, to become a morally responsible person, we should integrate our actions and decisions in life as a whole,[30] as they require a narrative configuration of a person. According to Illathuparambil, the narrative context of morality gives sufficient and mature expression of moral imagination. This is important because "otherwise, moral imagination might be reduced to a mere metaphoric exchange that occurs at the conceptual level or it could be underrated as a subjective fantasy."[31] Every action must have settings. Settings point toward a history. History is a narrative. Narrative includes both individual and social factors. It is clear from the writings of Maclntyre that "the story of my life is always embedded in the story of the communities from which I derive my identity. I am born with a past; and trying to cut myself off from the past, in the individualist mode, is to deform my present relationships."[32] Only a narrative can accommodate the above-mentioned social and individual factors and form the unity of life.

The narrative view of moral life emphasizes the unity of life and gives a clear picture of one's self and identity.[33] Human actions assume meaning

---

26 Johnson, *Moral Imagination*, 35–55.

27 Mark Johnson, *The Body in the Mind: The Bodily Basis of Meaning, Imagination, and Reason* (Chicago and London: The University of Chicago Press 1987): 74–75. See also Illathuparampil, *Technology and Ethical Ambiguity*, 170–171.

28 Johnson, *Moral Imagination*, 33.

29 Johnson, *Moral Imagination*, 174.

30 Johan Verstraeten, "Spirituality as Source of Inspired, Authentic and Innovative Leadership," in *Leadership, Innovation, and Spirituality*, eds. Patrick Nullens and Jack Barentsen (Leuven: Peeters, 2014): 88.

31 Illathuparampil, *Technology and Ethical Ambiguity*, 173.

32 Alasdair Maclntyre, *After Virtue: A Study of Moral Theory* (Notre Dame: University of Notre Dame Press, 1981): 205.

33 Maclntyre, *After Virtue*, 203.

in the context of a narrative unity. Moreover, an abstract moral concept can be made clear by a narrative unity. For instance, the virtue of charity becomes clear by the narrative unity of life of Mother Teresa. However, narrative continuity or unity of the life is not always a reality because there is a possibility for a rapid rapture in the narrative unity of life as seen in the life of St. Paul. The complexity of identity and different aspects and dimensions of human experiences are the challenges to having the narrative to situate one's identity or self. It is the real limitation to the understanding of one's self through the narrative. Of course, time is necessary to connect various events and experiences into a narrative unity.[34]

According to Illathuparambil, moral imagination operates in the context of narratives in a mature way. First, the everyday disconnected actions and experiences of human beings are connected to a meaningful whole by the use of moral imagination. Since we are unaware of the purposive element behind our actions i.e. survival, quest for meaning in life, or flourishing in a narrative context, imagination connects actions with purpose and forms all actions into a meaningful whole. Moreover, a narrative context is a necessary condition to become a responsible self.[35] Second, in a narrative context, moral imagination helps to distinguish morally silent elements in complex life events and actions. Third, in the context of narrative, based on experiences, moral imagination helps one to move toward a better future. Fourth, moral imagination helps discern the meaning of an action or an event in a narrative context.[36]

1.1.2 The Influencing Factors of Moral Imagination in Corporate Contexts

Various organizational and personal factors influence the moral imagination of the managers and employees of a corporation. Personal integrity (Expression of Moral Identity)[37] is a decisive influencing factor in the moral imagination of a person. A person can express creative action

[34] Illathuparampil, *Technology and Ethical Ambiguity*, 174–177. We have already explained the complexity of identity in previous chapters.

[35] Verstraeten, "Spirituality as Source of Inspired, Authentic and Innovative Leadership," 88.

[36] Illathuparampil, *Technology and Ethical Ambiguity*, 178–179.

[37] In chapter three, I explained the various terms used for the concept of personal integrity. Moral identity is one among them. Moral identity refers to the moral self of a person. Many authors define moral identity as a "self-conception organized around a set of moral traits." Cf. Karl Aquino and Americus Reed, "The Self-Importance of Moral Identity," *Journal of Personality and Social Psychology* 83, no. 6 (2002): 1424. My definition of personal integrity goes along the same line. Studies show that moral identity and actions of a person are related. Cf. Aquino and Reed, "The Self-Importance of Moral Identity," 1424–1425. My argument is that personal integrity influences action. Therefore, since both personal integrity and moral identity refer to the moral core of the person, I show that moral identity and personal integrity influence the moral imagination in the same way.

in an ethical or non-ethical manner. However, "An individual with a high level of moral identity will tend to be more likely to find moral significance in what he/she experiences and, consequently, to behave ethically."[38] A person with moral imagination needs to be creative. Moreover, persons with moral identity do not contradict their moral identity with creative action. An individual with strong moral identity is a person of integrity. Therefore, there is a positive relationship between moral imagination, personal integrity (Expression of Moral Identity), and the creative action of a person.[39] I believe that the moral imagination of a person depends on personal integrity (moral identity) of the person. If people have low personal integrity, then they may not be able to have a creative moral imagination.[40] Therefore, people with integrity will have a creative moral imagination to act in an ethical way in different circumstances because they know their central moral self and act in accordance with it.

The corporate culture and structure have a strong influence on the actions of managers and employees in corporate life. Corporate culture and structure are reflected in corporate informal rules and formal systems. According to many studies, if corporate culture and structure are "strong and create cognitive images that are distinctive, central, and enduring, individuals often adapt their behaviors to be consistent with them."[41] According to the empirical studies of David F. Caldwell and Dennis Moberg, managers and employees who work in a strong ethical organizational culture have higher moral imagination than individuals who work in an organizational culture where ethics is not so strong.[42]

The locus of control influences the moral imagination of managers and employees. It is defined as the "assumed internal reasons why some people try to deal willingly with difficult circumstances."[43] The locus of control can be perceived from internal and external perspectives. According to the internal perspective, outcomes of one's actions are influenced by one's abilities, efforts or skills, which are also the locus of control. According to an external perspective, the locus of control comes from outside of the individual, that is, powerful other chances or luck. Moral imagination is

38 Yang, "Linking Proactive Personality to Moral Imagination," 168.

39 Yang, "Linking Proactive Personality to Moral Imagination," 168.

40 Yang, "Linking Proactive Personality to Moral Imagination," 165–175.

41 David F. Caldwell and Dennis Moberg, "An Exploratory Investigation of the Effect of Ethical Culture in Activating Moral Imagination," *Journal of Business Ethics* 73, no. 2 (2007): 195. See also Linda Klebe Treviño, Kenneth D. Butterfield, and Donald L. McCabe, "The Ethical Context in Organizations: Influences on Employee Attitudes and Behaviors," *Business Ethics Quarterly* 8, no. 3 (1998): 447–476.

42 Caldwell and Moberg, "An Exploratory Investigation of the Effect of Ethical Culture," 193–204.

43 Gülçimen Yurtsever, "Measuring Moral Imagination," *Social Behavior and Personality* 34, no. 3 (2006): 214.

closely related to the creativity of the person. Creativity is thus related to an internal locus of control. According to empirical studies, if managers and employees of an organization work under an external locus of control, then their moral imagination is negatively influenced. However, if the working condition is related to an internal locus of control, then managers and employees have a high level of moral imagination.[44]

Tolerance of ambiguity relates to the moral imagination of managers and employees. Generally, "An ambiguous situation is one that cannot be adequately structured or categorized by an individual because it lacks sufficient cues."[45] Rational decisions are difficult in ambiguous situations. Individuals with tolerance for ambiguity will not compromise with unethical values. Unethical decisions can be a result of making ethical decisions in a situation with unclear information. Moral imagination can provide alternate choices and possibilities in ambiguous situations. Studies depict that there is a correlation between moral imagination and tolerance of ambiguous situations. People with a mentality permitting them to tolerate ambiguous situations have a high range of moral imagination.[46]

Empathy can be defined as a "reaction of one individual to the observed experience of another."[47] Moral imagination covers the feelings of other individuals. According to empirical studies, there is a positive correlation between empathy and moral imagination. Empathetic concern for others has a positive influence by increasing the tendency for the functioning of moral imagination. However, people with a Machiavellian mentality[48] have a lower tendency to use moral imagination. This means that Machiavellianism negatively correlates with moral imagination.[49]

These factors, which positively influence moral imagination, can be summarized by the following two perspectives: the moral qualities of the person and the ethical corporate structure and culture. Corporate integrity theories neglect the influencing elements of moral imagination based on the moral quality of managers and employees. The proposed personalist integrity approach gives equal importance to both and, therefore,

44 Yurtsever, "Measuring Moral Imagination," 214–215.

45 Stanley Budner, "Intolerance of Ambiguity as a Personality Variable," *Journal of Personality* 30, no. 1 (1962): 30. See also Yurtsever, "Measuring Moral Imagination," 215.

46 Yurtsever, "Measuring Moral Imagination," 215–216. See also Denis G. Arnold and Laura P. Hartman, "Moral Imagination and the Future of Sweatshops," *Business and Society Review* 108, no. 4 (2003): 425–461.

47 Mark H. Davis, "Measuring Individual Differences in Empathy: Evidence for a Multidimensional Approach," *Journal of Personality and Social Psychology* 44, no. 1 (1983): 113.

48 A Machiavellian mentality holds that since the world is imperfect, for achieving good ends we have to use any means. It is a duplicitous way of life. Cf. Martyn Hammersley and Anna Traianou, "Moralism and Research Ethics: A Machiavellian Perspective," *International Journal of Social Research Methodology* 14, no. 5 (2011): 384.

49 Yurtsever, "Measuring Moral Imagination," 216–217.

the personalist approach to corporate integrity theory incorporates the possibility of moral imagination into the corporate decision making process. I think it is important to balance ethics and economic rationality in corporate decisions. In the following section, I shall explain how moral imagination works in corporate life.

1.1.3 Moral Imagination in Ethical Decisions of Corporate Life

In this section, I shall present two claims: first, that moral imagination is an essential element in corporate ethics, which justifies my proposal of the personalist approach to corporate integrity theory. Second, the exercise of moral imagination is the best solution to overcome corporate unethical act. My claims are based on the arguments advocated by Johnson and Werhane.

According to Johnson, moral law theory states that morality is a matter of keeping absolute moral laws and applying them in each context. Although he does not deny the usefulness of moral laws, he states that limiting morality to the application of absolute moral laws misses what really matters in morality. He writes that, "An exclusive focus on moral laws and rational principles is a threat to human well-being because it blinds us to the cultivation of moral imagination that is necessary if we are to be morally sensitive and fully responsible to other people."[50] Johnson is critical of extreme positions such as moral absolutism and moral relativism. Moral absolutism sees morality as just laws. On the contrary, moral relativism holds the view that morality is not related to universal laws but to the particular cultural group and within a particular historical context. In both these views, there is no space for moral imagination and individual creativity. Johnson presents moral imagination as the "juxtaposition of two incompatible or contradictory concepts."[51] Moreover, moral imagination is neither subjective nor unconstrained nor irrational. It takes seriously the above-mentioned opposite views.

Conflict of interests or moral dilemmas, and illegal connections between political and corporate sector, and cultural elements are the main causes of corporate unethical act. Corporate integrity theories suggest codes, corporate ethical structure, and culture as a solution. I concur with Johnson that codes, ethical corporate culture, and structure of corporate integrity theories are the prototypes. Since cultural elements, conflicts of interest and immoral corporate political connections are so complex and diverse, it is not an easy task to have a universally applicable moral stance or prototypical case. In this context, we require a morally imaginative reason to overcome corporate unethical conduct. As Johnson states, "What

[50] Johnson, *Moral Imagination*, 5.

[51] Johnson, *Moral Imagination*, 2.

we need in such cases is a cultivated moral imagination for exploring various courses of action open to us, for rehearsing possible relationships and forms of action, and for doing our best to harmonize our often conflicting values and conceptions of reason."[52] How does moral imagination work in a corporate context? I shall explain this in the following section, based on the writings of Werhane.

In order to understand the role of moral imagination in the corporate context, according to Werhane, we should understand systems thinking in relation to moral imagination. According to her view, "Systems thinking presupposes that most of our thinking, experiencing, practices and institutions are interrelated and interconnected."[53] A system is a whole with many parts, sub systems, networks of relationships and interactions. The system approach in decision-making is a holistic approach.[54] Since in a system, all elements are closely connected, no systemic problems can be solved in an isolated way. A constituent part of the system is not the whole. Werhane states that in order to make a decision in a system or corporation, a multiple-perspective approach is needed.[55] As discussed in the preceding chapters, the systemic nature of corporations gives birth to various relationships, interests, and dilemmas. The failure to keep a balance among the various interests of stakeholders is the cause of corporate unethical conduct. A multiple-perspective approach is a proposed solution.

Initially, a multiple-perspective system of decision-making accepts that a system or an organization is a network of interrelationships. Second, the boundaries of an organization have to be outlined in order to make clear the roles, rights, and duties of the all stakeholders of an organization. Consequently, the organization is accountable to the stakeholders for its decision. However, it is possible that "different stakeholders will outline the boundary conditions differently because of the way each prioritizes stakeholders. For example, a Western-trained Bangladeshi banker will calculate loans to the poor differently than, say, someone working for an NGO."[56] Finally, we have to set the goal of the system and make decisions in an evaluative way keeping in mind the boundaries of an organization.[57]

The fixing of a boundary condition and its evaluation is problematic. A boundary condition is limited because of operative mental models or different mind-sets. Operative mental models or mind-sets are the mental representations or mental pictures of human beings, which are framed by

52 Johnson, *Moral Imagination*, 125.

53 Patricia Werhane, "Moral Imagination and Systems Thinking," *Journal of Business Ethics* 38, no. 1 (2002): 36.

54 Werhane, "Moral Imagination and Systems Thinking," 33.

55 Werhane, "Moral Imagination and Systems Thinking," 36.

56 Werhane, "Moral Imagination and Systems Thinking," 37.

57 Werhane, "Moral Imagination and Systems Thinking," 37–39.

the experiences and learning situations of each person and with which human beings see problems and make decisions.[58] Werhane uses various terms to denote mind-sets including "world view" or "conceptual schemes."[59] Our mind-sets have a social realm because "the schema we employ are socially learned and altered through religion, socialization, culture, educational upbringing, and other experiences."[60] Due to the operative mental models or mind-sets, "Managers locked into fixed ways of viewing organizational problems become unable to either envision the moral ramifications of the issues at stake, or to conceptualize alternative solutions to the problems they confront."[61] Even our experiences and moral theories would gradually become a part of our operational mind-sets.[62] Moreover, because of the ambiguous nature of the corporate context, the application of moral laws in a corporate dilemma situation is a difficult task.[63]

Operative mental models exist both at individual and organizational levels. At the organizational level, "we are trapped within an organizational culture that creates mental habits that preclude creative thinking."[64] It is worthwhile to note that both are related because organizational culture, structure, and working individuals are mutually influencing. Moreover, due to the various operative mental models, there is a possibility of having the various framings of a particular given corporate situation and as a result, different conclusions might follow.

According to Werhane, we need to break the operative mental models at the individual and organizational level to overcome corporate conflicts of interest and dilemmas in a better way. Those who break the operative mental models can go beyond self-interests and economic rationality and see new ways for resolving corporate unethical conduct. We need to break this model otherwise it will be systematically sustained and promoted.

---

58 Patricia H. Werhane, "Mental Models, Moral Imagination and System Thinking in the Age of Globalization," *Journal of Business Ethics* 78, no. 3 (2008): 463–464.

59 Patricia H. Werhane, "Moral Imagination and the Search for Ethical Decision-Making in Management," *Business Ethics Quarterly* (1998): 75–98 see also Werhane, "Moral Imagination and Systems Thinking," 39.

60 Werhane, "Moral Imagination and Systems Thinking," 39.

61 Deborah Vidaver-Cohen, "Moral Imagination in Organizational Problem-Solving: An Institutional Perspective," *Business Ethics Quarterly* 7, no. 4 (1997): 2.

62 Werhane, "Moral Imagination," 79.

63 According to proportionate reasoning, as far as there is a good to be achieved by an action, such actions can be permitted despite the presence of a certain evil side of the act. It indicates that there should be a balance. In such cases, one has to evaluate all the possible and potential good and bad results of an action. To have an evaluation of all possible and potential outcomes of a corporate decision is a very difficult task. Cf. Illathuparampil, *Technology and Ethical Ambiguity*, 112–124.

64 Werhane, "Mental Models, Moral Imagination and System Thinking," 464.

Werhane suggests moral imagination as a tool to break operative mental models or conceptual schemes.[65]

Moral imagination works in three different stages. First, the stage of reproductive imagination, which consists of the various kinds of awareness such as context, mind-sets, or script, or schema operating in thc context of possible conflicting interests or moral dilemmas. Second, the stage of productive imagination wherein we re-think our own schema and find new possibilities within a given context. Third, the stage of creative imagination that entails framing a morally accepted alternative solution to solve a problem. This stage entails "the ability to envision and actualize possibilities that are not context-dependent but are (a) encouraged by or project a fresh schema, and/or (b) the ability to envision possibilities that other reasonable persons could envision, and (c) evaluation."[66]

Moral imagination is a tool to overcome rigid mind-sets or operative mental models and moral amnesia[67] in the corporate context. As a result of the exercise of moral imagination, we will have better morally justified solutions in the context of conflicts of interest or dilemmas because moral imagination helps us to go beyond existing mind-sets. Moreover, I believe that a moral imagination is a tool to avoid the instrumenalization of ethics at individual and corporate levels for selfish interests. As Verstraeten observes, moral imagination enables managers to adopt the attitude of an impartial spectator, which leads managers beyond the bias of "managerial discourse and the culture of distrust." It enables them to see all stakeholders in a new light, human beings as human beings, not merely as productive engines or simply as means for profit.[68] It is important to note that one of the main influencing factors of moral imagination is the moral identity or the personal integrity of a person. This is why I argue for a personalist approach to corporate integrity as a solution to corporate unethical conduct and the instrumentalization of corporate ethics.

The main criticism against moral imagination is that it would destroy objectivity in morality. However, moral imagination is not equal to one's fantasy. Moral imagination happens within a framework of narratives. Therefore, moral imagination is always in accordance with the moral framework of one's own community. A Catholic cannot exercise his/her moral imagination against Catholic moral tradition. In fact, people

---

65 Werhane, "Mental Models, Moral Imagination and System Thinking," 446. See also Vidaver-Cohen, "Moral Imagination in Organizational Problem-Solving," 2.

66 Werhane, "Moral Imagination," 85.

67 It can be defined as "an inability to remember past mistakes and to transfer that knowledge when fresh challenges arise." Cf. Werhane, "Moral Imagination," 75.

68 Verstraeten, "Spirituality as Source of Inspired, Authentic and Innovative Leadership," 86.

are making use of their own imagination to apply moral principles in a context.[69]

1.2 Inner Freedom

One can look at freedom from two perspectives: the freedom of being and the freedom of doing.[70] According to Rollo May, "'freedom of doing' refers to the act, the 'freedom of being' refers to the context out of which the urge to act emerges. It refers to the deeper level of one's attitudes and is the fountain out of which 'freedom of doing' is born. Hence, I call this second kind of freedom *essential freedom*."[71] Freedom of being precedes the freedom of doing but both are nevertheless closely related. Freedom of being is explained as an inner or core personal freedom. Freedom of being "is what gives the person a sense of being; it gives one the experience of autonomy, identity, the capacity to use the pronoun "I" with its full range of meaning."[72] May calls freedom of being as the inner freedom of a person.[73] That means inner freedom exists at a level of being or that inner freedom is the capacity to exercise one's own being. In other words, inner freedom is the freedom to live as one's core being.

The personal integrity of a person is related to inner freedom because personal integrity also exists at the level of being. A person who is morally oriented and has formed a fundamental stance or self, is a person with integrity. An exercise of personal integrity exists at the level of the exercise of inner freedom and it influences the actions and reflections of the person. Since personal integrity is the moral core of the person, a person with integrity will have a morally oriented inner freedom. In this section, I argue that the exercise of inner freedom is a source to overcome conflicts of interest and corporate unethical decisions and conduct. In order to substantiate my claim, I shall use the arguments advocated by Verstraeten. I shall begin with the fundamental question of how inner freedom works in an individual's life or how one person can acquire inner freedom.

Based on the Ignatian tradition, Verstraeten explains that self-awareness is the first step to attain inner freedom. Self-awareness makes people aware of who they are and what they value in life. Moreover, it makes them aware of their own fundamental stance in life. Similarly, through self-awareness one can become aware of a blind spot or a weakness that

---

69 Illathuparampil, *Technology and Ethical Ambiguity*, 184–186.

70 Since I have given a detailed description about this division of freedom in the third chapter, I will not discuss it in detail here.

71 Rollo May, *Freedom and Destiny* (New York: Dell Publishing, 1981): 55.

72 May, *Freedom and Destiny*, 57.

73 May, *Freedom and Destiny*, 57. See also Jennifer A. Rountree, "Joining Inner and Outer Approaches to Freedom: Meeting the Needs of Developing Communities," *Journal of Humanistic Psychology* 51, no. 3 (2011): 298.

hinders the exercise of one's inner freedom.[74] Continuous self-reflection and learning are required to have the real self-awareness.[75] Ignatian spiritual exercise is an attempt "to help people look at their lives, pray, take note of what's going on in themselves and their lives, and make a decision."[76] In short, self-awareness, which is a result of self-reflection, is the first step to actualize inner freedom in the day-to-day life of people.

Self-awareness is one of the qualities of personal integrity. A person with integrity knows who he or she is and what he or she wants to do. This means that a person with integrity is well aware of his or her core self. Moreover, to live with self-awareness helps managers or employees with integrity make decisions and actions in corporate life in accordance with their moral core.

The second step is discernment. It comes from the Latin word *discernere*, which means to separate or to distinguish. It "involves 'sifting through' interior and exterior experiences to know which helps one stay centered and which pulls one away from centeredness."[77] Discernment is a process by which we go deep into our self to see the context of decision making in a holistic way. Simultaneously, it goes beyond and includes the intellectual analysis and emotional intelligence of the decision maker. It brings together all the faculties of the person for making decisions by which one can separate the *wheat from the chaff* because it gives one clear vision.[78]

Discernment has a long history. Although it is rooted in Christian tradition, a similar line of thought can be seen in other religious traditions. For instance, in the Buddhist tradition Buddha teaches that the "opening of the eye of Dhamma allows one to see things just as they are."[79] According to Buddhist tradition, the goal of a spiritual exercise is to achieve internal clarity. To attain internal clarity, a right perception, the right understanding, and right thoughts about real life contexts, is an imperative. This internal clarity is the source of discernment in real life, which is the result of spiritual exercise.[80] In the Christian tradition, discernment is considered

---

74 Verstraeten, "Spirituality as Source of Inspired, Authentic and Innovative Leadership," 91.

75 Chris Lowney, *Heroic Leadership: Best Practices from a 450-Year-Old Company That Changed the World* (Chicago: Loyola Press, 2003): 27.

76 Ronald Modras, *Ignatian Humanism: A Dynamic Spirituality for the 21st Century* (Chicago: Loyola Press): 23; See also Verstraeten, "Spirituality as Source of Inspired, Authentic and Innovative Leadership," 91.

77 Margaret Benefiel, "Using Discernment to Make Better Business Decisions," in *Leadership and Business Ethics*, ed. Gabriel Flynn (Dublin: Springer, 2008): 32.

78 Benefiel, "Using Discernment to Make Better Business Decisions," 32.

79 Tejadhammo Bhikku, "Making a Cup of Tea: Some Aspects of Spiritual Direction within a Living Buddhist Tradition," in *Tending the Holy: Spiritual Direction across Traditions*, ed. Norvene Vest (Harrisburg: Morehouse, 2003): 6.

80 Rafael Luévano, "Catholic Discernment with a View of Buddhist Internal Clarity," *Buddhist-Christian Studies* 29 (2009): 39–51.

as finding and following the will of God in every context of life or it is listening to the voice of God in every life situation. The Christian tradition proposes preconditions for discernment such as trust in God, the capacity for listening to one's inner voice, humility, prayer, and Scripture meditation. Self-interest, desire for security, and attachment or greed are considered to be impediments to discernment.[81] Later in the sixteenth century, Ignatius Loyola gave a systematic and developed method of discernment for the Western Christian tradition. He proposed spiritual exercises for having a right discernment.[82]

Discernment can be practiced both at the individual and corporate level. Although corporations have a collective existence, individuals are the real decision makers and constitutive elements of corporations. Discernment is not a subjective and an isolated act. It "requires the support of a community, nurturing and grounding the person's spiritual life. Individual discernment also requires the accountability of a community, offering checks and balances to the individual's discernment."[83] That means discernment has both subjective and objective dimensions.

1.2.1 Discernment at the Organizational Level

In the discernment process, managers and employees make use of their inner freedom to reach a right decision. In other words, they try to live as their being or in accordance with their personal integrity. As Verstraeten observes, "One of the greatest obstacles to leadership is a dependency on the expectations of others."[84] If managers and employees are concerned with recognition, approval, and personal achievement as interior motivation of their decision, the exercise of inner freedom will be far away because they do not give importance to who they are but they try to satisfy the company where they work. As a result, managers and employees attempt to rearrange their behavior in order to satisfy the company or employer so as to attain promotion or salary increases, for example. Although managers and employees should be good listeners, they have to be free from the division of the self.[85]

Discernment unites the moral self of managers and employees and their day-to-day decisions in corporate life. Managers and employees have two options when making decisions: they either make a decision on the side of life and humanity; or the one that is negative to life and humanity.[86] By using inner freedom, people with integrity can always

81 Benefiel, "Using Discernment to Make Better Business Decisions," 34.
82 Luévano, "Catholic Discernment with a View of Buddhist Internal Clarity," 41.
83 Benefiel, "Using Discernment to Make Better Business Decisions," 32.
84 Verstraeten, "Spirituality as Source of Inspired," 90.
85 Verstraeten, "Spirituality as Source of Inspired," 89–91.
86 Verstraeten, "Spirituality as Source of Inspired," 92.

make decisions to humanize the world because they are positively oriented toward humanity. According to Lowney, one has to engage in the self-examination of one's own decisions and actions and ascertain whether these actions and decisions are in accordance with their fundamental orientation to life. This examination is part of discernment and it will help us to learn from our successes and failures.[87]

André L. Delbecq et al., propose five principles for the practice of discernment in corporate life. First, managers and employees should undergo the decision making process with a reflective inner disposition. Second, managers and employees must take enough time to make the decision, as it helps them discover various alternative possibilities for a decision. Third, along with patience in decision making they should work hard at collecting information regarding issues of decision. Fourth, reflection and prayers are necessary to pick the important matters underlying the issue of decisions. Finally, managers and employees must make a tentative decision and wait for the outcome. Waiting for the outcome would help evaluate and, if it is necessary, modify the tentative decision.[88]

As explained earlier, inner freedom works through self-awareness and discernment. It is obvious that the process of the use of inner freedom depends on who the person is and how the person functions in society. In corporate life, the correct use of inner freedom is only possible when managers and employees have a moral self. Managers and employees with personal integrity have a moral self or positive fundamental orientation of the self. Therefore, I argue that in situations of conflicting interests or dilemmas, the personal integrity of managers and employees would help them to use their inner freedom in a correct way. As a result, the possibility of occurrence of unethical conduct decreases because, due to the use of the inner freedom, a decision is made in conformity with one's own moral self through self-awareness and discernment.

1.3 Moral Courage to Use Power Rightly

Shane J. Lopez et al., define moral courage as "the expression of personal views and values in the face of dissension and rejection."[89] The exercise of moral courage depends upon various situations such as the practice of injustice, human rights violation, unfair treatment, or illegal business

[87] Lowney, *Heroic Leadership*, 294.

[88] André L Delbecq et al., "Discernment and Strategic Decision Making: Reflections for a Spirituality of Organizational Leadership," in *Spiritual Intelligence at Work: Meaning, Metaphor, and Morals*, eds. Moses Pava and Patrick Primeaux (London: Emerald Group Publishing Limited, 2003): 139–174. See also Benefiel, "Using Discernment to Make Better Business Decisions," 34–38.

[89] Shane J. Lopez et al., "Profiling Courage," in *Positive Psychological Assessment: A Handbook of Models and Measures*, eds. Shane J. Lopez and C. R. Snyder (Washington: American Psychological Association, 2003): 184.

practices. In all these situations, there are possibilities of conflicts between people and between the inner values of others.[90] Morally courageous actions are different from other pro-social actions such as helping, sharing, or donating because morally courageous actions tend to attract high social costs such as opposition, insulation, or an attack. While moral courage is a brave behavior to enforce one's own moral values and ethical norms irrespective of the consequences, there may not be a direct reward to the actor.[91] In this section, I claim that since personal integrity of managers and employees is the real source of moral courage, the incorporation of personal integrity into corporate integrity would, therefore, reduce the possibility of corporate unethical conduct occurring as we currently know it.

The motivation of a person is important, but to have moral courage is more important. In conflicting situations, people can act differently depending on their motivation. First, one can be motivated by one's self-interest. In this case, one acts in a way to fulfill one's own interest without being concerned about morality. Second, the inner motivation of a person can be moral as an end in itself, which is in keeping with moral integrity. Third, motivation of a person can be made to appear as moral without taking the cost of being moral, which is a moral hypocrisy. Fourth, an overpowered integrity surrenders the moral goal when the cost of being moral becomes clear.[92] Studies show that an ethical act is not possible if a person is motivated by selfish interests, moral hypocrisy, and overpowered integrity.[93]

Moral courage stems from the fundamental moral disposition (moral integrity) or motivation of the person. The fundamental orientation of people is the determining factor of moral courage because moral courage is an attempt to establish one's own basic moral stance in a given situation of a conflict. In the exercise of personal integrity, an individual is not concerned with the consequence of an action but will act in accordance with personal integrity in any situation.[94] Therefore, managers and employees with the personal integrity display moral courage in their corporate

90 Silvia Osswald, Dieter Frey, and Bernhard Streicher, "Moral Courage," in *Justice and Conflicts: Theoretical and Empirical Contributions*, eds. Elisabeth Kals and Ju¨rgen Maes (Berlin Heidelberg: Springer, 2012): 392.

91 Osswald, Frey, and Streicher, "Moral Courage," 393. See also Tobias Greitemeyer et al., "Civil Courage and Helping Behavior," *European Psychologist* 11, no. 2 (2006): 90–98.

92 Daniel Batson and Elizabeth R. Thompson, "Why Don't Moral People Act Morally? Motivational Considerations," *Current Directions in Psychological Science* 10, no. 2 (2001): 54–56.

93 Batson and Thompson, "Why Don't Moral People Act Morally? Motivational Considerations," 56.

94 Daniela Niesta Kayser et al., "Why Mood Affects Help Giving, but Not Moral Courage: Comparing Two Types of Prosocial Behaviour," *European Journal of Social Psychology* 40, no. 7 (2010): 1138–1139. See also Batson and Thompson, "Why Don't Moral People Act Morally? Motivational Considerations," 54–57.

existence, which will reduce the possibility of conflicts of interest and corruption.

According to De George, a corporate act with integrity comes from moral courage, both from the side of business and from the side of individuals within the business. From the level of a corporation, moral courage is essential to accepting that ethical behaviors are not always profitable and sometimes, they are costly because often the ethically right action and economic rationality do not go together. In such a case, moral courage and commitment to ethics are needed at the corporate level. Moreover, moral courage can also empower one to avoid unethical policies and missions. For instance, the policy of International Business Machines Corporation (IBM) is not to pay bribes.[95] Although De George makes a distinction between moral courage of firms and individuals within the business, I think that the moral courage of firms depends upon the moral courage of the people who are responsible internally for the operation of the business.

Furthermore, corporate managers and employees need moral courage. Senior managers experience conflicts of interest, challenges, and temptations in their corporate lives. Shareholders can insist that senior managers act unethically. Similarly, senior managers may compel employees to act corruptly. In such instances they require moral courage to overcome the pressure.[96] Similarly, "employees need moral courage to say no when corporate superiors instruct them to falsify documents, backdate reports or orders, or produce goods that fall below contracted specifications."[97] Moreover, working in corrupt environments and systems raise the need of moral courage to act ethically.[98] Furthermore, moral courage is vital for the well-functioning of moral imagination and the creativity of managers and employees in conflicting situations. The "ultimate expression of moral courage is the courage to be visionary toward the future in spite of inevitable uncertainties and the fears that they understandably raise."[99] In corporate environments, managers and employees require moral courage along with an ethical corporate structure and culture to go beyond the present situation, so that they can do this with a vision of a good future and, therefore, to use their power appropriately to ensure a brighter future for all concerned. Moral courage is an outcome of the personal integrity of a person. Therefore, I propose to incorporate personal integrity in

95 Richard T. DeGeorge, *Competing with Integrity in International Business* (Oxford: Oxford University Press, 1993): 110–111.

96 Adrian Furnham, "Managers as Change Agents," *Journal of Change Management* 3, no. 1 (2002): 23.

97 DeGeorge, *Competing with Integrity in International Business*, 110.

98 DeGeorge, *Competing with Integrity in International Business*, 111.

99 Jack Mahoney, "Editorial Adieu: Cultivating Moral Courage in Business," *Business Ethics: A European Review* 7, no. 4 (1998): 191.

corporate integrity theories as a practical solution to overcome corporate unethical acts.

It is worthwhile to realize the paradoxical nature to corporate unethical act especially in corporate corruption. Corruption, while universally accepted as unethical, to a great extent still exists in corporate life.[100] Paradoxically, corruption exists in corporate life because often managers and employees are compelled to compromise their principles within the workplace for unethical actions and decisions.[101] I believe that in such situations moral courage is needed from both individual and corporate perspectives. The moral courage of managers and employees has to be strengthened at the corporate level through ethical corporate policies and missions. This is why De George proposes that "competing with integrity in a corrupt environment requires moral courage, both personal and corporate."[102] Therefore, we give equal importance to personal and corporate moral courage in the personalist approach to corporate integrity theories.

1.4 A Greater Possibility for Dialogue

Volition, choice, and mutual dialogue are the characteristics of personal integrity or the integrated self or authenticity. A person with integrity does not find it difficult to have a mutual discussion with other colleagues in conflicting situations to find an optimal solution often in the form of a compromise. Therefore, the incorporation of personal integrity into corporate integrity theory gives a better possibility for dialogue in corporate life than without it. In this section, I argue for more dialogue in the corporate decision making processes in order to reduce the possibility of corporate corruption or unethical corporate behavior.

Dialogue is a critical element to build a trustworthy relationship as it divides clear mutual attentiveness and respect between the parties. Dialogue clarifies the given situation in corporate life because we can thereby gather information from different departments and colleagues from within the corporation. Dialogue has the power of making people feel very obliging and open as opposed to a situation where there is no dialogue.[103] Openness is an underlying principle in a corporate dialogue between stakeholders. "The defining characteristic of dialogic communication is that all of these

---

[100] David Hess and Thomas W. Dunfee, "Fighting Corruptions: A Principled Approach," *Cornell Internaltional Law Journal* 33 (2000): 595.

[101] Debra R. Comer and Gina Vega, "Introduction: Why Moral Courage Matters in Organizations," in *Moral Courage in Organizations: Doing the Right Thing at Work*, eds. Debra R. Comer and Gina Vega (New York: Routledge, 2011): 17.

[102] DeGeorge, *Competing with Integrity in International Business*, 118.

[103] Bill Puka, "Taking Care of Business: Caring in Competitive Corporate Structures," in *Applying Care Ethics to Business*, eds. Maurice Hamington and Maureen Sander-Staudt (Dordrecht Heidelberg: Springer, 2011): 192.

speech acts are done in ways that hold one's own position but allow others space to hold theirs, and are profoundly open to hearing others' positions without needing to oppose or assimilate them."[104] According to Pearson, openness is an inevitable characteristic of a high-integrity culture, in which there is no need for whistle-blowers because such a need indicates a closed and repressive culture.[105]

Open dialogue and corporate ethics go hand in hand. Open dialogue exists within the corporation and between the corporation and society. Openness "gives those with an interest in a particular decision the chance to make their views known and opens to argument the basis on which the decision is finally taken. This in turn enables the decision makers to learn from experience and to improve their powers of judgment."[106] Open dialogue before a corporate decision removes suspicion regarding the corporate motive. It would strengthen the relationship between the corporation and society. Corporations should be open to the views of society (local communities) as this would help create mutual trust.[107]

Dialogues within corporations are also important. It is not usual in normal corporate practice, particularly in hierarchical corporate structures. Workers and employees provide their abilities for the business in order to fulfill the goal of its shareholders. As history teaches, companies pay attention to a democratic debate within the company only if government, trade unions, and public opinions compel them to do so.[108] Dialogue within the business is also important to have ethical decisions in conflicting situations and to establish a personalist corporate view.

The core of a dialogue is the openness to listen and understand the other from their perspective. Dialogue in the corporate context is a collective attempt to find a good solution to the fundamental issues corporations face. In dialogue, everyone analyzes the problems in the light of their experience and perspectives. The fundamental thing is that everyone should understand the issue under discussion in considerable detail. In the decision making process, we have to reach a mutual understanding.[109]

---

104 W. Barnett Pearce and Kimberly A. Pearce, "Taking a Communication Perspective on Dialogue," in *Theorizing Difference in Communication Studies*, eds. R. Anderson, L. A. Baxter, and K. N. Cissna (Thousand Oaks, CA: Sage Publications, 2004): 192.

105 Gordon Pearson, *Integrity in Organizations: An Alternative Business Ethic* (New York: McGraw-Hill Book Company, 1995): 149–151. I have already discussed openness in the second chapter as the vital quality of corporate integrity theory. Therefore, I will not discuss this in detail here.

106 Sir Adrian Cadbury, "Ethical Managers Make Their Own Rules," *Harvard Business Review* 65, no. 5 (1987): 72.

107 Cadbury, "Ethical Managers Make Their Own Rules," 72.

108 Bouckaert, "Economic Democracy," 15–16.

109 Stan van Hooft, "Overcoming Principles: Dialogue in Business Ethics," *Teaching Business Ethics* 5, no. 1 (2001): 96–99.

As a result, "People learn how to think together, not just in the sense of analyzing a shared problem or creating new pieces of shared knowledge, but in the sense of occupying a collective sensibility, in which the thoughts, emotions, and resulting actions belong not to one individual, but to all of them together."[110] If a decision is made as a result of a dialogue, then the participants of the dialogue attribute more meaning to their decisions as they are part of the decision itself by virtue of their contribution to the decision making process.[111] This paves the way to act in accordance with the decision and decreases the chances that employees and managers will act in selfish ways.

Dialogue also leads to corporate transparency, which involves openness, availability, and disclosure of information. Corporate transparency can be understood from two perspectives, the static and the dynamic view. The static view of corporate transparency indicates the publication of information regarding corporate activities through documents and reports. However, the dynamic view "refers to transparency as an Information Technology (IT)-driven dialogue, in which firms and stakeholders interact to share information and cooperate."[112] According to empirical studies, transparency would strengthen the team behavioral integrity. Team behavioral integrity means that the members of the team act in accordance with the values and mission of the whole team.[113] Moreover, transparency in a corporate culture and structure reduces the possibility of corporate unethical conduct because a transparent atmosphere by its very nature decreases the possibility of hiding things from one another.[114]

Personal integrity is a precondition to having a better participatory decision making process within the corporate life. According to Wempe and Kaptein, a person of integrity always seeks a justifiable solution through dialogue and discussion with others in conflicting situations. The dialogues and discussions would never diminish one's integrity.[115] Therefore, top-level managers and employees with integrity feel comfortable to make decisions through dialogue, and this leads to transparency and a lower possibility for corporate unethical decision and conduct.

110 Peter M. Senge et al., *The Fifth Discipline Fieldbook: Strategies and Tools for Building a Learning Organization* (London: Nicholas Brealey, 1994): 358. See also Hooft, "Overcoming Principles," 97.

111 Senge et al., *The Fifth Discipline Fieldbook*, 358.

112 João César das Neves and Antonino Vaccaro, "Corporate Transparency: A Perspective from Thomas Aquinas' Summa Theologiae," *Journal of Business Ethics* 113, no. 4 (2013): 641.

113 Michael E. Palanski, Surinder S. Kahai, and Francis J. Yammarino, "Team Virtues and Performance: An Examination of Transparency, Behavioral Integrity, and Trust," *Journal of Business Ethics* 99, no. 2 (2011): 2201–216.

114 Ivar Kolstad and Arne Wiig, "Is Transparency the Key to Reducing Corruption in Resource-Rich Countries?," *World Development* 37, no. 3 (2009): 521–532.

115 Kaptein and Wempe, *The Balanced Company*, 96.

Conclusion

In the personalist approach to corporate integrity, the ethical corporate structure and culture are the same as corporate integrity theories. The additional element of the personalist approach is the personal integrity of managers and employees. The personal integrity of managers and employees works in the corporate life through moral imagination, inner freedom, courage to use power rightly, and dialogue. Moral imagination and inner freedom enables managers to have the attitude of an impartial spectator. This leads managers beyond the biases of "managerial discourse and the culture of distrust" and would help managers to overcome conflict of interests. Moral imagination and inner freedoms give one the ability to evaluate different possibilities and to make a decision in accordance with one's own moral self. The quality of personal integrity such as the ability to dialogue and courage to do the right thing would help managers and employees to overcome political pressures to practice unethical act, the social and corporate structural and cultural reasons of corporate unethical conduct.

CONCLUSION

The primary goal of the book was to elucidate the crucial role of personal integrity in corporate ethics. This is often neglected as a necessary condition for the solution of corporate misconduct. I have argued for this theme against the backdrop of its potential input for enriching corporate ethics, moral formation of managers and employees, and the creation of a new leadership style. The book has shown that the personalist approach to corporate integrity is a viable and valuable solution. This proposal takes seriously the significant role played by the personal integrity of managers and employees in obtaining corporate integrity. Thereby, the personal integrity of managers and employees as well as ethical corporate structures and cultures are considered to be necessary conditions to achieve corporate integrity.

I have developed this thesis in three parts. In the first part, I critically analyzed corporate integrity theories as the proposed solution to corporate misconduct. Corporate integrity is an attempt to integrate the various demands of the stakeholders and, as a result, it is a precondition for morally justifiable corporate decision making and conduct. I evaluated the corporate integrity theories of Kaptein, Wempe, and Brown. In my analysis, I found two types of corporate integrity theories that are based on either a social contract or a civic perspective. The assumption of an implicit contract between society and corporations for corporate existence is the foundation of the social contract-based corporate integrity theory. The social contract-based corporate integrity theory attempts to create an ethical corporate culture, and behavioral principles and structure hoping that this would lead to ethical corporate behavior. The corporate ethical structure and culture are related to, or embedded within, corporate codes of conduct. According to Kaptein and Wempe, corporate integrity is completely dependent upon these codes of conduct. However, in their later writings they have accepted the importance of personal integrity in corporate ethics.

Civic-based corporate integrity perceives corporations as members of civil society. Since corporations are citizens of a civil society, corporate integrity includes the relational aspects of integrity. From this perspective, corporate integrity is the sum total of the relational dimensions of corporate integrity, namely the cultural, interpersonal, organizational purpose, civic, and the natural dimensions. The cultural dimension of corporate integrity demands open communication between the corporation and its stakeholders. An effective cultural dimension of corporate integrity creates a strong interpersonal relationship between stakeholders and is known as the interpersonal dimension of corporate integrity. The cultural and interpersonal dimensions of corporate integrity delegate a worthwhile purpose to corporate decisions and actions, as well as human flourishing or *eudaimonia*. Furthermore, civic based corporate integrity demands strong relationships between the corporation, the environment, and the local government. The above-mentioned five dimensions of civic based corporate integrity are implemented by proper corporate missions, codes, policies, structures, and culture.

When corporate codes are implemented, the personal integrity and responsibility of managers and employees are not sufficiently addressed in corporate moral agency models or responsibility theories. The corporate amoral-moral agency model states that corporations are legal beings but not moral entities. The association model reduces corporate moral agency to individuals who work within the corporation. This view, therefore, attributes an ontological priority to individuals. Generally, the moral person view equates corporations with human beings, and stands for methodological collectivism. Among the various moral person views, I argued for the secondary actor theory as a holistic approach because secondary actor theory includes methodological collectivism and gives ontological priority to the person. This is a strong foundation for incorporating full-fledged corporate integrity. Similarly, no corporate social responsibility theories attribute a sufficient regard to the personal integrity of managers and employees since they are aligned with methodological collectivism. It is my contention that personal integrity is missing in corporate integrity theories, and it needs to be incorporated. The inclusion of personal integrity in corporate integrity theories would make it a holistic method, thus helping to prevent corporate unethical conduct.

In the second part of the book, I critically analyzed the role of personal integrity in corporate ethics. While there is little agreement as to the meaning and scope of personal integrity and it is defined in different ways such as the integration of self, authenticity, word/action consistency, and virtue, the cited authors interpreted these definitions either from a subjective or an objective perspective. Integrity as authenticity refers to the condition of people who stand for something or attempt to attain something while remaining true to their ideals. However, Taylor argues that the ideal of authenticity does not free us from our obligations in relation to others (communal dimension). Taylor objects to contemporary perspectives of a purely self-centered view of authenticity and suggests that human authenticity is created dialogically through interacting with others. Authenticity presupposes a moral quality of one's self that is determined by the community and tradition where one happens to conduct one's social engagement. Similar to Taylor's authenticity view, I have interpreted personal integrity from both subjective and objective perspectives.

The common element in all the above-mentioned descriptions of personal integrity is that it is the moral core of the self or identity. It manifests itself when one makes decisions, especially in conflicting situations. I concluded that personal integrity is the moral core of the self, and it works as a source of inspiration or practical wisdom that impels the person to make a right and objectively justifiable decision or choice in conflicting situations. Furthermore, I see a correlation between the concepts of personal integrity and the Christian ethical notion of the fundamental option. Although we cannot equate the Christian interpretation of the fundamental option with personal integrity, both share common elements as both concepts denote a self, which identifies itself with society's positive morality. Additionally, both concepts contain subjective and objective dimensions because the status of the self is formed in community with personal evaluation. The actions, which are a result of the exercise of a positive fundamental option and personal integrity, affirm the moral core of the self.

Conflicts of interests are a real problem in business. In conflicting situations, the final decision is crucial. The integrity approach was proposed as a solution since it takes into consideration both the people and their contexts to arrive at a solution. There is no absolute moral theory to be applied in the integrity approach. It takes seriously all ethical theories, persons involved, conflicting values and obligations and interests, and the circumstances of the conflict into account. It enables one to make the best possible justifiable decision in conflicting situations. If these obligations are equally valuable to a decision maker, then the selection of obligation depends upon the integrity of the person who is acting, leading to a valuation of personal integrity in business. Since corporate integrity theories neglect the relevance of the personal integrity of managers and employees, I propose a personalist approach to corporate integrity as a better solution to corporate unethical conduct.

In the final part of the book, I proposed a few additional ethical reasons for a personalist approach to corporate integrity. First, business ethics is more than simply codes of conduct, duties, sanctions, and limitations. According to many ethicists, a good life is the primary concern in ethics. In order to achieve a good life, managers and employees require not only codes of conduct but also a living context that allows them to act according to their own values and ends in organizational life, which also provides them with opportunities to give meaning to their work. This ensures that individuals are given more opportunities to participate in the management of their company's affairs with more freedom and responsibility. Second, there is no all-embracing and comprehensive moral theory, which allows for clear solutions to corporate problems. Third, codes of conduct can instrumentalize employees and managers for the benefit of the company. The corporate actor can make dangerous agricultural pesticides in an efficient way, even by motivated employees; nevertheless this does not mean that the company has a high degree of corporate integrity. Corporate integrity demands more than mere efficiency or obedience to codes of conduct.

Finally, corporate integrity does not leave sufficient space for personal integrity when it neglects links between the moral acts of managers and employees and the moral quality of their lives as a whole. Present corporate integrity theories attempt to separate corporate integrity from personal integrity. When employees and managers blindly follow their role integrity through codes of conduct, they become unaware of the consequences of their professional behavior and this may in turn lead to unethical behavior. Personal integrity along with corporate codes of conduct enables managers to foresee the broader consequences of their professional activities, because personal integrity is a connective link between the role of responsibility and moral motivation, which connects different theories, values, interests, and role responsibilities in the business arena.

I have presented the personalistic economics view of Bouckaert as the basis for describing a personalist approach to corporate integrity. According to Bouckaert, "personalistic economics refers to normative economics [...] that is based on human dignity and social justice."[1] He has proposed four assumptions for the project of personalistic economics, which I found very relevant for my investigation.

First, a human's basic needs do not coincide with his subjective preferences. Meeting the basic needs must be the first norm of an economy that aims at the development of every person, involving the entire person. Second, ethical commitment is an important source of innovative and creative economic behavior. As a result, economics must model a human being not only as a calculating being, but also as a reflective meaning-seeking being. The priority of commitment over self-interest is essential. Third, the market is a social system made up of relations of free exchange. In order to have a sustainable market, the free exchange must not only rest on mutual advantage but also on mutual trust. Fourth, a company is a community of people who cooperatively invest in the accomplishment of a meaningful and profitable project. Hence, a personalistic business ethics

1 Bouckaert, "The Project of a Personalistic Economics," 21.

strives for real forms of economic democracy and the responsible participation of everyone concerned.

While corporate integrity theories focus only on corporate efficiency, the personalist approach for corporate integrity takes care of different aspects. First, corporate decisions must see a person as an end in itself not as a means. Second, corporate decisions must be based on an ethical commitment. Third, mutual trust needs to exist among the stakeholders. Fourth, decision must occur as a participatory process.

The additional element of the personalist approach to corporate integrity is personal integrity. The question to be answered here is, how would personal integrity help to interpret the personalist economic vision in corporate integrity. I have proposed four qualities of personal integrity—moral imagination, inner freedom, moral courage, and dialogue—as legitimate reasons to adopt a personalistic vision in corporate decision-making processes and implementations.

Moral imagination enables managers to develop the attitude of the impartial spectator, which leads managers beyond the biases of "managerial discourse and the culture of distrust." It enables managers to see all stakeholders in a brand new light, to see human beings as human beings and not merely as productive engines or means for profit. Moreover, since moral concepts and theories are metaphoric by nature, there are interpretative and creative ventures of morality. This generates sufficient room for creativity and imagination in morality because a metaphor is one of the principal mechanisms of imaginative cognition.

Various organizational and personal factors influence the moral imagination of managers and employees. Personal integrity is the expression of moral identity, which is a decisive influencing factor. Imagination leads to a creative action, and this creative action can be either ethical or non-ethical. People with integrity do not contradict their moral identity in creative action. Therefore, there is a positive correlation between moral imagination and personal integrity. Second, people who work in an ethical corporate culture with an ethical structure tend to have a higher moral imagination than their counterparts. Third, the locus of control of an action of a person can be either external or internal. If it is internal to the person, managers and employees will have a higher level of moral imagination. People with integrity always act in accordance with their convictions. Fourth, managers and employees with a tolerance for ambiguity and empathy in corporate life will have a higher tendency to exercise moral imagination. Conflicts of interest and ambiguity are common in corporate existence. The elements of the personalist approach to corporate integrity are personal integrity and corporate ethical structure and culture, which enhance the use of moral imagination by managers and employees in corporate ethical decision making.

Based on the arguments of Johnson and Werhane, I have argued that moral imagination is indispensable to overcome Indian corporate dilemma. Following Johnson's approach, I drew upon the notion that codes, ethical structure, and the culture of corporate integrity theories matter to a certain extent as the prototype for overcoming corporate unethical conduct. In order to extend these prototypes to non prototypical causes, one needs moral imagination to explore various courses of action to be followed up as well as for doing one's best to harmonize various conflicting values. On the notion of moral imagination in corporate life, I have followed Werhane's multiple-perspective approach in systems thinking. First, a multiple-perspective system of decision-making accepts that a corporation is a network of interrelationships. Second, managers and employees have to outline the boundaries of the organization including the roles, rights, and duties of all stakeholders. Finally, by considering the goal of organizations and their boundaries, the managers and employees have to make decisions in an evaluative manner.

Fixing boundary conditions and their evaluation depends upon operative mental mind-sets or the conceptual schemes of managers and employees, which are framed by the experience and learning situation of each person. Mental mind-sets exist at both the personal and organizational level. Organizational mind-sets are based on existing corporate culture, stories, rituals, and structural behavioral patterns. Managers and employees have to break operative rigid mental mind-sets at a personal and organizational level in order to overcome the causes of corporate unethical decisions. Those who break operative mental mind-sets can think beyond self-interest, instrumentalization of ethics, and economic rationality. In this context, moral imagination works in three stages: First, the stage of reproductive imagination consisting of an awareness of the mind-sets, contexts and dilemmas present; Second, the stage of productive imagination wherein managers and employees re-think their own schemas or mind-sets and find new possibilities within the given context; Third, the stage of creative imagination that entails framing a morally acceptable alternative solution to the problem.

Inner freedom is the second quality of personal integrity. Human freedom can be divided into freedom of being and freedom of doing. The freedom of being can be called inner freedom, which is the capacity to exercise one's own being. Personal integrity is the expression of one's moral core of self or being. People with integrity can exercise their inner freedom. I have argued that the exercise of inner freedom is an effective means to overcome conflicts of interest and corporate dilemma.

Based on the Ignatian tradition, Verstraeten explains that self-awareness is the first step to exercise inner freedom in daily life. Personal integrity is an expression of the moral core of the people who are aware of who they are and what they want to do. Indeed, self-awareness makes people of integrity cognizant about the blind spots or weaknesses that hinder the work of their personal integrity. The next step is discernment, where the people of integrity must ask how they can live in accordance with their personal integrity amidst conflicts of interest. Discernment brings harmony between their being and actions or decisions in professional life. As a result, managers and employees are more engaged, and find more meaning in their organizational or professional life. By using inner freedom, managers and employees with integrity can always make decisions that humanize the world because they are positively oriented toward humanity. As a result, corporate unethical conduct becomes less probable.

Moral courage is also a result of personal integrity. I have argued that the incorporation of personal integrity into corporate integrity would generate the moral courage that is necessary to overcome corporate unethical conduct. Moral courage is a brave behavior where one realizes one's own moral values, irrespective of the consequences that follow. Managers and employees have the power to make and execute their decisions. This power can be used differently in accordance with various conflicts of interest and temptations. It can be used to satisfy the interests of the self or firm without considering the worth of all stakeholders. However, the opposite is also possible, where moral courage is an outcome of the moral disposition of a person.

Moral courage should, however, come from both the side of business and the side of individuals within the business. At the level of the business, moral courage is needed to accept that ethical behavior is not always profitable. From the individual's perspective, it may lead to conflicts of interest. Shareholders can insist that senior managers act unethically. Sometimes, senior managers compel employees to act corruptly. If managers and employees do not have sufficient integrity, they may compromise their principles to corrupt decision-making. Managers with integrity would have courage to use power rightly by considering all stakeholders as persons in the midst of temptations and dilemmas because moral courage is the outcome of a moral self and its expression is found in personal integrity.

Other components of personal integrity are volition, choice, and mutual dialogue. A person with integrity would not find it difficult to have a mutual discussion with other colleagues in conflicting situations to find an optimal solution that implies a right/ethical compromise. Incorporation of personal integrity into corporate integrity theory permits a greater possibility for dialogue. I have argued that a greater possibility for dialogue in the corporate decision-making process or corporate culture and structure would reduce the possibility of unethical corporate behavior.

Openness is an underlying principle in a corporate dialogue between different stakeholders. It allows people to listen and to share viewpoints with one another. In the corporate context, however, openness is a collective attempt to find a good solution to fundamental issues. If a decision is the result of a dialogue, then the participants of the dialogue may find their decision more meaningful and remain committed to its implementation. Dialogues lead to corporate transparency that implies openness, availability, and disclosure of information. Unethical corporate conducts are risky acts if there is transparency in corporate life. Moreover, personal integrity is a precondition for a better participatory decision making process in corporate life. According to Wempe and Kaptein, a person of integrity always seeks a justifiable solution through dialogue and discussion with others in conflicting scenarios.

Even after I have clarified why the personalist approach to corporate integrity is indispensable, theories about the complementarity between ethics of being and ethics of doing have to be further investigated. Furthermore, it is also necessary to investigate how the general corporate and social environment can be created so that it promotes the personalist corporate integrity theory. Therefore, the role of political, social, and economic institutions requires further investigation.

BIBLIOGRAPHY

A. Books

Alatas, Syed Hussein. *Corruption: Its Nature, Causes and Functions*. Aldershot: Avebury, 1990.

Alvesson, Mats. *Understanding Organizational Culture*. London: Sage Publications, 2002.

Aquinas, Thomas. *Summa Theologica*, edited by Fathers of English Dominican Province. New York: Benziger Brothers, 1947.

Aristotle. *Nichomachean Ethics*. Translated by Martin Ostwald. Indianapolis: The Bobbs-Merrill Company, 1962.

———. *The Nicomachean Ethics*. Translated by Martin Ostwald. New Jersey: Prentice Hall, 1999.

Bakan, Joel. *The Corporation: The Pathological Pursuit of Profit and Power*. New York: Free Press, 2004.

Barnett, Pearce W. *Communication and the Human Condition*. Carbondale: Southern Illinois University Press, 1989.

Baron, Marcia W., Philip Pettit, and Michael Slote. *Three Methods of Ethics*. Oxford: Blackwell Publishers, 1997.

Barry, Vincent. *Moral Issues in Business*. Belmont: Wadsworth, 1986.

Batelaan, Volkert Johannes. *Organizational Culture and Strategy: A Study of Cultural Influences on the Formulation of Strategies, Goals and Objectives in Two Companies*. Amsterdam: Thesis Publishers, 1993.

Batni, Kiran. *The Pyramid of Corruption: India's Primitive Corruption and How to Deal with It*. Chennai: Notion Press, 2014.

Beauchamp, Tom L., and James F. Childress. *Principles of Biomedical Ethics*. New York: Oxford University Press, 2009.

Becker, Lawrence C. *Reciprocity*. Chicago: University of Chicago Press, 1986.

Bellah, Robert. *The Good Society*. New York: Knopf, 1992.

Bentham, Jeremy. *An Introduction to the Principles of Morals and Legislation*, edited by J.H. Burns & H.L.A. Hart. New York: Methuen, 1982.

Bergson, Henri. *The Two Sources of Morality and Religion*. Translated by R. Ashley Audra and Cloudesley Brereton. Garden: Doubleday and Company, 1956.

Boatright, John R. *Ethics and the Conduct of Business*. New Jersey: Prentice Hall, 1993.

Boersma, Martine. *Corruption: A Violation of Human Rights and a Crime under International Law*. Cambridge: Intersentia, 2012.

Bowen, Howard H. *Social Responsibilities of the Businessman*. New York: Harper&Row, 1953.

Bratman, Michael. *Intention, Plans, and Practical Reason*. Cambridge: Harvard University Press, 1987.

Brewer, Lynn, Robert Chandler, and O.C. Ferrell. *Managing Risks for Corporate Integrity: How to Survive an Ethical Misconduct Disaster*. Ohio: Thomson Higher Education, 2006.

Brown, Marvin T. *Corporate Integrity: Rethinking Organizational Ethics and Leadership*. Cambridge: Cambridge University Press, 2005.

Buber, Martin. *I and Thou*. Translated by R. Gregor Smith. New York: Charles Scribner's Sons, 1958.

Carter, Stephen. *Integrity*. New York: HarperCollins, 1996.

Cheal, David. *The Gift Economy*. London: Routledge, 1988.

Clarkson, Max. *Principles of Stakeholder Management*. Toronto: The Clarkson Centre for Business Ethics, 1999.

Cohen, Allen, and David Bradford. *Influence without Authority*. New York: John Wiley, 1991.

Cohen, Jean L., and Andrew Arato. *Civil Society and Political Theory*. Cambridge: MIT Press, 1992.

Colby, Anne, and William Damon. *Some Do Care: Contemporary Lives of Moral Commitment*. New York: Macmillan, 1992.

Cox, Damian, Marguerite La Caze, and Michael P. Levine. *Integrity and the Fragile Self*. Burlington: Ashgate Publishing, 2003.

Crane, A., and D. Matten. *Business Ethics*. 3rd ed. Oxford: Oxford University Press, 2004.

———. *Business Ethics: A European Perspective*. Oxford: Oxford University Press, 2004.

Crane, Andrew, and Dirk Matten. *Business Ethics: Managing Corporate Citizenship and Sustainability in the Age of Globalization*. 2nd ed. Oxford: Oxford University Press, 2007.

Curran, Charles E. *The Catholic Moral Tradition Today: A Synthesis*. Washington: Georgetown University Press, 1999.

DeGeorge, Richard T. *Competing with Integrity in International Business.* Oxford: Oxford University Press, 1993.

Deigh, John. *An Introduction to Ethics.* Cambridge: Cambridge University Press, 2010.

Digeser, Peter. *Our Politics, Our Selves? Liberalism, Identity, and Harm.* New Jersey: Princeton University Press, 1995.

Doig, Alan. *Fraud.* Devon: Willan Publishing, 2006.

Donaldson, Thomas. *Corporations and Morality.* New York: Prentice-Hall, 1982.

———. *The Ethics of International Business.* New York: Oxford University Press, 1989.

Donaldson, Thomas, and Thomas W. Dunfe. *Ties That Bind: A Social Contracts Approach to Business Ethics.* Harvard: Harvard Business School Press, 1999.

Doorley, John, and Helio Fred Garcia. *Reputation Management: The Key to Successful Public Relations and Corporate Communication.* 2nd ed. New York: Routledge, 2011.

Drucker, Peter F. *Innovation and Entrepreneurship.* New York: Harper and Row, 1985.

Edel, Abraham, Elizabeth Flower, and Finbarr W. O'Connor, eds. *Morality, Philosophy, and Practice: Historical and Contemporary Readings and Studies.* New York: Random House, 1989.

Eterovich, Francis H. *Aristotle's Nichomachean Ethics: Commentary and Analysis.* Washington: University Press of America, 1980.

Etzioni, Amitai. *The Moral Dimension: Toward a New Economics.* New York: Free Press, 1998.

Ewing, A.C. *Second Thoughts in Moral Philosophy.* London: Routledge amd Kegan Paul, 1959.

Feinberg, Joel. *Social Philosophy.* New Jersey: Prentice Hall, 1973.

Frank, Robert H. *Passions within Reasons: The Strategic Role of the Emotions.* New York: Norton and Company, 1988.

Frankena, William K. *Ethics.* 2nd ed. New Jersey: Prentice-Hall, 1973.

Freeman, R. Edward. *Strategic Management: A Stakeholder Approach.* Boston: Pitman Publishing, 1984.

French, Peter A. *Collective and Corporate Responsibility.* New York: Columbia University Press, 1984.

———. *Corporate Ethics.* New York: Harcourt Brace, 1995.

Friedman, Milton. *Capitalism and Freedom.* Chicago: Chicago University Press, 1963.

Froding, Barbro. *Virtue Ethics and Human Enhancement*. London: Springer, 2013.

Fuchs, Josef. *Human Values and Christian Morality*. Dublin: Cahill & Co. Limited, 1970.

Fukuyama, Francis. *Trust: The Social Virtues and the Creation of Prosperity*. New York: The Free Press, 1995.

Furrow, Dwight. *Ethics: Key Concepts in Philosophy*. New York: Continuum International Publishing Group, 2005.

Galbraith, John Kenneth. *The Age of Uncertainty*. Boston: Houghton Mifflin, 1977.

Gawande, Eknath N. *Value Oriented Education: Vision for Better Living*. New Delhi: Sarup & Sons, 2002.

George, Richard T. De. *Business Ethics*. New Jersey: Pearson Prentice Hall, 2006.

Gill, S.S. *The Pathology of Corruption*. New Delhi: Harper Collins, 1998.

Goodpaster, Kenneth E. *Conscience and Corporate Culture*. Oxford: Blackwell Publishing, 2007.

Gove, Philip Babcock, ed. *Webster's Third New International Dictionary*. Massachusetts: Merriam-Webster, 1993.

Guire, Joseph Mc. *Business and Society*. New York: McGraw-Hill, 1963.

Gutmann, Amy, and Sigal Ben-Porath. *Democratic Education*. Princeton: Princeton University Press, 1987.

Hackman, J. Richard. *Leading Teams: Setting the Stage for Great Performances*. Boston: Harvard Business School Press, 2002.

Häring, Bernhard. *Free and Faithful in Christ: Moral Theology for Priests and Laity*. Vol. 1. London: Billing and Sons, 1978.

Hayek, Friedrich. *Studies in Philosophy, Politics and Economics*. London: Routlegde, 1967.

Hessen, Robert. *In Defence of the Corporation*. Stanford: Hoover Institution Press, 1979.

Hewitt, John. *Self and Society: A Symbolic Interactionist Social Psychology*. Boston: Allyn and Bacon, 1997.

Hofstede, Geert. *Cultures and Organizations: Software of the Mind*. London: McGraw-Hill, 1991.

———. *Culture's Consequence*. 2nd ed. California: Sage Publications, 2001.

Hooft, Stan Van. *Understanding Virtue Ethics*. Chesham: Acumen, 2006.

Hosmer, LaRue Tone. *The Ethics of Management*. New York: McGraw, 2008.

Illathuparambil, Mathew. *Business Ethics*. Tiruvalla: Macfast Publications, 2005.

———. *Technology and Ethical Ambiguity*. New Delhi: Global Vision Publishing, 2009.

Iozzio, Mary Jo. *Self Determination and the Moral Act*. Leuven: Peeters, 1995.

Jacoby, Neil H., Peter Nehemkis, and Richard Eells. *Bribery and Extortion in World Business: A Study of Corporate Political Payments Abroad*. New York: Macmillan Publishers, 1977.

Joe, Martin. *Environmental Ethics and Politics in the Developing Countries*. Wien: Ferdinand Schoningh, 2003.

Johnson, Mark. *The Body in the Mind: The Bodily Basis of Meaning, Imagination, and Reason*. Chicago: The University of Chicago Press, 1987.

———. *Moral Imagination: Implications of Cognitive Science for Ethics*. Chicago: The University of Chicago Press, 1993.

Kaptein, Muel. *Ethics Management: Auditing and Developing the Ethical Content of Organizations*. Boston: Kluwer Academic Publishers, 1998.

———. *The 6 Principles of Managing with Integrity: A Practical Guide for Leaders*. Trowbridge: The Cromwell Press, 2008.

Kaptein, Muel, and Johan Wempe. *The Balanced Company: A Theory of Corporate Integrity*. Oxford: Oxford University Press, 2002.

Keenan, James F. *A History of Catholic Moral Theology in the Twentieth Century: From Confessing Sins to Liberating Consciences*. New York: Continuum International Publishing Group, 2010.

Keynes, John Maynard. *The General Theory of Employment, Interest and Money*. London: Macmillan, 1967.

Klitgaard, Robert. *Controlling Corruption*. Berkeley: University of California Press, 1988.

Knudson, Albert C. *The Philosophy of Personalism: A Study in the Metaphysics of Religion*. New York: Kraus, 1969.

Kochen, Nick, and Robin Goodyear. *Corruption: The New Corporate Challenge*. New York: Macmillan, 2011.

Krishan, Yuvraj. *The Doctrine of Karma in the Vedic Literature*. Delhi: Motilal Banarsidass Publishers, 1997.

Kumar, Rajesh, and Anand Kumar Sethi. *Doing Business in India: A Guide for Western Managers*. New York: Palgrave Macmillan, 2005.

Lakoff, George, and Mark Johnson. *Philosophy in the Flesh: The Embodied Mind and Its Challenge to Western Thought*. New York: Basic Books, 1999.

Lambsdorfe, Johann Graf. *The Institutional Economics of Corruption and Reform: Theory, Evidence, and Policy*. Cambridge: Cambridge University Press, 2007.

Landau, Russ Shafer. *The Fundamentals of Ethics*. Oxford: Oxford University Press, 2010.

Little, Daniel. *Varieties of Social Explanations*. New York: Westview Press, 1991.

Lowney, Chris. *Heroic Leadership: Best Practices from a 450-Year-Old Company that Changed the World*. Chicago: Loyola Press, 2003.

Lutz, Mark A., and Kenneth Lux. *Humanistic Economics: The New Chellenge*. New York: The Bootstrap Press, 1988.

MacIntyre, Alasdiar. *Whose Justice Which Rationality*. Notre Dame: University of Notre Dame Press, 1998.

———. *After Virtue: A Study of Moral Theory*. Notre Dame: University of Notre Dame Press, 1981.

Maslow, Abraham H. *Toward a Psychology of Being*. New York: Van Nostrand Reinhold, 1968.

Maslow, Abraham Harold. *Motivation and Personality*. New York: Harper & Row, 1954.

May, Larry. *The Morality of Groups: Collective Responsibility, Group-Based Harm, and Corporate Rights*. Indiana: University of Notre Dame Press, 1987.

May, Rollo. *Freedom and Destiny*. New York: Dell Publishing, 1981.

Menzel, Donald C. *Ethics Management for Public Administrators: Leading and Building Organizations of Integrity*. New York: M.E. Sharpe, 2012.

Migne, Jacques-Paul. *Patrologia Latina*. Vol. 72. Paris: J.P. Migne, 1844.

Mill, John Stuart. *Utilitarianism*. Auckland: The Floating Press, 1879.

Modras, Ronald. *Ignatian Humanism: A Dynamic Spirituality for the 21st Century*. Chicago: Loyola Press, 2004.

Moran, Gabriel. *No Leader to the Sky: Education and Morality*. New York: Harper and Row, 1987.

Mulgan, Tim. *Understanding Utilitarianism*. Stocksfield: Acumen Publishing Limited, 2007.

Nagel, Thomas. *Mortal Questions*. New York: Cambridge University Press, 1979.

Nash, Laura L. *Good Intentions Aside: A Manager's Guide to Resolving Ethical Problems*. Boston: Harvard Business School Press, 1990.

Nash, Ronald H. *Freedom, Justice and the State*. Washington: University Press of America, 1980.

Noonan, Johnson. *Bribes*. New York: MacMillan, 1984.

Novak, Michael. *Business as a Calling: Work and the Examined Life*. New York: The Free Press, 1996.

Nussbaum, Martha C. *Love's Knowledge: Essays on Philosophy and Literature.* New York: Oxford University Press, 1990.

O'Connell, Timothy E. *Principles for a Catholic Morality.* New York: The Seabury Press, 1978.

O'Gara, John D. *Corporate Fraud: Case Studies in Detection and Prevention.* New Jersey: John Wiley & Sons, 2004.

Oliveira, Agamenon R.E. *A History of the Work Concept: From Physics to Economics.* Dordrecht: Springer, 2014.

Paine, Lynne Sharp. *Value Shift.* New York: McGraw-Hill, 2003.

Painter-Morland, Mollie. *Business Ethics as Practice: Ethics as the Everyday Business of Business.* Cambridge: Cambridge University Press, 2008.

Palmier, Leslie H. *The Control of Bureaucratic Corruption: Case Studies in Asia.* New Delhi: Allied Publishers, 1985.

Pearson, Gordon. *Integrity in Organizations: An Alternative Business Ethic.* New York: McGraw-Hill Book Company, 1995.

Peikoff, Leonard. *Objectivism, the Philosophy of Ayn Rand.* New York: Meridiam, 1991.

Petrick, Joseph A., and John F. Quinn. *Management Ethics: Integrity at Work.* London: Sage Publications, 1997.

Phansalkar, S.J. *Opportunities and Strategies for Indian Business: Preparing for a Global India.* New Delhi: Response Books, 2005.

Pirovolakis, Eftichis. *Reading Derrida and Ricoeur: Improbable Encounters between Deconstruction and Hermeneutics.* New York: State University of New York Press, 2010.

Rahner, Karl. *Grace in Freedom.* London: Burns&Oates, 1968.

———. *Theology of Freedom.* New York: The Seabury Press, 1974.

———. *Foundations of Christian Faith: An Introduction to the Idea of Christianity.* Translated by William V. Dych. New York: The Seabury Press, 1978.

Ramsay, Hayden. *Beyond Virtue: Integrity and Morality.* London: Macmillan Press, 1997.

Ricoeur, Paul. *Time and Narrative.* Translated by Kathleen McLaughlin and David Pellauer. Vol. 1. Chicago: University of Chicago Press, 1984.

———. *Oneself as Another.* Translated by Kathleen Blarney. Chicago: The University of Chicago Press, 1992.

———. *The Just.* Chicago: The University of Chicago Press, 2000.

Robbins, Stephen P., and Mary Coulter. *Management.* New Jersey: Pearson Prentice, 2009.

Ross, W.D. *The Right and the Good*. Oxford: Oxford University Press, 1930.

Rudman, Stanley. *Concepts of Person and Christian Ethics*. New York: Cambridge University Press, 1997.

Ryken, Leland, James C. Wilhoit, and Tremper Longman, eds. *Dictionary of Biblical Imagery: An Encyclopaedic Exploration of the Images, Symbols, Motifs, Metaphors, Figures of Speech and Literary Patterns of the Bible*. Illinois: Inter Varsity Press, 1998.

Sen, Amartya. *Resources, Values and Development*. Oxford: Basil Blackwell, 1984.

———. *Commodities and Capabilities*. Oxford: Elsevier Science Publishers, 1985.

———. *On Ethics and Economics*. Oxford: Basil Blackwell, 1990.

Senge, Peter M., Charlotte Roberts, Richard B. Ross, Bryan J. Smith, and Art Kleiner. *The Fifth Discipline Fieldbook: Strategies and Tools for Building a Learning Organization*. London: Nicholas Brealey, 1994.

Sharma, Laxmi. *Corruption in India: Problems and Solutions*. Jaipur: Prateeksha Publications, 2012.

Shaw, W.H., and Vincent Barry. *Moral Issues in Business*. Belmont: Wadsworth Publishing Company, 1998.

Shaw, William H. *Contemporary Ethics: Taking Account of Utilitarianism*. Massachusetts: Blackwell Publishers, 1999.

Skousen, Mark. *The Big Three in Economics: Adam Smith, Karl Marx, and John Maynard Keynes*. New York: M.E. Sharpe, 2007.

Smith, Adam. *An Inquiry into the Nature and Causes of the Wealth of Nations*. Vol. 1. London: J.M. Dent and Sons, 1964.

———. *An Inquiry into the Nature and Causes of the Wealth of Nations*. Vol. 2. London: J.M. Dent and Sons, 1964.

———. *The Theory of Moral Sentiments*. New York: Arlington House, 1969.

Solomon, Robert. *Ethics and Excellence: Cooperation and Integrity in Business*. Oxford: Oxford University Press, 1992.

———. *A Better Way to Think About Business: How Personal Integrity Leads to Corporate Success*. Oxford: Oxford University Press, 1999.

Spinosa, Charles, Fernando Flores, and Hubert L. Dreyfus. *Disclosing New Worlds*. Cambridge: The MIT Press, 1997.

Stanford, Naomi. *Corporate Culture Getting It Right*. New Jersey: John Wiley & Sons, 2011.

Stonich, Paul J. *Implementing Strategy: Making Strategy Happen*. Cambridge: Ballinger Publishing Company, 1982.

Sullivan, Roger J. *Morality and the Good Life: A Commentary on Aristotle's Nicomachean Ethics*. Memphis: Memphis State University Press, 1980.

Swamy, Subramanian. *Corruption and Corporate Governance in India: Satyam, Spectrum and Sundaram*. New Delhi: Har Anand Publications, 2009.

Swanton, Christine. *Freedom: A Coherence Theory*. Cambridge: Hackett Publishing Company, 1990.

Tanzi, Vito, and Hamid Davoodi. *Roads to Nowhere: How Corruption in Public Investment Hurts Growth*. Washington: IMF Publication, 1998.

Taub, Richard P. *Bureaucrats under Stress: Administrators and Administration in an Indian State*. Berkeley: University of California Press, 1969.

Taylor, Charles. *Sources of the Self: The Making of Modern Identity*. Cambridge: Harvard University Press, 1989.

———. *The Ethics of Authenticity*. Cambridge: Harvard University Press, 1991.

———. *A Secular Age*. Cambridge: The Belknap Press, 2007.

Velasquez, Manuel G. *Business Ethics: Concepts and Cases*. New York: Prentice Hall, 1992.

———. *Business Ethics: Concepts and Cases*. Upper Saddle River: Prentice Hall, 2002.

Vittal, N. *Corruption in India: The Roadblock to National Prosperity*. New Delhi: Academic Foundation, 2003.

Walton, Clarence C. *Corporate Social Responsibilities*. Belmont: Wadsworth, 1967.

Weber, Max. *The Protestant Ethic and the Spirit of Capitalism*. London: Taylor & Francis e-Library, 2005.

Wells, Joseph T. *Corporate Fraud Handbook: Prevention and Detection*. 3rd ed. New Jersey: John Wiley & Sons, 2011.

———. *Principles of Fraud Examination*. 3rd ed. New Jersey: John Wiley and Sons, 2011.

Wempe, Johan. *Market and Morality: Business Ethics and the Dirty and Many Hands Dilemma*. Amsterdam: Eburon, 1998.

Werhane, Patricia H. *Persons, Rights and Corporations*. New York: Prentice Hall, 1985.

———. *Adam Smith and His Legacy for Modern Capitalism*. Oxford: Oxford University Press, 1991.

———. *Moral Imagination and Management Decision Making*. New York: Oxford University Press, 1999.

Wogaman, J. Philip. *Moral Dilemma: An Introduction to Christian Ethics*. Kentueky: Westminister John Knox Press, 2009.

Ziegler, Alexandre. *A Game Theory Analysis of Options: Contributions to the Theory of Financial Intermediation in Continuous Time*. Heidelberg: Springer, 1999.

B. Articles

Abdalla, Hagen F., Ahmed S. Maghrabi, and Bel G. Raggad. "Assessing the Perceptions of Human Resource Managers toward Nepotism: A Cross-Cultural Study." *International Journal of Manpower* 19, no. 8 (1998): 554–570.

Abdulai, Abdul-Gafaru. "Political Will in Combating Corruption in Developing and Transition Economies." *Journal of Financial Crime* 16, no. 4 (2009): 387–417.

Acevedo, Alma. "Personalist Business Ethics and Humanistic Management: Insights from Jacques Maritain." *Journal of Business Ethics* 105, no. 2 (2012): 197–219.

Agboola, Alirat Olayinka. "Neoclassical Economics and New Institutional Economics." *Property Management* 33, no. 5 (2015): 412–429.

Agrawal, Chetan. "Right to Information: A Tool for Combating Corruption in India." *Journal of Management & Public Policy* 3, no. 2 (2012): 26–38.

Aguilera, Ruth V., and Abhijeet K. Vadera. "The Dark Side of Authority: Antecedents, Mechanisms, and Outcomes of Organizational Corruption." *Journal of Business Ethics* 77 (2008): 431–449.

Ahmad, Shahbaz. "Humanistic Economics Needed to Sustain Society." *Indian Journal of Economics and Development* 1, no. 4 (2013): 98–99.

Aidt, Toke S. "Economic Analysis of Corruption: A Survey." *The Economic Journal* 113, no. 491 (2003): 632–652.

Akbar, Yusaf H., and Vukan Vujic. "Explaining Corruption: The Role of National Culture and Its Implications for International Management." *Cross Cultural Management* 21, no. 2 (2014): 191–218.

Allee, Verna. "Value Network Analysis and Value Conversion of Tangible and Intangible Assets." *Journal of Intellectual Capital* 9, no. 1 (2008): 5–24.

Amba-Rao, Sita C., Joseph A. Petrick, Jatinder N. D. Gupta, and Thomas J. Von Der Embse. "Comparative Performance Appraisal Practices and Management Values among Foreign and Domestic Firms in India." *The International Journal of Human Resource Management* 11, no. 1 (2000): 60–89.

Andersen, Poul Houman, and Rajesh Kumar. "Emotions, Trust and Relationship Development in Business Relationships: A Conceptual Model for Buyer-Seller Dyads." *Industrial Marketing Management* 35 (2006): 522–535.

Anyinam, Charles C. "Ecology and Ethnomedicine: Exploring Links between Current Environmental Crisis and Indigenous Medical Practices." *Social Science and Medicine* 40, no. 3 (1995): 321–329.

Aquino, Karl, and Americus Reed. "The Self-Importance of Moral Identity." *Journal of Personality and Social Psychology* 83, no. 6 (2002): 1423–1440.

Aquino, Ranhilio Callangan. "The Dialectics of Power, Rights, and Responsibility." *Kritike* 3, no. 1 (2009): 1–9.

Ardichvili, Alexandre, Douglas Jondle, Brenda Kowske, Edgard Cornachione, Jessica Li, and Thomas Thakadipuram. "Ethical Cultures in Large Business Organizations in Brazil, Russia, India, and China." *Journal of Business Ethics* 105 (2012): 415–428.

Arjoon, Surendra. "Virtue Theory as a Dynamic Theory of Business." *Journal of Business Ethics* 28 (2000): 159–178.

Arneback, Emma. "Moral Imagination in Education: A Deweyan Proposal for Teachers Responding to Hate Speech." *Journal of Moral Education* 43, no. 3 (2014): 269–281.

Arnold, Denis G. "Corporate Moral Agency." *Midwest Studies in Philosophy* 30, no. 1 (2006): 279–291.

Arnold, Denis G., and Laura P. Hartman. "Moral Imagination and the Future of Sweatshops." *Business and Society Review* 108, no. 4 (2003): 425–461.

Arrow, Kenneth. "Social Responsibility and Economic Efficiency." *Public Policy* 21, no. 3 (1973): 300–317.

Arunthanes, Wiboon, Patriya Tansuhaj, and David J. Lemak. "Cross-Cultural Business Gift Giving: A New Conceptualization and Theoretical Framework." *International Marketing Review* 11, no. 4 (1994): 44–55.

Ashford, Elizabeth. "Utilitarianism, Integrity, and Partiality." *The Journal of Philosophy* 97, no. 8 (2000): 421–439.

Ashforth, Blake E., and Vikas Anand. "The Normalization of Corruption in Organizations." *Research in Organizational Behavior* 25 (2003): 1–52.

Ashforth, Blake E., Dennis A. Gioia, Sandra L. Robinson, and Linda K. Treviño. "Introduction to Special Topic Forum: Re-Viewing Organizational Corruption." *The Academy of Management Review* 33, no. 3 (2008): 670–684.

Ashley, Benedict M. "Fundamental Option and/or Commitment to Ultimate End." *Philosophy & Theology* 10, no. 1 (2010): 113–139.

Ashman, Ian, and Diana Winstanley. "For or against Corporate Identity? Personification and the Problem of Moral Agency." *Journal of Business Ethics* 76, no. 1 (2007): 83–95.

Audi, Robert. "Virtue Ethics as a Resource in Business." *Business Ethics Quarterly* 22, no. 2 (2012): 273–291.

Audi, Robert, and Patrick E. Murphy. "The Many Faces of Integrity." *Business Ethics Quarterly* 16, no. 1 (2006): 3–21.

Baack, Donald, Christine Fogliasso, and James Harris. "The Personal Impact of Ethical Decisions: A Social Penetration Theory." *Journal of Business Ethics* 24, no. 1 (2000): 39–49.

Bardhan, Pranab. "Corruption and Development: A Review of Issues." *Journal of Economic Literature* 35, no. 3 (1997): 1320–1346.

Barnett, Michael L., John M. Jermier, and Barbara A. Lafferty. "Corporate Reputation: The Definitional Landscape." *Corporate Reputation Review Volume* 9, no. 1 (2006): 26-38.

Basdeo, Dax K., Ken G. Smith, Curtis M. Grimm, Violina P. Rindova, and Pamela J. Derfus. "The Impact of Market Actions on Firm Reputation." *Strategic Management Journal* 27, no. 12 (2006): 1205–1219.

Batson, Daniel, and Elizabeth R. Thompson. "Why Don't Moral People Act Morally? Motivational Considerations." *Current Directions in Psychological Science* 10, no. 2 (2001): 54–57.

Beatty, Sharon E., Lynn R. Kahle, and Pamela Homer. "Personal Values and Gift-Giving Behaviors: A Study across Cultures." *Journal of Business Research* 22, no. 2 (1991): 149–157.

Becker, Gerhold K. "Integrity as a Moral Ideal and Business Benchmark." *Journal of International Business Ethics* 2, no. 2 (2009): 70–84.

Becker, Thomas E. "Integrity in Organizations: Beyond Honesty and Conscientiousness." *Academy of Management Review* 23, no. 1 (1998): 154–161.

Beckhard, Richard, and W. Gibb Dyer. "Managing Continuity in the Family-Owned Business." *Organizational Dynamics* 12, no. 1 (1983): 5–12.

Beekun, Rafik, Yvonne Stedham, James W. Westerman, and Jeanne H.Yamamura. "Effects of Justice and Utilitarianism on Ethical Decision Making: A Crosscultural Examination of Gender Similarities and Differences." *Business Ethics: A European Review* 19, no. 4 (2010): 309–325.

Benson, George C.S. "Codes of Ethics." *Journal of Business Ethics* 8, no. 5 (1989): 305–319.

Benz, Matthias. "Not for the Profit, but for the Satisfaction?—Evidence on Worker Well—Being in Non-Profit Firms." *KYKLOS* 58, no. 2 (2005): 155–176.

Berger, Ron, and Ram Herstein. "The Evolution of Business Ethics in India." *International Journal of Social Economics* 41, no. 11 (2014): 1073–1086.

Bernardi, Richard A., and Ikki Hayashi. "The Association between Bribery and Unethical Actions: An Asian Perspective." *European Journal of Business and Innovation Research* 1, no. 2 (2013): 70–84.

Bernardi, Richard A., and Katie M. Vassill. "The Association among Bribery and Unethical Corporate Actions: An International Comparison." *Business Ethics: A European Review* 13, no. 4 (2004): 342–353.

Bertland, Alexander. "Virtue Ethics in Business and the Capabilities Approach." *Journal of Business Ethics* 84 (2009): 25–32.

Bhasin, Madan. "Corporate Accounting Scandal at Satyam: A Case Study of India's Enron." *European Journal of Business and Social Sciences* 1, no. 12 (2013): 25–47.

Bhasin, Madan Lal. "Corporate Accounting Fraud: A Case Study of Satyam Computers Limited." *Open Journal of Accounting* 2 (2013): 23–38.

Bijoy, C.R. "Kerala's Plachimada Struggle: A Narrative on Water and Governance Rights." *Economic and Political Weekly* 41, no. 41 (2006): 4332–4339.

Bishara, Norman D., and Cindy A. Schipani. "Strengthening the Ties That Bind: Preventing Corruption in the Executive Suite." *Journal of Business Ethics* 88 (2009): 765–780.

Biss, Mavis. "Moral Imagination, Perception, and Judgment." *The Southern Journal of Philosophy* 52, no. 1 (2014): 1–21.

Blowers, Andrew, Jan Boersema, and Adrian Martin. "Is Sustainable Development Sustainable?" *Journal of Integrative Environmental Sciences* 9, no. 1 (2012): 1–8.

Boatright, John R. "Aristotle Meets Wall Street: The Case for Virtue Ethics in Business Ethics and Excellence: Cooperation and Integrity in Business by Robert C. Solomon." *Business Ethics Quarterly* 5, no. 2 (1995): 353–359.

Bolino, Mark C., William H. Turnley, and James M. Bloodgood. "Citizenship Behavior and the Creation of Social Capital in Organizations." *The Academy of Management Review* 27, no. 4 (2002): 505–522.

Bommer, Michael, Clarence Gratto, Jerry Gravander, and Mark Tuttle. "A Behavioral Model of Ethical and Unethical Decision Making." *Journal of Business Ethics* 6, no. 4 (1987): 265–280.

Bouckaert, Luk. "The Project of a Personalistic Economics." *Ethical Perspectives* 6, no. 1 (1999): 20–33.

———. "Spirituality as a Public Affair." *Ethical Perspectives* 10, no. 2 (2003): 106–117.

Bowen, Shannon A. "Expansion of Ethics as the Tenth Generic Principle of Public Relations Excellence: A Kantian Theory and Model for Managing Ethical Issues." *Journal of Public Relations Research* 16, no. 1 (2004): 65–92.

———. "Autonomy in Communication Inclusion in Strategic Management and Ethical Decision-Making, a Comparative Case Analysis." *Journal of Communication Management* 10, no. 4 (2006): 330–352.

Bowen, Shannon A., and Robert L. Heath. "Issues Management, Systems and Rhetoric: Exploring the Distinction between Ethical and Legal Guidelines at Enron." *Journal of Public Affairs* 5 (2005): 84–98.

Boyd, Brian K., Donald D. Bergh, and David J. Ketchen. "Reconsidering the Reputation—Performance Relationship: A Resource-Based View." *Journal of Management* 36, no. 3 (2010): 588–609.

Bozeman, Barry. "A Theory of Government 'Red Tape'." *Journal of Public Administration Research and Theory* 3, no. 3 (1993): 273–303.

Bragues, George. "Seek the Good Life, Not Money: The Aristotelian Approach to Business Ethics." *Journal of Business Ethics* 67, no. 4 (2006): 341–357.

Branco, Manuel Couret. "Economics against Democracy." *Review of Radical Political Economics* 44, no. 1 (2012): 23–39.

Bratman, Michael. "Two Faces of Intention." *The Philosophical Review* 93, no. 3 (1984): 375–405.

———. "Shared Intention." *Ethics* 104, no. 1 (1993): 97–113.

Breuer, Roland. "Individualism and Personalism." *Ethical Perspectives* 6, no. 1 (1999): 67–81.

Brown, Marvin T. "Corporate Integrity and Public Interest: A Relational Approach to Business Ethics and Leadership." *Journal of Business Ethics* 66, no. 1 (2006): 11–18.

Brown, Randall B. "Organizational Commitment: Clarifying the Concept and Simplifying the Existing Construct Typology." *Journal of Vocational Behavior* 49, no. 3 (1996): 230–251.

Brundin, Ethel, Holger Patzelt, and Dean A. Shepherd. "Managers' Emotional Displays and Employees' Willingness to Act Entrepreneurially." *Journal of Business Venturing* 23 (2008): 221–243.

Buchholz, Rogene A., and Sandra B. Rosenthal. "Integrating Ethics All the Way Through: The Issue of Moral Agency Reconsidered." *Journal of Business Ethics* 66, no. 2/3 (2006): 233–239.

Budhwar, Pawan S. "Indian and British Personnel Specialists' Understanding of the Dynamics of Their Function: An Empirical Study." *International Business Review* 9 (2000): 727–753.

Budhwar, Pawan S., and Paul R. Sparrow. "Strategic HRM through the Cultural Looking Glass: Mapping the Cognition of British and Indian Managers." *Organization Studies* 23, no. 4 (2002): 599–638.

Budhwar, Pawan S., Arup Varma, Virender Singh, and Rohin Dhar. "HRM Systems of Indian Call Centres: An Exploratory Study." *The International Journal of Human Resource Management* 17, no. 5 (2006): 881–897.

Budner, Stanley. "Intolerance of Ambiguity as a Personality Variable." *Journal of Personality* 30, no. 1 (1962): 29–50.

Burdenski, H.M., and D.H. Dunson. "Acquiring Economic Justice for All: An Ongoing Struggle." *Journal of Business Ethics* 20, no. 2 (1999): 93–99.

Burggraeve, Roger. "Prohibition and Taste: The Bipolarity in Christian Ethics." *Ethical Perspectives* 1, no. 3 (1994): 130–144.

———. "The Holistic Personalism of Professor Magister Louis Janssens." *Louvain Studies* 27, no. 1 (2002): 29–38.

Burke, Lee, and Jeanne M. Logsdon. "How Corporate Social Responsibility Pays Off." *Long Range Planning* 29, no. 4 (1996): 495–502.

Butler, John K. "Toward Understanding and Measuring Conditions of Trust: Evolution of Conditions of Trust Inventory." *Journal of Management History* 17, no. 3 (1991): 643–663.

Cadbury, Sir Adrian. "Ethical Managers Make Their Own Rules." *Harvard Business Review* 65, no. 5 (1987): 69–73.

Caldwell, David F., and Dennis Moberg. "An Exploratory Investigation of the Effect of Ethical Culture in Activating Moral Imagination." *Journal of Business Ethics* 73, no. 2 (2007): 193–204.

Calhoun, Cheshire. "Standing for Something." *The Journal of Philosophy* 92, no. 5 (1995): 235–260.

Calhoun, Laurie. "The Problem of 'Dirty Hands' and Corrupt Leadership." *The Independent Review* 8, no. 3 (2004): 363–385.

Calton, Jerry M., and Lawrence J. Lad. "Social Contracting as a Trust-Building Process of Network Governance." *Business Ethics Quarterly* 5, no. 2 (1995): 271–295.

Camerer, Colin. "Gifts as Economic Signals and Social Symbols." *American Journal of Sociology* 94 (1988): 180–214.

Camfield, Laura, and Monica Guillen-Royo. "Wants, Needs and Satisfaction: A Comparative Study in Thailand and Bangladesh." *Social Indicators Research* 96, no. 2 (2010): 183–203.

Carroll, Archie B. "A Three-Dimensional Conceptual Model of Corporate Performance." *The Academy of Management Review* 4, no. 4 (1979): 497–505.

———. "In Search of the Moral Manager." *Business Horizons* 4 (1987): 7–15.

———. "The Pyramid of Corporate Social Responsibility: Toward the Moral Management of Organizational Stakeholders." *Business Horizons* 34, no. 4 (1991): 39–51.

———. "Corporate Social Responsibility: Evolution of a Definitional Construct." *Business & Society* 38, no. 3 (1999): 286–295.

Carson, Thomas L. "Bribery, Extortion, and The Foreign Corrupt Practices Act." *Philosophy and Public Affairs* 14, no. 1 (1985): 66–90.

Carter, David L. "Drug-Related Corruption of Police Officers: A Contemporary Typology." *Journal of Criminal Justice* 18, no. 2 (1990): 85–98.

Cartwright, Susan, and Nicola Holmes. "The Meaning of Work: The Challenge of Regaining Employee Engagement and Reducing Cynicism." *Human Resource Management Review* 16, no. 2 (2006): 199–208.

Carvaja, Raul. "Large-Scale Corruption: Definition, Causes, and Cures." *Systemic Practice and Action Research* 12, no. 1 (1999): 335–353.

Chakraborty, S. K. "Business Ethics in India." *Journal of Business Ethics* 16, no. 14 (1997): 1529-1538.

Chalupnicek, Pavel. "From an Individual to a Person: What Economy Can Learn from Theology About Human Beings." *Econ Journal Watch* 11, no. 2 (2014): 120–126.

Chandrasekaran, V. "Corruption in India and Mechanism to Control—a Study." *Journal of Radix International Educational and Research Consortium* 1, no. 12 (2012): 1–10.

Chatterjee, Samir R., and Cecil A. L. Pearson. "Indian Managers in Transition: Orientations, Work Goals, Values and Ethics." *Management International Review* 40, no. 1 (2000): 81–95.

Chattopadhyay, Chandrani. "Indian Philosophy and Business Ethics: A Review" *Advances in Management & Applied Economics* 2, no. 3 (2012): 111–123.

Chen, Charles J.P., Yuan Ding, and Chansog Kim. "High-Level Politically Connected Firms, Corruption, and Analyst Forecast Accuracy around the World." *Journal of International Business Studies* 41, no. 9 (2010): 1505–1524.

Chennattu, Mary M. "The Dignity of Women: Christian Perspectives." *Journal of Dharma* 37, no. 1 (2012): 435–450.

Chrisman, James J., Esra Memili, and Kaustav Misra. "Nonfamily Managers, Family Firms, and the Winner's Curse: The Influence of Noneconomic Goals and Bounded Rationality." *Entrepreneurship Theory and Practice* 38, no. 5 (2013): 1103–1127.

Christensen, Clayton M., and Michael Overdorf. "Meeting the Challenge of Disruptive Change." *Harvard Business Review* 78, no. 2 (2000): 66–71.

Christie, Maria Joseph, Ik-Whan G. Kwon, Philipp A. Stoeberl, and Raymond Baumhart. "A Cross-Cultural Comparison of Ethical Attitudes of Business Managers: India, Korea and the United States." *Journal of Business Ethics* 46, no. 3 (2003): 263–287.

Ciepley, David. "Beyond Public and Private: Toward a Political Theory of the Corporation." *American Political Science Review* 17, no. 1 (2013): 139–158.

Clark, Alice W., and T.V. Sekher. "Can Career-Minded Young Women Reverse Gender Discrimination? A View from Bangalore's High-Tech Sector." *Gender Technology and Development* 11, no. 3 (2007): 285–319.

Clarkson, Max B. E. "A Stakeholder Framework for Analyzing and Evaluating Corporate Social Performance." *The Academy of Management Review* 20, no. 1 (1995): 92–117.

Coase, R. H. "The Nature of the Firm." *Economica* 4, no. 16 (1937): 386–405.

Coffey, David. "Rahner's Theology of Fundamental Option." *Philosophy and Theology* 10 no. 1 (1997): 255–284.

Cohen, Jeffrey, Yuan Ding, Cédric Lesage, and Hervé Stolowy. "Corporate Fraud and Managers' Behavior: Evidence from the Press." *Journal of Business Ethics* 95 (2010): 271–315.

Colander, David. "The Death of Neoclassical Economics." *Journal of the History of Economic Thought* 22, no. 2 (2000): 127–143.

Coleman, James S. "Social Capital in the Creation of Human Capital." *American Journal of Sociology* 94 (1988): S95–S120.

Collins, Jamie D., Klaus Uhlenbruck, and Peter Rodriguez. "Why Firms Engage in Corruption: A Top Management Perspective." *Journal of Business Ethics* 87 (2009): 89–108.

Cooper, Eugene J. "The Fundamental Option." *Irish Theological Quarterly*, no. 39 (1972): 383–392.

Cooter, Robert, and Melvin A. Eisenberg. "Fairness, Character, and Efficiency in Firms." *University of Pennsylvania Law Review* 149, no. 6 (2001): 1717–1733.

Copp, David. "Collective Actions and Secondary Actions." *American Philosophical Quarterly* 16, no. 3 (1979): 117–186.

Corlett, Angelo J. "Collective Punishment and Public Policy." *Journal of Business Ethics* 11, no. 3 (1992): 207–216.

Cosgrave, William. "Basic Choice and Basic Stance: Explaining the Fundamental Option." *The Furrow* 35, no. 8 (1984): 508–518.

Cottingham, John. "Integrity and Fragmentation." *Journal of Applied Philosophy* 27, no. 1 (2010): 1–13.

Craft, Jana L. "A Review of the Empirical Ethical Decision-Making Literature: 2004–2011." *Journal of Business Ethics* (2012): 1–39.

Crane, Andrew, and Trish Ruebottom. "Stakeholder Theory and Social Identity: Rethinking Stakeholder Identification." *Journal of Business Ethics* 102, no. 1 (2011): 77–87.

Crossan, Mary, Daina Mazutis, and Gerard Seijts. "In Search of Virtue: The Role of Virtues, Values and Character Strengths in Ethical Decision Making." *Journal of Business Ethics* 113 (2013): 567–581.

Cullinan, Paul P. "Epidemiological Assessment of Health Effects from Chemical Incidents." *Occupational and Environmental Medicine* 59, no. 8 (2002): 568–572.

D'Souza, Victor S. "Sociology and Social Transformation in India. The Neglect of the Idea of Fraternity." *Sociological Bulletin* 37, no. 1/2 (1988): 1–9.

D'Souza, Clare. "An Inference of Gift-Giving within Asian Business Culture." *Asia Pacific Journal of Marketing and Logistics* 15, no. 1/2 (2003): 27–38.

Dailey, R.C., and L.T Reuschling. "Managing Continuity in the Family-Owned Company." *Journal of General Management* 5 (1980): 49–56.

Daniel, Shirley J., Joshua K. Cieslewicz, and Hamid Pourjalali. "The Impact of National Economic Culture and Country-Level Institutional Environment on Corporate Governance Practices: Theory and Empirical Evidence." *Management International Review* 52, no. 3 (2012): 365–394.

David B. Greenberger, Marcia P. Miceli and, and Debra J. Cohen. "Oppositionists and Group Norms: The Reciprocal Influence of Whistle-Blowers and Co-Workers." *Journal of Business Ethics* 6, no. 7 (1987): 527–542.

Davis, James H., and John A. Ruhe. "Perceptions of Country Corruption: Antecedents and Outcomes." *Journal of Business Ethics* 43, no. 4 (2003): 275–288.

Davis, Keith. "Can Business Afford to Ignore Social Responsibilities?" *California Management Review* 2, no. 3 (1960): 70–78.

———. "The Case for and against Business Assumption of Social Responsibilities." *The Academy of Management Journal* 16, no. 2 (1973): 312–322.

Davis, Mark H. "Measuring Individual Differences in Empathy: Evidence for a Multidimensional Approach." *Journal of Personality and Social Psychology* 44, no. 1 (1983): 113–126.

Dehejia, Rajeev H, and Vivek H. Dehejia. "Religion and Economic Activity in India: An Historical Perspective." *American Journal of Economics and Sociology* 52, no. 2 (1993): 145–153.

Denison, Daniel R., Robert Hooijberg, and Robert E. Quinn. "Paradox and Performance: Toward a Theory of Behavioral Complexity in Managerial Leadership." *Organization Science* 6, no. 5 (1995): 524–540.

Desai, Sonalde, and Devaki Jain. "Maternal Employment and Changes in Family Dynamics: The Social Context of Women's Work in Rural South India." *Population and Development Review* 20, no. 1 (1994): 115–136.

Dik, Bryan J., and Ryan D. Duffy. "Calling and Vocation at Work: Definitions and Prospects for Research and Practice." *The Counseling Psychologist* 37, no. 3 (2009): 424–450.

———. "Calling and Vocation in Career Counseling: Recommendations for Promoting Meaningful Work." *Professional Psychology: Research and Practice* 40, no. 6 (2009): 625–632.

Dinda, Soumyananda. "Social Capital in the Creation of Human Capital and Economic Growth: A Productive Consumption Approach." *The Journal of Socio-Economics* 37, no. 5 (2008): 2020–2033.

Dion, Michel. "Are Ethical Theories Relevant for Ethical Leadership?" *Leadership & Organization Development Journal* 33, no. 1 (2012): 4–24.

Dirksen, Kevin M., and Paul Schotsmans. "The Historical Roots of Personalism: Borden Parker Bowne and the Boston Tradition on Personal Identity and the Moral Life." *Bijdragen, International Journal in Philosophy and Theology* 73, no. 4 (2012): 388–400.

Djankov, Simon, Rafaella Porta, Florencio Lopezde Silanes, and Anderi Shleifer. "The Regulation of Entry." *The Quarterly Journal of Economics* 117, no. 1 (2000): 1–37.

Dobel, J. Patrick. "The Corruption of a State." *The American Political Science Review* 72, no. 3 (1978): 958–973.

Donaldson, Thomas. "Precis for Ties That Bind." *Business and Society Review* 105, no. 4 (2000): 436–443.

Donaldson, Thomas, and Thomas W. Dunfee. "Toward a Unified Conception of Business Ethics: Integrative Social Contracts Theory." *The Academy of Management Review* 19, no. 2 (1994): 252–284.

———. "Integrative Social Contract Theory." *Economics and Philosophy* 11 (1995): 85–111.

Donaldson, Thomas, and Lee E. Preston. "The Stakeholder Theory of the Corporation: Concepts, Evidence, and Implications." *The Academy of Management Review* 20, no. 1 (1995): 65–91.

Dudzinski, Denise M. "Integrity: Practical Coherence, Virtue, or Both?" *The Journal of Value Inquiry* 38 (2004): 299–313.

Duff, Antony. "Intention, Responsibility and Double Effect." *The Philosophical Quarterly* 32, no. 126 (1982): 1–16.

Dunn, Craig P. "Integrity Matters." *International Journal of Leadership Studies* 5, no. 1 (2009): 102–126.

Duschinsky, Michael Pinto. "Financing Politics: A Global View." *Journal of Democracy* 13, no. 4 (2002): 69–86.

Dwivedi, O. P. "Bureaucratic Corruption in Developing Countries." *Asian Survey* 7, no. 4 (1967): 245–253.

Dykstra, Craig Richard. "No Longer Strangers: The Church and Its Educational Ministry." *The Princeton Seminary Bulletin* 6, no. 6 (1985): 188–200.

Dyllick, Thomas, and Kai Hockerts. "Beyond the Business Case for Corporate Sustainability." *Business Strategy and the Environment* 11, no. 2 (2002): 130–141.

Edgar, Andrew, and Stephen Pattison. "Integrity and the Moral Complexity of Professional Practice." *Nursing Philosophy* 12, no. 2 (2011): 94–106.

Eggert, Andreas, and Sabrina Helm. "Exploring the Impact of Relationship Transparency on Business Relationships: A Cross-Sectional Study among Purchasing Managers in Germany." *Industrial Marketing Management* 32, no. 8 (2003): 101–108.

Elangovan, A.R., Craig C. Pinder, and Murdith McLean. "Callings and Organizational Behavior." *Journal of Vocational Behavior* 76, no. 3 (2010): 428–440.

Elankumaran, Srinivasan. "Corporate Codes of Conduct in India: A Survey." *Journal of Human Values* 12, no. 1 (2006): 65–80.

Emanuel, David, Jilnaught Wong, and Norman Wong. "Efficient Contracting and Accounting." *Accounting and Finance* 43, no. 2 (2003): 149–166.

Epstein, Brian. "Ontological Individualism Reconsidered." *Synthese* 166, no. 1 (2009): 187–213.

Epstein, Edwin M. "Business Ethics, Corporate Social Citizenship and the Corporate Social Policy Process: A View from the United States." *Journal of Business Ethics* 8, no. 8 (1989): 583–595.

Etzioni, Amitai. "Toward a New Socio-Economic Paradigm." *Socio-Economic Review* 1, no. 1 (2003): 105–118.

Evensky, Jerry. "Retrospectives: Ethics and the Invisible Hand." *The Journal of Economic Perspectives* 7, no. 2 (1993): 197–205.

Ewin, R. E. "The Moral Status of the Corporation." *Journal of Business Ethics* 10, no. 10 (1991): 749–756.

Eyerson, Debram, and Joanne Martin. "Cultural Change: An Integration of Three Different Views." *Journal of Management Studies* 24, no. 6 (1987): 623–647.

Faccio, Mara. "Politically Connected Firms." *The American Economic Review* 96, no. 1 (2006): 369–386.

———. "Differences between Politically Connected and Nonconnected Firms: A Cross Country Analysis." *Financial Management* 39, no. 3 (2010): 905–927.

Faccio, Mara, Ronald W. Masulis, and John J. McConnella. "Political Connections and Corporate Bailouts." *Journal of Finance* 61, no. 6 (2006): 2597–2635.

Fahey, Michael. "Janssens, Louis, 1908–2001." *Theological Studies* 63 (2002): 1–2.

Falkenberg, Loren, and Irene Herremans. "Ethical Behaviours in Organizations: Directed by the Formal or Informal Systems?" *Journal of Business Ethics* 14, no. 2 (1995): 133–143.

Fassin, Yves. "The Reasons Behind Non-Ethical Behaviour in Business and Entrepreneurship." *Joumal of Business Ethics* 60, no. 3 (2005): 265–279.

Fehr, Ernst, and Urs Fischbacher. "Why Social Preferences Matter—the Impact of Non-Selfish Motives on Competition, Cooperation and Incentives." *The Economic Journal* 112, no. 478 (2002): C1–C33.

Fehr, Ernst, and Klaus M. Schmidt. "A Theory of Fairness, Competition, and Cooperation." *The Quarterly Journal of Economics* 114, no. 3 (1999): 817–868.

Fisher, Colin M., Raj Shirolé, and Ashutosh P. Bhupatkar. "Ethical Stances in Indian Management Culture." *Personnel Review* 30, no. 6 (2001): 694–711.

Fleming, John E. "A Suggested Approach to Linking Decision Styles with Business Ethics." *Journal of Business Ethics* 4, no. 2 (1985): 137–144.

Ford, Robert C., and Woodrow D. Richardson. "Ethical Decision Making: A Review of the Empirical Literature." *Journal of Business Ethics* 13, no. 3 (1994): 205–221.

Fraedrich, John Paul. "The Ethical Behavior of Retail Managers." *Journal of Business Ethics* 12, no. 3 (1993): 207–218.

Frankfurt, Harry G. "Freedom of the Will and the Concept of a Person." *The Journal of Philosophy* 68, no. 1 (1971): 5–20.

———. "The Faintest Passion." Proceedings and Addresses of the American Philosophical Association 66, no. 3 (1992): 5–16.

Fransen, Piet. "Pour Une Psychologie De La Grace Divine." *Lumen vitae* 12 (1957): 209–240.

Frederick, William C. "The Growing Concern over Business Responsibility." *California Management Review* 2, no. 4 (1960): 54–63.

———. "The Moral Authority of Transnational Corporate Codes." *Journal of Business Ethics* 10, no. 3 (1991): 165–177.

———. "From CSR1 to CSR2: The Maturing of Business and Society Thought." *Business & Society* 33, no. 2 (1994): 150–164.

Freeman, R. Edward. "The Politics of Stakeholder Theory: Some Future Directions." *Business Ethics Quarterly* 4, no. 4 (1994): 409–421.

French, Peter A. "The Corporation as a Moral Person." *American Philosophical Quarterly* 16, no. 3 (1979): 207–215.

———. "Integrity, Intentions, and Corporations." *American Business Law Journal* 34, no. 2 (1996): 141–155.

Furnham, Adrian. "Managers as Change Agents." *Journal of Change Management* 3, no. 1 (2002): 21–29.

Garofalo, Charles. "Toward a Global Ethic Perspectives on Values, Training and Moral Agency." *The International Journal of Public Sector Management* 16, no. 7 (2003): 490–501.

Garrett, Jan Edward. "Unredistributable Corporate Moral Responsibility." *Journal of Business Ethics* 8, no. 7 (1989): 535–545.

Garriga, Elisabet, and Domènec Melé. "Corporate Social Responsibility Theories: Mapping the Territory." *Journal of Business Ethics* 53, no. 1/2 (2004): 51–71.

Gatewood, Elizabeth, and Archie B. Carroll. "The Anatomy of Corporate Social Response: The Rely, Firestone 500, and Pinto Cases." *Business Horizons* 24, no. 5 (1981): 9–16.

Gathii, James Thuo. "Defining the Relationship between Human Rights and Corruption." *Journal of International Law* 31, no. 1 (2009): 125–202.

Gaynesford, Maximilian de. "Integrity over Time: Korsgaard and the Unity Criterion." *The Harvard Review of Philosophy* 18, no. 1 (2012): 50–72.

Getz, Kathleen A. "International Codes of Conduct: An Analysis of Ethical Reasoning." *Journal of Business Ethics* 9, no. 7 (1990): 567–577.

Gibson, Kevin. "Toward an Intermediate Position on Corporate Moral Personhood." *Journal of Business Ethics* 101 (2011): 71–81.

Giesler, Markus. "Consumer Gift Systems." *Journal of Consumer Research* 33, no. 2 (2006): 283–290.

Gillespie, Kate, and Gwenn Okruhlik. "The Political Dimensions of Corruption Cleanups: A Framework for Analysis." *Comparative Politics* 24, no. 1 (1991): 77–95.

Gladwin, Thomas N., James J. Kennelly, and Tara-Shelomith Krause. "Shifting Paradigms for Sustainable Development: Implications for Management Theory and Research." *The Academy of Management Review* 20, no. 4 (1995): 874–907.

Goel, Rajeev K., and Michael A. Nelson. "Economic Freedom Versus Political Freedom: Cross-Country Influences on Corruption." *Australian Economic Papers* 44, no. 2 (2005): 121–133.

Goodpaster, Kenneth E. "The Concept of Corporate Responsibility." *Journal of Business Ethics* 2, no. 1 (1983): 1–22.

———. "Tenacity: The American Pursuit of Corporate Responsibility." *Business and Society Review* 118, no. 4 (2013): 577–605.

Gosling, Mark, and Heh Jason Huang. "The Fit between Integrity and Integrative Social Contracts Theory." *Journal of Business Ethics* 90, no. 3 (2009): 407–417.

Gotsi, Manto, and Alan M. Wilson. "Corporate Reputation: Seeking a Definition." *Corporate Communications: An International Journal* 6, no. 1 (2001): 24–30.

Gotsis, George N., and Zoe Kortezi. "Ethical Considerations in Organizational Politics: Expanding the Perspective." *Journal of Business Ethics* 93 (2010): 497–517.

Gramlich, Edward M. "A Natural Experiment in Styles of Capitalism: Professional Sports." *Quarterly Review of Economics and Finance* 34, no. 2 (1994): 121–130.

Grampp, William D. "What Did Smith Mean by the Invisible Hand?" *Journal of Political Economy* 108, no. 3 (2000): 441–465.

Green, Ronald M. "When Is 'Everyone's Doing It' A Moral Justification?" *Business Ethics Quarterly* 1, no. 1 (1991): 75–93.

Greitemeyer, Tobias, Peter Fischer, Andreas Kastenmüller, and Dieter Frey. "Civil Courage and Helping Behavior." *European Psychologist* 11, no. 2 (2006): 90–98.

Greyser, Stephen A. "Advancing and Enhancing Corporate Reputation." *Corporate Communications: An International Journal* 4, no. 4 (1999): 177–181.

Groves, Kevin, Charles Vance, and Yongsun Paik. "Linking Linear/Nonlinear Thinking Style Balance and Managerial Ethical Decision-Making." *Journal of Business Ethics* 80, no. 2 (2008): 305–325.

Guerrette, Richard H. "Environmental Integrity and Corporate Responsibility." *Journal of Business Ethics* 5, no. 5 (1986): 409–415.

Gupta, Akhil. "Blurred Boundaries: The Discourse of Corruption, the Culture of Politics, and the Imagined State." *American Ethnologist* 22, no. 2 (1995): 375–402.

Habib, Mohsin, and Leon Zurawicki. "Corruption and Foreign Direct Investment." *Journal of International Business Studies* 23, no. 2 (2002): 291–307.

Hacker-Wright, John. "Virtue Ethics without Right Action: Anscombe, Foot, and Contemporary Virtue Ethics." *Journal Value Inquiry* 44, no. 2 (2010): 209–224.

Halstead, Mark J. "Moral Education in Family Life: The Effects of Diversity." *Journal of Moral Education* 28, no. 3 (1999): 265–281.

Hamann, Ralph, and Nicola Acutt. "How Should Civil Society (and the Government) Respond to 'Corporate Social Responsibility'? A Critique of Business Motivations and the Potential for Partnerships." *Development Southern Africa* 20, no. 2 (2003): 255–270.

Hammersley, Martyn, and Anna Traianou. "Moralism and Research Ethics: A Machiavellian Perspective." *International Journal of Social Research Methodology* 14, no. 5 (2011): 379–390.

Hansmann, Henry. "When Does Worker Ownership Work? ESOPs, Law Firms, Codetermination, and Economic Democracy." *The Yale Law Journal* 99, no. 8 (1990): 1749–1816.

Hanson, Eileen. "Integrity and Identity." *Macalester Journal of Philosophy* 6, no. 1 (2011): 19–30.

Haq, Rana. "Intersectionality of Gender and Other Forms of Identity Dilemmas and Challenges Facing Women in India." *Gender in Management: An International Journal* 28, no. 3 (2013): 171–184.

Harman, Gilbert. "Moral Relativism Defended." *The Philosophical Review* 84, no. 1 (1975): 3–22.

Hart, Stuart L. "A Natural-Resource-Based View of the Firm." *The Academy of Management Review* 20, no. 4 (1995): 986–1014.

Haslam, S. Alexander, Rachael A. Eggins, and Katherine J. Reynolds. "The Aspire Model: Actualizing Social and Personal Identity Resources to Enhance Organizational Outcomes." *Journal of Occupational and Organizational Psychology* 76 (2003): 83–113.

Haslip, Susan. "Aristotle's Theory of the Good Life: A Consideration of the Role of Luck in the Good Life and the Concept of Self-Sufficiency." *Quodlibet Journal* 5, no. 1 (January 2003): 1–5.

Hasnas, John. "The Normative Theories of Business Ethics: A Guide for the Perplexed." *Business Ethics Quarterly* 8, no. 1 (1998): 19–42.

Haxhi, Ilir, and Hans van Ees. "Explaining Diversity in the Worldwide Diffusion of Codes of Good Governance." *Journal of International Business Studies* 41, no. 4 (2010): 710–726.

Hayton, James C., Gerard George, and Shaker A. Zahr. "National Culture and Entrepreneurship: A Review of Behavioral Research." *Entrepreneurship Theory and Practice* 26, no. 4 (2002): 33–52.

Heald, Morrell. "Management's Responsibility to Society: The Growth of an Idea." *Business History Review* 31, no. 4 (1957): 375–384.

Herman, Barbara. "Integrity and Impartiality." *The Monist* 66, no. 2 (1983): 233–250.

Hess, David, and Thomas W. Dunfee. "Fighting Corruptions: A Principled Approach." *Cornell Internaltional Law Journal* 33 (2000): 593–626.

Hessen, Robert "A New Concept of Corporations: A Contractual and Private Property Model." *Hastings Law Journal* 30, no. 5 (1979): 1327–1350.

Heywood, Paul P. "Political Corruption: Problems and Perspectives." *Political studies* 45, no. 3 (1997): 417–235.

Highhouse, Scott, Margaret E. Brooks, and Gary Gregarus. "An Organizational Impression Management Perspective on the Formation of Corporate Reputations." *Journal of Management* 35, no. 6 (2009): 1481–1493.

Hildebrand, Dietrich von. "Sittlichkeit Und Sittliche Werterkentnis." *Jahrbuch für Philosophie und Phänomenologische Forschung* 5 (1992): 463–502.

Hirota, Shinichi, Katsuyuki Kubo, Hideaki Miyajima, Paul Hong, and Young Won Park. "Corporate Mission, Corporate Policies and Business Outcomes: Evidence from Japan." *Management Decision* 48, no. 7 (2010): 1134–1153.

Hitlin, Steven. "Values as the Core of Personal Identity: Drawing Links between Two Theories of Self." *Social Psychology Quarterly* 66, no. 2 (2003): 117–138.

Hodgkinson, Peter. "The Sociology of Corruption—Some Themes and Issues." *Sociology* 31, no. 1 (1997): 17–35.

Hofmann, Paul B. "Performing an Ethics Audit." *Healthcare Executive* 10, no. 6 (1995): 47.

Hofstede, Geert. "The Cultural Relativity of Organizational Practices and Theories." *Journal of International Business Studies* 14, no. 2 (1983): 75–89.

———. "Cultural Constraints in Management Theories." *The Executive* 7, no 1 (1993): 81–94.

Hogan, Suellen J., and Leonard V. Coote. "Organizational Culture, Innovation, and Performance: A Test of Schein's Model." *Journal of business research* 67, no. 8 (2014): 1609–1621.

Hooft, Stan van. "Overcoming Principles: Dialogue in Business Ethics." *Teaching Business Ethics* 5, no. 1 (2001): 89–106.

Hooker, John. "The Case against Business Ethics Education: A Study in Bad Arguments." *Journal of Business Ethics Education* 1, no. 1 (2004): 73–86.

Hosmer, LaRue-Tone. "Lessons from the Wreck of the Exxon Valdez." *Business Ethics Quarterly* 8, no. 1 (1998): 109–122.

Hulla, Clyde Eiríkur, and Brian H. Lio. "Innovation in Non-Profit and for-Profit Organizations: Visionary, Strategic, and Financial Considerations." *Journal of Change Management* 6, no. 1 (2006): 53–65.

Hunt, Geoffrey. "Moral Crisis, Professionals and Ethical Education." *Nursing Ethics* 4, no. 1 (1997): 31–38.

Hunt, Shelby D., and Scott Vitell. "A General Theory of Marketing Ethics." *Journal of Macromarketing* 6, no. 5 (1986): 5–15.

———. "A General Theory of Marketing Ethics." *Journal of Macromarketing* 6, no. 1 (1986): 5–15.

Husted, Bryan W. "Wealth, Culture, and Corruption." *Journal of International Business Studies* 30, no. 2 (1999): 339–360.

———. "Is It Ethical to Use Ethics as Strategy?" *Journal of Business Ethics* 27, no. 1/2 (2000): 21–31.

Hutton, James G., Michael B. Goodman, Jill B. Alexander, and Christina M. Genest. "Reputation Management: The New Face of Corporate Public Relations?" *Public Relations Review* 25 (2001): 247–261.

Ichniowski, T. "The New Nepotism: Why Dynasties Are Making a Comeback." *Business Week* 31 (1988): 106–109.

Ingley, C. B., and N. T. Van Der Walt. "Corporate Governance, Institutional Investors and Conflicts of Interest." *Corporate Governance: An International Review* 12, no. 4 (2004): 534–551.

Izraeli, Dove. "Ethical Beliefs and Behavior among Managers: A Cross-Cultural Perspective." *Journal of Business Ethics* 7, no. 4 (1988): 263–271.

Jackson, Kevin T. "Towards Authenticity: A Sartrean Perspective on Business Ethics." *Journal of Business Ethics* 58, no. 4 (2005): 307–325.

Jain, Arvind K. "Corruption: A Review." *Journal of Economic Surveys* 15, no. 1 (2002): 71–121.

James, Harvey S. "Reinforcing Ethical Decision Making through Organizational Structure." *Journal of Business Ethics* 28, no. 1 (2000): 43–58.

———. "When Is a Bribe a Bribe? Teaching a Workable Definition of Bribery." *Teaching Business Ethics* 6 (2002): 199–217.

———. "On Finding Solutions to Ethical Problems in Agriculture." *Journal of Agricultural and Environmental Ethics* 16 (2003): 239–457.

James, Harvey S., and Farhad Rassekh. "Smith, Friedman, and Self-Interest in Ethical Society." *Business Ethics Quarterly* 10, no. 3 (2000): 659–667.

Janićijević, Nebojša. "The Mutual Impact of Organizational Culture and Structure." *Economic Annals* 58, no. 198 (2013): 35–60.

Janssens, Louis. "Personalist Morals." *Louvain Studies* 3 (1970): 5–16.

———. "Ontic Evil and Moral Evil." *Louvain Studies* 4 (1972): 115–156.

———. "Artificial Insemination: Ethical Considerations." *Louvain Studies* 8, no. 1 (1980): 3–30.

———. "Particular Good and Personalistic Morals." *Ethical Perspectives* 6, no. 1 (1999): 55–59.

Jaskiewicz, Peter, Klaus Uhlenbruck, David B. Balkin, and Trish Reay. "Is Nepotism Good or Bad? Types of Nepotism and Implications for Knowledge Management." *Family Business Review* 26, no. 2 (2013): 121–139.

Jones, Thomas M. "Corporate Social Responsibility Revisited, Redefined." *California Management Review* 22, no. 2 (1980): 59–67.

———. "An Integrating Framework for Research in Business and Society: A Step toward the Elusive Paradigm?" *The Academy of Management Review* 8, no. 4 (1983): 559–564.

———. "Ethical Decision Making by Individuals in Organizations: An Issue-Contingent Model." *The Academy of Management Review* 16, no. 2 (1991): 366–395.

———. "Instrumental Stakeholder Theory: A Synthesis of Ethics and Economics." *The Academy of Management Review* 20, no. 2 (1995): 404–437.

Jong-sung, You, and Sanjeev Khagram. "A Comparative Study of Inequality and Corruption." *American Sociological Review* 70, no. 1 (2005): 136–157.

Jonsen, Albert R. "Casuistry: An Alternative or Complement to Principles?" *Kennedy Institute of Ethics Journal* 5, no. 3 (1995): 237–251.

Joseph, Augustine. "The Relevance of Personal Integrity in Corporate Ethics: A Study Based on Indian Scenario." *Indian Theological Studies* 52, no. 1 (2015): 77–90.

Joseph, Augustine. "The Conceptual Link between Personal Integrity and Positive Fundamental Option: A Christian Interpertation of Personal Integrity Conceptualization," *Eastern Journal of Dialogue and Culture* 8, no. 1 (2015): 108–126.

Joseph, Augustine. "The Need of Personal Responsibility and Integrity in Corporate Social Responsibility Theories," *International Journal of Recent Advances in Organizational Behaviour and Decision Science* 1, no. 1 (2014): 45–65.

Kahn, Jeffrey D. "Organizations' Liability for Torts of Volunteers." *University of Pennsylvania Law Review* 133, no. 6 (1985): 1433–1452.

Kanagasabapathi, P. "Ethics and Values in Indian Economy and Business." *International Journal of Social Economics* 34, no. 9 (2007): 577–585.

Kannan-Narasimhan, Rangapriya, and Barbara S. Lawrence. "Behavioral Integrity: How Leader Referents and Trust Matter to Workplace Outcomes." *Journal of Business Ethics* 111 (2012): 165–178.

Kaptein, Muel. "The Ethics Thermometer: An Audit-Tool for Improving the Corporate Moral Reputation." *Corporate Reputation Review* 2, no. 1 (1998): 10–15.

———. "Integrity Management." *European Management Journal* 17, no. 6 (1999): 625–634.

———. "The Diamond of Managerial Integrity." *European Management Journal* 12, no. 1 (2003): 99–108.

———. "Business Codes of Multinational Firms: What Do They Say?" *Journal of Business Ethics* 50, no. 1 (2004): 13–31.

———. "Developing and Testing a Measure for the Ethical Culture of Organizations: The Corporate Ethical Virtues Model." *Journal of Organizational Behavior* 29, no. 7 (2008): 923–947.

———. "From Inaction to External Whistleblowing: The Influence of the Ethical Culture of Organizations on Employee Responses to Observed Wrongdoing." *Journal of Business Ethics* 98 (2011): 513–530.

———. "Understanding Unethical Behavior by Unraveling Ethical Culture." *Human Relations* 63, no. 6 (2011): 843–869.

Kaptein, Muel, and Scott Avelino. "Measuring Corporate Integrity: A Survey-Based Approach." *Corporate Governance* 5, no. 1 (2005): 45–54.

Kaptein, Muel, and Jan Van Dalen. "The Empirical Assessment of Corporate Ethics: A Case Study." *Journal of Business Ethics* 24 (2000): 95–114.

Kaptein, Muel, and Piet van Reenen. "Integrity Management of Police Organizations." *International Journal of Police Strategies & Management* 24, no. 3 (2001): 281–300.

Kaptein, Muel, and Mark S. Schwartz. "The Effectiveness of Business Codes: A Critical Examination of Existing Studies and the Development of an Integrated Research Model." *Journal of Business Ethics* 77 (2008): 111–127.

Kaptein, Muel, and Rob Van Tulder. "Toward Effective Stakeholder Dialogue." *Business and Society Review* 108, no. 2 (2003): 203–224.

Kaptein, Muel, and Johan Wempe. "The Ethics Report: A Means of Sharing Responsibility." *A European Review* 7, no. 3 (1998): 131–139.

Karpoff, Jonathan M., and John R. Lott. "The Reputational Penalty Firms Bear for Committing Criminal Fraud." *Journal of Law and Economics* 34, no. 2 (1993): 757–802.

Kaufmann, Daniel, and Pedro C. Vicente. "Legal Corruption." *Economics & Politics* 23, no. 2 (2011): 195–219.

Kaur, Manpreet. "Corporate Governance in India: Case Study of Satyam." *Indian Journal of Research* 2, no. 11 (2013): 29–31.

Kaushik, Neeraj, Anita Sharma, and Veerander Kumar Kaushik. "Equality in the Workplace: A Study of Gender Issues in Indian Organisations." *Journal of Management Development* 33, no. 2 (2014): 90–106.

Kayser, Daniela Niesta, Tobias Greitemeyer, Fischer Peter, and Dieter Frey. "Why Mood Affects Help Giving, but Not Moral Courage: Comparing Two Types of Prosocial Behaviour." *European Journal of Social Psychology* 40, no. 7 (2010): 1136–1157.

Keenan, James F. "Virtue, Grace and the Early Revisionists of the Twentieth Century." *Studies in Christian Ethics* 23, no. 4 (2010): 365–380.

Kerlin, Michael J. "Peter French, Corporate Ethics and the Wizard of Oz." *Journal of Business Ethics* 16 (1997): 1431–1438.

Kernis, Michael H. "Toward a Conceptualization of Optimal Self-Esteem." *Psychological Inquiry* 14, no. 1 (2003): 1–26.

Khandekar, Aalok. "An Indian Summer: Corruption, Class, and the Lokpal Protests." *Journal of Consumer Culture* 15, no. 2 (2015): 221–247.

Khwaja, Asim Ijaz, and Atif Mian. "Do Lenders Favor Politically Connected Firms? Rent Provision in an Emerging Financial Market." *The Quarterly Journal of Economics* 120, no. 4 (2005): 1371–1411.

Kimbro, Marinilka Barros. "A Cross-Country Empirical Investigation of Corruption and Its Relationship to Economic, Cultural and Institutional Variables: An Examination of the Role of Accounting and Financial Statements Quality." *Journal of Accounting Auditing and Finance* 17, no. 4 (2002): 325–349.

Kimmel, Allan J., N. Craig Smith, and Jill Gabrielle Klein. "Ethical Decision Making and Research Deception in the Behavioral Sciences: An Application of Social Contract Theory." *Ethics and Behavior* 21, no. 3 (2011): 222–251.

Kingston, Christopher. "Social Structure and Cultures of Corruption." *Journal of Economic Behavior & Organization* 67 (2008) 90–102.

Kinjerski, Val M., and Berna J. Skrypnek. "Defining Spirit at Work: Finding Common Ground." *Journal of Organizational Change Management* 17, no. 1 (2004): 26–42.

Kling, Blair B. "The Origin of the Managing Agency System in India." *The Journal of Asian Studies* 26, no. 1 (1966): 37–47.

Knack, Stephen, and Philip Keefer. "Does Social Capital Have an Economic Payoff? A Cross-Country Investigation." *The Quarterly Journal of Economics* 112, no. 4 (1997): 1251–1288.

Koehn, Daryl. "A Role for Virtue Ethics in the Analysis of Business Practice." *Business Ethics Quarterly* 5, no. 3 (1995): 533–539.

———. "Integrity as a Business Asset." *Journal of Business Ethics* 58, no. 1/3 (2005): 125–136.

Kohls, John, and Sandra L. Christensen. "The Business Responsibility for Wealth Distribution in a Globalized Political-Economy: Merging Moral Economics and Catholic Social Teaching." *Journal of Business Ethics* 35, no. 3 (2002): 223–234.

Kok, Peter, Ton van der Wiele, Richard McKenna, and Alan Brown. "A Corporate Social Responsibility Audit within a Quality Management Framework." *Journal of Business Ethics* 31 (2001): 285–297.

Kolstad, Ivar. "Corruption as Violation of Distributed Ethical Obligations." *Journal of Global Ethics* 8, no. 2/3 (2012): 239–250.

Kolstad, Ivar, and Arne Wiig. "Is Transparency the Key to Reducing Corruption in Resource-Rich Countries?" *World Development* 37, no. 3 (2009): 521–532.

Komter, Aafke Elisabeth. "The Disguised Rationality of Solidarity: Gift Giving in Informal Relations." *The Journal of Mathematical Sociology* 25, no. 4 (2001): 385–401.

Konar, Arup Kanti. "A Paradox of Corporate Perception and Perpetuation of Corruption." *Journal of Social Science* 18, no. 2 (2009): 81–93.

Kong, Eric. "The Development of Strategic Management in the Non-Profit Context: Intellectual Capital in Social Service Non-Profit Organizations." *International Journal of Management Reviews* 10, no. 3 (2008): 281–299.

Kopecký, Petr, and Cas Mudde. "Rethinking Civil Society." *Democratization* 10, no. 3 (2003): 1–14.

Kovacs, Gyongyi, and Karen M. Spens. "Abductive Reasoning in Logistics Research." *International Journal of Physical Distribution & Logistics Management* 35, no. 2 (2005): 132–144.

Kuin, Pieter. "Magic of Multinational Management." *Harvard Business Review* 50, no. 6 (1972): 89–99.

Kujala, Johanna, Anna-Maija La¨msa¨, and Katriina Penttila. "Managers' Moral Decision-Making Patterns over Time: A Multidimensional Approach." *Journal of Business Ethics* 100 (2011): 191–207.

Kulshreshtha, Praveen. "Business Ethics Versus Economic Incentives: 'Contemporary Issues and Dilemmas.'" *Journal of Business Ethics* 60, no. 4 (2005): 393–410.

Kumar, Krishan. "Civil Society: An Inquiry into the Usefulness of an Historical Term." *The British Journal of Sociology* 44, no. 3 (1993): 375–395.

Kumar, Udaya. "Self, Body and Inner Sense: Some Reflections on Sree Narayana Guru and Kumaran Asan." *Studies in History* 13, no. 2 (1997): 247–270.

Kuntz, J. R. C., J. R. Kuntz, Detelin Elenkov, and Anna Nabirukhina. "Characterizing Ethical Cases: A Cross-Cultural Investigation of Individual Differences, Organizational Climate, and Leadership on Ethical Decision-Making." *Journal of Business Ethics* 113 (2013): 317–331.

Ladd, John. "Morality and the Ideal of Rationality in Formal Organizations." *The Monist* 54, no. 4 (1970): 488–516.

Lambooy, Tineke. "Corporate Social Responsibility: Sustainable Water Use." *Journal of Cleaner Production* 19 (2011): 852–866.

Lan, Luh Luh, and Loizos Heracleous. "Rethinking Agency Theory: The View from Law." *Academy of Management Review* 35, no. 2 (2010): 294–314.

Lange, Donald, and Peggy M. Lee. "Organizational Reputation: A Review." *Journal of Management* 37, no. 1 (2011): 153–184.

Ledford, Gerald E., Jon R. Wendenhof, and James T. Strahley. "Realizing a Corporate Philosophy." *Organizational Dynamics* 23, no. 3 (1995): 5–19.

LeFebvre, Rebecca. "Cross-Cultural Comparison of Business Ethics in the U.S. And India: A Study of Business Codes of Conduct." *Journal of Emerging Knowledge on Emerging Markets* 3, no. 11 (2011): 390–409.

Leff, Nathaniel H. "Economic Development through Bureaucratic Corruption." *American Behavioral Science* 8, no. 8 (1964): 8–14.

Leroy, Hannes, Michael E. Palanski, and Tony Simons. "Authentic Leadership and Behavioral Integrity as Drivers of Follower Commitment and Performance." *Journal of Business Ethics* 107 (2012): 255–264.

Lindgren, James. "Elusive Distinction between Bribery and Extortion: From the Common Law to the Hobbs Act." *UCLA Law Review* 35 (1987): 815–909.

Linnane, Brian F. "Rahner's Fundamental Option and Virtue Ethics." *Philosophy & Theology* 15, no. 1 (2003): 229–254.

Logsdon, Jeanne M., and Donna J. Wood. "Business Citizenship: From Domestic to Global Level of Analysis." *Business Ethics Quarterly* 12, no. 2 (2002): 155–187.

Lorin, Henry G., and Per E.J. Kulling. "The Bhopal Tragedy—What Has Swedish Disaster Medicine Planning Learned from It?" *The Journal of Emergency Medicine* 4, no. 4 (1986): 311–316.

Love, E. Geoffrey, and Mathew Kraatz. "Character, Conformity, or the Bottom Line? How and Why Downsizing Affected Corporate Reputation." *Academy of Management Journal* 52, no. 2 (2009): 314–335.

Lowenberg, Anton D. "Neoclassical Economics as a Theory of Politics and Institutions." *Cato Journal* 19, no. 3 (1990): 619–637.

Luévano, Rafael. "Catholic Discernment with a View of Buddhist Internal Clarity." *Buddhist-Christian Studies* 29 (2009): 39–51.

Luo, Yadong Y. "An Organizational Perspective of Corruption." *Management and Organization Review* 1, no. 1 (2005): 119–154.

Lyshaug, Brenda. "Authenticity and the Politics of Identity: A Critique of Charles Taylor's Politics of Recognition." *Contemporary Political Theory* 3 (2004): 300–320.

Maak, Thomas. "Undivided Corporate Responsibility: Towards a Theory of Corporate Integrity." *Journal of Business Ethics* 82 (2009): 353–368.

Macaro, Antonia. "Aristotle and the Good Life." *Practical Philosophy* 7, no. 2 (2005): 4–6.

MacCallum, Gerald C. "Negative and Positive Freedom." *The Philosophical Review* 76, no. 3 (1967): 312–334.

Mahoney, Jack. "Editorial Adieu: Cultivating Moral Courage in Business." *Business Ethics: A European Review* 7, no. 4 (1998): 187–192.

Manikutty, S. "Family Business Groups in India: A Resource-Based View of the Emerging Trends." *Family Business Review* 13, no. 4 (2000): 279–292.

Manning, Rita C. "Corporate Responsibility and Corporate Personhood." *Journal of Business Ethics* 3 (1984): 77–84.

———. "Dismemberment, Divorce and Hostile Takeovers: A Comment on Corporate Moral Personhood." *Journal of Business Ethics* 7 (1988): 639–643.

Mansbach, Abraham, and Yaacov G Bachner. "Internal or External Whistleblowing: Nurses' Willingness to Report Wrongdoing." *Nursing Ethics* 17, no. 4 (2010): 483–490.

Marciukaityte, Dalia, Samuel H. Szewczyk, Hatice Uzun, and Raj Varma. "Governance and Performance Changes after Accusations of Corporate Fraud." *Financial Analysts Journal* 62, no. 3 (2006): 32–41.

Maritain, Jacques, and John J. FitzGerald. "The Person and the Common Good." *The Review of Politics* 8, no. 4 (1946): 419–455.

Marrewijk, Marcel van, and Marco Werre. "Multiple Levels of Corporate Sustainability." *Journal of Business Ethics* 44, no. 2 (2003): 107–119.

Martin, Kelly D., John B. Cullen, Jean L. Johnson, and K. Praveen Parboteeah. "Deciding to Bribe: A Cross-Level Analysis of Firm and Home Country Influences on Bribery Activity." *The Academy of Management Journal* 50, no. 6 (2007): 1401–1422.

Mattem, Drik, Andrew Crane, and Wendy Chapple. "Behind the Mask: Revealing the True Face of Corporate Citizenship." *Journal of Business Ethics* 45, no. 1/2 (2003): 109–120.

Mauro, Paolo. "Corruption and Growth." *The Quarterly Journal of Economics* 110, no. 3 (1995): 681–712.

May, William F. "Doing Ethics: The Bearing of Ethical Theories on Fieldwork." *Social Problems* 27, no. 3 (1980): 358–370.

McCain, Roger A. "Commitment and Weakness of Will in Game Theory and Neo-Classical Economics." *The Journal of Socio-Economics* 38, no. 4 (2009): 549–556.

McFall, Lynne. "Integrity." *Ethics* 98, no. 1 (1987): 5–20.

McLaughlin, Terence H. "Parental Rights and the Religious Upbringing of Children." *Journal of Philosophy of Education* 18, no. 1 (1984): 75–83.

McPherson, David. "Vocational Virtue Ethics: Prospects for a Virtue Ethic Approach to Business." *Journal of Business Ethics* 116, no. 2 (2013): 283–296.

McSweeney, Brendan. "Hofstede's Model of National Cultural Differences and Their Consequences: A Triumph of Faith—a Failure of Analysis." *Human Relations* 55, no. 1 (2002): 89–118.

Melé, Domènec. "The Challenge of Humanistic Management." *Journal of Business Ethics* 44, no. 1 (2003): 77–88.

Melé, Domènec. "Integrating Personalism into Virtue-Based Business Ethics: The Personalist and the Common Good Principles." *Journal of Business Ethics* 88 (2009): 227–244.

Menard, Julie, and Luc Brunet. "Authenticity and Well-Being in the Workplace: A Mediation Model." *Journal of Managerial Psychology* 26, no. 4 (2011): 331–346.

Miceli, Marcia P., Janet P. Near, and Charles R. Schwenk. "Who Blows the Whistle and Why?" *Industrial and Labor Relations Review* 45, no. 1 (1991): 113–130.

Michie, Susan, and Janaki Gooty. "Values, Emotions, and Authenticity: Will the Real Leader Please Stand Up?" *The Leadership Quarterly* 16 (2005): 441–457.

Miles, Samantha. "Stakeholder: Essentially Contested or Just Confused?" *Journal of Business Ethics* 108 (2012): 285–298.

Miller, Marisal L., and Barry R. Schlenker. "Integrity and Identity: Moral Identity Differences and Preferred Interpersonal Reactions." *European Journal of Personality* 25 (2011): 2–15.

Mingers, John, and Geoff Walsham. "Toward Ethical Information Systems: The Contribution of Discourse Ethics." *MIS Quarterly* 34, no. 4 (2010): 833–854.

Mintzberg, Henry. "The Design School: Reconsidering the Basic Premises of Strategic Management." *Strategic Management Journal* 11, no. 3 (1990): 171–195.

Mo, Pak Hung. "Corruption and Economic Growth." *Journal of Comparative Economics* 29 (2001): 66–79.

Monga, Manjit. "Managers' Moral Reasoning: Evidence from Large Indian Manufacturing Organisations." *Journal of Business Ethics* 71, no. 2 (2007): 179–194.

Monks, Robert A.G. "Creating Value through Corporate Governance." *Corporate Governance: An International Review* 10, no. 3 (2002): 116–123.

Moore, Geoff. "Corporate Character: Modern Virtue Ethics and the Virtuous Corporation." *Business Ethics Quarterly* 15, no. 4 (2005): 659–685.

Morand, David A., and Kimberly K. Merriman. "'Equality Theory' As a Counterbalance to Equity Theory in Human Resource Management." *Journal of Business Ethics* 111, no. 1 (2012): 133–144.

Morse, John. "The Missing Link between Virtue Theory and Business Ethics." *Journal of Applied Philosophy* 16, no. 1 (1999): 47–58.

Morsing, Mette, and Majken Schultz. "Corporate Social Responsibility Communication: Stakeholder Information, Response and Involvement Strategies." *Business Ethics: A European Review* 15, no. 4 (2006): 323–338.

Murphy, Patrick E. "Corporate Ethics Statements: Current Status and Future Prospects." *Journal of Business Ethics* 14, no. 9 (1995): 727–740.

Musschenga, Albert W. "Education for Moral Integrity." *Journal of Philosophy of Education* 35, no. 2 (2001): 221–235.

Mynatty, Hormis. "The Concept of Social Sin." *Louvain Studies* 16, no. 1 (1991): 3–26.

Myrsiades, Linda Suny. "Corporate Stories as Cultural Communications in the Organizational Setting." *Management Communication Quarterly* 84, no. 1 (1987): 83–120.

Nachi, Mohamed. "The Morality in/of Compromise: Some Theoretical Reflections." *Social Science Information* 43, no. 2 (2004): 291–305.

Nandy, Sarmistha, and Shalini Kumar. "Women Entrepreneurship in 21st Century India." *Global Journal of Finance and Management* 6, no. 9 (2014): 967–976.

Narasimhan, Niranjan, Kumar Bhaskar, and Srinivas Prakhya. "Existential Beliefs and Values." *Journal of Business Ethics* 96, no. 3 (2010): 369–382.

Natale, Samuel Michael, and Sebastian A. Sora. "Ethics in Strategic Thinking: Business Processes and the Global Market Collapse." *Journal of Business Ethics* 94, no. 3 (2010): 309–316.

Neves, João César das, and Antonino Vaccaro. "Corporate Transparency: A Perspective from Thomas Aquinas' Summa Theologiae." *Journal of Business Ethics* 113, no. 4 (2013): 639–648.

Newman, Karen L., and Stanley D. Nollen. "Culture and Congruence: The Fit between Management Practices and National Culture." *Journal of International Business Studies* 27, no. 4 (1996): 753–779.

Noggle, Robert. "Integrity, the Self, and Desire-Based Accounts of the Good." *Philosophical Studies* 96, no. 3 (1999): 303–331.

Norrisa, Gweneth, and Brendan O'Dwyer. "Motivating Socially Responsive Decision Making: The Operation of Management Controls in a Socially Responsive Organisation." *The British Accounting Review* 36, no. 2 (2004): 173–196.

Nussbaum, Martha C. "Mill between Aristotle & Bentham." *Daedalus* 133, no. 2 (2004).

O'Boyle, Edward J. "Personalist Economics: Unorthodox and Countercultural." *Review of Social Economy* 59, no. 4 (2001): 367–393.

O'Boyle, Edward J., and Patrick J. Welch. "Tracing the Origins of Personalist Economics to Aristotle and Aquinas." *Forum for Social Economics* 45, no. 1 (2015): 1–16.

O'Keefe, Mark. "Social Sin and Fundamental Option." *Irish Theological Quarterly* 58 (1992): 85–94.

Ochulor, and Chinenye Leo. "Ethical and Moral Implications of Corruption/ Corruption D'implications Ethiques Et Morales." *Canadian Social Science* 7, no. 5 (2011): 223–228.

Ong, Wan Kah, and Peng Chan. "Business Ethics and Buddhism." *Review of Business Research* 12, no. 4 (2012): 139–150.

Organ, David L. "Leadership: The Great Man Theory Revisited." *Business Horizons* 39, no. 3 (1996): 1–4.

Osei-Afoakwa, Kofi. "What Makes Corruption in the Public Procurement Process Awful?" *International Journal of Development and Sustainability* 1, no. 3 (2012): 622–633.

Ozar, David T. "Do Corporations Have Moral Rights?" *Journal of Business Ethics* 4, no. 4 (1985): 277–281.

Paine, Lynn sharp. "Managing for Organizational Integrity." *Harvard Business Review* 72, no. 3/4 (1994): 106–117.

Painter-Morland, Mollie. "Triple Bottom-Line Reporting as Social Grammar: Integrating Corporate Social Responsibility and Corporate Codes of Conduct." *Business Ethics: A European Review* 15, no. 4 (2006): 352–364.

Pajankar, Vishal D., and Pranali V. Pajankar. "Development of School Education Status in India." *Journal of Social Science* 22, no. 1 (2010): 15–23.

Palanski, Michael E, and Francis J. Yammarino. "Integrity and Leadership: A Multi-Level Conceptual Framework." *The Leadership Quarterly* 20 (2009): 405–420.

Palanski, Michael E., Surinder S. Kahai, and Francis J. Yammarino. "Team Virtues and Performance: An Examination of Transparency, Behavioral Integrity, and Trust." *Journal of Business Ethics* 99, no. 2 (2011): 201–216.

Palanski, Michael E., and Francis J. Yammarino. "Integrity and Leadership: Clearing the Conceptual Confusion." *European Management Journal* 25, no. 3 (2007): 171–184.

———. "Impact of Behavioral Integrity on Follower Job Performance: A Three-Study Examination." *The Leadership Quarterly* 22 (2011): 765–786.

Paldam, Martin M. "The Cross-Country Pattern of Corruption: Economics, Culture and the Seesaw Dynamics." *European Journal of Political Economy* 18, no. 2 (2002): 215–240.

Panda, Abinash, and Rajen K. Gupta. "Mapping Cultural Diversity within India: A Meta-Analysis of Some Recent Studies." *Global Business Review* 5, no. 1 (2004): 27–49.

Panini, M. N. "Corporate Culture in India." *Economic and Political Weekly* 23, no. 35 (1988): 86–94.

Parry, Jonathan. "The Gift, the Indian Gift and the 'Indian Gift.'" *Man, New Series* 21, no. 3 (1986): 453–473.

Paxton, Joseph M., and Joshua D. Greene. "Moral Reasoning: Hints and Allegations." *Cognitive Science* 2, no. 3 (2010): 511–527.

Payne, Dinah, and Frédéric Dimanche. "Towards a Code of Conduct for the Tourism Industry: An Ethics Model." *Journal of Business Ethics* 15, no. 9 (1996): 997–1007.

Peace, Pontifical Council for Justice and Peace. "Vocation of the Business Leader: A Reflection." (2018): 1–29.

Peurala, J. "Assessing the Corruption Prevention Measures and the Bribery Criminalisations in the Finnish Anti-Corruption Framework." *European Journal of Crime, Criminal Law and Criminal Justice* 19, no. 4 (2011): 319–362.

Pfeiffer, Raymond S. "The Central Distinction in the Theory of Corporate Moral Personhood." *Journal of Business Ethics* 9, no. 6 (1990): 473–480.

Phillips, Michael J. "Corporate Moral Personhood and Three Conceptions of the Corporation." *Business Ethics Quarterly* 2, no. 4 (1992): 435–459.

Phillips, Robert A. "Stakeholder Theory and a Principle of Fairness." *Business Ethics Quarterly* 7, no. 1 (1997): 51–66.

———. "Stakeholder Theory and a Principle of Fairness." *Business Ethics Quarterly* 7, no. 1 (1997): 51–66.

Pianalto, Matthew. "Integrity and Struggle." *Philosophia* 40 (2012): 319–336.

Pieterse, Jan Nederveen. "Globalisation as Hybridisation." *International Sociology* 9, no. 2 (1994): 161–184.

Place, Katic R. "A Qualitative Examination of Public Relation Practitioner Ethical Decision Making and the Deontological Theory of Ethical Issues Management." *Journal of Mass Media Ethics* 25, no. 3 (2010): 226–245.

Porte, Todd R. La. "High Reliability Organizations: Unlikely, Demanding and at Risk." *Journal of Contingencies & Crisis Management* 4, no. 2 (1996): 60–71.

Porter, Jean. "Moral Language and the Language of Grace: The Fundamental Option and the Virtue of Charity." *Philosophy and Theology* 10 (1997): 171–181.

Prahalad, C.K. "Strategies for the Bottom of the Economic Pyramid: India as a Source of Innovation." *Reflections* 3, no. 4 (2002): 6–16.

Preston, Anne E. "The Nonprofit Worker in a for-Profit World." *Journal of Labor Economics* 7, no. 4 (1989): 438–463.

Preston, Lee E., and James E. Post. "Private Management and Public Policy." *California Management Review* 23, no. 3 (1981): 56–64.

Provis, Chris. "Virtuous Decision Making for Business Ethics." *Journal of Business Ethics* 91 (2010): 3–16.

Quah, Jon S. T. "Comparing Anti-Corruption Measures in Asian Countries: Lessons to Be Learnt." *Asian Review of Public Administration* 11, no. 2 (1999): 71–90.

Quah, Jon S.T. "Curbing Corruption in India: An Impossible Dream?" *Asian Journal of Political Science* 16, no. 3 (2008): 240–259.

Qureshi, Paul. "Sin, Fundamental Option and Conversion." *Irish Theological Quarterly* 71 (2006): 272–284.

Rahman, Shafiqur. "Evaluation of Definitions: Ten Dimensions of Corporate Social Responsibility." *World Review of Business Research* 1, no. 1 (2011): 166–176.

Rajan. P. Varadarajan, and Anil Menon. "Cause-Related Marketing: A Coalignment of Marketing Strategy and Corporate Philanthropy." *The Journal of Marketing* 52, no. 3 (1998): 58–74.

Rajeev, Priya. "Wisdom from Ancient Indian Philosophy for the Corporate World." *International Management Review* 3, no. 1 (2007): 72–81.

Ranken, Nani L. "Corporations as Persons: Objections to Goodpaster's Principle of Moral Projection." *Journal of Business Ethics* 6, no. 8 (1987): 633–637.

Reisert, Joseph R. "Authenticity, Justice, and Virtue in Taylor and Rousseau." *Polity* 33, no. 2 (2000): 305–330.

Reuvers, Mark, Marloes L van Engen, Claartje J Vinkenburg, and Elisabeth Wilson-Evered. "Transformational Leadership and Innovative Work Behaviour: Exploring the Relevance of Gender Differences." *Creativity and Innovation Management* 17, no. 3 (2008): 227–244.

Richards, Donald G. "Eudaimonia, Economics and the Environment: What Do the Hellenistic Thinkers Have to Teach Economists About 'the Good Life'?" *Ethics & the Environment* 18, no. 2 (2013): 33–53.

Rijckeghem, Caroline Van, and Beatrice Weder. "Bureaucratic Corruption and the Rate of Temptation: Do Wages in the Civil Service Affect Corruption, and by How Much?" *Journal of Development Economics* 65 (2001): 307–331.

Rindova, Violina P., Ian O. Williamson, Antoaneta P. Petkova, and Joy Marie Sever. "Being Good or Being Known: An Empirical Examination of the Dimensions, Antecedents, and Consequences of Organizational Reputation." *The Academy of Management Journal* 48, no. 6 (2005): 1033–1049.

Robert, R. Phillips, Edward Freeman, and Andrew C. Wicks. "What Stakeholder Theory Is Not." *Business Ethics Quarterly* 13, no. 4 (2003): 479–502.

Rodriguez, Peter, and Donald S. Siegel. "Three Lenses on the Multinational Enterprise: Politics, Corruption, and Corporate Social Responsibility." *Journal of International Business Studies* 37, no. 6 (2006): 733–746.

Roels, Shirley J. "The Christian Calling to Business Life." *Theology Today* 60, no. 3 (2003): 357–369

Rose-Ackerman, Susan. "Grand Corruption and the Ethics of Global Business." *Journal of Banking & Finance* 26 (2002): 1889–1918.

Rosthorn, John. "Business Ethics Auditing: More Than a Stakeholder's Toy." *Journal of Business Ethics* 27, no. 1/2 (2000): 9–19.

Rothstein, Bo, and Eric M. Uslaner. "All for One: Equality, Corruption, and Social Trust." *World Politics* 58, no. 1 (2005): 41–72.

Rountree, Jennifer A. "Joining Inner and Outer Approaches to Freedom: Meeting the Needs of Developing Communities." *Journal of Humanistic Psychology* 51, no. 3 (2011): 291–317.

Rozuel, Cécile. "Moral Imagination and Active Imagination: Searching in the Depths of the Psyche." *Journal of Management Development* 31, no. 5 (2012): 488–501.

Rugman, Alan M., and Alain Verbeke. "A Note on the Transnational Solution and the Transaction Cost Theory of Multinational and Strategic Management." *Journal of International Business Studies* 23, no. 4 (1992): 761–771.

Sadler-Smith, Eugene. "Toward Organizational Environmental Virtuousness." *The Journal of Applied Behavioral Science* 49, no. 1 (2013): 123–148.

Sakamoto, Yoshikazu. "An Alternative to Global Marketization: East Asian Regional Cooperation and the Civic State." *Alternatives: Global, Local, Political* 24, no. 2 (1999): 143–165.

Salbu, Steven R. "Transnational Bribery: The Big Questions." *Northwestern Journal of International Law & Business* 21, no. 2 (2001): 435–470.

Sandberg, Joakim. "Moral Economy and Normative Ethics." *Journal of Global Ethics* 11, no. 2 (2015): 176–187.

Sanyal, Rajib, and Turgut Guvenli. "The Propensity to Bribe in International Business: The Relevance of Cultural Variables." *Cross Cultural Management* 16, no. 3 (2009): 287–300.

Sargeant, Adrian, and Lucy Woodliffe. "Gift Giving: An Interdisciplinary Review." *International Journal of Nonprofit and Voluntary Sector Marketing* 12, no. 4 (2007): 275–307.

Schauber, Nancy. "Integrity, Commitment and Concept of a Person." *American Philosophical Quarterly* 33, no. 1 (1996): 119–129.

Schminke, Marshall, Maureen L. Ambrose, and Jeffrey A. Miles. "The Impact of Gender and Setting on Perceptions of Others' Ethics." *Sex Roles* 48, no. 7/8 (2003): 361–374.

Schneewind, Jerome B. "The Misfortunes of Virtue." *Ethics* 101, no. 1 (1990): 42–63.

Schwartz, Shalom H. "A Theory of Cultural Value Orientations: Explication and Applications." *Comparative Sociology* 5, no. 2/3 (2006): 137–182.

Scott, Johnston James. "Dewey's Critique of Kant." *A Quarterly Journal in American Philosophy* 42, no. 4 (2006): 518–551.

Sejersted, Francis. "Managers and Consultants as Manipulators: Reflections on the Suspension of Ethics." *Business Ethics Quarterly* 6, no. 1 (1996): 67–86.

Seleim, Ahmed, and Nick Bontis. "The Relationship between Culture and Corruption: A Cross-National Study." *Journal of Intellectual Capital* 10, no. 1 (2009): 165–184.

Sen, Amartya. "Does Business Ethics Make Economic Sense?" *Business Ethics Quarterly* 30, no. 1 (1993): 45–56.

———. "Economics, Business Principles and Moral Sentiments." *Business Ethics Quarterly* 7, no. 3 (1997): 5–15.

———. "Rational Fools: A Critique of the Behavioral Foundations of Economic Theory." *Philosophy & Public Affairs* 6, no. 4 (1977): 317–344.

Shafqat, Saeed. "Review of Public Office, Private Interest: Bureaucracy and Corruption in India." *The Journal of Asian Studies* 61, no. 3 (2002): 1085–1087.

Shanka, Tekle, and Brian Handley. "Gift Giving: An Exploratory Behavioural Study." *Asia Pacific Journal of Tourism Research* 16, no. 4 (2011): 359–377.

Shin, Yuhyung, Sun Young Sung, Jin Nam Choi, and Min Soo Kim. "Top Management Ethical Leadership and Firm Performance: Mediating Role of Ethical and Procedural Justice Climate." *Journal of Business Ethics* 129, no. 1 (2015): 43–57.

Shrivastava, Paul. "The Role of Corporations in Achieving Ecological Sustainability." *Academy of Management Review* 20, no. 4 (1995): 936–960.

Shrivastava, Paul, and Stuart Hart. "Creating Sustainable Corporations." *Business Strategy and the Environment* 4 (1995): 154–165.

Simons, Tony. "Behavioral Integrity: The Perceived Alignment between Managers' Words and Deeds as a Research Focus." *Organizational Science* 13, no. 1 (2002): 18–35.

Sims, Randi L., Baiyun Gong, and Cynthia P. Ruppel. "A Contingency Theory of Corruption: The Effect of Human Development and National Culture." *The Social Science Journal* 49 (2012): 90–97.

Singh, J. P. "Managerial Culture and Work-Related Values in India." *Organisation Studies* 11, no. 1 (1990): 75–101.

Singh, Kunwar P., Amrita Malik, and Sarita Sinha. "Water Quality Assessment and Apportionment of Pollution Sources of Gomti River (India) Using Multivariate Statistical Techniques—A Case Study." *Analytica Chimica Acta* 538, no. 1/2 (2005) 355–374.

Singha, Shoran. "Ram Mohan Roy: The Father and Founder of Modern India." *The Contemporary Review* 144, no. 1 (1933): 439–445.

Sinha, Jai B. P. "Power in Indian Organizations." *Indian Journal of Industrial Relations* 17, no. 3 (1982): 339–352.

Sinhaac, Jai B.P., and D. Sinha. "Role of Social Values in Indian Organizations." *International Journal of Psychology* 25, no. 3/6 (1990): 705–714.

Solomon, Robert C. "The Corporation as Community: A Reply to Ed Hartman." *Business Ethics Quarterly* 4, no. 3 (1994): 271–285.

———. "Aristotle, Ethics and Business Organizations." *Organization Studies* 25, no. 6 (2004): 1023–1043.

Sparrow, Paul R., and Pawan S. Budhwar. "Competition and Change: Mapping the Indian HRM Recipe against World-Wide Patterns." *Journal of World Business* 32, no. 3 (1997): 224–242.

Sparrowe, Raymond T. "Authentic Leadership and the Narrative Self." *The Leadership Quarterly* 16 (2005): 419–439.

Spicer, Andrew, and Wendy J. Bailey. "When Does National Identity Matter? Convergence and Divergence in International Business Ethics." *The Academy of Management Journal* 50, no. 6 (2007): 1462–1480.

Srivastava, Sanjay. "Organizational Culture and Work Related Values." *Delhi Business Review* 4, no. 1 (2003): 1–9.

Steidlmeier, P. "Gift Giving, Bribery and Corruption: Ethical Management of Business Relationships in China." *Journal of Business Ethics* 20, no. 2 (1999): 121–132.

Stevulak, Cathy, and Jeffrey Campbell. "Supply-Side Corruption." *The Journal of corporate citizenship* 29, no. 4 (2008): 33–48.

Streicher, Bernhard, Verena Graupmann, and Silke Weisweiler. "A Spoonful of Fairness: Training in Fairness Principles Helps Communicate Bad News." *International Journal of Training Research* 12, no. 1 (2014): 71–82.

Sugden, Robert. "Mutual Advantage, Conventions and Team Reasoning "*International Review of Economics* 58, no. 1 (2011): 9–20.

Sukhtankar, Sandip. "Sweetening the Deal? Political Connections and Sugar Mills in India." *American Economic Journal* 4, no. 3 (2012): 43–63.

Suria, Gurpreet Singh, and Pamela Yvette Abbott. "Cultural Enclaves and Social Change: The Interplay between Indian Cultural Values and Western Ways of Working in an Indian Organization." *Information Technology for Development* 19, no. 3 (2013): 193–214.

Svensson, Jakob. "Who Must Pay Bribes and How Much? Evidence from a Cross Section of Firms." *The Quarterly Journal of Economics* 118, no. 1 (2003): 207–230.

Swedberg, Richard. "The Market." *Contexts* 6, no. 4 (2007): 64–66.

Tablan, Ferdinand. "Catholic Social Teachings: Toward a Meaningful Work." *Journal of Business Ethics* 128, no. 2 (2015): 291–303.

Tavernier, Johan De. "The Historical Roots of Personalism: From Renouvier's Le Personnalisme, Mounier's Manifeste Au Service Du Personnalisme and Maritain's Humanisme Integral to Janssens' Personne Et Societe." *Ethical Perspectives* 16, no. 3 (2009): 361–392.

Taylor, Gabriele, and Raimond Gaita. "Integrity." *Proceedings of the Aristotelian Society, Supplimentary Volumes* 55 (1981): 143–176.

Taylor, Jerry. "Sustainable Development: A Dubious Solution in Search of a Problem." *Policy Analysis* 26, no. 449 (2002): 1–49.

Tharenou, Phyllis. "Women's Self-Initiated Expatriation as a Career Option and Its Ethical Issues." *Journal of Business Ethics* 95 (2010): 73–88.

Thite, Mohan. "Ethics and Human Resource Management and Development in a Global Context: Case Study of an Indian Multinational." *Human Resource Development International* 16, no. 1 (2013): 106–115.

Tholkappian, C, and S Rajendran. "Pesticide Application and Its Adverse Impact on Health: Evidences from Kerala." *International Journal of Science and Technology* 1, no. 2 (2011): 56–59.

Thomasset, Alain. "Narrativity and Hermeneutics in Professional Ethics." *Ethical Perspectives* 3, no. 4 (1996): 168–174.

Thompson, Edward Palmer. "The Moral Economy of the English Crowd in the Eighteenth Century." *Past & Present* 50, no. 2 (1971): 76–136.

Tillman, Robert. "Making the Rules and Breaking the Rules: The Political Origins of Corporate Corruption in the New Economy." *Crime Law Soc Change* 51 (2009): 73–86.

Trevino, Linda Klebe. "Ethical Decision Making in Organizations: A Person-Situation Interactionist Model." *The Academy of Management Review* 11, no. 3 (1986): 601–617.

———. "Moral Reasoning and Business Ethics: Implications for Research, Education, and Management." *Journal of Business Ethics* 11, no. 5 (1992): 445–459.

Treviño, Linda Klebe, Kenneth D. Butterfield, and Donald L. McCabe. "The Ethical Context in Organizations: Influences on Employee Attitudes and Behaviors." *Business Ethics Quarterly* 8, no. 3 (1998): 447–476.

Trevino, Linda Klebe, Laura Pincus Hartman, and Michael Brown. "Moral Person and Moral Manager: How Executives Develop a Reputation for Ethical Leadership." *California Management Review* 42, no. 4 (2000): 128–142.

Trevino, Linda Klebe, Weaver, Gary R. Gibson, David G, and Barbara Ley Toffler. "Managing Ethics and Legal Compliance: What Works and What Hurts." *California Management Review* 41, no. 2 (1999): 131–151.

Trevino, Linda Klebe, and Gary R. Weaver. "Business Ethics/Business Ethics: One Field or Two?" *Business Ethics Quarterly* 4, no. 2 (1994): 113–128.

Trevinyo-Rodrı´guez, Rosa Nelly. "Integrity: A Systems Theory Classification." *Journal of Management History* 13, no. 1 (2007): 74–93.

Trice, Harrison M., and Janice M. Beyer. "Studying Organizational Cultures through Rites and Ceremonials." *The Academy of Management Review* 9, no. 4 (1984): 653–669.

Trotter, R. Clayton, Susan G. Day, and Amy E. Love. "Bhopal, India and Union Carbide: The Second Tragedy." *Journal of Business Ethics* 8, no. 6 (1989): 439–454.

Tsalikis, John, and David Fritzsche. "Business Ethics: A Literature Review with a Focus on Marketing Ethics." *Journal of Business Ethics* 8, no. 9 (1989): 695–744.

Tsuchiya, Shigehisa. "Utility Deregulation and Business Ethics: More Openness through Gaming/Simulation." *Simulation & Gaming* 36, no. 1 (2005): 114–133.

Tuan, Luu Trong. "Corporate Social Responsibility, Ethics, and Corporate Governance." *Social Responsibility Journal* 8, no. 4 (2012): 547–560.

Tyler, Tom R. "Social Justice: Outcome and Procedure." *International Journal of Psychology* 35, no. 2 (2000): 117–125.

Tyler, Tom R., and Steven L. Blader. "Can Businesses Effectively Regulate Employee Conduct? The Antecedents of Rule Following in Work Settings." *The Academy of Management Journal* 48, no. 6 (2005): 1143–1158.

Uhlenbruck, Klaus, Peter Rodriguez, Jonathan Doh, and Lorraine Eden. "The Impact of Corruption on Entry Strategy: Evidence from Telecommunication Projects in Emerging Economies." *Organization Science* 17, no. 3 (2006): 402–414.

Ulrich, Peter, and Ulrich Thielemann. "How Do Managers Think About Market Economies and Morality? Empirical Enquiries into Business-Ethical Thinking Patterns." *Journal of Business Ethics* 12, no. 11 (1993): 879–898.

Valentine, Sean R., and Connie R. Bateman. "The Impact of Ethical Ideologies, Moral Intensity, and Social Context on Sales-Based Ethical Reasoning." *Journal of Business Ethics* 102 (2011): 155–168.

Vallejo, Manuel Carlos. "Is the Culture of Family Firms Really Different? A Value-Based Model for Its Survival through Generations." *Journal of Business Ethics* 81, no. 2 (2008): 261–279.

Veiga, John F., Timothy D. Golden, and Kathleen Dechant. "Why Managers Bend Company Rules." *Academy of Management Executive* 18, no. 2 (2004): 84–90.

Velasquez, Manuel. "Debunking Corporate Moral Responsibility." *Business Ethics Quarterly* 13, no. 4 (2003): 531–562.

Verhezen, Peter. "The (Ir)Relevance of Integrity in Organizations." *Public Integrity* 10, no. 2 (2008): 133–149.

Verkerk, M.A, J. J. V. Busschbach, and E.D. Karssing. "Health-Related Quality of Life Research and the Capability Approach of Amartya Sen." *Quality of Life Research* 10, no. 1 (2001): 49–55.

Verma, Arvind. "Cultural Roots of Police Corruption in India." *An International Journal of Police Strategies & Management* 22, no. 3 (1999): 264–279.

Verstraeten, Johan. "Narrativity and Hermeneutics in Applied Ethics: Some Introductory Considerations." *Ethical Perspectives* 1, no. 1 (1994): 51–55.

———. "From Business Ethics to the Vocation of Business Leaders to Humanize the World of Business." *Business Ethics: A European Review* 7, no. 2 (1998): 111–124.

———. "How Faith Makes a Difference: Business as a Calling or the Calling of Christians in Business." *Estudios Empresariales* 113, no. 3 (2003): 56–68.

Vidaver-Cohen, Deborah. "Moral Imagination in Organizational Problem-Solving: An Institutional Perspective." *Business Ethics Quarterly* 7, no. 4 (1997): 1–26.

Vijayakumar, and A. G. Khan. "Critical Review of Family Life Education in India." *Indian Streams Research Journal* 5, no. 1 (2015): 1–5.

Viramgama, Nikunj M. "Influence of Corruption on Economic and Finacial Development of the Country." *Indian Social Science Journal* 3, no. 2 (2014): 40–52.

Vytautas Juščius. "Corporate Social Responsibility and Sustainable Development." *Management of Organizations: Systematic Research,* no. 44 (2007): 35–44.

Waddell, Steve. "New Institutions for the Practice of Corporate Citizenship: Historical, Intersectoral, and Developmental Perspectives." *Business and Society Review* 105, no. 1 (2000): 107–126.

Waddock, Sandra A., Charles Bodwell, and Samuel B. Graves. "Responsibility: The New Business Imperative." *The Academy of Management Executive* 16, no. 2 (2002): 132–148.

Wang, Eric T. G. "Transaction Attributes and Software Outsourcing Success: An Empirical Investigation of Transaction Cost Theory." *Information Systems Journal* 12 (2002): 153–181.

Waters, James A., and Frederick Bird. "The Moral Dimension of Organizational Culture." *Journal of Business Ethics* 6, no. 1 (1987): 15–22.

Waters, William. R. "Social Economics: A Solidarist Perspective." *Review of Social Economy* 46, no. 2 (1998): 113–143.

Watson, George W., Robyn A. Berkley, and Stevend D. Papamarcos. "Ambiguous Allure: The Value-Pragmatics Model of Ethical Decision Making." *Business and Society Review* 114, no. 1 (2009): 1–29.

Weaver, Gary R. "Ethics Programs in Global Businesses: Culture's Role in Managing Ethics." *Journal of Business Ethics* 30 (2001): 3–15.

Weaver, Gary R., Linda Klebe Treviño, and Philip L. Cochran. "Integrated and Decoupled Corporate Social Performance: Management Commitments, External Pressures, and Corporate Ethics Practices." *The Academy of Management Journal* 42, no. 5 (1999): 539–552.

Weber, James, and Kathleen Getz. "Buy Bribes or Bye-Bye Bribes: The Future Status of Bribery in International Commerce." *Business Ethics Quarterly* 14, no. 4 (2004): 695–711.

Wei, Shang-Jin. "How Taxing Is Corruption on International Investors?" *The Review of Economics and Statistics* 82, no. 1 (2000): 1–11.

Werhane, Patricia. "Moral Imagination and Systems Thinking." *Journal of Business Ethics* 38, no. 1 (2002): 33–42.

Werhane, Patricia H. "Corporate and Individual Moral Responsibility: A Reply to Jan Garrett." *Journal of Business Ethics* 8, no. 10 (1989): 821–822.

——— "Moral Imagination and the Search for Ethical Decision-Making in Management." *Business Ethics Quarterly* (1998): 75–98.

———. "Business Ethics and the Origins of Contemporary Capitalism: Economics and Ethics in the Work of Adam Smith and Herbert Spencer." *Journal of Business Ethics* 24, no. 3 (2000): 185–198.

———. "Moral Imagination and Systems Thinking." *Journal of Business Ethics* 38 (2002): 33–42.

———. "Mental Models, Moral Imagination and System Thinking in the Age of Globalization." *Journal of Business Ethics* 78, no. 3 (2008): 463–474.

Wernerfelt, Birger. "A Resource-Based View of the Firm." *Strategic Management Journal* 5, no. 2 (1984): 171–180.

Wheeler, David, Barry Colbert, and R. Edward Freeman. "Focusing on Value: Reconciling Corporate Social Responsibility, Sustainability and a Stakeholder Approach in a Network World." *Journal of General Management* 28, no. 3 (2003): 1–29.

Whetstone, J. Thomas. "How Virtue Fits within Business Ethics." *Journal of Business Ethics* 33 (2001): 101–114.

———. "Personalism and Moral Leadership: The Servant Leader with a Transforming Vision." *Business Ethics: A European Review* 11, no. 4 (2002): 385–392.

White, Bruce M. "'Give Us a Little Milk': The Social and Cultural Meanings of Gift Giving in the Lake Superior Fur Trade." *Minnesota History* 48, no. 2 (1982): 60–71.

Windsor, Duane. "The Future of Corporate Social Responsibility." *International Journal of Organizational Analysis* 9, no. 3 (2001): 225–256.

Wolcott, Gregory. "The New (Old) Case for the Ethics of Business." *Journal of Business Ethics* 132, no. 1 (2015): 127–146.

Worden, Skip. "The Role of Integrity as a Mediator in Strategic Leadership: A Recipe for Reputational Capital." *Journal of Business Ethics* 46, no. 1 (2003): 31–44.

Wu, Xun. "Determinants of Bribery in Asian Firms: Evidence from the World Business Environment Survey." *Journal of Business Ethics* 87 (2009): 75–88.

Wynne, Edward A. "Great Traditions in Education: Transmitting Moral Values." *Educational Leadership* 43, no. 4 (1985): 4–9.

Yang, Jianfeng. "Linking Proactive Personality to Moral Imagination: Moral Identity as a Moderator." *Social Behavior and Personality* 41, no. 1 (2013): 165–175.

Yanga, Chenlung, John G. Wackerb, and Chwen Sheuc. "What Makes Outsourcing Effective? A Transaction-Cost Economics Analysis." *International Journal of Production Research* 50, no. 16 (2012): 4462–4476.

Yeganeh, Hamid. "Culture and Corruption: A Concurrent Application of Hofstede's, Schwartz's and Inglehart's Frameworks." *International Journal of Development Issues* 13, no. 1 (2014): 2–23.

Yilmaz, A., and M. Akif. "Determinants of Economic Corruption: A Cross-Country Data Analysis." *International Journal of Business and social Science* 2, no. 13 (2011): 161–169.

Yunus, Muhammad, Bertrand Moingeon, and Laurence Lehmann-Ortega. "Building Social Business Models: Lessons from the Grameen Experience." *Long Range Planning* 43 (2010): 308–325.

Yurtsever, Gülçimen. "Measuring Moral Imagination." *Social Behavior and Personality* 34, no. 3 (2006): 205–219.

Zafirovski, Milan. "Reconsidering Equilibrium: A Socio-Economic Perspective." *Journal of Socio-Economics* 31 (2002): 559–579.

Zhu, Weichun, Bruce J. Avolio, Ronald E. Riggio, and John J. Sosik. "The Effect of Authentic Transformational Leadership on Follower and Group Ethics." *The Leadership Quarterly* 22 (2011): 801–817.

C. Book Sections

Albrow, Martin. "Introduction." In *Globalization, Knowledge and Society*, edited by, Martin Albrow and Elizabeth King, 3–17. London: Sage Publications, 1990.

Annas, Julia. "Virtue Ethics." In *The Oxford Handbook of Ethical Theory*, edited by, David Copp, 515–537. Oxford: Oxford University Press, 2006.

Backhaus, Kristin B. "Organizational Identity, Corporate Social Performance and Corporate Reputation: Their Roles in Creating Organizational Attractiveness." In *Corporate Reputation: Managing Opportunities and Threats*, edited by, Ronald J. Burke, Graeme Martin and Cary L. Cooper, 111–129. Burlington: Ashgate Publishing company, 2011.

Barcelona, Antonio. "Introduction: Cognitive Theory of Metaphor and Metonymy." In *Metaphor and Metonymy at the Crossroads: A Cognitive Perspective*, edited by, Antonio Barcelona, 1–28. Berlin & New York: Mouton/ de Gruyter, 2003.

Benefiel, Margaret. "Using Discernment to Make Better Business Decisions." In *Leadership and Business Ethics*, edited by, Gabriel Flynn, 31–39. Dublin: Springer, 2008.

Berlin, Isaiah. "Two Concepts of Liberty." In *Four Essays on Liberty*, edited by, Isaiah Berlin, 166–218. London: Oxford University Press, 1969.

Bhikku, Tejadhammo. "Making a Cup of Tea: Some Aspects of Spiritual Direction within a Living Buddhist Tradition." In *Tending the Holy: Spiritual Direction across Traditions*, edited by, Norvene Vest, 3–19. Harrisburg: Morehouse, 2003.

Black, Henry Campbell. "Corporation." In *Black's Law Dictionary*, 340–343. New York: West Publishing, 1999.

Blundell, Boyd. "Refiguring Virtue." In *A Passion for the Possible: Thinking with Paul Ricoeur*, edited by, Brian Treanor and Henry Isaac Venema, 158–172. New York: Fordham University Press, 2010.

Boersma, Martine. "Corruption as a Violation of Economic, Social and Cultural Rights: Reflections on the Right to Education." In *Corruption and Human Rights: Interdisciplinary Perspectives*, edited by, Martine Boersma and Hans Nelen, 51-90. Mortsel: Intersentia Publishers, 2010.

Bouckaert, Luk. "Reducing Opportunism through Moral Commitment: The Ethical Paradox of Management." In *Moral Leadership in Action*, edited by, Heidi von Weltzein Hoivik, 84-96. Cheltenham: Edward Elgar, 2002.

———. "Humanity in Business." In *Sustaining Humanity: An Ethics Agenda for European Leaders Today*, edited by, Johan Verstraeten and Maria Duffy, 99–109. Leuven: Bibliotheek Faculteit Godgeleerdheid with European Ethics Network Co-Ordination Centre, 2004.

———. "When More Ethics Create Less Ethics—Some Fruther Clarifications on the Ethics Management Paradox." In *Interdisciplinary Yearbook for Business Ethics*, edited by, László Zsolnai, 1, 215–218. Oxford: Peter Lang, 2006.

———. "Spirituality in Economics." In *Spirituality as a Public Good*, edited by, Luk Bouckaert and Laszlo Zsolnai, 11–25. Antwerp: Garant, 2007.

———. "Doing Business Ethics in Europe: Before and after the Financial Crisis." In *Imagine Europe: The Search for European Identity and Spirituality*, edited by, Luk Bouckaert and Jochanan Eynikel, 79-88. Antwerpen: Garant, 2009.

———. "Economic Democracy as a Social and Spiritual Utopia." In *Respect and Economic Democracy*, edited by, Luk Bouckaert and Pasquale Arena, 13-28. Antwerp: Grant Publishers, 2010.

———. "From Business Ethics to Business Spirituality: The Socratic Model of Leadership." In *Spirituality and Business: Exploring Possibilities for a New Management Paradigm*, edited by, Sharda S. Nandram and Margot Esther Borden, 73-87. Heidelberg: Springer, 2010.

———. "Personalism." In *The Palgrave Handbook of Spirituality and Business*, edited by, Luk Bouckaert and Laszlo Zsolnai, 155-162. Basingstoke: Palgrave Macmillan, 2011.

———. "Spirituality and Economic Democracy." In *Spirituality and Ethics in Management*, edited by, Laszlo Zsolnai, 41-49. London: Springer, 2011.

———. "Spirituality and Rationality." In *The Palgrave Handbook of Spirituality and Business*, edited by, Luk Bouckaert and Laszlo Zsolnai, 18-25. Basingstoke: Palgrave Macmillan, 2011.

________ and Laszlo Zsolnai. "Spirituality and Business." In *The Palgrave Handbook of Spirituality and Business*, edited by, Luk Bouckaert and Laszlo Zsolnai, 3-8. Basingstoke: Palgrave Macmillan, 2011.

Brady, F. Neil. "Profit." In *Blackwell Encyclopedic Dictionary of Business Ethics*, edited by, Patricia H. Werhane and Edward Freeman, 518-520. Oxford: Blackwell Publishers, 1997.

Bulger, Carrie A., and Gwenith G. Fisher. "Ethical Imperatives of Work/Life Balance." In *Work and Quality of Life: Ethical Practices in Organizations*, edited by, Nora P. Reilly, M. Joseph Sirgy and C. Allen Gorman, 181-203. Dordrecht: Springer, 2012.

Burke, Ronald J. "Corporate Reputations: Development, Maintenance, Change and Repair." In *Corporate Reputation: Managing Opportunities and Threats*, edited by, Ronald J. Burke, Graeme Martin and Cary L. Cooper, 3-45. Burlington: Ashgate Publishing Company, 2011.

Buyens, Dirk, and Jasmijn Verbrigghe. "Adding Value and HRM Practice: Evidence-Based HR." In *Human Resource Management Practices: Assessing Added Value*, edited by, Maike Andresen and Christian Nowak, 15-31. Heidelberg: Springer, 2015.

Cain, Glen G. "The Economic Analysis of Labour Market Discrimination: A Survey." In *Handbook of Labour Economics*, edited by, O. Ashenfelter and R. Layard, 1, 693-785. Amsterdam: Elsevier, 1986.

Carson, Thomas L. "Milton Friedman." In *The Blackwell Encyclopedic Dictionary of Business Ethics*, edited by, Patricia H. Werhane and Edward Freeman, 291-292. Oxford: Blackwell Publishers, 1997.

Chatterji, Madhumita. "Humanizing the Economic Man." In *Spiritual Humanism and Economic Wisdom*, edited by, Hendrik Opdebeeck and Laszlo Zsolnai, 89-98. Antwerpen: Garant, 2011.

Childress, James F. "Just-War Criteria." In *War or Peace? The Search for New Answers*, edited by, A. Shannon, 40-58. New York: Orbis Books, 1980.

Christopher, John. "How Normative Is the Past? Rediscovering Gurukul Education and Its Virtue Approach as Alternative for Value Education." In *Redefining Education: Expanding Horizons*, edited by, Mintu Sinha, 561-573. New Delhi: Alfa Publications, 2013.

________ and Johan De Tavernier. "Educating Virtues in Order to Prevent Crimes?: Strategies to Minimize Interpersonal Crimes among Children and Youth." In *Second International Conference of the South Asian Society of Criminology and Victimology*, edited by, K. Jaishankar and Natti Ronel, 234-242. Tirunelveli: SASCV & Department of Criminology and Criminal Justice, Manonmaniam Sundaranar University, 2013.

Clarkson, Max, and Michael Deck. "Stockholder." In *Encyclopedic Dictionary of Business Ethics*, edited by, Patricia H. Werhane and R. Edward Freeman, 608. Oxford: Blackwell Publishers, 1998.

Coffey, Betty Smith. "Corporate Philanthropy." In *Encyclopedic Dictionary of Business Ethics*, edited by, Patricia H. Werhane and R. Edward Freeman, 151-152. Oxford: Blackwell Publishers, 1998.

Comer, Debra R., and Gina Vega. "Introduction: Why Moral Courage Matters in Organizations." In *Moral Courage in Organizations: Doing the Right Thing at Work*, edited by, Debra R. Comer and Gina Vega, 15-23. New York: Routledge, 2011.

Danley, John. "Corporate Moral Agency." In *A Companion to Business Ethics*, edited by, Robert E. Frederick, 243-256. Malden: Blackwell Publishers, 1999.

Dare, Tim. "Detachment, Distance and Integrity." In *Personal Ethics and Integrity*, edited by, Tim Dare and W. Bradley Wendel, 100-124. Newcastle upon Tyne: Cambridge Scholars Publishing, 2010.

Dauenhauer, Bernard P. "Response to Rawls." In *Ricoeur as Another: The Ethics of Subjectivity*, edited by, Richard A. Cohen and James L. Marsh, 203-221. New York: State University of New York Press, 2002.

Delbecq, André L, Elizabeth Liebert, John Mostyn, Paul C Nutt, and Gordan Walter. "Discernment and Strategic Decision Making." In *Spiritual Intelligence at Work: Meaning, Metaphor, and Morals*, edited by, Moses L. Pava and Patrick Primeaux, 139-174. Brandford: Emerald Group Publishing, 2003.

———. "Discernment and Strategic Decision Making: Reflections for a Spirituality of Organizational Leadership." In *Spiritual Intelligence at Work: Meaning, Metaphor, and Morals*, edited by, Moses Pava and Patrick Primeaux, 139-174. London: Emerald Group Publishing Limited, 2003.

Deneulin, Séverine, Mathias Nebel, and Nicholas Sagovsky. "Introduction: Transforming Unjust Structures: The Capability Approach." In *Transforming Unjust Structures: The Capability Approach*, edited by, Séverine Deneulin, Mathias Nebel and Nicholas Sagovsky, 1-17. Dordrecht: Springer, 2006.

Diamond, Cora. "Integrity." In *Encyclopedia of Ethics*, edited by, Lawrence C. Becker and Charlotte B. Becke, 618-623. New York: Garland Publishing, 1992.

Donaldson, Thomas. "Multinational Decision-Making: Reconciling International Norms." In *Business Ethics: A Philosophical Reader*, edited by, Thomas I. White, 799-809. New York: Macmillan publishers, 1933.

———. "Personalizing Corporate Ontology: The French Way." In *Shame, Responsibility and the Corporation*, edited by, Hugh Curtler, 99-112. New York: Haven, 1986.

Dunfee, Thomas W. "Social Contract Theory." In *Encyclopedic Dictionary of Business Ethics*, edited by, Patricia H. Werhane and R. Edward Freeman, 585-588. Oxford: Blackwell Publishers, 1998.

Dunfee, Thomas W., and Thomas J. Donaldson. "Untangling the Corruption Knot: Global Bribery Viewed through the Lens of Integrative Social Contract Theory." In *The Blackwell Guide to Business Ethics*, edited by, Norman E. Bowie, 60-74. Malden: The Blackwell Publishers, 2002.

Eaker, Mark. "Free Enterprise." In *Encyclopedic Dictionary of Business Ethics*, edited by, Patricia H. Werhane and R. Edward Freeman, 283-284. Oxford: Blackwell Publishers, 1998.

Eicher, Sharon. "Introduction: What Corruption Is and Why It Matters." In *Corruption in International Business: The Challenge of Cultural and Legal Diversity*, edited by, Sharon Eicher, 1-15. Farnham: Ashgate Publishers, 2009.

Flynn, Thomas R. "Authenticity." In *The Blackwell Encyclopedic Dictionary of Business Ethics*, edited by, Patricia H. Werhane and Edward Freeman, 30. Malden: Blackwell Publishers, 1997.

Fombrun, Charles J. "Three Pillars of Corporate Citizenship: Ethics, Social Benefit, Profitability." In *Corporate Global Citizenship: Doing Business in the Public Eye*, edited by, Noel M. Tichy, Andrew R. McGill and Lunda St. Clair, 27-42. San Francisco: New Lexington Press, 1997.

Frankfurt, Harry G. "Taking Ourselves Seriously: Getting It Right." In *Taking Ourselves Seriously: Getting It Right*, edited by, Debra Satz, 169-202. California: Stanford University Press, 2006.

———. "Identification and Wholeheartedness." In *Responsibility, Character, and the Emotions: New Essays in Moral Psychology*, edited by, Ferdinand Schoeman, 159-176. New York: Cambridge University Press, 1987.

Freeman, R. Edward. "Stakeholder Theory." In *Encyclopedic Dictionary of Business Ethics*, edited by, Patricia H. Werhane and R. Edward Freeman, 602-606. Oxford: Blackwell Publishers, 1998.

Freeman, R. Edward, and William M. Evan. "A Stakeholder Theory of the Modern Corporation: Kantian Capitalism." In *Ethical Issues in Business: A Philosophical Approach*, edited by, Thomas Donaldson and Patricia H. Werhane, 311-315. New Jersey: Prentice-Hall, 1996.

French, Peter A. "Corporate Moral Agency." In *Business Ethics: Readings and Cases in Corporate Morality*, edited by, W. Michael Hoffman and Jennifer Mills Moore, 194-201. New York: MCgraw-Hill, 1990.

———. "Corporate Moral Agency." In *Encyclopedic Dictionary of Business Ethics*, edited by, Patricia H. Werhane and R. Edward Freeman, 148-151. Oxford: Blackwell Publishers, 1998.

Friedman, Milton. "The Social Responsibility of Business Is to Increase Its Profits." In *Business Ethics: Readings and Cases in Corporate Morality*, edited by, W. Michael Hoffman and Jennifer Mills Moore, 153-157. New York: McGraw-Hill, 1990.

Fuchs, Josef. "Good Acts and Good Persons." In *Understanding Veritatis Splendor: The Encyclical Letter of Pope John Paul 2 on the Church's Moral Teaching*, edited by, John Wilkins, 21-27. Melksham: The Cromwell Press, 1994.

Funderburk, Charles. "Political Corruption: Causes and Consequences." In *Political Corruption in Comparative Perspective: Sources, Status and Prospects*, edited by, Charles Funderburk, 1-19. Farnham: Ashgate Publishing, 2012.

Garofalo, Charles, and Dean Geuras. "Administrative Leadership and Transparency." In *Ethics and Integrity in Public Administration Concepts and Cases*, edited by, Raymond W. Cox, 69-77. London: M. E. Sharpe, 2009.

George, Richard De. "Corporations and Morality." In *Shame, Responsibility and the Corporation*, edited by, Hugh Curtler, 57-75. New York: Haven, 1986.

Goodpaster, Kenneth E. "Business Ethics and Stakeholder Analysis." In *Ethical Issues in Business: A Philosophical Approach*, edited by, Thomas Donaldson and Patricia H. Werhane, 316-330. New Jersey: Prentice-Hall, 1996.

________ and John B. Matthews. "Can a Corporate Have a Conscience?" In *Business Ethics: Readings and Cases in Corporate Morality*, edited by, W. Michael Hoffman and Jennifer Mills Moore, 183-192. New York: McGraw-Hill, 1998.

Häring, Bernhard. "Sin in Post-Vatican II Theology." In *Personalist Morals: Essays in Honor of Professor Louis Janssens*, edited by, Joseph Selling, 87-107. Leuven: Leuven University Press 1988.

Hodgson, D.H. "Is Act-Utilitarianism Self-Defeating?" In *Utilitarianism and Its Critics*, edited by, Jonathan Glover, 204-210. New York: Macmillan Publishing Company, 1990.

Holton, Richard. "How Is Strength of Will Possible?" In *Weakness of Will and Practical Irrationality*, edited by, Sarah Stroud and Christine Tappolet, 39-68. Oxford: Oxford University Press, 2003.

Hursthouse, Rosalind. "Normative Virtue Ethics." In *Ethical Theory: An Anthology*, edited by, Russ Shafer Landau, 701-710. Malden: Blackwell Publishing, 2007.

Jackson, Frank. "Decision-Theoretic Consequentialism and the Nearest and Dearest Objection." In *Consequentialism*, edited by, Philip Pettit, 305-327. Vermont: Dartmouth Publishing Company, 1993.

Janssens, Louis. "Time and Space in Morals." In *Personalist Morals: Essays in Honor of Professor Louis Janssens*, edited by, Joseph A. Selling, 10-21. Leuven: Leuven University Press, 1988.

Johnson, Henry C. "Moral Education, Cultural Inheritance and the Transmission of Values: Moral Development as Nurturing the Moral Imagination." In *Moral Imagination in Personal Formation and Character Development*, edited by, George F. McLean and Richard Knowles, 139-155. Washington: The Council for Research in Values and Philosophy, 2003.

Jordan, Mark D. "Scholasticism." In *The New Dictionary of Theology*, edited by, Joseph A. Komonchak, Marry Collins and Dermot A. Lane, 936-938. Dublin: Gill and Macmillan, 1990.

Kallenberg, Brad J. "The Master Argument of Maclntyre's after Virtue." In *Virtues and Practices in the Christian Tradition: Christian Ethics after Maclntyre*, edited by, Nancey Murphy, Brad J. Kallenberg and Mark Thiessen Nation, 7-30. Notre Dame: University of Notre Dame Press, 1997.

Kant, Immanuel. "Groundwork of the Metaphysics of Morals." In *Rethinking the Western Tradition*, edited by, Allen. W. Wood, 1-63. New Haven: Yale University Press, 2002.

Kantha, Pramod K. "Corruption and Governance in South Asia." In *Political Corruption in Comparative Perspective: Sources, Status and Prospects*, edited by, Charles Funderburk, 117-140. Farnham: Ashgate Publishers, 2012.

Keane, John. "Despotism and Democracy." In *Civil Society and the State: New European Perspectives*, edited by, John Keane, 35-72. New York: Verso, 1998.

Kent, Bonnie. "Habits and Virtues." In *Aquinas's Summa Theologiae: Critical Essays*, edited by, Brian Davies, 223-245. New York: Rowman and Littlefield Publishers, 2006.

Kirkpatrick, Jerry. "Ethical Theory in Marketing." In *Marketing Education: Challenges, Opportunities and Solutions*, edited by, Doug Lincoln and Jeffery Doutt, 50-54. Hightstown: McGraw-Hill Book Company, 1989.

Kohlberg, Lawrence. "Moral Education, Religious Education, and the Public Schools." In *Religion and Public Education*, edited by, Theodore R. Sizer, 164-183. New York: Houghton Mifflin Company, 1967.

Kohli, Suresh. "The Psychology of Corruption." In *Corruption in India*, edited by, Suresh Kohli, 32-39. New Delhi: Chetana Publications, 1975.

Kopfensteiner, Thomas. "The Theory of Fundamental Option." In *Christian Ethics: An Introduction*, edited by, Bernard Hoose, 123-134. London: Cassell, 1998.

Kruschwitz, Robert B., and Robert C. Roberts. "Introduction." In *The Virtues: Contemporary Essays on Moral Character*, edited by, Robert B. Kruschwitz and Robert C. Roberts, 1-21. Belmont: Wadsworth, (1987).

Kuklys, Wiebke, and Ingrid Robeyns. "Sen's Capability Approach to Welfare Economics." In *Amartya Sen's Capability Approach: Theoretical Insights and Empirical Applications*, edited by, Wiebke Kuklys, 9-29. Berlin: Springer, 2005.

Landau, Russ Shafer. "Introduction." In *Ethical Theory: An Anthology*, edited by, Russ Shafer Landau, 3-7. Malden: Blackwell Publishers, 2007.

Larmer, Robert. "Improper Payments and Gifts." In *Encyclopedia of Applied Ethics*, edited by, Ruth Chadwick, 2, 659-664. New York: Academic Press, 1998.

Leff, Nathaniel H. "Economic Development through Bureaucratic Corruption." In *Political Corruption Concepts and Contexts*, edited by, Arnold J. Heidenheimer and Michael Johnston, 307-320. Brunswick: Transaction, 2002.

Lewicki, Roy J., Carolyn Wiethoff, and Edward C.Tomlinson. "What Is the Role of Trust in Organizational Justice?" In *Handbook of Organizational Justice*, edited by, Jerald Greenberg and Jason A. Colquitt, 247-270. Mahwah: Lawrence Erlbaum, 2005.

Lopez, Shane J., Kristin Koetting O'Byrne, and Stephanie Petersen. "Profiling Courage." In *Positive Psychological Assessment: A Handbook of Models and Measures*, edited by, Shane J. Lopez and C. R. Snyder, 185-198. Washington: American Psychological Association, 2003.

Louden, Robert B. "Virtue Ethics." In *Encyclopedia of Applied Ethics*, edited by, Ruth Chadwick, 491-499. New York: Academic Press, 1998.

Luijk, Henk Van. "Integrity in the Private, the Public, and the Corporate Domain." In *Corporate Integrity and Accountability*, edited by, George G. Brenkert, 38-55. London: Sage Publications, 2004.

———. "Facing the Ethics Management Paradox." In *Interdisciplinary Yearbook for Business Ethics*, edited by, László Zsolnai, 202-204. Oxford: Peter Lang, 2006.

MacIntyre, Alasdair. "Existentialism." In *The Encyclopedia of Philosophy*, edited by, Paul Edwards, 3-4, 147-156. New York: Macmillan Publishing 1967.

———. "The Virtues, the Unity of a Human Life, and the Concept of a Tradition." In *Memory, Identity, Community: The Idea of Narrative in the Human Sciences*, edited by, L. P. Hinchman and S. K. Hinchman, 241-264. Albany: State University of New York Press, 2001.

Mann, J.A. "Personalism." In *New Catholic Encyclopedia*, edited by, Berard L. Marthaler, Gregory F. Lavave, Jonathan Y. Tan and Richard E. McCarron, 152-153. New York: Gale, 2003.

Marsh, James L. "The Right and the Good: A Solution to the Communicative Ethics Controversy." In *Ricoeur as Another: The Ethics of Subjectivity*, edited by, Richard A. Cohen and HJames L. Marsh, 223-239. New York: State University of new York Press, 2002.

McDonagh, E. "Fundamental Option." In *New Catholic Encyclopedia*, edited by, Bernard L. Marthaler, Gregory F. Lanave, Joonathan Y. Tan and Richard E. McCarron, 6. New York: Gale Group, 2003.

McNaughton, David, and Piers Rawling. "Deontology." In *The Oxford Handbook of Ethical Theory*, edited by, David Copp, 424-458. Oxford: Oxford University Press, 2006.

Mitnick, Barry M. "Agency Theory." In *Encyclopedic Dictionary of Business Ethics*, edited by, Patricia H. Werhane and Edward Freeman, 14-15. Oxford: Blackwell Publishers, 1998.

Mothersill, Mary. "The Moral Dilemmas Debate." In *Moral Dilemmas and Moral Theory*, edited by, H.E. Manson, 66-86. Oxford: Oxford University Press, 1996.

Muchinsky, Paul M. "The Nepotistic Organization: What Is This Place and How Do the People Make It?" In *Nepotism in Organizations*, edited by, Robert G. Jones, 43-67. New York: Routledge, 2012.

Musschenga, Albert W. "Integrity—Personal, Moral, and Professional." In *Personal and Moral Identity*, edited by, Albert W. Musschenga, Wouter Van Hafften, Ben Spiecker and Marc Slors, 169-203. London: Kluwer Academic Publishers, 2001.

O'Connell, Timothy E. "An Understanding of Conscience." In *Conscience*, edited by, Charles E. Curran, 25-39. New York: Paulist Press, 2004.

Osborne, Kenan B. "Existentialism." In *The New Dictionary of Theology*, edited by, Joseph A. Komonchak, Mary Collins and Dermot A. Lane, 366-369. Dublin: Gill and Macmillan.

Osswald, Silvia, Dieter Frey, and Bernhard Streicher. "Moral Courage." In *Justice and Conflicts: Theoretical and Empirical Contributions*, edited by, Elisabeth Kals and Ju¨rgen Maes, 391-407. Berlin Heidelberg: Springer, 2012.

Paine, Lynn Sharp. "Integrity." In *Encyclopedic Dictionary of Business Ethics*, edited by, Patricia H. Werhane and R. Edward Freeman, 335-336. Oxford: Blackwell Publishers, 1998.

Patrick, Gnana. "Civil Society and Church as Critical Interrogators." In *Church's Engagement in Civil Society*, edited by, Antony Kalliath and Francis Gonsalves, 1-28. Bangalore: Indian Theological Association, 2009.

Paul, Samuel, and Manubhai Shah. "Corruption in India: Agenda for Action." In *Corruption in Public Service Delivery*, edited by, S. Guhan and S. Pau, 144-163. New Delhi: Vision Books, 1997.

Pearce, W. Barnett, and Kimberly A. Pearce. "Taking a Communication Perspective on Dialogue." In *Theorizing Difference in Communication Studies*, edited by, R. Anderson, L. A. Baxter and K. N. Cissna, 39-56. Thousand Oaks, CA: Sage Publications, 2004.

Pellauer, David. "At the Limit of Practical Wisdom." In *Ricoeur as Another: The Ethics of Subjectivity*, edited by, Richard A. Cohen and James L. Marsh, 187-201. New York: State University of New York Press, 2002.

Post, Robert C., and Nancy L. Rosenblum. "Introduction." In *Civil Society and Government*, edited by, Robert C. Post and Nancy L. Rosenblum, 1-6. Oxford: Oxford University Press, 2002.

Puka, Bill. "Taking Care of Business: Caring in Competitive Corporate Structures." In *Applying Care Ethics to Business*, edited by, Maurice Hamington and Maureen Sander-Staudt, 175-201. Dordrecht Heidelberg: Springer, 2011.

Puri, Rajinder. "The Anatomy of Corruption." In *Corruption in India*, edited by, Suresh Kohli, 22-25. New Delhi: Chetana Publications, 1975.

Rasmussen, David. "Rethinking Subjectivity: Narrative Identity and the Self." In *Ricoeur as Another: The Ethics of Subjectivity*, edited by, Richard A. Cohen and James L. Marsh, 57-69. Albany: State University of New York, 2002.

Raphael, D.D., and A.L. Macfie. "Introduction." In *Smith, an Inquiry into the Nature and Causes of the Wealth of Nations*, edited by, D. D. Raphael A.L. Macfie, 1-7. Indianapolis: Liberty Classics, 1987.

Reagan, Charles E. "Personal Identity." In *Ricoeur as Another: The Ethics of Subjectivity*, edited by, Richard A. Cohen and James L. Marsh, 1-31. New York: State University of New York Press, 2002.

Ricoeur, Paul. "Ethique Et Morale: Visee Theologique Et Perspective Deontologique." In *Ragione Pratica Liberta Normativita*, edited by, Marcello Sanchez Sorondo, 353-366. Roma: Universita Lateranense, 1991.

Rose-Ackerman, Susan. "Corruption and Conflicts of Interest." In *Corruption and Conflicts of Interest: A Comparative Law Approach*, edited by, Jean Bernard Auby, Emmanuel Breen and Thomas Perroud, 3-15. Massachusetts: Edward Elgar Publishing, 2014.

Rose, Cecily. "Corruption and Conflicts of Interests in the United Kingdom." In *Corruption and Conflicts of Interest: A Comparative Law Approach*, edited by, Jean Bernard Auby, Emmanuel Breen and Thomas Perroud, 150-166. Massachusetts: Edward Elgar Publishing, 2014.

Selling, Joseph. "The Human Person." In *Christian Ethics: An Introduction*, edited by, Bernard Hoose, 95-110. Continnum: London, 1998.

———. "Introduction." In *Personalist Morals: Essays in Honor of Professor Louis Janssens*, edited by, Joseph A. Selling, 1-7. Leuven: Leuven University Press, 1988.

———. "The Context and the Arguments of Veritatis Splendor." In *The Splendor of Accuracy: An Examination of the Assertions Made by Veritatis Splendor*, edited by, Joseph A. Selling and Jan Jans, 11-71. Kampen: Kok Pharos Publishing House, 1994.

———. "The Human Person." In *Christian Ethics: An Introduction*, edited by, Bernard Hoose, 95-110. New York: The Liturgical Press, 2003.

Sen, Amartya. "Development as Capability Expansion." In *Readings in Human Development. Concepts, Measures and Policies for a Development Paradigm*, edited by, Sakiko Fukuda-Parr and A.K. Shiva Kumar, 3-16. Oxford: Oxford University Press, 2003.

Shaw, Bill. "Profit and the Profit Motive." In *Blackwell Encyclopedic Dictionary of Business Ethics*, edited by, Patricia H. Werhane and R. Edward Freeman, 517-518. Malden: Blackwell Publishers, 1997.

Shore, Cris, and Dieter Haller. " Introduction—Sharp Practice: Anthropology and the Study of Corruption." In *Corruption: Anthropological Perspectives*, edited by, Dieter Haller and Cris Shore, 1-29. London: Pluto Press, 2005.

Singh, Khushwant. "Are We a Corrupt People?" In *Corruption in India*, edited by, Suresh Kohli, 9-16. New Delhi: Chetana Publications, 1975.

Sirgy, M. Joseph. "Employee Well-Being: An Integrative Perspective." In *Work and Quality of Life: Ethical Practices in Organizations*, edited by, Nora P. Reilly, M. Joseph Sirgy and C. Allen Gorman, 35-65. Dordrecht: Springer, 2012.

Skole, David, and Compton Tucker. "Tropical Deforestation and Habitat Fragmentation in the Amazon: Satellite Data from 1978 to 1988." In *Environmental Management Readings and Case Studies*, edited by, Lewis Owen and Tim Unwin, 205-212. Oxford: Oxford Blackwell Publishers, 1997.

Solomon, Robert. "Corporate Roles, Personal Virtues: An Aristotelian Approach to Business Ethics." In *Virtue Ethics: A Critical Reader*, edited by, Daniel Stratman, 205-226. Edinburgh: Edinburgh University Press, 1997.

Statman, Daniel. "Introduction to Virtue Ethics." In *Virtue Ethics*, edited by, Daniel Statman, 1-42. Edinburgh: Edinburgh University Press, 1997.

Tajfel, Henri. "La CatéGorisation Sociale." In *Introduction a` La Psychologie Sociale*, edited by, S. Moscovici, 272-302. Paris: Larouse, 1972.

Taran, Leonard. "Monism and Presocratic Philosophy." In *Monism*, edited by, Andreas Bachli and Klaus Petrus, 11-29. Frankfurt: Die Deutsche Bibliothek, 2003.

Tavernier, Johan De. "Personalism and the Natural Root of Morality." In *Questioning the Human: Towards a Theological Anthropology for the Twenty-First Century*, edited by, Lieven Boeve, Yves De Maeseneer and Ellen Van Stichel, 42-59. New York: Fordham University Press, 2014.

Taylor, Charles. "The Dialogical Self." In *The Interpretive Turn: Philosophy, Science, Culture*, edited by, David R. Hiley, James F. Bohman and Richard Shusterman, 305-314. London: Cornell University Press, 1991.

———. "The Politics of Recognition." In *Multiculturalism: Examining the Politics of Recognition*, edited by, Amy Gutmann, 25-73. New Jersey: Princeton University Press, 1994.

Tyler, Tom R. "Managing Conflicts of Interest within Organizations: Does Activating Social Values Change the Impact of Self Interest on Behavior?" In *Conflicts of Interest Challenges and Solutions in Business, Law, Medicine, and Public Policy*, edited by, Don A. Moore, Daylian M. Cain, George Loewenstein and Max H. Bazerman, 13-36. Cambridge: Cambridge University Press, 2005.

Vargas-Hernández, José G. "The Multiple Faces of Corruption: Typology, Forms and Levels." In *Contemporary Legal and Economic Issues Iii*, edited by, Ivana Barkovic Bojanic and Mira Lulic, 269-291. Osijek: Josip Juraj Strossmayer University, 2011.

Verma, Arvind, and R. K. Tiwari. "Organized Crime: A Perspective from India." In *Organized Crime: World Perspectives*, edited by, Jay S. Albanese, Dilip K. Das and Arvind Verma, 240-267. New Jersey: Pearson Education, 2003.

Verstraeten, Johan. "Business Ethics and Personal Moral Responsibility." In *Business Ethics: Broadening the Perspectives*, edited by, Johan Verstraeten, 97-113. Leuven: Peeters, 2000.

———. "Integriteit in een context van geïnstitutionaliseerde corruptie. Een sociaal-ethische en christelijke benadering van een complex probleem." In *Witboek over Corruptie en Integritiet*, edited by, Roger Burggraeve, Johan De Tavernier, Didier Pollefeyt and Jo Hanssens, 111-131. Leuven: Davidsfonds, 2008.

———. "Responsible Leadership Beyond Managerial Rationality: The Necessity of Reconnecting Ethics and Spirituality." In *Leadership and Business Ethics*, edited by, Gabriel Flynn, 131-151. Heidelberg: Springer, 2008.

———. "Non E Solo Questione Di Applicare De Principi." In *L'etica Negli Ambiti Di Vita*, edited by, Simone Morandini, 37-61. Padova: Proget Edizioni, 2010.

———. "Spirituality as Source of Inspired, Authentic and Innovative Leadership." In *Leadership, Innovation, and Spirituality*, edited by, Patrick Nullens and Jack Barentsen, 81-97. Leuven: Peeters, 2014.

———. "Institutionalised Corruption and Integrity: A Theological-Ethical Clarification of the Issue." In *Financial Crimes: Psychological, Technological, and Ethical Issues*, edited by, Michel Dion, David Weisstub and Jean-Loup Richet, 235-249. Basel: Springer, 2016.

Viner, Jacob. "Adam Smith." In *Essays on the Intellectual History of Economics*, edited by, Irwin, 248-262. Princeton: Princeton University Press, 1968.

Wallace, Kent. "Fundamental Option." In *Encyclopedia of Catholic Social Thought, Social Science, and Social Policy*, edited by, Michael L. Coulter, Stephen M. Krason, Richard S. Myers and Joseph A. Varacalli, 1, 456-457. Toronto: The Scarecrow Press, 2007.

Warnock, Geoffrey James. "The Correspondence between Virtues and Principles." In *Philosophical Ethics: An Introduction to Moral Philosophy*, edited by, Tom L. Beauchamp, 163-170. New York: McGraw-Hill Book Company, 1982.

Werhane, Patrica H. "Corporate Social Responsibility/Corporate Moral Responsibility: Is There a Difference and the Difference It Makes." In *The Debate over Corporate Social Responsibility*, edited by, Steve May, George Cheney and Juliet Roper, 459-475. Oxford: Oxford University Press, 2007.

Yukl, Gray A, and David D. Van Fleet. "Theory and Research on Leadership in Organizations." In *Handbook of Industrial and Organizational Psychologists*, edited by, M. D. Dunnette and L. M. Hough. Palo, 147-219. Alto: Consulting Psychologists Press, 1992.

D. Theses and Dissertations

Palelil, Thomas. "Conversion a Positive Fundamental Option: A Critical Developmental Interpretation." Unpublished Advanced Masters Thesis, Faculty of Theology and Religious Studies, KU Leuven, 1997.

E. Internet Sources

Amundsen, Inge. "Political Corruption: An Introduction to the Issues," 1-32, accessed November 14, 2014, http://www.cmi.no/publications/file/1040-political-corruption.pdf.

Australian Trade Commission. "Doing Business in India: Managing Business Risks—Bribery and Corruption," 1-6, accessed December 1, 2014, https://www.austrade.gov.au/ArticleDocuments/.

Bhatt, Anjali. "Legal Method and Legal Reasoning Mass Tort: Bhopal Gas Tragedy," 1-22, accessed April 21, 2015, http://www.scribd.com/doc/55412373/Bhopal-Gas-Tragedy-Project#scribd.

Barclays Wealth Insights Survey Report, "Family Business: In Safe Hands," accessed December 18, 2014, https://www.uvm.edu/business/vfbi/documents/2009BarclaysFamilyBusinessInsights.pdf.

Carter, Ian. "Positive and Negative Liberty." In *The Stanford Encyclopedia of Philosophy,* edited by, Edward N. Zalta, 2012, accessed September 18, 2013, http://plato.stanford.edu/archives/spr2013/entries/integrity.

Caze, Marguerite La, Damian Cox, and Michael Levine. "Integrity." edited by, Uri Nodelman Edward N. Zalta, and Colin Allen. Stanford: Stanford University, 2008, accessed September 18, 2013, http://plato.stanford.edu/archives/spr2013/entries/integrity.

Chauhan, Rishika. "Corruption a Structural Defect," 1-27, accessed September 25, 2015, http://paperroom.ipsa.org/papers/paper_14867.pdf.

Control Risk, "International Business Attitude Corruption Survey" (2013): 1-22, accessed December 1, 2014, http://www.controlrisks.com/~/media/Public%20Site/Files/Oversized%20Assets/International_business_attitudes_to_corruption.pdf.

Coca Cola Case, 2003, Judgement of the High Court of Kerala in *Perumatty Grama Panchayat vs State Of Kerala,* accessed July 26, 2014, http://www.indiankanoon.org/doc/1161084/.

Feldt, Allan G. "General System Theory," accessed January 9, 2016, http://www.holisticwisdom.org/hwpages/chapt%202%20-%20GST.htm.

Pope Francis. "Laudato Si" 1-82, accessed April 17, 2016, http://w2.vatican.va/content/francesco/en/encyclicals/documents/papa-francesco_20150524_enciclica-laudato-si.pdf.

Grieger, Jürgen. "Corruption in Organizations Some Outlines for Research," 1-46, accessed March 12, 2015, http://elpub.bib.uni-wuppertal.de/servlets/DerivateServlet/Derivate776/ab0502 pdf.

John Paul II. "Laborem Exercens," accessed March 9, 2015, http://w2.vatican.va/content/john-paul-ii/en/encyclicals/documents/hf_jp-ii_enc_14091981_laborem-exercens.html.

John Paul II, "Veritatis Splendor," 66, accessed February 1, 2017, http://w2.vatican.va/content/john-paul-ii/en/encyclicals/documents/hf_jp-ii_enc_06081993_veritatis-splendor.html.

Jenkins, Rhys. "Corporate Codes of Conduct: Self-Regulation in a Global Economy," accessed October 7, 2014, http://www.adapttech.it/old/files/document/18111JENKINS.pdf.

Kaptein, Muel. "The Servant of the People: On the Power of Integrity in Politics and Government," accessed February 4, 2017, http://www.rsm.nl/about-rsm/news/detail/3304-new-book-on-integrity-in-politics-and-government-written-by-rsm-professor/http://ssrn.com/abstract=2498730.

Kar, Prati. "Fighting Abusive Related Party Transactions in Asia: Workshop on Implementation." Background document, OECD-Asian Roundtable on Corporate Governance, accessed June 28, 2014, http://www.oecd.org/daf/ca/corporategovernanceprinciples/46435512.pdf.

Klynveld Peat Marwick Goerdeler (KPMG), "India Fraud Survey 2012," 1-96, accessed December 2, 2014, http://www.kpmg.com/FR/fr/IssuesAndInsights/ArticlesPublications/Documents/India-Fraud-Survey-2012.pdf.

"Kroll Annual Global Fraud Survey, 2013/2014," accessed December 10, 2014, http://fraud.kroll.com/wp-content/uploads/2013/10/GlobalFraudReport_2013-14_WEB.pdf.

Menon, Mahesh. "Lessons from Plachimada for Water Law: Who should Own the Groundwater," 5-6, accessed June 27, 2014, http://www2.lwr.kth.se/Publikationer/PDF_Files/LWR_EX_13_ 44.pdf.

Naughton, Michael J. "Business as a Calling: Overcoming the Divided Life," 1-5, accessed December 10, 2015, http://www.stthomas.edu/media/catholicstudies/center/ryan/publications/publicationpdfs/businessasacallingpdf/I.pdf.

Pethe, Abhay, Vaidehi Tandel, and Sahil Gandhi. "Unravelling the Anatomy of Legal Corruption in India: Focusing on the 'Honest Graft' by the Politicians," 1-32, accessed November 16, 2014, http://mpra.ub.uni-muenchen.de/39306/1/MPRA_paper_39306.pdf.

Pontifical Council for Justice and Peace, "Vocation of the Business Leader: A Reflection," accessed December 10, 2015, http://www.pcgp.it/dati/2012-05/04-999999/Vocation%20ENG2.pdf.

Sharma, Akshay. "From Hawala Scam to Coalgate: An Analysis of Scams in India: White Collar Crime." accessed April 14, 2015, file:///C:/Users/user/Downloads/From+Hawala+Scam+to+Coalgate-An+Analysis+of+Financial+Scams+in+India.pdf.

Schwenke, Stephen. "The Moral Critique: Corruption in Developing Countries," 146-147, accessed February 15, 2015, https://www.princeton.edu/jpia/past-issues-1/2000/8.pdf.

Sun, Yan. "China Versus India: Why Does a Poor Democracy Not Do Better on Corruption?" 1-28, accessed September 28, 2015, http://www.indiana.edu/~rccpb/china/papers/sun.pdf.

Tenth Plan Report of the Planning Commission of India, 2002-2007, 180, accessed September 20, 2015, http://planningcommission.nic.in/plans/planrel/fiveyr/10th/volume1/10th_vol1.pdf.

Visser, Wayne. "Revisiting Carroll's Pyramid: An African Perspective," 1-8, accessed February 18, 2012, http://www.waynevisser.com/wp-ontent/uploads/2012/07/article_africa_pyramid_ wvisser.pdf.

Zafirovski, Milan. "Human Rational Behavior and Economic Rationality." *Electronic Journal of Sociology*, accessed February 18, 2016, http://www.sociology.org/content/vol7.2/02_zafirovski.html.